ROAD SHOW

ROAD SHOW

IN AMERICA, ANYONE CAN
BECOME PRESIDENT.
IT'S ONE OF THE
RISKS WE TAKE

ROGER SIMON

Farrar ☆ *Straus* ☆ *Giroux*
NEW YORK

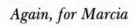

Again, for Marcia

CONTENTS

PREFACE

ALONE IN HIS BEDROOM on a dark and stormy night, the presidential candidate was putting the finishing touches on his announcement speech when the devil appeared before him.

"Worry not," the devil said. "I can grant you a victory in the Iowa caucuses. I can give you the New Hampshire primary, the South, New York, California and all the rest. I will even guarantee you the nomination of your party. But in return, you must sell me your soul.

"You must betray all decent principles. You must pander, trivialize and deceive. You must gain victory by exploiting bigotry, fear, envy and greed. And you must conduct a campaign based on lies, sham, hype and distortion."

"So?" the presidential candidate replied. "What's the catch?"

INTRODUCTION

WE ARE TAUGHT as schoolchildren that choosing a national leader is about issues and policies and agendas. But then we are taught a lot of nonsense as schoolchildren.

Today, choosing a President seems to have more to do with sex, lies and videotape.

And that last one may be the most important. Twenty years ago, when I was still in college, I read Joe McGinniss' *The Selling of the President 1968*. In it, Roger Ailes, then a young producer helping to package Richard Nixon for the TV cameras, said: "This is the beginning of a whole new concept. This is it. This is the way they'll be elected forevermore. The next guys up will have to be performers."

That Presidents would have to perform for the public was not a new concept. Though George Washington never consented to kiss a baby, he did once pat the head of six-year-old Washington Irving. And every President since has, to one extent or another, performed, transforming the electoral process into the longest-running road show in American history.

But today we are talking about something far more alarming than just pleasing the crowd. We are talking about candidates who give themselves over to the concept of continual performance until the person can no longer be distinguished from the persona.

And we are talking about a public and press who, far from decrying it, seem to demand it.

This is not a campaign book; it is not a comprehensive account of the presidential race of 1988. Although I was out in the hustings for twenty-two months, covering every major event and an unforgivable array of minor ones, I have, out of a sense of mercy, spared the reader some events, characters and even whole candidates.

This book would not have been possible without the support of my newspaper, the Baltimore *Sun*. I am especially grateful to Reg Murphy, the publisher, and James I. Houck, the managing editor.

I am also indebted to my researchers: Nancy Balz, Alexa O'Meara, Ariane DeVogue, Alan Cohen and Roman Ponos; as well as Susan Baer of the Baltimore *Sun* for her interview with Clifford and Angela Barnes; and to Raphael Sagalyn, Linda Healey, and Sean O'Loinsiagh.

Along with the presidential candidates, I would like to thank: Marcia Kramer, Mark Starr, Ann McDaniel, Dan Balz, Bob Hillman, Warren Steibel and the staff of *Firing Line*, Tom Brokaw, Michael Kelly, Madelyn Greenberg, Roger Ailes, Lee Atwater, T. R. Reid, Terry Michael, David Axelrod, Mark Gearan, Rick Kogan, Jennifer Boznos, Stephen Studdert, Linda Breakstone, Phil Roeder, Sarah Barnes, Andrew Casell, Michael Tackett, Scott and Craig Timberg, Michael Crick, Kate Kelly, Brian Kelly, Walt Riker, Elaine London, Joe McQuaid, Susan Feeney, David Hoffman, Pat Wingert, Paul Galloway, H. L. Benenson, Stephen Wigler, Joan Gartlan, Carl Leubsdorf, Fern Simon, Fred Sainz, Michael Oreskes, Bill Peterson, Fred Barnes, Milton Starr, Tony Fuller, Ed Fouhy, David Runkel and the Institute of Politics at Harvard University's John F. Kennedy School of Government, the Presidential Campaign Hotline, Donald S. Lamm, Amy Peck and Mark London.

The subtitle of this book is taken from a quotation by Adlai Stevenson and is one of the many sensible things he said.

Needless to say, he never became President.

ROAD SHOW

☆ **1** ☆

THE REGULAR GUY

*"Wimp — Weak, unmanly, indecisive men have been called
wimps since the 1970s and the term is still frequently used.
Although the Popeye cartoon character Wimpy (of ham-
burger fame) may have influenced the coinage, it more likely
comes from whimper."*
—Encyclopedia of Word and Phrase Origins, *1987*

"THE DAY BUSH ANNOUNCED, the *Newsweek* cover came out,
the Wimp Cover," Roger Ailes was saying, his fists clenching and
unclenching on the tablecloth in front of him. "*Newsweek* had been
trying to get a picture of him playing tennis so they could make him
look wimpy. They lied and said they wanted to take a picture to
make him look good on the cover, but that was false. They just
wanted a shitty picture of him, the sons of bitches."

Roger Ailes, media consultant, had been hired to sculpt an image
for George Bush. A President was many things to many people, but
whatever he was in the eighties, a decade in which Rambo and Rocky
had become folk heroes, he was not a wimp.

"I went down to George's room at 5 a.m., because we had to go
on the morning TV shows and I wanted to prepare him," Ailes said.
"I got to his room and the Secret Service agent was outside and the
door was ajar. I asked the agent what was going on."

The agent shook his head slowly. "He's been up a while," he said.

Ailes pushed open the door and looked inside the darkened room.

"He's there in his bathrobe and the magazine is there," Ailes said.
"*Newsweek* is there on the floor at his feet. He'd been up all night."

October 12, 1987, was supposed to be one of the best days of
George Bush's life. He would announce his candidacy and then he
would go on the TV shows and take his first steps on the long,
winding staircase to the presidency. The day had been planned,
prepared for, choreographed. It was the day on which Bush would

begin to prove once and for all that he was more than a résumé, more than a ticket puncher, more than Ronald Reagan's lapdog.

Then *Newsweek* hit the stands. Although the cover was dated October 19, it was distributed nationally on October 12, and available in airports as early as Sunday night, October 11. Bush had no trouble getting a copy.

Now it was on the floor of his room, cover down, so he would not have to see the hated word. There on the cover was his name in small type. But below it, dominating the page in type more than twice the size, were the words: "Fighting the 'Wimp Factor.' " *Newsweek* had put "Wimp Factor" in quotation marks to make clear that the magazine wasn't calling Bush a wimp; others were. It is the kind of distinction that journalists consider highly significant and few readers even notice.

George Bush didn't notice. All he could see was the word "wimp" swimming up before him, even when he shut his eyes against it. He had not slept. He had not yet shaved. He sat there in his bathrobe in the predawn gloom looking like a sick, tired man.

"Goddammit," he said to Ailes, "I've spent my whole life serving my country and they do *this* to me. And in a half hour I've got to go on TV!"

Ailes is a big man and he stood over Bush, towering above him. The color rose in Ailes's face. His whiskers twitched. He thrust out his chin as he spoke slowly and deliberately. "Look, we're going to ride this out," he said. "I don't believe this is the way this country perceives you. How you perform will make all the difference. If they ask you about it you say, you say . . ." Ailes thought for a second. He was good at this. He was paid to produce the killer lines, the ones that got quoted in the papers and made the network news, the ones that, over time, formed an image of the candidate like paint daubed on a canvas.

"O.K.," Ailes said. "You say: 'The guys on my carrier didn't believe it. The people in my business didn't believe it. The President doesn't believe it. The people won't believe it.' "

Bush looked at him, hope flickering across his face. After all, he had enlisted in the Army at eighteen, right out of high school (O.K., prep school). He had flown fifty-eight combat missions in a torpedo bomber in the Pacific in World War II and had been awarded the Distinguished Flying Cross, one of the military's highest honors. He was a hero, not a wimp. But he couldn't go around just saying that. He needed a way to say it. And men like Ailes taught him the ways, gave him the lines. He had picked a crackerjack staff, hadn't he?

Super guys. Smart. Tough. Knew their stuff. And there was no point in hiring these people if you didn't listen to them.

"*Stick* to that," Ailes said, knowing how important it was to keep Bush from wandering off into his own flights of vocabulary. "If you don't give a reporter anything new to write about, he won't write about it." Translation: Deliver the line and shut up.

Later that morning, George Bush announced for the presidency. ABC, NBC and CBS all mentioned the wimp factor. Reporters, flying around the country with Bush, asked him about it, too.

"The people on my carrier didn't feel that way in combat," Bush replied. "The people I helped build a business didn't feel that way. The people I served with at the CIA didn't feel that way. My record of leadership is well established."

Now he had the lines. He felt confident. He knew how to deal with the wimp factor. But the hurt wouldn't go away. Even people close to him were a little bit surprised by this. Bush had been in politics a long time and had been attacked before. But this was different. To him, the *Newsweek* cover had been deeply personal. It gnawed at him and he would not let it go.

In Red Oak, Iowa, two weeks later, he was still talking about it. The *Newsweek* cover was "a lousy, cheap shot . . ." he said. "The American people don't make up their minds over what some elite publication in the East is going to think." The audience applauded loudly though few, even in Iowa, considered *Newsweek* "elite" or particularly "Eastern."

Bush did get some sympathy. I wrote a column about the wimp factor in the Baltimore *Sun*. I had said there were many things you could criticize Bush for: his flip-flops on abortion and on Ronald Reagan's voodoo economics. (That last was a double flip-flop. Bush coined the phrase and then denied ever using it, challenging "anybody to find it." Ken Bode of NBC did, on a videotape, and broadcast it. Bush wrote him a note: "NBC 1, Bush 0.")

But I also wrote that challenging Bush's manhood, which is what the term was really all about, was unfair and I suggested a solution for him. "George Bush should confront his accusers," I wrote. "He should walk into newsrooms across this country and go right up to the columnists and cartoonists who call him a wimp. He should tap them on the shoulder and say: 'I've sent the Secret Service home. It's just you and me. Outside. In the alley. Right now. Let's go.' And then we'll find out who the real wimps are."

Two weeks later, a letter arrived on my desk. It was on heavy, cream-colored stationery. At the top, engraved (not merely embossed) was the seal of the Vice President. It was hand-signed by George Bush. "The *Newsweek* cover was devastating in that the editors elected on the very day I announced to inject themselves into the political process," he wrote. "I'm told the editors debated whether to use the w-word on the cover recognizing that they were editorializing there. But frankly, they went ahead and did it and that was their own call. As for me, I'm plowing ahead basing my case on the fairness of the American people and my own record."

What struck me about the letter was that weeks after the cover had come out, and after dealing with it in interview after interview, George Bush still could not use the word. He could not bring himself to say it or to write it. To him, it forever would be the w-word.

Eventually, most people forgot about it. As a political issue, it largely faded away. But it remained an obsession with Bush. Bush ordered that *Newsweek* was to be cut off from his campaign, nobody was to talk to *Newsweek* reporters. (Lee Atwater, his campaign manager, was the first to violate this. You didn't freeze out the media, he knew, you manipulated them.)

Even eleven months later, with most of his major battles won, with the nomination of his party in hand, with the polls showing him that the presidency was his and with nobody talking about his being a wimp, even then Bush remained furious. He still would not give one-on-one interviews to *Newsweek* and had given *Time* magazine preferential treatment as extra punishment.

Newsweek wanted a truce. It was doing a book on the campaign and had committed a half dozen full-time people and hundreds of thousands of dollars to the effort. And it needed Bush, especially because it looked like he was going to be the winner. So on September 17, 1988, a meeting was arranged at the Vice President's residence in Washington, D.C. In attendance were Bush, James Baker, his campaign chairman, and Craig Fuller, his chief of staff, on one side, and Katharine Graham, chairman of the board of the Washington Post Company, which owns *Newsweek*, Rick Smith, the magazine's editor, and Evan Thomas, chief of the Washington bureau, on the other. Though the byline on the wimp article was Margaret Garrard Warner's, she had not used the word "wimp" in her original story. It was inserted by Thomas and the decision to run it on the cover—which was what really had sent Bush "ballistic," to use one of his favorite terms—had been made by Smith.

While the story was progressing through the *Newsweek* editing system, sources at *Newsweek* were informing the Bush campaign how things were proceeding. (Though the public reads stories only about the press having sources within campaigns, in reality information flows both ways. The smart campaigns look upon information as a commodity: it is hoarded, exchanged and bartered.) And when Bush's aides learned the word "wimp" might be on the cover, Atwater called *Newsweek* in an attempt to persuade the magazine not to use it. He argued, he cajoled, he threatened. But it did not work.

The editors pointed out that the word had been around for a long time—it was how Reagan had felt about Bush in the New Hampshire primary in 1980, in fact—and that Garry Trudeau's *Doonesbury* comic strip had already used the word in print. Besides, the article was not intended as a campaign profile, it was an exploration of how Bush would deal with his image problem. In retrospect, the article was tough, but fair. The word was used only two times in the main article (though seven more times in the headlines and accompanying articles), and when introduced into the article it was referred to as a "mean word."

None of that mattered to Bush. All he cared about was that the editors had used *that* word on the cover on the day he announced. And now he wanted their guts for garters.

"We knew we were sticking our necks out, but we felt it was justifiable," a *Newsweek* source said of the article. "There was internal debate about whether we were going too far by using the word on the cover, but the decision was made that it was justifiable. And we did little things to soften it: putting the word in quotes, using the cover picture of Bush in his speedboat to make him look forceful, etc.

"The Bushies had excellent sources in *Newsweek*. I think they actually had the hard [that is, printed as opposed to electronic] copy in advance and they were blowing up because it offended Bush that it came out on his announcement day. I thought that was a weird thing. Why was it unfair to write a negative piece on his announcement day? When else were we going to run it?

"Bush prides himself on thick skin, but, for him, this crossed the line. He thought it was a cheap shot. He thought it was editorializing, but that's what we do. Newsmagazines do that all the time. Doro [his daughter, Dorothy, twenty-seven] had burst into tears and had called her father crying. Mrs. Bush was upset. Nancy Ellis [his sister] was upset. It really got to Bush."

As Ailes had claimed, *Newsweek* had wanted a picture of Bush in a tennis outfit for the cover, though mainly, *Newsweek* contends, because it wanted an action shot of Bush, who was known as a good tennis player. Pete Teeley, then Bush's director of communications, had set aside fifteen minutes for a photo shoot for a *Newsweek* photographer. But just before the shoot was scheduled to take place, Teeley called a source at *Newsweek*. "We hear you're going to use 'wimp' on the cover," he said. "I just want to know: Are you about to fuck us? Because if you are, I don't want to make Bush go through with the shoot."

The source, though loyal to *Newsweek*, felt Teeley's future with Bush might be endangered if the truth was withheld. He confirmed that "wimp" was probably going to be used on the cover. Teeley canceled the shoot. And the eventual cover picture, Bush at the helm of his speedboat, a grim, manly expression on his face looking like John Paul Jones on the deck of the *Bon Homme Richard*, was provided by the White House. (After the cover came out, Bush told the Detroit *Free Press*: "I kind of like that cover picture, but I'd like to take the guy who wrote that headline out in that boat.")

"We thought it would pass," a *Newsweek* source said. "It didn't pass. It hung around."

At the September 17 meeting with the *Newsweek* brass, Bush should have been in good humor. For the first time, media tracking polls were showing him with a double-digit lead over Michael Dukakis. And four days earlier, Dukakis had insisted on taking a ride in an M-1 tank at a General Dynamics plant in Sterling Heights, Michigan. The resulting photos of Dukakis in a tank helmet made him look like Snoopy or Alfred E. Neuman or, well, a wimp. So Bush should have been in high spirits.

He wasn't. He was looking for an apology from *Newsweek*. "He wanted his honor assuaged," one source said. But *Newsweek* was not about to apologize. It wanted Bush's freeze to end, mainly because of its book and because the editors wanted a working relationship with the man who might be the next President, but it was not willing to sell out its principles to do so. Fortunately, the magazine had a powerful figure on its side, a person used to standing up to Presidents, let alone Vice Presidents. Kay Graham was known not only for her toughness (it would have been hard for her newspaper, the Washington *Post*, to have gotten through Watergate without it) but also for her charm. Few people find it easy to stay angry with her face to face.

Bush, however, seemed to be managing quite well. It was 9 a.m. on a Saturday and Bush was wearing a work shirt and an icy expression. "He was frosted," the source said. "Very frosted." The *Newsweek* people tried to explain that it was not *Newsweek* that had called Bush a wimp but that "the word was out there and [his own] aides recognized it as a problem." They also said they were proud of the story and that it had been balanced.

"You used that w-word," Bush said. "That awful word. That

dreadful word. That ugly word." He went on for forty-five minutes. He said he was personally offended and that his family had been hurt, his daughter had cried and his whole family had been embarrassed. He turned to Evan Thomas, the Washington bureau chief, and asked: "How many times is that ugly word in the story?"

Thomas wasn't sure. "Ten times?" he replied.

Jim Baker, who wanted the breach repaired, intervened. "No, no, not that many!" he said. "Three or four at the most."

And then, men who would soon negotiate language with the Soviets over arms reduction began negotiating for a nonapology apology that would satisfy Bush.

"They were trying to find some language," the source said, "like how *Newsweek* 'recognized in retrospect it wasn't the best thing to do' or something like that."

The *Newsweek* people wanted to show Bush they realized he felt badly and that they could sympathize with his feelings. They just didn't want to apologize. By the time the meeting ended, Bush did seem somewhat mollified. "Kay," he said to Mrs. Graham at the end of the meeting, "we'll work this out."

So later, Rick Smith had to fly back to Washington to have lunch with Baker to work out details. Baker still sought an apology and Smith still refused. "In the end, *Newsweek* never actually apologized, but Baker sort of put words in our mouth to the President [that is, Bush]," the source said. "He told him, 'Well, they concede this and that,' and, in effect, Baker apologized on *Newsweek*'s behalf." Bush said it was now O.K. for his people to cooperate with the magazine. But he would often talk about that Saturday meeting and how he "really put the editors in their place."

THAT WOULD BE in the future, however. Now, at 5:30 in the morning on the day Bush's official campaign began, the wound was deep and fresh. And it actually pained Ailes to see Bush looking this way. Ailes was a professional who certainly could work for men he did not like. But he actually liked George Bush. And when George Bush hurt, it showed all over him. "It was a deep, deep hurt," Ailes said. "And a very deep hurt to Barbara. I saw her with tears in her eyes after that cover. And it steeled my resolve to fight to the bitter end."

Ailes stood over Bush in the hotel room. "Hey!" Ailes said.

Bush looked up at him.

"*Fuck* those guys," said Ailes. "*Fuck* 'em. We'll show them. You and me. We'll *show* them."

George Bush's face brightened. That was the ticket! These men, these good, talented men like Ailes, they could help him show everybody. Because they all knew the unspoken truth:

In 1980, Ronald Reagan had been called too old, too dim and too right-wing to become President. Now, nobody said those things. There was but one way to wipe out all the negatives, to wipe the smiles and the smirks off the faces of the people who said awful, ugly things about you and made your wife and children cry.

All you had to do was win. Because if you won, they never called you wimp.

They called you Mr. President.

IN THE IOWA CAUCUSES, Bush got clobbered. He had won the state eight years before, but now he came in third, losing not only to his one serious opponent, Bob Dole, but also to Pat Robertson. It was a disaster. Dan Rather called it a "nightmare." Tom Brokaw: "an embarrassing defeat." Bernard Shaw: "a stunning upset." The Des Moines *Register*: "a worst-case situation." *The New York Times*: "humbling."

The New Hampshire primary was just eight days away. If Bush lost to Dole again, he might be finished. There was a solution, however: George Bush would have to be recast. Whatever he was in Iowa had not worked, had not played.

Bernard Weinraub of *The New York Times* had identified one of Bush's main problems in a piece that ran the day before the Monday-night Iowa caucuses:

> Sioux City, Iowa, Feb. 6 — In the front cabin of Air Force Two, Vice President Bush sits quietly, invisible to most of the passengers in the rear. After the plane lands, Mr. Bush climbs into a limousine, and a 20-car motorcade then moves to carefully staged rallies and Rotary Club luncheons crammed with supporters.
>
> Questions are rarely asked by the audience. Reporters are kept behind barricades by Secret Service agents. The Vice President uses back entrances to avoid questions and then returns to the cocoon of Air Force Two. Nearly 100 aides, Secret Service agents and journalists and technicians accompany him.

The key words were all there: "invisible," "barricades," "cocoon." What kind of image was that for a man who was selling himself to the people? It was such a serious problem that Bush had to be pulled home for some lessons in remedial human being. On Tuesday night, with the clock ticking, Bush left New Hampshire, where he had been campaigning, and flew to Washington to meet with his handlers. Among themselves, they had already begun asking (one contest too late) some basic questions: Who is George Bush? What is his image?

Well, that was the problem. He didn't seem to have one. People couldn't even tell you where he came from. In the *New York Times* story on Bush's announcement for the presidency in Houston, the fourth paragraph began: "Mr. Bush, who was born in Connecticut, made his announcement in his adopted home state . . ." The little box next to the story got it right: Bush had been born in Massachusetts. But a man who seemed to be from everywhere also could seem to be from nowhere. As *Spy* magazine would later put it, Bush was a man "claiming to be a Texan although he was born in Massachusetts, grew up in Connecticut, lives in Washington, D.C., and pays taxes in Maine."

So that was a negative. As was the wimp thing. As was his cloudy involvement in the Iran-contra scandal . . . but, hey, forget that, let's look on the plus side. What were the guy's positives? The handlers looked at each other. Well, people who knew him liked him. He was a nice guy. To some, this seemed a thin reed upon which to base a presidential campaign. But others felt Ronald Reagan had proven the strength of it.

The men around George Bush (there were few high-ranking women in the campaign) liked George Bush. And those like Atwater, who could tend toward fanaticism, liked him fanatically. Atwater had been equally devoted to Ronald Reagan when he was running against George Bush in 1980. But there was no conflict here. Fanatics are devoted to the emotion itself more than the object of the emotion.

O.K., so they all liked Bush because Bush was a nice guy. But how do you sell that? New Hampshire Governor John Sununu, whom Atwater had recruited for the Bush campaign, came up with it. They all had liked Bush just as soon as they had seen him up close. So let the people of New Hampshire see Bush that way. The press, too. Drop the velvet rope, in effect. Break him out of the cocoon. Let the people see George Bush up close and personal. Sununu would come to call it the "see me, touch me, feel me" strategy.

" 'Smell me,' " he said, "is for our opponents."

BUT WHILE THEY BEGAN WORKING on the positive aspects of the Bush campaign, they did not forget the negative. Atwater and Ailes were clear on that. Sell George Bush, sure. But destroy Bob Dole, too. That went without saying.

"George knew he was in trouble after Iowa," Ailes said. "Oh yeah, we got our ass handed to us in Iowa. So we had to get focused and strategize in our media. The advantage I had is that George and I genuinely like each other as people. He knows I am a tough son of a bitch and I will drive hard to win. After Iowa, I had a 102 fever. I had walking pneumonia and the doctor told me I couldn't go to New Hampshire. I said: 'You better nuke me with something, because I'm going.' I could barely speak. I would just gulp. But I put together the Straddle ad."

The thirty-second Straddle ad (on December 14, 1987, ABC had done a profile of Dole calling him "Senator Straddle") would become the best-known TV ad of the 1988 primary season. It was a triumph of negative advertising. It was not pretty or slick. But it was direct. Sort of like a kick to the balls. Ailes loved it:

VISUAL: Portraits of Bush and Dole.
SOUND: "George Bush and Bob Dole on leadership."

VISUAL: Portrait of Bush, with the words: "Led Fight for INF."
SOUND: "George Bush led the fight on the INF treaty for Ronald Reagan."

VISUAL: Two Dole portraits facing each other (as in two-faced) with the word: "Straddled."
SOUND: "Bob Dole straddled, until Iowans pushed him into supporting INF."

VISUAL: Bush portrait, with the words: "Against Oil Import Tax."
SOUND: "George Bush is against an oil import tax."

VISUAL: Dole pictures—"Straddled."
SOUND: "Bob Dole straddled, but now says he's for an oil import fee."

VISUAL: Bush: "Won't Raise Taxes." A period is added after "Taxes."
SOUND: "George Bush says he won't raise taxes, period."

VISUAL: Dole pictures—"Straddle."
VISUAL: Word dissolves to: "Taxes — He can't say no."
SOUND: "Bob Dole straddles, and he just won't promise not to raise taxes. And you know what that means."

VISUAL: Portrait of Bush and flag.
LOGO: "Bush/Presidential Leadership"
SOUND: "George Bush—ready on Day One to provide presidential leadership."

What was so good about Straddle was that it implied that no matter what Dole said, he could not be trusted. He was two-faced, a "straddler." The ad was a classic case of poisoning the well. But it also lightly camouflaged its negative thrust by making references to real issues. That mattered. "Voters today tend to be repulsed by anti-intellectual negatives but attracted toward information-gathering types of television advertisement or those which tend to point out sharp differences between the candidates," wrote V. Lance Tarrance, Jr., in his monograph *Negative Campaigns and Negative Votes: The 1980 Elections*. And that was one of the beauties of Straddle. It seemed to be presenting real information and it certainly pointed out sharp differences. All while calling Dole a dirty, rotten liar. And at least according to the man who was on the receiving end, it did its job. "In my own mind it was all over because of the Straddle ad," Bob Dole said later. "It really worked."

"AFTER IOWA," George Bush would say, "we were staring into the abyss." Atwater was similarly gloomy: "Nothing focuses your mind like your own impending hanging."

So there was no risk that was not worth taking in New Hampshire. "At first, they didn't want me to make Straddle," Ailes said. "I said, 'Look, I'll eat the cost if it never runs. Because when we need this, it's going to be too late to make it.' So we make it and Bush looked at it and he rejected releasing it."

In some campaigns, that would have been that. But in the Bush campaign, Bush was merely the candidate.

"So we have this meeting in a garage as Bush is about to go out and campaign," Ailes said, "and Teeter [Robert Teeter, Bush's pollster] tells him: 'You know, you're down seven points.'

"And Bush says: 'What? I thought I was *up* seven points!'

"And Teeter says: 'Where'd you get that?'

"And Bush says: 'Shit. We're down?'

"And I say: 'I happen to have this little ad.' " Ailes tilted back his head and laughed, remembering it.

"But it's Saturday," Bush told them. "The primary is Tuesday. How're you going to get it on the air in time?"

Ailes was ready for that. It was like reading from a script. "I got it wired," he said. "I got it wired."

"And I'll tell you, Atwater earned his spurs that day," Ailes said later. "He spoke up. He said: 'Sir, I may get fired for this, I know how you feel about this sort of stuff, but Ailes is right.' "

Bush said: "If we go negative, it's going to look like we're desperate, that we're hitting Dole out of desperation."

"Hell, Dole is hitting *us*," Ailes said.

Later, Atwater would say: "The two things you have to remember about Bush is that he is a counterpuncher—he attacks only after he is attacked—and he is a survivor, he responds to a crisis."

They had already convinced Bush he was in a crisis. Now they had to convince him that Dole had thrown the first punch. Luckily, Dole had. Though few would later remember Dole's negative ads, he had begun running one in Iowa that showed a vanishing picture of Bush. But Dole, sensing victory in New Hampshire, decided to take the high road, and he stopped his negative advertising.

Bush now looked around the garage. Barbara Bush spoke up and said she didn't think the Straddle ad was *that* negative.

Then Sununu joined in. "I don't see anything wrong with it," he said. "What's to worry?"

Bush relaxed. He was off the hook. He had voiced his objections to negative campaigning, but his aides and advisers and even his wife had said the ad wasn't really that bad. And there was one other factor, of course. "Attacking was good for us because of Bush's perceived wimp image," Atwater said. "Every time we attacked, we were cutting against our worst stereotype." It was a message not lost on Bush, who still seethed over the *Newsweek* cover. If attacking made him look tough and unwimplike, then he would attack.

"And I'll tell you," Atwater said, "George Bush is damn good on the attack."

THE NEGATIVE TAKEN CARE OF, now it was time to sell the positive. "We knew we had to change in New Hampshire," Ailes said. "We had to get to people. Campaign 'close to the ground,' that's what we called it. We wanted to 'let George be George.' Nobody didn't think he could enter a room and not make a good impression."

But all campaigns say that, I said.

"Yeah, but we *meant* it," Ailes said. "We wanted to let people be in the room with him, let people touch him. We were going to do the same thing in California, Michigan and Ohio, but by then we didn't need it.

"George is a genuinely likable guy. A kinder, gentler guy. You know, he is much more complex than people give him credit for. This was the Year of the Cartoon: Dole was mean. George was a wimp. Dukakis had a computer heart. The media spends a great deal of time creating cartoons and then reinforcing the image they have created. It is the natural extension of the nine-second sound bite: if one word can describe a person, why go beyond that one word? And it was my job to define the word. To develop a crisp image. Develop two or three words, but not more than that."

In New Hampshire the image would be: the Regular Guy.

Forget about what you usually thought about when you thought about George Bush. Forget about the gray suits and button-down shirts and striped ties. ("I haven't owned a button-down shirt in ten years," Bush told *The New York Times* in 1986. "I might have, I don't want to be going into much depth on my wardrobe, but I'd say three, possibly two percent of the ties I've got are striped.") Forget about his privileged upbringing and his preppy schooling. Forget about him being a . . . w--p. A new George was being fashioned. A new George who was as easygoing and down-home as the guy down the block.

"In New Hampshire, it was my role to make him laugh," Ailes recalled. "I tend to see things in weird ways and he loves a good dirty joke. I'd tell a few; he'd tell a few. In debate prep, he'd be serious and say, 'What happens if So-and-so says such-and-such?' and I'd say: 'Why, George, you just go over and beat the shit out of him.' He'd rear back and laugh. After Iowa, we had the worst week of both our lives, but we were still able to laugh and keep going.

"See, I am just the flip side of journalists. I get up and try to figure out how to make my client look better. You get up and try to figure out how to humiliate him in front of his family. And I sleep at night and make more money than you and you hate me for it."

One large factor in Bush's wimp image was his loyalty to Ronald Reagan. He had run against Ronald Reagan, attacked Reagan, and then loyally had served and defended him for eight years. To some, that was being a patsy and a flunky.

"The press hates loyalty," Ailes said. "They see it as a betrayal of personal ethics to be loyal to your boss. But the people like loyalty. They understand loyalty. We'd have these focus groups and people would say: 'Well, this Bush is slavish to the President.' And others would say: 'Hey, he *works* for the guy. What's he supposed to do?' In a sense we were running against the national press corps.

"We all advised him to distance himself from Reagan early on. He said: 'After the convention, when I am the nominee of the party, I will. But now I am the Vice President.' We told him he might never *get* the nomination if he didn't, but he still refused. That's loyalty."

Lee Atwater figured the campaign could survive just about anything, even loyalty, as long as Bush won New Hampshire. "We figured if we could win in New Hampshire, we could win in the South and that would give us a good chance to come back. In our business, a bona fide front-runner inevitably wins, but he gets in trouble early. But if he gets back through herculean effort, he makes it. Look at Reagan [losing to Bush in Iowa in 1980] and look at Mondale [losing to Gary Hart in New Hampshire in 1984]. That's the new model.

"We met at 7 a.m. the day after we lost Iowa and I was personally devastated. I had been up all night thinking up ways to offer my resignation. Bush said he didn't want any handwringing, we were a good team. That to me was the day I knew he was going to be President. Because that was grace under pressure. Had the candidate fallen apart then, as another candidate did a week later [that is, Dole claiming in a live TV interview with Tom Brokaw that Bush had lied about Dole's record], he would have lost.

"Dole couldn't weather a crisis and Hart couldn't weather a crisis. We could. We had Iran, we had Iowa, we had the wimp thing and we weathered it all. There was no doubt we never could have gotten through the Iranian crisis without that experience."

On Tuesday night after the loss in Iowa, Bush flew to Washington and the next day had lunch with Ronald Reagan. The White House released a picture of the two men eating together. Reagan was good news in New Hampshire, just as he was bad news in Iowa. Times were tough in Iowa, unemployment was up and population was down. The opposite was true in New Hampshire. There loyalty to Ronald Reagan could pay off. And the Bush campaign quickly put out a new brochure urging voters to "give George Bush the same trust given him by Ronald Reagan."

Bush did one other thing in Washington: he sat down with Peggy Noonan, who would later write his "thousand points of light" speech (a phrase he freely admitted he did not understand), and began learning how to be a Regular Guy.

"In New Hampshire, we tore the barricades down so he could get closer to the people," Atwater said.

At first, things did not go well.

BEING A MAN OF THE PEOPLE was not the easiest role for Bush to play. This was the man who, when asked after returning as envoy to China if he had met any ordinary Chinese citizens, replied: "Oh yes. They gave me a boy to play tennis with."

And flying back to New Hampshire from Washington, Bush got national TV coverage, not for being a man of the people, but for one of his most bizarre campaign utterances. Talking at a Lincoln Day dinner in Nashua about the environmental advantages of the Alaskan oil pipeline, Bush said: "The caribou love it. They rub up against it and they have babies. There are more caribou in Alaska than you can shake a stick at."

The press did begin noticing a difference, however. Events were less orchestrated than in Iowa. Bush would reach across the ropes and shake hands more. Bush "is beginning to act like a real candidate, instead of the crown prince of the '88 campaign," the Philadelphia *Inquirer* noted.

By Thursday, five days before the New Hampshire primary, the transformation was complete. Bush took off his coat and tie and put on a parka and a green-and-white baseball cap from East Coast Lumber and went to Cuzzin Ritchie's Truck Stop. There he drove an eighteen-wheel Mack truck—slowly and with two Secret Service agents clinging to the sides and looking somewhat ill. After all, it was Barbara Bush who later said: "George Bush said if he loses, on January 20, he is going to get in a car and drive away from the White House and I said you'll be by yourself. Because I'm not leaving the White House in a car with a man who's never driven in eight years."

The reporters rushed to the souvenir counter and bought black baseball caps printed with the words "Shit Happens," which they found apt commentary on the campaign so far. While the cameras were rolling, Bush looked at the caps and gave a disapproving moue. But when the cameras turned away, Bush motioned a reporter over. "Can you get me one of those caps?" he said.

Inside the truck stop, Bush even pulled out his wallet from his right-hand back pocket and paid for his own cup of coffee. Still, some fine tuning was needed. When the waitress asked if he wanted some more, Bush said: "Just a splash."

His handlers winced. They felt that "splash" was a wimpy word. (Apparently he was supposed to say something like: "Fill my mug with java, you sweet thang.") And Johnny Carson was to joke: ". . . he went into a truck stop wearing a pair of overalls, but he had a little alligator sewn over the pocket."

The press wanted to know what had motivated the transformation. Was the campaign running scared in New Hampshire? "Hell, yeah, we're running scared," Pete Teeley said.

The next day, Friday, a snowstorm paralyzed the state. People knew it was going to be a real blizzard when the AP sent out the advisory: "With snow expected to continue all day, be sure to clean out your satellite dishes several times." It was a classic nor'easter. Winds gusted to 60 miles per hour and two feet of snow fell throughout the state. The day before, as the storm rolled eastward, stretching from Texas to Michigan, twenty-two traffic deaths had been blamed on it. But that was not important. What was important was that the presidential campaigns could not move in New Hampshire. Candidates and reporters were trapped in their hotels. A few people could get around in four-wheel-drives. But motorcades? Press buses? Forget it. The campaigns would just have to halt for twenty-four hours.

Except that George Bush could not afford to lose twenty-four hours. He would have to do something, anything. "I have a touch of cabin fever," Bush announced with the snow still falling. Then he bundled up and plunged outside of his hotel, the new and massive Clarion Somerset Hotel outside Nashua, a building so out of scale with its surroundings that it looked like it had been built as part of a Soviet five-year plan. Reporters suddenly got word that Bush was on the move. They groaned, pulled on their boots and took off after him. Dusk was approaching as Bush tramped through the drifts, challenged reporters to snowball-throwing contests and took any questions they wanted to ask. There were no velvet ropes here. Reporters asked and asked and Bush answered and answered. Did he feel good about New Hampshire? Yes, he felt good about New Hampshire. Was he going to win? Well, he sure hoped so. But after forty-five minutes, the questions began to dribble off and then, well, the reporters just couldn't think of anything more to ask. It was as if they actually had too much of George Bush.

Which made Lee Atwater very happy. Often he couldn't get Bush to sit down with reporters and establish the informal contacts that he believed so important to a successful campaign. One night, Atwater found Bush at dinner with some local politicians from Maine and grew furious. "Call Gerry Boyd [of *The New York Times*] and have dinner with him!" Atwater told Bush afterward. "Call David Hoffman [of the Washington *Post*] and eat with him. They're going to elect you President, not these guys from Maine!"

Later, Atwater brought it up again, but Bush had been getting advice so fast and furious, he grew confused. His aides also had been telling him he needed a woman press secretary to fight his "gender gap" problem and Bush thought Atwater was criticizing him for that. "Are you complaining about the woman thing?" Bush said after Atwater was done.

"No, the press thing, the press thing!" Atwater said.

But when Bush did go to dinner with reporters, he showed a side the public never saw. He was funny. Relaxed. And had a good sense of himself. "I get such a bad reputation for being rich," he joked at one meal, "but there were days in 1939 when my limo had trouble getting through the snow to school."

He also could tell one heck of a dirty joke. He knew hundreds of them, maybe thousands. It was his job in the Reagan White House to amuse the President with them at the weekly national security briefings. Bush would solicit these jokes from state legislators around the country (it was also a way to maintain ties to people who could help him politically later) and he would write them down on a piece of paper taped to a pull-out shelf in his desk.

"A woman is taking a shower and the doorbell rings," Bush would say.

"And the woman hears the guy shout: 'Blind man! Blind man!'

"So, she figures, what the heck, and she gets out of the shower and answers the door naked.

" 'Hi, lady,' " the guy says. " 'I'm here to fix your venetian blinds. Nice tits!' "

Bush told raunchier jokes, ones with the f-word, but he cleaned them up around women. He liked to tell dirty jokes around women, but he took care about the "woman thing."

"He would use the word 'screw,' nothing harsher," one woman said, "and he would make sure the jokes were not sexist. There was one about some guy who stopped at a gas station and asks some advice about screwing his wife—I really can't remember it all—but the point was the guy in the gas station already had been screwing his wife or something like that. Anyway, it struck me that in the dirty jokes Bush told around women, it was always the man who was the butt of the joke. He seemed careful about that."

Trailing staff, Secret Service and the press, Bush slogged through the foot of snow already on the ground over to the Somerset condominiums adjacent to his hotel. When Bush said he was heading for a nearby shopping mall, Barbara told him he knew darn well the stores were all closed. But it didn't matter. This was a photo op, a chance to be seen being one of the guys, slogging—manfully—through the snow.

The flakes continued to fall heavily. A few people came out into the parking lot to try to dig out their cars. Bush charged over to each one, offering to help. Sununu, the wind lashing his face and snow sticking to his eyelashes, shouted: "Come meet the Vice President! Come meet the Vice President!"

Person after person refused help from Bush.

"New Hampshire people are independent," Sununu opined.

"Only in New Hampshire," Bush concurred. Then he spied a man walking his dog and rushed over to pet it.

At about the one-hour mark, there seemed nothing left to do or say. But Bush would not go back to his room. Coming upon a snowplow that had just finished clearing a stretch of road, he asked if he could drive it a little way. The driver allowed Bush to climb behind the wheel and drive about ten yards—down the stretch that had already been cleared.

Bush's vice presidential limousine followed slowly behind.

(The limo was a problem for Bush, but it was very difficult for him to abandon it. As Vice President, Bush had to be guarded carefully and the limo was armored. It was so large and heavy, however, it had to be flown around the nation in its own C-141 transport plane and it often made as much news as Bush. When it landed in Mason City, Iowa, in December 1987, it was the largest plane ever to land there. A hundred people came out to the airport to watch and a picture of this historic event made the front page of the local newspaper.)

Eventually, Bush went in the hotel and the reporters returned, exhausted, to their rooms. They wanted a shower, time to work on their stories, a good meal, sleep, whatever. Instead, they got a phone call. Would they like to come down to the Vice President's suite for a drink?

They groaned. They moaned. And then they went down to the Vice President's suite for a drink. Bush was a jovial host. He stood in an open-necked shirt with a margarita in his hand. (This was his "casual" drink. His real drink was a martini with olives and he usually had at least one a night. In the South, in public, he would drink Tecate beer, expertly forcing a chunk of lime down into the can. He knew all the moves.) He chatted. Made small talk. Bush liked to have an exercise cycle in his hotel suite and he worked out on it religiously. He looked over to where Barbara was eating something. "I just wish I could get Barbara to use it," he chuckled, swigging his margarita. Just guy talk, you understand.

Some reporters felt just a little uncomfortable. Was this the real George Bush? they wondered. *Is* there a real George Bush? they wondered. Earlier, when he had been throwing snowballs with them, he kept trying to hit a sign a few yards away and had kept missing to the right. "I never could hit the side of a barn," he said. When he was on the Yale baseball team, however, he was a considerably better fielder than hitter. He batted .167 one season. They made him captain anyway. When asked what kind of player Bush was, Ethan Allen, eighty-six, the former Yale baseball coach, said: "If you told him to bunt, he bunted."

IT IS SATURDAY and the Bush campaign pulls out of the garage where the candidate has just given permission to release the Straddle ad. Bush is wearing his blue Patagonia windbreaker over a red sweater and an open-necked white shirt. He has on gray suit slacks and big, black, floppy boots, the kind your mother told you to take off as soon as you got to school or else they'd make your feet flat. When reporters see him, they immediately know something is up. You always know something is up when the Secret Service is dressed better than the candidate.

It will be the strangest and one of the most important days of the Bush campaign. It will be the day of the Regular Guy.

His plans for this day, three days before the primary, are filled with "impromptus," events that ostensibly have not been "advanced" by his staff. The advance team of a major campaign resembles the landing party of a military invasion. There are people who gather intelligence. (Who are the local people the candidate will be seen with? Whom should he praise by name? Have any ever been indicted? Arrested for flashing? Voted Democrat?) And people who handle logistics. (Signs and balloons and sound systems that don't squeal have to be purchased and delivered and then packed up and moved to the next stop.) And people who handle crowds. (Crowds often must be purchased and delivered pretty much like the balloons.) And people who stand out in the cold holding signs that say "Press—This Way" and "Follow Me" and "Washrooms" and "Phones." Jack Kemp's advance staff always had to scout up local footballs—Kemp brought his own just in case, but he preferred local ones—for the former quarterback to throw. And all the campaigns searched madly for the perfect backdrop, the perfect "visual" that the candidate could stand in front of for the TV cameras. The Wayfarer Hotel in Bedford, just outside Manchester, was very popular because of its pond and waterfall. They looked swell on TV and you could not tell they were fake or that the hotel sat in the middle of a shopping-center parking lot.

A candidate never wants to look ill at ease, he never wants to get to an event and have to stand around. A candidate learned to get out of the car and follow the back of his advance person blindly. "You know how baby ducks bond with the first thing they see after they hatch?" an advance man told *The New York Times Magazine*. "That's the way it is. Sometimes I think I could lead him into a broom closet."

But it could work too well. Bush had looked too programmed in Iowa, too slick, too neat. Professionalism began working against him. At each stop in Iowa, Bush had been surrounded by what was called TMBS: Too Many Blue Suits.

In New Hampshire, that had to be changed. The careful planning had to be eliminated. No, scratch that. The *appearance* of careful planning had to be eliminated. Instead, the campaign had to create events that looked impromptu and casual. Although planned in advance, they were kept off the schedule to give reporters the impression that they were truly last-minute.

George Bush gets out of his car and walks down the sidewalk of a strip shopping center in Bedford, his big boots flapping on his feet. In an empty storefront, about fifty kids are sitting cross-legged on a bare floor making campaign signs that say: "Iowa's First and New Hampshire's Right" and "Bush '88." Standing around the kids is a Bush advance team that has baseball legend Ted Williams, the former Boston Red Sox left fielder, in tow.

The kids are teenagers with scrubbed faces. An aide gets a signal and he begins leading them in a cheer: "Are we gonna win New Hampshire?"

"Yeah!" shout the kids.

"Can't hear ya!"

"YEAH!"

Bush's entire campaign staff has come up from Washington and 500 volunteers have been brought into the state. By primary day, Bush campaign workers will have called every registered Republican in the state at least once and all likely Bush supporters will have been identified and have been sent at least one letter. Between 50,000 and 100,000 calls are now being made to likely Bush supporters. Sununu also has created a network of county sheriffs to help get out the vote. Ron Kaufman, a Bush coordinator, says the Bush organization in New Hampshire has been built to withstand a "worst-case scenario." The teenagers begin singing "Hail to the vee-pee, hail to vic-tor-ee" as Bush walks into the room. Then they break into the chant: "Bush '88! Bush '88!"

Bush unzips the front of his windbreaker. He puts his hands in his pockets, but when he sees Ted Williams he reaches up and hugs him. (Bob Dole has Nick Lowery, a placekicker for the Kansas City Chiefs, campaigning with him. "But he's a *very good* placekicker," a Dole aide explains.) Bush will campaign with numerous celebrities as the campaign progresses, and each is selected carefully. Williams is a superstar and a he-man. Considered by some to be the greatest hitter of all time, he also served his country in World War II and Korea. In his last turn at bat, he hit a home run. And then he not only refused to tip his hat to the crowd but also refused to come out of the dugout and recognize the ovation. He once spat at the crowd. He was never known as a friendly man, but in New Hampshire he is now affable and giving interviews to the press. He seems to have undergone a strange transformation. In New Hampshire, everybody associated with Bush seems to have undergone a strange transformation.

"Hey, Ted Williams, by golly!" Bush says as he hugs him. Bush then releases Williams and immediately thrusts his hands back in his pockets. He is very sensitive about his hands. Ailes has complained about his effeminate hand gestures. *Newsweek* quoted Ailes yelling at Bush: "There you go with that fucking hand again. You look like a fucking *pansy!*"

Now Bush begins to speak to the assembled teenagers. "As an old ball fan, I'd be remiss if I didn't mention the big guy here, Ted Williams." Williams is dressed in a short black trench coat over a khaki jacket, black sweater and blue shirt. He is chewing gum.

"If you want to get an inferiority complex," Bush goes on, "go around shopping centers with this guy." Bush takes his hands out of his pockets and makes shoving motions with them. He changes his voice to imitate a voter. " 'Hey, would you get out of the picture and let us see *Ted?*' "

He laughs; we all laugh. Then it dawns on us that the Vice President of the United States is actually doing shtik. He is doing stand-up comedy.

This day, as Bush will later joke, Williams will be asked to sign ten times as many autographs as Bush. But Bush does not care. He clearly enjoys basking in Williams' glow. And later, at the dogsled races in Laconia, a small kid, one of the racers with a No. 30 pinned to his jersey, will go up to old No. 9 of the Red Sox, hand him a piece of paper and ask for his autograph. Williams takes the paper and looks for a place to rest it on in order to sign it. Bush immediately intervenes. "Hey, Ted," he shouts, "use my back!" And then he hunches over, hands on knees, and lets Williams sign on his back.

Whatta guy. Whatta regular guy.

Bush is asked to go next door to his phone bank. In this room, there is row after row of telephones and people checking off names from long lists as they make calls.

Bush sits down in a chair in front of a telephone, takes his wire-framed glasses out of his pocket, puts them on, reads a number from a list and takes up a Bic pen in his left hand. Finger poised over the telephone as the TV cameras zoom in on him, he turns to Faith Donovan, eighteen, his phone bank supervisor from Nashua.

"How's it been going?" he asks.

"It's been going great," she says.

"Really?" he asks, mild disbelief in his voice. "Really?"

She nods. Bush punches the number into the phone. He waits a moment and begins to speak. "This is George Bush calling from headquarters to solicit your vote. Over and out. Good luck to you."

He turns toward the cameras. "Answering machine," he says.

He is given another number. He dials again. "Is Margaret Packet of Plaistow there?" he asks. "This is the Vice President calling. I am hoping you'd be able to vote for me on Tuesday."

He pauses, listening.

"You will?" The same note of disbelief in his voice. "That's *wonderful*." Bush turns toward the press, making sure the TV crews are picking this up. Heck, this is good news. She could have hung up on him. "Drag a couple of friends with you, will you?" he asks. Then he listens again. "I think we will. I feel good about it. And now I feel *better* about it."

GEORGE BUSH WALKS with his hands in both back pockets through the Fishing and Outdoor Show at the Manchester Armory. He is a big guy ("I've made money betting people my dad is taller than Ronald Reagan," his son Jeb says), but he walks with his shoulders slightly hunched.

Gray light weakly filters through the high windows of the large, echoing hall. There are all sorts of booths, tables and exhibits. Rods and reels, boats, rifles and fishing lures are on display. The Secret Service has been ordered back, far back, and though the procedures for protecting a Vice President are more stringent than those for the other candidates (an ambulance always is included in his motorcade; a helicopter always hovers nearby), the agents have been told to allow the people to get close to George Bush. So people are coming up to him, whomping him on the back, grabbing his hand, asking him to pose for snapshots with their kids. It is a nightmare for the agents. Bush appears to love it.

He stops in front of the Yamaha booth, where a powerful jet ski is on display.

"Ever been on one?" Sununu asks Bush.

Bush looks at him.

"A jet ski," the governor says. "Been on one?"

"Never," Bush says.

"Really?" says the governor, as if just everyone could picture George Bush up on his jet ski, his hard body glistening in the sun as he crashes through the surf.

"Really," says Bush. He moves on to safer territory, the Johnson Woolen Mills table. On it are two stacks of pants. On the left is a stack of forest-green pants and on the right is a stack of zany plaid pants, gray with large red checks. They are $30, marked down from $49.99.

Bush rubs a pair of the green slacks between his thumb and forefinger. "Got a 38?" he asks.

The man behind the table shakes his head.

"Got a 37?" Bush asks.

The man shakes his head again. "A 36," the man says. "We got a 36."

Bush smiles. "I can't do that anymore," he says, straightening up and sucking in his gut. "Don't you have any pants for *fat* guys?"

The man behind the table hesitates, looks at Bush to make sure he has told a joke, and then laughs. The governor of New Hampshire also laughs. Then the people around Bush put their heads back and laugh.

Bush writes down an address and asks that a pair of size 38 pants be sent to him.

"The green pants, right?" the man behind the table says.

"No," says Bush. "Gimme the plaid."

Ab-so-*lute*-ly! The plaid! You can see it now: Sitting around the horseshoe pit at Kennebunkport in his plaid pants, Bush hands Mikhail Gorbachev an ice-cold Tecate and says, "Hey, Mickey, don't go chokin' on the lime!"

Bush moves on, picks up a fishing rod and flexes it expertly. He puts it down and picks up a lure. Al Peters, who is nearby selling hats, shouts over to him: "Tuesday's your day!"

Bush brightens. Tuesday is primary day. Tuesday is victory or . . . the abyss.

A Bush aide appears genie-like at Bush's side, hands him a card with the vice presidential seal on it and Bush autographs it with a black felt-tip pen and hands it to Peters.

At the fly-tie booth run by Stan Fudala and John Heath, Bush sits down and tries to tie a fly. This involves delicate work, tying line around some red squirrel fur clamped in a tiny vise. Bush squints, giving it his full attention. Fudala reaches over from behind him and moves his hands, helping him.

After about thirty seconds, Bush holds up something that looks like a very tiny red squirrel that has been squashed in the road. "A fish would have to be real hungry to go after this," he says. Then he hands vice presidential tie bars to Fudala and Heath.

Bush moves through the crowd. Some people are just realizing they have a celebrity in their midst. A woman charges up to Bush with a clipboard and pen in her hand. The Secret Service agents stiffen, but do not move forward. They stand poised, staring at her, watching her hands.

"This is a petition to ensure public access on Lake Wentworth," she says at high speed. "We would like you to sign this petition on this very important matter, because it is very important to the people of this state."

Bush looks at the woman and then looks at Sununu with an expression that says: Where the hell is Lake Wentworth and how do I get out of this?

"Sign it," Sununu says.

Bush signs it without question.

After he moves on, I ask the woman to let me see the petition. Bush has signed it: "George Bush. Washington/Houston, Texas."

THE PRESIDENTIAL ELECTION of 1840 pitted incumbent Martin Van Buren, a Democrat, against William Henry Harrison, a Whig. Harrison was a military hero, the "victor" in a battle against the Shawnee Indians at Tippecanoe Creek on November 7, 1811. After beating back an Indian attack, Harrison razed an Indian village and then retreated. But the engagement was good enough to create one of the most famous slogans in political history: "Tippecanoe and Tyler Too" was the ticket of Harrison and his running mate, John Tyler.

"William Henry Harrison's 1840 campaign produced a series of firsts . . . including the first systematic and widespread use of what today would be called image advertising," wrote Kathleen Hall Jamieson in *Packaging the Presidency*. Before 1840, campaign advertising emphasized American symbols: the eagle, Lady Liberty, the Constitution, etc. But Harrison's forces were out to create an image, a good old boy image, an image that would transform Harrison into a man of the people.

"Harrison's supporters appropriated the log cabin and cider [barrel] to transform the wealthy son of a governor into a farmer and backwoodsman," Jamieson wrote.

Just as the George Bush campaign would transform the wealthy son of a U.S. senator into just plain folks by emphasizing his love of pork rinds (in reality, Bush much preferred popcorn), horseshoe pitching, hunting and fishing.

"The symbol of the log cabin was a potent one, for it identified Harrison with the pioneers who cut the country from the wilderness and with rural voters still residing in log cabins," Jamieson pointed out. At the time, opposition Democrats revealed the truth: Harrison lived in a palatial Georgian mansion. He owned 2,000 lush acres farmed by tenant farmers. He had been born not in a log cabin but in a fine two-story brick home. He was no rustic. "But the voters would have none of it," wrote Jamieson. "Enveloped by propaganda picturing a log-cabin-dwelling farmer, they clung tenaciously to the fabricated image."

It should not surprise us. Nearly 150 years later, Americans had not changed. When reality was at odds with a pleasant image, Americans took the image every time. Everyone knew that Bush, by manner, speech and upbringing, was a Northeastern preppy. But the image of the horseshoe-pitching, beer-swigging Texan was too much fun to abandon. Bush even had his own version of the log cabin: a hotel suite in Houston that made him an official resident of Texas and a son of the South. Early on, the press exposed the ridiculous nature of renting a hotel room to make oneself a Texan. Few seemed to care.

KINGSWOOD REGIONAL JUNIOR HIGH is a red-brick two-story box in Wolfeboro, New Hampshire. In the gymnasium, the basketball hoops have been cranked out of the way and a few hundred people are sitting on folding chairs on the parquet floor. Many of them are wearing white "George Bush for President" headbands with red feathers sticking up behind. A sign strung across the front of the gym uses the letters of Bush's name to spell out: "B-est U-nited S-tates H-ope." There is a man dressed as Uncle Sam walking on stilts. There is a clown with a painted face. A jazz band. And pretty young cheerleaders dressed in green-and-white sweaters. There are mesh bags full of balloons. ("Balloons," Bush says when he sees them.)

This is not an "impromptu." This has been advanced. The word has gone out to the press that this will be a major speech. The Bush campaign wants this punch telegraphed. This is it, the handlers are saying. Don't miss it.

Sununu enters the gymnasium first, while Bush waits outside in the hall. Bush has put on a black-and-red-striped tie. He strips off his windbreaker and tosses it to a Secret Service agent. Sununu introduces Bush by saying he is about to give an important speech. There are six TV camera crews in the press pen.

Bush walks to the lectern and opens a blue leather folder with the vice presidential seal on it. Before he begins, he glances toward the press pen and looks at us intently as if to say: "O.K., wake up."

Excluding his thanks to the local dignitaries, his thanks to the band and his thanks to "the Splendid Splinter," Ted Williams, his speech lasts twelve minutes and fifteen seconds. In it, he attacks Bob Dole indirectly by stressing his own executive experience over Dole's legislative experience. "Executive leadership is where you call the shots and move the country forward," Bush says. "In the executive, you don't just look out for the interest of one constituent or one district back home; when you're President, back home is the whole nation."

(Bush briefly was America's chief executive. When Ronald Reagan had to undergo general anesthesia for intestinal surgery on July 13, 1985, he transferred constitutional authority to Bush. And so Bush was head of state and commander in chief for seven hours and fifty-four minutes. During that time, he played tennis at his home, slipped, hit his head and, in the words of one aide, had to "sleep it off.")

Bush also directly attacks Dole ten times by name in his speech, but that is not important. The true import of the speech comes near the end, when the audience has fallen deathly silent and all that can be heard in the room is the quiet note of desperation in George Bush's voice.

He grasps the lectern with both hands now and, head down, reads his speech.

"Now let me tell you why I want to lead," he says. "I've been in the White House almost eight years now and I'm not through yet. I'm not done yet doing the work of the people. And that's a big statement, but that's what I want to do.

"I want to keep us strong . . . keep our economy growing . . . end once and for all the sadness of racial division . . . be the education President, the one who schoolchildren look at and know that he cares." And when he says the word "cares," he taps his chest with his hand. It is not one of Bush's stock gestures. Everyone in the gym stares at the hand that now rests lightly upon his heart.

Bush looks up and into their eyes.

"I don't have to do this," he says. "I'm sixty-three years old. I've got some years of mileage on me and a few lines. And I could be over here, sixty, eighty, a hundred miles east in Maine, listening to the waves pound in on the shore over there. My feet up and have a beer. Tell Dorothy's children what it was like to sit across from Gorbachev and take part in a great revolution."

Now he leans forward and grips the lectern so hard you can see his knuckles go white.

"But . . . I'm . . . not . . . done . . . yet! I'm going . . ." But his words are drowned out. People are on their feet applauding, their red feathers bobbing wildly as they beat their hands together, hooting, yelling: "Yeah, George! Ge-orr-gge!" And when has any crowd ever called him by his first name?

". . . giving to my country, giving absolutely everything that I've got," he says. A muscle on the side of his face tenses and untenses. "And I may not seem *passionate* about these things sometimes. I'm not one for the *high-sounding phrases* or the *eloquent declarations*. But don't"—he looks around the room; there is pleading in his voice—"but don't mistake quietness for lack of conviction, lack of belief. I'm not a talker, I'm a doer. And I'm not done doing what I can to help this country. To stand beside it. To guide it. And I want your help."

He stops. He takes a deep, almost shuddering breath. "And one year from now, in the snowy winter of 1989, I'm going to be taking the oath of office. And I'm going to be thinking four words: 'Thank you, New Hampshire.' "

He finishes and steps back from the lectern. There are men and women standing, wiping their cheeks with the back of their hands, clearing their throats, standing and applauding and calling, endlessly calling, the name of their friend. George Bush has done it. He has pulled it off. And it may not even be an act. It may be real. Maybe for the first time it is real.

To lose New Hampshire would be to lose his chance at redemption. For that is what this election is to him. It is to redeem himself in the eyes of his family and the public and history. To win would be the equivalent of the high school geek, the kid with pens sticking out of his shirt pocket, who got pantsed in the locker room and then thrown out into the hall, coming back to the high school reunion as the most successful guy in the class.

George Bush has to win. So, yes, he would let his aides run the negative ads. Yes, he would let people get close. Yes, he would let them peer inside him and see his worst fears. He had to. There was no other way.

George Bush. See him. Touch him. Feel his pain.

BUSH WON NEW HAMPSHIRE, of course. Big. More than 9 points over Dole. Many of the polls had been wrong: the final Gallup poll was off by 17 points.

Bob Dole never really knew what hit him. "I don't know what happened," he said. "Bush was being very effective. He would blanket the news. He had this very tough ad and he was out there shoveling the snow. Bush pulled it off. You know, Wirthlin [Richard Wirthlin, Dole's pollster] told me once, if you win New Hampshire, it's 60–40 you're going to be the nominee. If you lose, it drops back to 40–60. That's about right.

"They all sat around, trying to decide whether to run the Straddle ad. Mrs. Bush was there and Teeter and Ailes, and whoever, and they finally decided to do it. We sat around and didn't decide anything. So I guess that's the difference."

Atwater would emphasize it over and over: unity. Unity equaled strength. He carried a heavily underlined copy of Sun Tzu's *The Art of War* wherever he went and he would quote: "Harmony among people is the basis of the way of military operations." And a campaign was a military operation, wasn't it? You achieved victory, at least in part, by destroying the enemy.

"I think it's almost impossible to avoid negative campaigning," Dole said. "They were more skilled in their attacks. The Straddle ad. It was that one ad. And we weren't prepared. But I hope that this campaign doesn't mean that you go out and destroy your opponent and you win at any cost. Then when it's over, everybody's supposed to cheer you on, saying, well, you wiped that guy out." He snorted. "It paid off, I'll say that. We were told that people in New Hampshire didn't like negative advertising. Well, maybe they didn't like it. But they watched it."

THE "SEE ME, TOUCH ME, feel me" campaign did not last long. Now George Bush was looking good and he didn't need it anymore. The carefully crafted aspects of the Regular Guy would be retained. But not the rest.

The day after the New Hampshire primary, Bush went to a truck stop in Missouri and handed a tie clip to one trucker, saying: "If your old lady makes you wear a tie, slide that on." But that was just about the last time he went to a truck stop. There would be no more snowball fights with the press either. Casual contact would be maintained, but when it was, it often would be off the record. His on-the-record meetings with reporters would eventually go from occasional to sporadic to virtually none. The velvet ropes would go back up for press and public alike.

There would be no more opening up and letting people gaze into his soul. For one brief moment, born of dire need, he had let down the barriers and shown how badly he wanted it, how vulnerable, hurting, desperate a human being he could be.

He would never let it happen again.

2

LIFE AMONG
THE JELL-O EATERS

"Just because your voice reaches halfway around the world doesn't mean you are wiser than when it reached only to the end of the bar."

—*Edward R. Murrow*

TOM BROKAW PULLS UP to the Hotel Savery in Des Moines in a rented blue Thunderbird. He is without aides or entourage. He parks in the taxi zone at the side of the hotel and ducks inside. He is wearing a black turtleneck sweater under a dark windbreaker and brown corduroy pants, cowboy boots and a plaid scarf. He is slightly hung over, having spent the previous night in New York at the theater watching humorist Roy Blount's one-man show and then going to a party.

Because the New Hampshire primary and the Iowa caucuses are only eight days apart, the candidates and press have been bouncing back and forth between the two states. Now, however, it is time for Brokaw to settle in Iowa. It is the last week before the caucuses and he must prepare for the first major telecast of the political season.

Brokaw checks in at the front desk and then takes one of the two old and slow elevators to the third floor, where NBC has set up its control center. Presidential candidates litter the landscape. For a voter, experiencing the campaign in Iowa is like going to the produce section of a supermarket: everything is grouped nicely in one place and you get to poke and prod and thump them to see which ones are ripe.

Few Iowans are really that interested, however. Only about 3 percent will bother to vote in the Monday-night caucuses. One reason is that the voting system has been made as bizarre as possible, which is to say as Democratic as possible. Unlike a primary that has voting booths and secret balloting, the Democrat precinct caucuses in Iowa are held in 2,493 living rooms, high school gymnasiums and basements all at the same hour on the same night. All those who want to vote for Michael Dukakis, for instance, march to one corner of the room under the moose head. All for Paul Simon, over by the potted plant. Those for Bruce Babbitt, into the kitchen. And the groups get to shout and argue and arm-twist as the TV camera crews walk among them, recording it all.

It is not a speedy process. On TV and radio all week, the same public service spot has been running over and over. It features two popular Iowa basketball coaches talking about the wonders of voting in the Hawkeye State. "Iowa has a big say in who will lead this country," one says to the other. "And in about the time it takes to watch a basketball game, Iowans can attend a caucus."

In about the time it takes to watch a basketball game? You mean like two hours? Gee, what a swell way to spend an evening.

Yet even though Iowa and New Hampshire possess less than 2 percent of the U.S. population, the two states accounted for about a third of all the media coverage in the 1984 primaries. The reason is not profound. Somebody has to be first. The curtain has to go up somewhere. And the critics are not about to miss an opening night.

The reason Iowa is first also tells you something about the crazy quilt that is America's electoral process. The precinct caucuses in Iowa are only the first step in selecting delegates that go to the national convention. After the precinct caucuses come the district caucuses and then the state caucus. And in between each, a great deal of information has to be printed up and handed out. In 1972 the Iowa Democratic Party had an old mimeograph machine that worked at a slow and deliberate speed. "We had to give it enough time to print the material between the precinct and district caucuses," Clif Larson, then chairman of the party, said. "The only way to do that was move up the precinct date."

And that is how Iowa became first. Now, in 1988, there are 3,000 newspeople in Iowa. Phil Roeder, the twenty-four-year-old press director for the Iowa Democratic Party, has been interviewed more than 1,200 times. The Los Angeles *Times* has twenty people and two condominiums in Iowa. NBC has 120 people. The thirteen candidates will spend a total of 999 days here. And though Jimmy Carter didn't come to Iowa until February 1975, about one year before the caucuses, Richard Gephardt, Democratic congressman from Missouri, got here in March 1985, about three years before the caucuses. His mother campaigned so much for him here that he got her an apartment in

Des Moines. The combined campaigns employ 656 paid staff members and use thousands of volunteers. By caucus night, about $60 million will have flowed into the state and all 6,000 hotel rooms in a ten-mile radius of Des Moines will be filled.

All because the mimeo machine was slow.

BROKAW CHECKS the long list of the candidates' schedules and notices that Jesse Jackson is speaking in Des Moines at this moment. Though Brokaw has no crew with him, he decides to go. He wants to get a feel for how Jackson is going over here and, even more than that, Brokaw just wants to get out and do something.

Coming here for the caucuses every four years is always somewhat of a homecoming for him. He grew up in the small town of Webster, South Dakota (current population: 2,417), in the northeastern part of the state not far from the Iowa border. And in high school he moved down to Yankton in the southeast near Sioux City, Iowa. He went to college at the University of Iowa in Iowa City for his freshman year—"At that age I believed, as Senator Alan Simpson once said, that beer was a food," Brokaw says—and to him Des Moines was a considerable metropolis. "I have a friend," Brokaw says, "a *New York Times* reporter, who whenever he sees me out here says: 'Ahh, that's right, Brokaw, you speak the *patois*.' "

Brokaw heads back outside and drives to the Prince Masonic Hall, where the Jackson rally is underway. There are no seats left and Brokaw stands to one side of the hall, taking notes in a spiral notebook with a black felt-tip pen as Jesse Jackson speaks. Jackson is dressed exquisitely in a light gray suit, light blue shirt and dark tie. He likes clothes and is always joking about other people's. In 1984, after a presidential debate that Brokaw moderated, Jackson motioned to him. "Brokaw, come here," he said in his commanding voice. Brokaw went over. "Now, Brokaw, tell me," Jackson said. "Where the *hell* did you get that tie?"

When he wants to be, Jackson can be downright playful. Noticing how hard Paul Simon always studied his note cards before each debate, Jackson began walking over to him before the debate, grabbing the cards and mixing them up. Moments before one debate began, Jackson left his seat, scooted across the stage and, with a huge grin on his face, grabbed one of Simon's note cards, stuck it in his jacket pocket and kept it. Then, perhaps as penance, at Faneuil Hall in Boston, Jackson wore a Simon bow tie campaign pin on his lapel for the entire ninety-minute debate without a word of explanation to anyone.

Now Jackson is saying: "Rural farmers and urban workers together will never be defeated. If we turn *to* each other and not *on* each other, we become the new majority." Jackson's crowds across Iowa are very large these days (he will end up with 9 percent of the vote in a state where blacks are only about 1 percent of the registered voters) and he doesn't care if people are coming out of curiosity. Though many are writing that Jackson will do worse in 1988 than he did in 1984—his "novelty" has supposedly worn off—Jackson is convinced he has a real chance. "I'm not looking for a job [in the cabinet] and I'm not looking for a role [in the party]," he will say later. "I could have all those without the sacrifice of the campaign. I want to win. I want to be President. I'm no mystery. What you see is what *is*."

"They told Rosa Parks she could not win!" Jackson is now booming from the stage. "An' she stood up. Two Jews and a black killed in Mississippi could not win! An' they stood up! Medgar Evers, they said he could not win. He stood up. They say *we* cannot win Monday night. Stand *up!* Stand *up!*"

The crowd leaps to its feet. "Jess-*eee!* Jess-*eee!* Jess-*eee!*"

Jackson's speeches often do not have clear-cut endings (you know they are over when he leaves the hall), and now he is going through his ritual of inviting children up on the stage while he tries to explain the complicated caucus voting process to the audience. "When you go to the caucus, they will try to confuse you, but it's just a get-together," Jackson says in his down-home Southern accent, which he employs at his convenience. "Po' folks *lie* and rich folks pre-*var*-i-cate. Rich folks *caucus* and po' folks get to-*geth*-er." While this is going on, a black man in a camel coat and gray hat stands up, moves to the aisle, turns his back on Jackson and heads directly for Brokaw. He reaches out his hand and Brokaw shakes it. "You are very popular here," the man says. Brokaw mumbles a word or two, but now a crowd is gathering, people are peering over each other's shoulders to get a look at him.

"He's goin' to run for President," the man says to the crowd now around Brokaw. "And he's goin' to win!"

It hasn't happened yet, though in the future it seems inevitable. If an actor can become the nation's chief executive, if a peanut farmer can, why not a network anchor? They are bright and good-looking and know how to play to the camera. Others have attained the presidency with only two out of these three.

THE BAR AT the Hotel Savery is long and dark and without ferns. It is off the main lobby and situated in such a way that one can sit at the bar, look out the doorway and watch anyone who enters or leaves the hotel. So you know when Michael Dukakis or Dick Gephardt or Jesse Jackson enters and who they are with. Like the hotel, the bar is nondescript yet famous. It has been remodeled into something that is not quite anything. It is rectangular with a dogleg to the right. There are mirrors along one wall, a long serving bar in the center and a grouping of low tables and chairs to the left as you walk in. Along the street side there is a long row of windows. In the far corner there is a small stage for the nightly jazz band. It is usually the civilians who pay attention to the jazz band. A civilian is anyone not directly connected to the Making of the President, the Campaign, the Road Show. Those who merely select the next President are civilians. Those who write about it, broadcast it and work in it are the players. And the Savery bar is the nexus, the nerve center for the players. The players crowd the Savery bar for a few weeks every four years. And during those weeks, expense account money flows freely and the talk goes on into the wee hours. The talk and not the drink is what is attractive about the Savery bar. The consumption of hard liquor is way down among the new, younger players in the game. But talk has filled the void. It flows, it burbles, it gushes. It never stops.

A campaign aide for Paul Simon, Democratic senator from Illinois, sits down next to me. The atmosphere is collegial in the Savery bar. General, though unspoken, rules apply: the reporters buy the booze. Nothing is strictly on the record, and nothing is strictly off. Slack is cut. Yet should an aide let slip that his candidate is currently upstairs in bed with a live boy or a dead woman, it will make headlines tomorrow.

"We need endorsements in New Hampshire," the Simon aide tells me. "You know of anybody in New Hampshire who's famous?"

I think for a moment. "Christa McAuliffe's husband," I say. "The husband of the schoolteacher who blew up on the space shuttle. How about him?"

"No good," he says.

"Too crass, huh?"

"Naw," he says. "He already endorsed Biden."

Paul Taylor and Bill Peterson, two reporters for the Washington *Post*, are discussing a bon mot somebody has cooked up to describe Gary Hart's lackluster performance in the most recent Democratic debate.

"Did you hear the line?" Taylor says. "It goes: 'Instead of Hart filling the void, he fell into it.' "

"That's good," says Peterson, "that's good. Let's get somebody to say it." He looks around and sees Joe Trippi, the political director of

the Gephardt campaign, talking to Steve Murphy, the campaign's
Iowa director.

"Hey, Trippi," Peterson says jokingly. "You want to be quoted
saying 'Instead of Hart filling the void, he fell into it'?"

Trippi chews the line over a moment and then shakes his head.
"Naw," he says, "give that one to Murphy."

The candidates themselves will sometimes make cameo appearances
in the Savery bar, though they approach it with some caution, like a
swimmer dipping a toe into the water to see if it contains piranha.
Michael Dukakis ducks in and spends just enough time to say the
wrong thing. "You guys were all sitting here when I left Iowa *two
days* ago," he says. "Now I come back and you're still all here."

"So where should we be?" a reporter mumbles. "Cleaning up
Boston Harbor?"

Other public officials, here to endorse candidates, also come in and
sit down and chat up the press. When Boston mayor Raymond Flynn,
who is known for visiting the scenes of disasters in his hometown,
walked into the bar one night, a reporter sat bolt upright and cried:
"Sweet Jesus, we must be on fire!"

The players like Iowa. Most of the stereotypes are true: The people
are friendly. Getting around is easy. Though the blizzards can be
fierce, unlike in New Hampshire there are no mountains to fly into.
Besides, the bars close at 2 a.m. and a Heineken costs only a buck
and a quarter. The reporters collect Iowa minutiae to drop into their
stories like small pearls: Iowa is the only state with more women
drivers than men. It leads the nation in motorcycles per capita and
the consumption of Jell-O. Only 8 percent of the people live on
farms, but 70 percent of the jobs in the state depend on agriculture.
Hogs outnumber the people seven to one. (The term "hog" is favored
over "pig" in Iowa. A grasp of such details is important here. Dick
Gephardt liked to joke that Michael Dukakis came to Iowa, looked
out over a farm and said to the farmer: "How much wool are you
planting this year?")

Still, the state has identity problems. "People still confuse us with
Idaho and Ohio," Governor Terry Branstad said before the caucuses.
"They ask me how the potato crop is doing."

Those must be civilians. The players know Iowa. The reporters
love to travel to small towns—the more rural-sounding the name, the
better—and write about the people. In the Savery bar the story is
being repeated once again. It is fundamentally true; only the details
improve with each retelling:

A reporter has staked out "his" Iowa town for months. He goes to
work with the people. Goes home with them. Helps their kids with

their homework. Finally, with caucus night approaching he lines up his big story. He goes to the farm family he has practically lived with and lays it out for them: he will go to the precinct caucuses with them, take down their every thought as they vote, then come back to the farmhouse with them, sit around the big kitchen table with the red-checked oilcloth and get some real down-home wisdom about What It All Means.

"Well, gosh, son," the farmer tells the reporter, "we'd like to, but we just can't."

The reporter is stunned. "Why not?" he cries.

"Because that night we got a live shot with Koppel," the farmer says.

IT IS 11:20 on a Thursday night, four days before the Iowa caucuses. I have brought my laundry down to the front desk of the Marriott Hotel to try to negotiate for its eventual return. Laundry is the single greatest problem of the traveling press. When you are on the road, bouncing around from city to city, state to state, sleeping in a different hotel bed each night, it is virtually impossible to get your undies washed.

In 1976, a candidate solved the problem. And even though he did not win the election that year, everyone who traveled with him was convinced he had what it took to go all the way. If Ronald Reagan could take care of our laundry, we figured, he could take care of our nation.

You'd get to your room at some motel in some New Hampshire hamlet at 1 a.m. or so. You'd get out your typewriter (no portable computers back then) and would be tapping away when the knock would come on the door. A fresh-faced teenager would be standing there, dressed in a white blouse with a blue skirt and a red sash that read: "Reaganette."

"Hi! I'm here for your laundry, Mr. Simon," she would say, reading the name off a clipboard. "I'll have it back to you by morning."

I never knew where they took the laundry. Could there possibly have been a laundromat open at that hour? No, they must have taken it home. Cindy (I always pretended that my Reaganette was named Cindy; life can be lonely on the road) and her mom and pop and gram and gramps would be stuffing clothes into the washer and dryer all night. And come dawn Cindy would be standing over the ironing board with a steaming iron, blowing away a wisp of hair that had fallen onto her glistening forehead (life can be *very* lonely on the road), just so we could have clean clothes.

"Would you like to come in?" I would always ask my Reaganette.

"No, sir, just the laundry, sir," Cindy would always say.

"There's a radio. We could dance."

"That's very funny, sir. We were told that you reporters would be very funny. Now, would you like these shirts with starch?"

So now I am in the modern and nearly empty lobby of the Marriott Hotel at 11:20 p.m. carrying a laundry bag. Iowa is good for laundry. You can stay in one place to cover the story, which means you can get your laundry done. The glass lobby doors hiss open, letting in a blast of frigid air, and I look up to see a dark and looming figure sweep through them. He is dressed in a long, very soft black coat. Cashmere at the very least, though the possibility of vicuña crosses my mind. He is wearing a gray-brown fedora with the brim snapped down low. He looks like Darth Vader as conceived by Ralph Lauren.

Only a small strip of his face is visible between the hat brim and the upturned collar of his coat, a narrow band, a small window of vulnerability. Still, it is unmistakably Dan Rather. You don't need to see the whole face to work out the puzzle.

Rather strides swiftly across the lobby, looking neither left nor right. A young man follows behind him, lugging a bulging black nylon suit bag. Rather has no bodyguards tonight, though he sometimes uses them. This is a surgical operation: the insertion of Rather into his hotel. It is dependent on stealth instead of muscle. Rather heads for the elevator as the young man darts over to the front desk. He gets Rather's key and hurries back to his side. Rather stands staring straight ahead, his eyes fixed on the blank wall above the elevator buttons.

If any civilian were in the lobby at this hour, he might take a first, faltering step toward Rather to ask for an autograph. But one withering look from those eyes that burn like coals from beneath that hat brim would almost certainly convince him to wait instead for Charles Kuralt.

These days, Dan Rather is not a happy camper. In the last two weeks, he has become the one thing journalists are not supposed to become: news.

What was supposed to be a hard-hitting, feet-to-the-fire interview with George Bush instead turned into what TV critic Tom Shales called "a strange interlude" that "will not help extinguish rumors that Rather has become emotionally unstable."

It began on January 5, 1988, with a letter from Richard M. Cohen, senior political producer at CBS News, to George Bush. The letter said that CBS had been doing a "series of candidate profiles" and "purposefully saved your profile for last, so it could be aired in January, as close to the actual [Iowa] caucus date as possible." Cohen also wrote: "Dan Rather is very interested in your profile and has decided to do it himself."

The letter was not exactly candid. CBS was not planning a "candidate profile" of George Bush. It had assembled a very tough five-minute taped segment bringing up some troubling questions about Bush's role in the Iran-contra scandal.

Still, a news organization does not have to telegraph its punches. It is expected that a presidential candidate should be able to field any question on any subject without being prepared in advance. So the letter, while somewhat disingenuous, was not totally outside the hazy boundary of journalistic ethics.

George Bush liked Dan Rather. When Bush had lived in Houston, Rather had been the news director for a Houston TV station. And Bush was a man who believed in old acquaintanceships. "I feel comfortable with Rather," Bush penned to his staff on the letter from CBS. "Make sure this guy gets a reply soon."

Roger Ailes was not happy with the decision. He looked upon Rather as just another journalist, which was to say the lowest rung on the food chain. "The night before, I got wind of what was going to happen," Ailes said. "Actually, a couple of weeks before, they said they wanted to tape a half-hour interview and use five minutes. I went nuts. No way, I said. You do it live. Then, the night before, Teeter [the Bush pollster] said: 'I think Rather is going to be worse than we thought.'

"I said: 'Well, then it's a good thing we've got George on for only five minutes.'

"He said: 'Well, I hear they're going to use half the news.'

"I said: 'Half the news? What have they got? Something new?' Teeter had this friend at CBS and he told him that the producer was running around saying: 'We're taking Bush out of the race tonight!'

"And Rather—he's managing editor of the show or something—was saying: 'I don't care about the rest of the show tonight. We're taking two-thirds of it on Bush and Iran.' And see, the letter they had sent us said this was going to be a political *profile*. So we were trapped. Sandbagged. If we backed out, it looked like we backed out of a profile."

In another sense, however, there was no reason for Bush to back out. If, as he kept insisting, he didn't know about the arms-for-hostages deal, or he couldn't talk about the details out of loyalty to Reagan, then that should have been good enough to see him through any interview.

But nobody was treating this as an ordinary interview, especially not CBS and Dan Rather. In one of the most extraordinary examples of journalism-as-performance, Rather was prepped for the interview as if he himself were a presidential candidate preparing for a head-to-head debate. On the day of the broadcast, Rather spent at least three one-hour sessions being prepared for the confrontation. "We spent most of the day [Monday, January 25] sitting briefing him, reading through material, going back and forth," said CBS Evening News producer Tom Bettag. Different staff members took different roles and there was a rehearsal of what Rather should do if Bush became "very aggressive." Rather was specifically warned that Bush might bring up the time that Rather walked off the set in Miami when he thought the U.S. Open tennis match was going to cut into the news broadcast. This resulted in CBS's "going black" for six minutes.

And Rather's preppers, his "war-gamers," were not just other journalists. They also included Tom Donilon, a Democratic Party activist who had been a top aide in Walter Mondale's 1984 campaign and had been working in the Joe Biden campaign until it folded. Now he was a paid consultant for CBS. (And later he would go to work for Michael Dukakis.)

To Ailes this was the last straw. He felt that when CBS hired a Democratic campaign operative to brief Rather to attack Bush, it was just another example of how little ethics the press had. Ailes agreed with the saying that journalistic ethics are to ethics what Velveeta is to cheese.

"George knows the press is not on his side and it doesn't bother him," Ailes said. "What bothers him is when it's personal. Rather got personal. CBS hires a liberal, Democratic consultant to coach Dan Rather and get George Bush. *That's* personal. And that piece they produced was McCarthyism. Five minutes of guilt by association. And the piece was wrong! That pissed George off."

After campaigning most of the day in New Hampshire, Bush had flown at 4:25 p.m. to Washington for the 6:30 p.m. interview. Unlike Rather, he had not spent the day being briefed. "I don't need a briefing," he told his aides. "I want to relax."

Because it was snowing heavily, Bush could not helicopter in from Andrews Air Force Base, and Ailes went out in the vice presidential limousine to get him. "I sat in the back of the car with Bush," Ailes said, "and I told him: 'It's going to get ugly tonight. CBS is going to take you out. They've got two Democrats out [Gary Hart and Joe Biden] and now they need a Republican to drive out and you're it.'

"And he says: 'Oh no, it won't be like that. It will just be questions about Iran and I don't know anything about it.' Well, you know George. So I told him: 'I have reason to believe it will not be pleasant.'

I told him to act in a normal, civilized manner, but if he gets sandbagged by Rather, he should kick the shit out of him."

Rather would be at the CBS studios in New York and Bush would be in his Capitol office. CBS's plan was to show the taped segment on Iran-contra, break for a commercial and then question Bush. They planned the Bush interview to last from three minutes to, at the outside, eight and a half minutes. But by the time it actually ended, nine minutes had passed and the producers were screaming into Rather's earpiece to end the segment. Altogether, the taped segment and the Bush interview took up fourteen minutes and forty-nine seconds, a very long time considering that the evening newscast minus commercials is only twenty-two minutes long. It is the kind of time usually reserved for a major disaster or an assassination.

CBS had been promoting the show that weekend, saying that it was going to be on Iran-contra, and Ailes had warned Bush of it. Still, when Rather introduced the taped segment and said the interview would be about "arms to Iran and money to the contras," Bush reacted as if he was surprised.

"Iran-contra affair?" Bush said into his microphone, which could not be heard on the air yet, but could be heard in the control booth in New York. "I didn't know this was about the Iran-contra affair. If he talks to me about the Iran-contra affair, they're going to see a seven-minute walkout here."

As ten million people watched, Rather and Bush then slugged it out. They sniped, they shouted, they insulted one another.

"Mr. Vice President, you've made us hypocrites in the face of the world!" Rather said in his toughest punch.

But what role was Rather playing when he said it? Was he a reporter? Commentator? Interviewer? Debater? On TV, the roles often seemed jumbled together.

Bush had his own rabbit punch ready: ". . . it's not fair to judge my whole career by a rehash on Iran. How would you like it if I judged your career by those seven minutes when you walked off the set in New York? Would you like that?"

The line had been scripted in advance by Ailes. And during the exchange, Ailes was standing by the side of the camera directly in front of Bush holding up homemade idiot cards.

So had he and Bush set up Rather instead of the other way around?

"Yeah, right," Ailes said later, his voice heavy with sarcasm. "Two guys in the back of a car for forty-five minutes and we sandbagged Rather? They spend a hundred thousand dollars and take a year and get a coach for Rather to produce five minutes and we have forty-five minutes to prepare, and *we* sandbagged *them*? We must be the smartest sons of bitches who ever lived. George Bush should have been elected by acclamation if we were that smart." (When asked the same question, Atwater played it a little closer to the vest. "We never talk about how we make sausage," he said.)

Ailes continued: "The fact is that George knocked Rather on his ass. And it was no ambush. It was a street fight. And we won."

You mean you won with the "walked off the set" line?

Ailes smiled. "If you slow it down and watch it in slow motion, Rather looks like a fighter taking a punch," Ailes said. Then Ailes blinked slowly, looked wide-eyed and snapped his head back in slow motion to imitate Rather. "Look at it sometime. Just look at it. Rather thought George would play the gentleman, because that's the way George is. But George knocked him on his ass. There was no way Bush could respond to the questions and I told him not to. And I'll tell you, George was pissed. This was not fair play."

Why not? Bush was a presidential candidate. What was unfair about asking him about Iran-contra?

"If I stick a microphone in your face," Ailes said, "and say, 'What were you doing on January 16 and who were you with and what was said?' you're going to blink and your eyes are going to roll and you're going to sweat and there is no way you're not going to look guilty. You can know an issue and still look bad. You can be asked in a way that confuses you. You may not have all the details, but TV doesn't allow for that. I can pause five seconds here and think of an answer and that's fine. If I pause five seconds on TV, I look guilty as hell. George was never worried about the questions. I was worried about how he would look answering them."

When the interview ended, Bush was energized, like a fighter who really had knocked Rather on his ass. "Well, I had my say, Dan," he said, off the air now, but with his mike still live. Then he turned to Ailes and said: "He makes Lesley Stahl look like a pussy!" And then back to Rather: "You can tell your goddamned network that if they want to talk to me, raise their hands at a press conference. No more 'Mr. Inside' stuff."

Initial public reaction favored Bush. Network anchors are Goliaths, and Rather had managed the neat trick of making the Vice President of the United States look like a David. Richard M. Cohen, the senior political producer who had written the letter to Bush, later gave an interview to Julie Gammack of the Des Moines *Register*. "Look, I think Dan made mistakes," he said. "I think his posture was probably too aggressive, but that's not the issue. I'd be the first to say we made a tactical error in agreeing to go live, because you can't control a live situation. We took a very heavy hit. I think it was very damaging to us. To Dan. To our credibility."

The newspaper interview appeared on caucus day and that night Cohen was barred from the CBS set. Less than four weeks later, he was fired.

"You know what it was with Rather?" Ailes said. "It was the first political debate and Rather was the Democratic debater. For the first time in political history, a newsman played the role of the opposing candidate. And I told George that. I said, 'Rather has been coached for two days to get you and trap you and that's a debate. CBS is not going to be in the news business tonight. It is going to be a debate and you need to go on the offensive. Don't do anything until he throws the first punch and then get him.' "

What about Bush's calling Lesley Stahl a "pussy"?

"Oh, I heard him say that behind me and I said: 'Oh no,' " Ailes said. "He didn't say it in anger. He wasn't riled. He was just saying it to me and his mike was on. That was my fault. I wasn't watching. I had turned away. Later, we said he meant she was a pussycat or something."

The pussy quote—it was immediately leaked—was a problem for the press. It is a word that does not usually appear in print. But a presidential candidate had said it. The press was divided. *Newsweek* used the quote; *Time* did not. The Baltimore *Sun* used it; the Washington *Post* did not, referring to it as a "vulgar" word instead. The Des Moines *Register* did not use it, but it did quote Bush's use of "goddamned," which, in Iowa, was bad enough. Bush later said: "If I had known the microphone was on I would not have taken the Lord's name in vain."

But letter after letter came in to the Des Moines *Register* like the one from Helen Denton of Slater, Iowa (population 1,312), who wrote: "Doesn't he know the Lord would have heard him even if the microphone had not been on or does he think a sin is not a sin if not heard or seen by anyone?"

What about the Iran-contra affair itself? In the aftermath of the Bush-Rather exchange, columnists and editorial writers kept saying that Iran-contra was the issue "that would not go away." In fact, however, it was an issue that never really went anywhere. To the public, there was no smoking gun. Iran-contra was complicated and confusing and messy. Who could really follow it all? All those countries, all those names. To Bush's Republican opponents, there was no way of using Iran-contra against Bush without also using it against Reagan. And nobody wanted to attack Ronald Reagan.

Bush also had a secret weapon on his side.

John Tower, former senator from Texas, had been recruited by Atwater in the spring of 1987. And he joined the Bush campaign after chairing a three-man committee investigating the role of the National Security Council—on which Bush sat—in the Iran-contra scandal. After the Tower Commission essentially exonerated Bush, Tower traveled from one end of the nation to the other telling people about it. Nobody campaigned harder for George Bush. And whenever someone brought up Iran-contra, Tower was trundled out to smother the flames. "There literally was not a surrogate in the country who did more than John Tower," Atwater said. "He was the best guy in the world to deal with the Iran questions. He'd knock them down firmly and quickly."

And Tower was rewarded for his knockdowns. After Bush's election, he was nominated to be Secretary of Defense. The Senate rejected the nomination, but Bush had tried. He believed in helping those who had helped him, especially those who had helped him in the dark, early days. Ask Sally Novetzke. In 1979, when Bush was running against Ronald Reagan, Sally Novetzke, a Republican activist, invited Bush into her Iowa home and campaigned hard for him. Then she again campaigned hard for Bush in 1988.

In 1989, Sally Novetzke was named Ambassador to Malta.

KATIE BOYLE, Bob Dole's spokesman in Iowa, had to keep "Pussygate" alive. As soon as Bush had used the word, Boyle had made her own official response. It was "very unpresidential and downright crude," she said.

When trouble hits, a campaign usually does whatever damage control it can and then hunkers down and waits forty-eight hours. In that time, the issue either will die and become just another blip on the radar screen or will snowball into a disaster.

Katie Boyle had to keep the snowball rolling. Two days after the Bush-Rather exchange, I made a routine call to her to arrange an interview with Dole.

"Did you hear what Bush called Lesley Stahl?" Boyle asked me.

I was tempted to say no. I was tempted to make Boyle actually say the word out loud, but I fessed up. Yes, I said, and my paper already printed the word.

"You did?" she said. "You really did? That's great. That's great! I think the feminists are going to be outraged, don't you?" Boyle wanted me to do a column on Bush and the word.

"Are you going to ask Bush about it?" Boyle said. "I think you should ask him about it."

Well, if he's in Iowa, I guess I could ask, I said.

"He's in South Dakota tonight," Boyle said, giving me Bush's schedule. It is not often you get George Bush's schedule from the Bob Dole campaign staff.

Uh, I think I'll just wait until he gets to Iowa, I said.

"It's only a five-hour drive," Boyle said.

And she was serious. After all, what was a five-hour drive at night in winter across Iowa compared with the seriousness of Bush's being a potty-mouth?

I think I'll wait for Bush to get to Iowa, I told Boyle. And I could just see it: Bush finishes up his speech to the Girl Scout Jamboree and is heading for the limousine and I am standing on the other side of the rope, waving my arms and shouting: "Yoo-hoo, Mr. Vice President! Just one more question on this pussy thing!"

"So you'll ask him in Iowa?" Boyle said.

If I see him, I'll ask him, I said. (I never did see Bush again in Iowa and Pussygate died, once again proving that the media rarely concentrate on the real issues.)

There was nothing wrong with Boyle pitching me on the story, however. Just as there was nothing wrong with Terry Michael, the highly respected communications director for the Paul Simon campaign, going to Dan Balz, the Washington *Post*'s national editor, and asking him if the *Post* was going to examine Bruce Babbitt's "regressive" tax proposals before the Iowa caucuses. One campaign trying to get negative ink for another campaign is just the way the game is played.

"There is nothing wrong with it and, in fact, it is part of the public's right to know," Michael said. "But you have to be credible. What you try to do when you approach a reporter with a negative story is present evidence and provide some neutral third party if you can. You have to be a skillful salesman."

Which is why the downfall of John Sasso, Michael Dukakis' campaign manager, was so strange. In September 1987, Sasso, one of Dukakis' closest advisers and a person Dukakis considered "like a brother," had found some dirt on Joe Biden, Democratic senator from Delaware. At the Iowa State Fair, Biden had used some of the same words in a speech that Neil Kinnock, leader of the British Labor Party, had previously used. It was not exactly a felony and in a previous speech Biden had given Kinnock credit. This time Biden had merely forgotten the rule that if you steal from one person it's called plagiarism and if you steal from many it's called research.

But the Dukakis campaign was keeping a close watch on Biden. That's because Biden was hitting Dukakis where it hurt the most: in the pocketbook. Dukakis' greatest claim to fame in the presidential campaign to date had been his amazing fund-raising abilities. In April 1987, when Dukakis formally declared his candidacy, he had no money, while Biden already had amassed $2.1 million. (Hart, leading in the polls, had $1.5 million.) But in one night, at a Boston fund-raiser in June, Dukakis raised $2 million. Then he launched a national fund-raising effort. At the bedrock of Dukakis' campaign was the theory that the guy who raised the most money had the best chance of winning.

Brian Sullam, a reporter for the Baltimore *Sun*, obtained a research grant from the Project for Investigative Reporting on Money in Politics to do a computer analysis of all the contributions to the Democratic candidates in 1987. "One fact leapt out of the data," Sullam said, "and that was that Joe Biden was going to all the same places that Dukakis was for money—and in some states Biden was beating him. It became clear to me that Dukakis had to knock off Biden or else risk his money drying up."

As Sullam wrote in *The New Republic* on March 14, 1988: "When Dukakis' staff knocked off Senator Joseph Biden last fall, they eliminated the only formidable candidate challenging him for fund-raising supremacy. . . . By forcing Biden out, Sasso had made Dukakis the front-runner."

By early 1988, Dukakis had raised $10.2 million, nearly $6 million more than any other Democrat. (That would be good enough to get Dukakis the nomination of his party, but after the Democratic convention his people had a hard time switching gears. "Since the general election is publicly funded," Sullam wrote, "the key to winning in November is not how skillfully you raise [money], but how you spend it.")

When Sasso got his hands on a videotape of the Kinnock speech and a videotape of the Biden speech using the same words, he knew he had a way of getting rid of Dukakis' chief opponent. Sasso put the two tapes together on one tape and leaked the "attack video," as it came to be known, to *The New York Times*, NBC and the Des Moines *Register*. All three went with the story. None revealed its source.

The story did not become a blip. It snowballed. Other Biden character flaws were discovered (he had inflated his academic record and had insulted a voter in New Hampshire) and Biden withdrew from the race.

But one question still remained on the table: Who had leaked the attack video? At first, Biden thought it was the Paul Simon campaign and then suspicion turned to the Dick Gephardt campaign. Eventually, attention turned to the Dukakis camp.

Now Sasso made his fatal error. He denied being behind the Biden attack. And so Dukakis denied it, too. Finally, Sasso went to Dukakis and admitted it. Dukakis held a news conference and apologized, saying he had no idea that Sasso had done it. He was reluctant to fire Sasso, the most important figure in his campaign. But this just kept the snowball rolling and Dukakis was forced to dump Sasso.

All of which led to one of the more esoteric jokes of the 1988 campaign: Jimmy Carter, Richard Nixon, Gary Hart, Joe Biden, and Michael Dukakis are all on a cruise ship when it hits an iceberg and begins to sink.

Carter says: "Women and children first!"

Nixon says: "Screw 'em!"

Hart says: "Do you think we have time?"

Biden says: "Do you think we have time?"

Dukakis says: "Did you hear what Joe Biden just said?"

One of the problems with the whole attack video episode, however, was that it just wasn't very believable. Which is not to say it wasn't true.

But to believe it, you have to believe that Sasso, who is like a brother to Dukakis, never tells Dukakis what he is up to. And then you have to believe that Dukakis never asks. The Biden attack video is all over TV and in the papers for days, but you have to believe Dukakis never turns to Sasso and says: "Gee, I wonder where the video came from."

Dukakis said he never asked and was never told. Perhaps, however, this was because he did not want to know. There were other things that Dukakis never knew about. Such as his wife's addiction to amphetamines for the first nineteen years of their marriage. Early in the campaign, Kitty Dukakis admitted to the addiction, which began when she was nineteen and before she met Dukakis. Campaigns are never hurt by confessions, only discoveries, and Kitty got a lot of sympathy for her admission. But, again, the real question is why Dukakis never knew. The two were clearly devoted to each other and very much in love with each other, but for nineteen years he doesn't know his wife is a speed freak?

When this question is asked of Dukakis' children, they provide an insight. No, that's just the way Dad is, one says. Dad just wouldn't notice something like that.

Sasso's departure from the campaign was a major blow, even though he would rejoin it after Dukakis' nomination. Some felt that without Sasso the campaign never went about the essential task of establishing a clear and appealing persona for Dukakis. But what had Sasso really done that was so terrible when he leaked the attack video? There was ample precedent. The Republicans had a "truth squad" following Harry Truman around the country in 1948, leaping on his every word and reporting its findings to the press. And in 1968, the Republican National Committee tape-recorded every Hubert Humphrey speech and provided reporters with lists of what it considered inconsistencies and errors.

"I don't know a campaign that doesn't have an opposition research staff," Kerry Moody, a press aide with the Pat Robertson campaign, said. "Why would you research the stuff if you weren't going to use it? Heck, if I had done that tape, I would have gotten a raise."

But Sasso got bounced. And soon afterward, Democratic representative Bruce Morrison of Connecticut, one of the brightest members of Congress, met with Dukakis. Dukakis was wooing congressmen, looking for their support. And it would have been logical for Morrison to endorse a candidate from a neighboring state.

"But I asked Dukakis the question that nobody else had asked him," Morrison said. "I asked: 'What would you have done if Sasso had come to you with the Biden tape?'"

"And Dukakis said: 'I would have burned it.'"

"And right then," Morrison said, "I knew Michael Dukakis would never be President."

ON THE SUNDAY before the Iowa caucuses, many of the presidential candidates went to church. Pete du Pont played miniature golf. I asked his press secretary, Fred Stern, why.

"Because," Stern said, "they don't allow TV cameras in church."

It is hard to argue with Stern's logic. Because eleven TV crews have shown up to record du Pont's stunt. Eleven TV crews! For Pete du Pont! Even though he has been formally campaigning longer than any candidate in either party—he officially announced on June 3, 1986—Pierre Samuel du Pont IV, former governor of Delaware, is a household name only in the MacNeil/Lehrer household.

Why do guys like du Pont bother to run? Well, they have an ego, for one thing. And they think they can do some good, for another. And, after all, Jimmy Carter was a long shot. But mostly they run because there is an entire industry that has urged them to. Pollsters, media consultants, campaign managers, fund-raisers, political directors, they all need somebody to employ them every four years. So they crunch a bunch of numbers and they cook up a mess of scenarios and they peddle them to whoever will listen: "You finish in the first tier in Iowa, Pete, and then we take that bounce into New Hampshire and finish no worse than third and we really break from the pack in the South on Super Tuesday and blah, blah, blah."

The operatives stroke the candidates and feed their egos and play to their ambitions and convince them they really have a chance. And, if possible, the operatives try to get paid up front.

So Pete du Pont was playing miniature golf on the Skywalk in Des Moines and looking into the lights of eleven camera crews. "When I proposed replacing welfare with work and phasing out farm subsidies, I couldn't get a camera to cover me," he said. "If I could get this many cameras to cover my campaign, I'd be doing better."

At the eighteenth hole, as du Pont was lining up his last putt, I asked Bob Perkins, his communications director, if he felt any embarrassment in cooking up such an obvious and issueless stunt.

"I have never read or seen an issues piece or substance piece in the media on the day before an election," Perkins said. "There is one purpose to this kind of thing: get your face one more time on the evening news."

Du Pont finished at eight under par and smiled for the cameras as his supporters waved signs behind him so the signs, too, would make the news. When it was all over, he turned to Perkins. "Did you ever think it would get to this?" du Pont asked, shaking his head a little ruefully. "A bunch of guys holding up signs at the eighteenth hole of a golf tournament on the Skywalk in Iowa?"

"Yes," Perkins said. "Yes, I did."

IN THE SAVERY BAR sit John Russonello and Sergio Bendixen of the Bruce Babbitt campaign. "Babbitt has been over at the Kirkwood Hotel since 9 a.m. making a new commercial," Russonello says, "and he just finished." It is ten minutes after 10 p.m., which means Babbitt has been making this commercial for more than thirteen hours.

Babbitt, the former Democratic governor of Arizona, has been getting very good press. Terry Michael has a theory that every four years the press gives its heart to the one candidate who runs his campaign the way the reporters would run a campaign: with candor, humor—and utterly no chance of winning.

Babbitt has practically lived in Iowa for eighteen months and his every word has been reported upon, even when he was reunited with his wife after a long time and he leaned over to her and whispered: "I'm horny."

A reporter asks Russonello how he is going to put his new commercial on the air and still stay under the spending limit. Each state has a maximum amount a campaign can spend there. The amount is fixed by law, but campaigns violate it with such frequency that it is considered a joke. If you get caught, you usually end up getting fined two or three years after the election.

The spending limit in Iowa is $775,217 per candidate. (For the whole nominating process, it is a staggering $26.6 million per candidate.) To stay under the limit, the campaigns rent cars in Missouri and drive them over the border or shuffle staff members in and out of the state. They also lie.

"Ask Sergio," Russonello says to the reporter. "He's in charge of that. Ask him about the spending limit and he'll tell you: 'What limit?' "

The reporter turns to Sergio and asks him how he is going to put the new Babbitt commercial on the air and not go over the spending limit.

"What limit?" Sergio says.

IN THE SAVERY BAR I am bragging. I have just pulled off a minor coup. Just to see if I can legally do it, I have registered to vote in Iowa. In reading over the voting requirements for the Iowa caucuses, I realized that many of the reporters had been in the state long enough to qualify. So I went out and got a voter registration application and I told the truth: I am a reporter staying at a hotel. Can I vote? A call is placed to Paulee Lippsman, the administrative assistant to the secretary of state of Iowa. Can a reporter, occupying a hotel room, legally register to vote? she is asked. Sure, comes the answer, why not? I fill out the card listing 700 Grand Avenue, Des Moines, as my address. That is the Marriott Hotel. A few days later, my voter registration card comes in the mail. I am officially registered in the 65th Precinct of the Third Ward of Polk County.

But when caucus night comes, I have second thoughts. I go to my precinct caucus site, Elsie Mason Manor, just a few blocks from the hotel, but one thought keeps crossing my mind: what if I vote and the whole election is decided by one vote? *My* vote. What if I change history? So I chicken out. I don't vote. Later, however, at the Savery bar, I pass around my voter registration card. And everyone gets a big laugh out of it.

But, hey, someone asks, what are you going to do when they call you for jury duty?

OUT AT ST. AUGUSTIN'S, the chapel filled up quickly and soon people had to stand in the back. The thin winter light picked up the bright colors from the stained-glass windows and cast them onto the faces of the mourners. The chapel had white walls and Gothic arches of dark wood. Up in front, there was a picture of Lisa Mack. It was one of those graduation pictures, all pastel shades and soft features.

Lisa Mack was twenty-four when she died. It happened sixteen days before the Iowa caucuses. That's how time was measured. Sixteen days before the caucuses. She died in a seventeen-car pileup in a blinding snowstorm. She had been a Bob Dole volunteer and had spent nearly her every waking hour trying to assure his victory in Iowa. Now Mrs. Dole was sitting quietly in the pew behind Lisa Mack's parents.

Lisa Mack was a volunteer; she got no money. All the work she did was done because she believed. She believed in the man, in the message, in the moment. We reporters tended to miss that. Belief? Who could possibly believe in these guys? It was all just politics, a game, a performance. Surely everyone knew that.

Lisa Mack was born in Minnesota and had graduated from Iowa State University in Ames. She was devoted to her sorority, Alpha Chi Omega, and returned there long after she had left the campus. Now her sorority sisters sat in the first pews, their pins over their hearts, weeping softly as the organist played "Amazing Grace."

Lisa Mack was a food editor at *Better Homes and Gardens* magazine, which is based in Des Moines. "The first day she was on the job, she put up a Dole sticker on her door," Pat Teberg, thirty-two, senior food editor at the magazine, said. "I couldn't believe it. Until then, I joked that out of the twenty-six food editors, I was the only Republican."

Teberg was not only a Republican; she was the Dole volunteer chairman for Polk County, the county that contains Des Moines. Lisa Mack went to work for Pat Teberg. "She would work at the magazine during the day and then come and work for Dole at night and on weekends," Teberg said. Lisa Mack's job was to go down long lists of registered Republican voters, call them, identify likely Dole supporters, persuade them to vote on caucus night and try to recruit others into the campaign.

"She was sitting here Thursday night, the last time I saw her alive, and she was phoning people," Teberg said, sitting now at her desk in Dole headquarters. "She was going home to Minnesota to see her sister in a high school play and then help out with the Dole campaign up there. The last thing I remember is giving her a Dole button so she could wear it home."

On the way back from that trip at around 4:30 p.m.—she wanted to get back to Des Moines early enough to do some more work for the campaign—Lisa Mack drove into a howling plains blizzard. She spun into the side of a bridge and she might have made it—she always wore her seat belt—but the semitrailer behind her drove over her car, flattening it.

I asked Teberg why the volunteers did it, why any of them did it. Why they spent so much time with so little hope of reward.

"Lisa believed in America," Teberg said, as if it were the most obvious thing in the world. "She believed you can't sit back and wait for things to happen. She believed that each person should try to make a difference."

There were a thousand Lisa Macks in Iowa and hundreds of thousands across the country. And they never thought it was all just a game played out for the benefit of the press and politicians. They did not see it as a matter of polls or commercials or who hired the best media wizard. They thought it was about America. About making things happen. About bearing the flame and dreaming the dream.

When the Mass for Lisa Mack was over, her sorority sisters rose, walked to the front of the chapel and faced the rest of us. They sang a slow, wistful song and fresh tears began flowing down their soft, unlined cheeks, making silver tracks in the flickering light of the chapel candles.

I did not go to the Savery bar that night. I left St. Augustin's and drove to Bob Dole headquarters. The phones were ringing there and the computers were humming. A group of new volunteers was being lectured on how to get out the vote on caucus night.

Some things never stop. And, for some, the dreams never die.

"I DON'T SPEAK these kids' language," Tom Brokaw is saying, speaking of the new generation of TV reporters. "They come up and say, 'Mr. Brokaw, I'm in the No. 19 market and I'd like to move to the No. 17 market. I've done live shots and my Q-ratings in Columbus are 69.2 and moving to 70.4. Can you help me?' I ask them what they're interested in and they say: 'Getting on the air.' Then they add: 'What agent should I use?' "

Later, he will walk past a long row of huge, boxy, satellite TV trucks, called mobile uplinks, or KUs. These are not the small microwave trucks that nearly every TV station in America has. These are trucks capable of beaming a signal up to a satellite in geosynchronous orbit 22,280 miles above the earth. There are only seventy-four such mobile uplinks in the United States. On caucus night, forty of them will be in Des Moines.

There is no good answer as to why. They are here for the same reason 3,000 newspeople are here. To be close to the action. To fly the flag. To show the folks back home that we care enough to send the very best: ourselves. But are the Iowa caucuses really worth this attention? The winners, Bob Dole and Dick Gephardt, will go nowhere. The third-place finishers, Bush and Dukakis, will go on to get the nominations of their parties in what will later be called the Revenge of the Thirds.

What do you suppose all these uplinks are really doing here? I ask Brokaw.

"I don't know," Brokaw says. "But I'll bet they're not covering their city halls."

IT IS 8:30 A.M. and Tom Brokaw goes up to Suite 900 of the Hotel Savery, which is Michael Dukakis' suite. The large living room is decorated with Mediterranean furniture and tall mirrors over a fake fireplace. Dukakis is standing, surrounded by a mini-entourage of five, including Kitty and Andrea, one of his daughters. Brokaw's crew has set up its equipment and now Brokaw takes his place next to Dukakis.

Dukakis is standing with his fingers laced across his stomach, a smile fixed on his face, looking very much like a Kewpie doll in a business suit. As he makes small talk with Brokaw, his makeup woman, Louise Miller, steps up to him and pats his cheeks with powder. He does not stop talking.

Brokaw gets the signal to begin and Dukakis turns to the other people in the room, who have been conversing in low tones. "Quiet on the set, everybody!" Dukakis says in a sharp, schoolmarm tone. "Quiet!"

Brokaw's crew look startled. If quiet is needed, one of them usually asks for it—and politely. But then people new to Dukakis are just getting to know his little quirks. "I once had to arrange an interview with Dukakis," a TV producer with another network said, "and this was early in the campaign when I still thought he was a normal human being. So I made a little joke. I said something like: 'They want to interview you because they really think you might be the leader of the free world.' And Dukakis looks at me with this deadly serious expression on his face and says: 'Yes, and it's a *grave* responsibility.' "

If Dukakis has a sense of humor, it is not discernible. He has replaced emotion with icy control. He is the man who can eat one potato chip. And though he talks about his pride in being a Greek-American, he acts as if he were a Yankee Puritan. In just one generation, he has become totally assimilated. Not for nothing is he called Zorba the Clerk.

The cameras roll and Brokaw begins. He asks Dukakis if this seems to be a campaign without passion. "Or is that a misreading?" Brokaw asks.

"I think it's a misreading," Dukakis says, gives one of his slow, almost lizard-like blinks and then takes off for the high country. "I think there's an enormous amount of passion about this country's values, about whether we're going to respect the law and the Constitution and have a President who understands that and respects the law and respects the Constitution both here and abroad. I think there's great uncertainty about our economic future. Where are we going? What are we doing? How can we live with a federal budget deficit of 150 to 200 billion dollars a year, year after year after year? And that's why I think the next President has got to be somebody who is tested and brings very strong fiscal and economic leadership to the White House."

What was the question again? Didn't it have something to do with passion?

Brokaw is professional enough not to wince, but he has run headlong into pol-speak. These are answers that have little or nothing to do with the questions. Presidential candidates are like Hollywood stars on movie tours (or authors on book tours) who have been told to mention the name of their new venture at least once every ninety seconds no matter what they are asked.

As Dukakis drones on and on, hitting every buzzword on his computer chip—schools, the environment, health care, strong leadership—Nick Mitropoulos, one of his closest friends, leans over to me. "He's doing this *without notes*," he whispers. "Can you believe this guy? No notes. None!"

Brokaw asks Dukakis how he will do when the campaign shifts to the South, a region where a Greek name may not play very well.

"Well, there was another guy from Massachusetts way back in 1960," Dukakis says, and bounces on his heels a little and smiles. "And he had a different name and was new and was young and people said he couldn't win in the South, Tom. But he did. Dramatically."

Dukakis loves this comparison. He brings it up all the time, as if it were actually meaningful. As if the American people looked at Dukakis and heard what he said and how he said it and then slapped themselves on their foreheads and said: "My God! Michael Dukakis and John Kennedy! Two peas in a pod!"

☆ **3** ☆

THE MAN WHO
FELL TO EARTH

*"Follow me around, I don't care. I'm serious. If anybody
wants to put a tail on me, go ahead. They'd be very bored."*
— *Gary Hart,* The New York Times Magazine,
May 3, 1987

*"In frustration, I said: 'Look, follow me around.' I obviously
didn't mean into my house."*

— *Gary Hart to author,*
December 10, 1988

A LAVENDER DAYBREAK over a line of scudding clouds. A wind
like a dagger to the heart. Snow so cold it squeaks underfoot. Twisted
icicles the color of martinis. Ridges of frozen snow like small mountain
ranges in the flat expanse of the parking lot of Kollsman Instruments
in Nashua, New Hampshire.

Kollsman is a series of long, low, well-guarded buildings. Like so
many factories here, it makes things best not talked about. Things
for the Defense Department. Hopefully *our* Defense Department.
Details are best left to the imagination. The sole detail that is important
to Bob Stewart, the security guard, is that no outsider gets inside
Kollsman Instruments. Not the press. Not the presidential candidates.
Not the Secret Service. To Stewart, the world is divided up neatly
into those with Kollsman security passes and potential saboteurs.

Pinpricks of cold tingle my lungs. Each breath vaporizes in the still
air and falls in little flakes toward my stamping boot tops. Gary Hart
is late. Gary Hart is always late.

After twenty minutes of watching me, Stewart throws open a glass
door and pokes his head out of the building. "You can come inside
this far," he says, motioning to a tiny area in front of the security

desk. He is not a man without compassion. Besides, should I freeze to death on the company parking lot, the paperwork would be horrendous. Inside, the warmth stabs at my toes as they thaw.

There are 2,000 employees working in six buildings at Kollsman, and 2,000 people in a state where only about a million live is not to be passed up. Asked why he robbed banks, Willie Sutton once said: "Because that's where the money is." Ask a presidential candidate why he goes to factories in New Hampshire and he'll tell you that's where the voters are, all in one place and unable to flee. To someone running for President, a captive audience is the best kind of audience.

Many factories will let the candidates come inside and tour in the belief that this is good publicity. A candidate, trailing a gaggle of minicams, photographers and reporters, squeezes down long assembly lines, jostling workers who are blinded by the TV lights just as they are trying to fit complex circuit boards together. On these tours, I always try to find out if they are putting together aircraft parts. And then I try to avoid those aircraft in the future.

But you don't tour Kollsman Instruments. A presidential candidate can stand outside and shake the hands of the workers. (One sign of a candidate's popularity is if workers bother to take their gloves off.) Experienced candidates know never to show up to shake the hands at the end of the day. At the end of the day, a person wants to go home or get a drink or do anything except stop and talk to a candidate in a parking lot. No, the smart candidates grab voters on their way in to work, when they are looking for an excuse to delay the day. Pete du Pont, a newcomer to presidential politics, had come to Kollsman at the end of the day and had been trampled by people trying to get home. Gary Hart was no neophyte, however. He had been around the track before, had upset Walter Mondale to win New Hampshire in 1984 and knew how the game was played.

But he was late. Inside, by the security desk, two young women, one in slacks and one in a miniskirt, have sneaked away from their jobs to peek out at the walkway that leads up from the parking lot. "I've never seen him up close before," the woman in slacks says to the woman in the miniskirt. "Maybe this is him in the taxi."

"Gary Hart can't afford a taxi," the woman in the miniskirt says with a giggle. "He'll probably hitchhike."

Two men join them. One man is wearing a red-and-white Kendall Motor Oil baseball cap and stands with his hands in his back pockets. "Can't keep his pants on," he says to his friend, but loud enough so everyone can hear. "That's what his problem is."

The woman in slacks takes offense. "They act like he's the only one ever to do it," she says to her friend in an equally loud voice.

Bob Stewart looks up at the clock behind the security desk. "For Al Haig, nobody was here," he says. "And Haig was on time."

A dark, plain car bumps over the frozen snow and pulls up to the foot of the walkway. A good-looking, short-haired man in a tan trench coat gets out of the car, sweeps the area with a practiced eye and then scans the snow-crusted rooftops. Even without looking for the bulge under his coat, you can tell he's Secret Service. He walks up the walk, pushes open the door and politely identifies himself to Stewart. The candidate is on his way. "Now," the agent says, "let's say Hart has to use the phone, could he get in the plant?"

Stewart stands with his arms crossed and shakes his head.

"Oooo-kay," the agent says. "But what if Hart has to use the bathroom?"

Stewart shakes his head again. "This is a class-i-fied building," he says, drawing out the syllables. "Classified. He wants to use the bathroom, I'd have to get permission." The Secret Service agent nods, shrugs. It's nothing to him. Not unless holding it in will endanger Hart's life.

Quickly and quietly, the crowd inside the entrance has grown. It is mainly made up of women, who step back from the blasts of cold air that sweep in every time someone comes in from the parking lot. There is a steady stream of employees reporting for work now, flashing their badges at Stewart, getting his nod and disappearing into the depths of the building. The new shift is reporting for work and if Hart doesn't show up soon, he will miss it.

After about ten minutes, a seven-car motorcade roars down the roadway and pulls to a halt in the Kollsman lot with a spray of snow. A Secret Service agent pops out of the front seat of the second car and opens the passenger door. Gary Hart gets out. As soon as he steps from the car, the door is slammed and the motorcade roars around in a tight circle to face back the way it came in case a quick getaway is needed. The maneuver is executed smoothly and without conversation. Everybody has done this before. The cars are left running and clouds of exhaust fumes billow into the still morning air.

Hart is coatless, hatless and gloveless. He is dressed in a herringbone sports jacket with leather buttons. He is wearing a pair of thin dress slacks, cut wide at the bottom to fit over his cowboy boots. In certain settings this would look rugged and manly, like Jack Kennedy refusing to wear hats except on state occasions. But this is New Hampshire in February and Hart looks foolhardy.

Hart grabs a few leaflets from his daughter, Andrea, and stands halfway up the walkway. I go outside to greet him. With scores of other reporters, I covered his campaign in 1984, and while I don't expect him to remember me, I anticipate he will at least say hello. Candidates and reporters are locked in a symbiotic relationship, and although there may not be love between them, there is a certain mutual dependency, a certain feeling that we are players in the same game. After my hearty hello and an obligatory comment about the weather—"Cold, huh?"—Hart lasers me with a look that could cut diamonds. He says nothing. To Gary Hart the press is the enemy. I stand about a yard away from him and a step back so I can hear what he says to people and what people say to him. All the tools of my trade—ballpoints, felt-tips, rolling writers—fail one after another in the subzero air. I unzip my parka and stick them under my armpit to thaw them. New Hampshire politics requires pencils. I should have remembered.

A few employees are still plodding up from the parking lot. They are on the verge of being late and they are walking purposefully, heads down, hands gripping their coats tight around their necks.

"Hi, nice to see you," Hart says to a woman who gets within range of him.

She looks up, startled to see a man standing in the wind and cold without a coat on. Then she does a double take as she realizes he is Somebody. Somebody famous.

Hart unleashes a fifty-kiloton smile at her, his tanned face crinkling pleasantly. "Hi," he says again. "I'm Gary Hart." He waits for the flash of recognition.

"You should wear *gloves*," she says to him. "A *hat. Something.*"

Hart's smile dims. "Never wear 'em," he says, and then he draws in an icy breath and throws out his chest, his jacket straining against the button. "This is a heat wave to me." The woman gives him a final glance, shakes her head, clutches the top of her coat more tightly and goes into work.

Hart turns his gaze back toward the parking lot, looking for more latecomers, when his peripheral vision catches some movement at the second-story window above him. The Secret Service agents immediately draw closer to him, but he waves them back. The window is filled with faces, all peering down at Hart. There are smiles and a few shy waves, and Hart waves back. In the window, a man turns to a friend and says something and they both laugh. Hart turns back to the parking lot.

It has taken me a moment to realize what is missing from the scene. There are no TV cameras with Hart, no crews, no crowd of reporters surrounding him with tape recorders, no boom mikes arching out to him. As it turns out, a few reporters are sitting in one car at the rear of his motorcade, but they don't bother to get out. Hart is no longer a big story. He is just a sideshow. A man going through the motions for reasons fully understood only by him. Gary Hart cannot become real news unless he wins New Hampshire or gets shot. Neither seems likely.

"I'm Gary Hart, nice to see you," Hart keeps saying to each straggler who passes. Most hurry on. The cold has made his hand involuntarily tighten around the campaign brochures and now they are bunched in a tight mass. The brochures are a relic from the year before, when he was running a real campaign. It seems like a memory now. He announced for the presidency on April 13, 1987, with the polls showing him slaughtering the other Democrats and beating George Bush. Twenty-six days later, he was caught in the sack (or at least in his house) with Donna Rice and withdrew from the race. Then, in the second greatest resurrection since perhaps, well, the Resurrection, he reannounced for the presidency on December 15. Now it is February 1988. He is running a presidential campaign, but each morning he seems to redefine the term. There is no press secretary and no press buses and no charter plane. There is virtually no planning. Hart just wakes up in the morning and . . . campaigns. Goes out. To a shopping mall maybe or a school or perhaps a senior citizens' center. Sometimes the people are expecting him and sometimes not. It doesn't matter much. The response is usually about the same either way.

A man in his fifties, wearing dark glasses and a knee-length burgundy stadium coat, walks up the sidewalk past Hart, then, almost as an afterthought, stops and turns toward him. "You're an embarrassment to the Democratic Party," he says, and then stands there, nostrils flaring, challenging Hart to do something about it.

"Good morning," Hart replies in a neutral tone of voice, looking squarely into the man's eyes. The man stares back at him. It becomes a contest, the kind kids have to see who will blink first. After a few seconds, the man gives up and moves on, muttering something we cannot hear.

Hart glances out of the corner of his eye over to where I am scratching this into my notebook, clumsily taking notes with gloved hands. He says nothing. Instead, even though there are no more workers in sight, he holds his ground, waiting for another moment. He stamps his feet against the cold. He coughs into his fist. Inside the lead car in the motorcade, the Secret Service driver wipes a clear spot through the frost on the window. Hart makes no move toward the warm and waiting vehicles. Candidates must have faith. More than faith in God or in country or in opinion polls, they must have faith in themselves. It is what separates them from normal people.

A dark dot approaches from the farthest reaches of the parking lot, and slowly, hesitantly, as it picks its way around snowdrifts and over ice patches, it turns into a woman in a blue cloth coat.

"Hi," Hart says to her when she finally has reached the walkway. "I'm Gary Hart."

She stops. She looks up. She blinks with shock. "I'm . . . I'm going to vote for you," she stammers. Then she ducks her head, as if she had just made some terrible admission. Her cheeks are already an apple red from the wind and it is impossible to tell if she is blushing.

"Thank you," Hart says in exactly the same tone in which he said "Good morning" to the man who had called him an embarrassment. "Thank you." He looks over at me to see if I have written this down. I have. O.K. Score even. Hart 1, Hart Haters 1.

Now can we get out of this frigging wind?

IN PROFILE AFTER PROFILE, the adjectives were always the same: "cerebral," "cool," "aloof," "shy," "lonely," "cold." A mystery. An enigma. A mystery wrapped in an enigma. The man who fell to earth. Distant. Brooding. A reader of Tolstoy and Dostoevski, Melville, Hawthorne, Poe and Kierkegaard. A man who carries around with him passages from Tennyson's "Ulysses" written out on a legal pad, a poem that begins: "It little profits that an idle king, / By this still hearth, among these barren crags, / Match'd with an aged wife, I mete and dole / Unequal laws unto a savage race, / That hoard, and sleep, and feed, and know not me."

He is a writer of spy novels and books on military reform. A man who appealed, according to pollsters, to "the young, the upscale, the better-educated Democrats who reject New Deal liberalism." In 1984, when he won twenty-nine primaries and caucuses, Hart was a clear alternative to the old-style FDR/Hubert Humphrey/Walter Mondale Democrats. Hart was high tech and high vision and high ideals. (Public ideals, anyway.) Rugged, tanned and good-looking, he had a head of hair that women wanted to run barefoot through.

Hart lost the primary battle in 1984, but he could afford to lose. There was now something called the Two-Timer Theory. Richard Nixon and Ronald Reagan had both run two times before winning. And Jimmy Carter won only because Humphrey didn't run two times, the theory went. (When George Bush eventually won, the theory also applied to him.) So Hart figured his day would come. After Mondale was crushed by Reagan in 1984, the Democratic Party would have nowhere else to turn, he felt, except to him and his ideas. And it wasn't particularly important if the voters even knew what his ideas were. Hart said: "The mistake analysts made in '84 after I won in New Hampshire and Mondale asked: 'Where's the beef?' was to stop factory workers and ask: 'Who are you going to vote for in the Ohio primary?' 'Hart.' 'Why?' 'Well, because I like his ideas.' 'What are his ideas?' 'I don't know, but I like 'em.' That is *not* a contradictory message. What you're trying to get across to people at that stage is that you *have* ideas. And it's not a test of the American people or the candidate for the voters not to be able to repeat back the details of military reform. The American people form a *sense* that you are a candidate with ideas and direction and that if you're elected, you're going to do things differently. They just can't tell you exactly how or what they are."

GARY HART STOOD in front of the class at Pelham High School in Pelham, New Hampshire, a small town near the Massachusetts border. Seated behind him was his wife of thirty years, Oletha, called Lee. She sat expressionless, almost glum, an attitude no one questioned. She, better than anyone, knew what role had been assigned her in the new Gary Hart for President campaign: she was a totem, a symbol. She was the woman who stood by her man—no matter what. And everybody knew what had mattered. Everybody who ever bought a newspaper or a supermarket tabloid or *People* magazine or watched Johnny Carson or David Letterman knew about her husband's sex life. It was not unlike what people used to read about the Aga Khan or Aristotle Onassis or Adnan Khashoggi. But none of them had ever run for President.

Lee's presence on the campaign trail also served another purpose: she was Gary's Kevlar vest, his bulletproof shield. While candidates and their spouses usually split up on the trail to cover more ground, Lee was kept close at hand. That's because her presence often kept the tough questions from being fired Gary's way. It took a great deal of nerve for a member of an audience to stand up at the end of one of Hart's speeches and ask him about his affair with Donna Rice. But with Lee sitting there on the stage by his side, it took more nerve than most people could muster.

In January, Hart, like all the candidates, had been summoned before the editorial board of the Des Moines *Register* for an interview. Unlike the other candidates, however, Hart brought his wife with him. And during the interview, he defended the soundness of their marriage. "I've been married almost thirty years," he said. "We have been married longer than the President in the White House today. We have kept our marriage together. One could argue—I wouldn't—that Ronald Reagan walked away from a marriage. I didn't."

Armchair psychologists would write that Hart had a death wish, but that seemed unlikely. He didn't want to fail; he wanted to succeed. But on his terms. Terms that allowed him to have it all. The presidency *and* love affairs. A sterling public life *and* a seamy private one. And when asked how this was possible, he would say: "I won't be the first adulterer in the White House. I may be the first one to have publicly confessed, but I won't be the first." And then he would talk about Franklin Roosevelt and John Kennedy and Dwight Eisenhower. They got away with it, didn't they? So why shouldn't he?

And who besides the press—those sanctimonious, hypocritical, self-appointed Keepers of the Public Morals—who besides them really objected to his behavior? Hart would ask privately. Not the people. No, the people still loved Gary Hart. He was sure of that. He had thousands of letters of support, he said, that had come to his home in Troublesome Gulch near Kittredge, Colorado, west of Denver, to prove it.

No, it was only the media that hated him. He could tell you the stories. When he had gotten back into the race for the presidency, the Atlanta *Constitution* had run an editorial cartoon showing a man exposing himself to two women. "Ignore him," one woman said to the other. "It's just Gary Hart with another new idea." The Baltimore *Sun*'s editorial had said: "Maybe he just thinks the campaign trail is a good place to meet some girls." The Des Moines *Register* had run a cartoon of the Seven Dwarfs with Hart labeled "Sleazy." And James Reston, senior columnist for *The New York Times*, said of the Democrats: "Their best men won't run and their worst won't quit." TV was just as bad. When Hart reannounced for the presidency, the networks had broadcast the now famous picture first published in the *National Enquirer* of Donna Rice sitting on Hart's lap, her dress riding high up on her thighs and Hart's hand around her hips. Her arm is around his neck and they are both holding drinks in plastic cups. He is wearing a sweatshirt that says: "Monkey Business Crew."

Presidential? Proper? Decent? Well, on *Nightline*, Ted Koppel asked Hart about the propriety of this woman sitting on his lap. "I chose not to dump her off," Hart solemnly replied.

Hart felt the attacks were a good sign. Because for the first time, people would pity him. People would feel sorry for him. People would identify with him. And that was the one thing that a cold and aloof man needed. He had told Hunter Thompson, columnist for the San Francisco *Examiner*, about this. "For the first time in my life," Hart said, "black people come up to me on the street and want to shake hands with me."

"What do we call it, Gary?" Thompson asked. "What kind of vote is it? The adulterer's vote? The sex fiend vote?"

"The victim's vote," Hart replied.

"Dear Gary," Richard Nixon had written him. "They [reporters] demand to ruthlessly question the ethics of anyone else. But when anyone else dares to question *theirs*, they hide behind the shield of freedom of speech."

"Dear Mr. President," Hart, who had managed the campaign of Nixon's 1972 opponent, George McGovern, wrote back. "My family and I want you to know how deeply we appreciate your thoughtful letter. It was considerate of you to write and to offer words of support and encouragement."

LEE HART SHIFTED UNCOMFORTABLY in her seat before the class at Pelham High. It was a typical school chair, wood and tubular steel, but it was not the chair that was causing her to fidget. Maybe it was because she would have to hear Gary give the Speech one more time. You could not even call it a speech, really. After he had reentered the race, he had abandoned normal forms of campaigning and he rarely gave normal speeches anymore. His task was now no less than to reeducate the American public. This was the New, Improved Gary Hart. Two days after his reentry, he was on a plane with David Shribman of *The Wall Street Journal* and had taken out his wallet and held it open. "Here is the campaign budget," he said, showing two twenty-dollar bills. "My daughter's the campaign manager, I'm the issues director and my son provides security. That's it. It will be the kind of campaign a lot of people said they wished we could go back to—genuinely grass-roots, genuinely directed to the people."

Shribman asked Hart about Donna Rice.

"It's none of your business," Hart said.

This was the New Gary Hart, too. That was what he *wished* he had said at the murderous press conference he had undergone back in May 1987 after his fling with Donna Rice had been exposed. After the story broke, the strategy behind his facing the press was to do "a Geraldine Ferraro," keep answering questions until the reporters had exhausted themselves. The difference was that in 1984 Ferraro, the Democratic vice presidential nominee, had answered questions about her campaign finances pretty much to the satisfaction of everyone for about ninety minutes. Hart barely lasted half that long before he escaped from the room.

"It was for an hour and fifteen minutes," Hart told me later, exaggerating by more than 66 percent. "And I answered everybody's questions but that one. I just said I'm not going to answer the question, but I *should* have said: 'It's none of your business.' Or: 'If you can relate how the answer to that question affects my ability to be President of the United States, then I'll answer it.' Because if you can make answers to questions like that integrity testers, then you are going to drive everybody out of the business. Because then the burden is either answer my question honestly about your personal life or you're a liar. And then we don't let liars in the White House. Well, that's ridiculous."

On May 1, the Miami *Herald*, acting on a tip, had begun a surveillance of Hart's Capitol Hill townhouse. On Sunday, May 3, it had printed a story saying Hart had spent "Friday night and most of Saturday" with Donna Rice. Assured by Hart it was untrue, his campaign manager had vigorously denied it. Rice had left by the back door, he explained, unseen by the reporters. (Two days later, after realizing Hart had not told him the whole story, the campaign manager resigned.)

Had it been the *National Enquirer* that had broken the story, the whole thing might have died. But the Miami *Herald* was a very respectable, highly respected newspaper. And reporters around the nation immediately accepted its account as true.

The Tuesday after the story appeared, Hart had spoken to a newspaper publishers' convention in New York and said he had done nothing "immoral." Later that night, at a fund-raiser, he described the whole account as a "stab in the back." Early Wednesday he prepared for his news conference with his press secretary, Kevin Sweeney. Sweeney fed him imaginary questions and Hart showed his calm, but righteous, indignation in his deft and semi-forthright answers. Hart was sure he could pull it off.

And contrary to the popular belief created by TV and movies, reporters are not usually aggressive at news conferences. Most reporters are somewhat shy in public. Harsh questions are rare. Even if reporters are privately contemptuous of the person being questioned, they are publicly respectful of his office. Hart, though now a private citizen, was called "Senator" by every reporter in the room that day. Donna Rice was invariably referred to as "Miss Rice." The pleasantries were observed.

But this press conference was to be different, even historic. Gary Hart soon realized that the reporters in the room not only thought him a liar but were willing to let that belief show.

On short notice, about 150 reporters, most of whom had come up from Washington, gathered in a small lounge in the Hanover Inn on the campus of Dartmouth College. The jokes were already circulating. Gary Hart's idea of safe sex? No press. Or try this one: Gary Hart calls his close friend Warren Beatty and tells him Donna Rice is in the house and the press is outside. What should he do? "No problem," Beatty says. "Get Ted Kennedy to drive her home."

Hart walked into the room and the murmuring was replaced by the incessant whirs of the motor drives on the still cameras. Throughout the press conference they would sound like wasps batting against a windowpane. By the time it was all over, Hart would have made only one clear point: Donna Rice was the only woman in America that he absolutely swore he had never slept with. (Would he take a lie detector test? "Oh no. Gimme a break," he replied.) As to all the other women, he refused to confirm or deny anything. He had to do this because he didn't know what other evidence the press had. If he said he had never slept with So-and-so and the press produced pictures the next day, he would be finished. He had to avoid the appearance of lying more than the appearance of infidelity. And since he had already denied having had sex with Rice, he had to stick to that. So his stance was that the one woman everyone was sure he had slept with was the one woman he had not slept with.

Hart began with a short statement, disputing some facts of the Miami *Herald*'s story, and then said Lee had flown to New Hampshire to join him (though she was not in the room). She had not been seen in public since the *Herald* story broke because, she said, of serious sinus swelling. Hart ended his statement on a passionate note: "I'll tell you, of the people I have met in the world, this is the most extraordinary human being I have had the pleasure of knowing. Not simply as a wife, but as a human being."

But the first question that told Hart this was not to be an ordinary press conference came from Carl Leubsdorf, a veteran political reporter and chief of the Washington bureau of the Dallas *Morning News*. Leubsdorf was known for his thoughtful, sober analysis of the issues. And he let Hart have it in the chops.

"Senator," he said, "in talking to a number of leading Democratic politicians yesterday about this, I was struck by the fact that a majority of the ones I talked to *did not believe your story*. And the reason they said they did not believe your story is that all of them either had heard rumors or claimed to know of previous incidents of this sort during the past fifteen years."

Leubsdorf's question fell on the room like a grenade. Now it was out in the open: nobody believed Hart and nobody believed him because everybody knew he had been screwing around for years. Leubsdorf had done, in effect, what is never done at press conferences:

he had called the candidate a liar. He had done it diplomatically, he had quoted others in doing it, but he had done it. There was now the sense that any question was fair game.

Leubsdorf concluded his question by asking: "Have there been times during the past fifteen years, other than periods when you were separated from your wife, when you have spent time with women in the manner that you did with Miss Rice this weekend?"

"The answer to the question is no, with this explanation: 'In the manner that I did this weekend,' " Hart said, splitting whatever hairs he could find. "I have dinner on the road with reporters of both genders. They have always been open, in the public. Someone reminded me today that in a recent campaign trip, a number of us after a hard day on the campaign trail, including staff, myself and some journalists, several journalists, ended up in having cocktails, dinner and ending up *dancing*. Now a news organization taking a picture of me on the dance floor with a woman could have made a great deal out of *that*. There is nothing there."

Hart had been rocked by Leubsdorf's question and it showed. Nobody was talking about Hart dancing with women reporters on a public dance floor. They were talking about a guy who had shtupped his career away.

Leubsdorf followed up. If the impression was false, he asked, why did so many people have it?

"I don't know," Hart began. "I can't . . . I would dispute the 'so many.' I have no way of knowing . . . Part of it goes with being in public life. It is not just politics. It is people in business, it is people in entertainment, it is even some media figures . . . It goes with the territory. My mistake, frankly, was underestimating that. If I had intended, um, a relationship with this woman—believe me, I have written spy novels, I am not stupid—if I wanted to bring someone into a house or an apartment or meet with a woman in secret, I wouldn't have done it this way."

Lawyers call this the Nobody Could Be That Stupid Defense: "Ladies and gentlemen of the jury, would my client be so stupid as to shoot his wife in the middle of Main Street at high noon with a hundred witnesses around?" It is not a very good defense. Juries often decide that, hell yes, some people *are* that stupid or arrogant enough to think they can get away with it.

Paul Taylor of the Washington *Post* also was at the press conference. He had been troubled by Hart's assertion the day before that he had done nothing "immoral" with Rice, and Taylor now wanted to find out just what Hart meant by the term.

"Let me be very specific," Taylor said. "I have a series of questions about this. When you said you did nothing immoral, did you mean you had no sexual relationships with Donna Rice last weekend or any other time?" There was a murmur from around the room. First honesty had been breached and now sex.

"That is correct," Hart replied.

"Do you believe that adultery is immoral?" Taylor asked.

"Yes," Hart replied.

"Have you ever committed adultery?" Taylor asked.

The question should not have caught Hart by surprise. He had, in fact, been asked this question by Sweeney in his practice session. But Hart had been so unnerved by the questions so far, so surprised that the press was doing this to him—him, the only man who could reform the political process and save the country!—that he blew it.

"Um, I do not have to answer that," he said. "Because it gets into some really fine definitions."

It does? The definition of "sexual relationships" sounded pretty simple to most people in the room. There are men and women, see, and the man has a . . .

"It seems the question of morality was raised by you," Taylor said.

"That's right," Hart said.

"And I think it is incumbent upon us to find out what your definition of morality really is . . . You believe adultery is immoral?" Taylor asked.

"Yes, I do," Hart replied.

"Have you ever committed adultery?" Taylor repeated.

In the context of the press conference, it was a logical, even an inevitable question. Only later did reporters realize it had never been asked of a presidential candidate before.

"I do not know. I am not going into theological definitions of what is adultery," Hart said. "In some people's minds it's people being married and having relationships with other people."

"Can I ask you whether you and your wife have an understanding about whether or not you can have sexual encounters?" Taylor asked.

"My inclination is to say, no, you can't answer [sic] that question," Hart said, rattled, "because my answer is no, I don't have such an understanding. We have an understanding of faithfulness, fidelity and loyalty."

The rest of the press conference scurried downhill from there. Tom Oliphant of the Boston *Globe*, another respected political reporter, felt Hart had not been fully pinned down. All the reporters in the room sensed that Hart might never again subject himself to another such press conference (he would not) and this might be their last chance to get answers. "Senator," Oliphant began, "I would like to follow up on Paul Taylor's question in a way that perhaps doesn't raise theological distinctions into a discussion of morality, as you see it. Except for times when you and your wife were separated, has your marriage been monogamous?"

Hart still didn't have a good answer. But he knew when he had had enough. "Um, I do not need to answer that question," he said, and then added a few moments later, his voice openly angry: "Now I'm going to *insist* that this be a fair system. You can ask me about adultery, you can ask me any question you want . . . but I am going to *demand* that this be fair. And I have a *right* to demand it. And if somebody's going to follow me around they better follow me around and they better print all the facts!"

But Hart was insisting on a technicality. His point was that the Miami *Herald* had not been 100 percent scrupulous in staking out his house. That it was theoretically possible for Rice to have slipped out the back. But in the end, it didn't matter. The paper may not have come up with every fact, but it had come up with the truth.

So the only question left was the death wish question.

"Accepting your version of events," a reporter asked, "some people in politics suggest that the episode suggests sort of a recklessness on your part, sort of flirting with danger, if you will. Can you address that issue?"

"I once said I loved danger," Hart said in what might have been the only poignant moment of the press conference. "I don't love it that much."

Press secretary Kevin Sweeney (who would soon be serving pasta in a San Francisco restaurant after the Hart campaign collapsed) leaped in at one point during the press conference to shout: "Just a few more questions!" Abandoned was the Geraldine Ferraro strategy of letting the reporters ask questions until they were exhausted. It was Hart who was getting exhausted.

"No!" came the shouts from the reporters. "No, Kevin." "No way!" "Forget it!" And so Hart had to continue, trapped in the spotlight like an escaping prisoner caught against a wall.

A reporter asked Hart if having Rice over to his house was risky.

"I didn't think at the time that inviting people into my house was risky," Hart said. "I just did what seemed to come naturally."

Say good night, Gary.

When he could stand it no longer, he ended his own press conference. "We've got to go," he said. "Thank you." And he left the room.

Afterward, Hart's staff knew the campaign was in deep trouble.

"When you have papers like the Washington *Post* and the Boston *Globe* asking questions like that, it didn't take a rocket scientist to figure out what was going on," one staff member said.

What was going on was that the press was going to continue to pursue the story of Gary Hart as liar, which was more important than Gary Hart as sex fiend. Not all reporters were comfortable with the sexual aspects of the story anyway. To them, Hart's sex life genuinely was his own business. And many reporters were downright uncomfortable with the stakeout of Hart's house, believing this was not the proper role of the press. But the bigger story was Hart's lack of candor. Presidential candidates lie (just as Presidents do). But it is usually fatal to get caught at it.

Hart had not been swept up, as he believed, in some new standard of journalism, some extension of the boundaries of what is a printable story. For the press, the standard had always been one of proof. Sure, reporters "knew" which candidates screwed around, just as they "knew" about John Kennedy's affairs. But you didn't print or broadcast what you "knew." You printed or broadcast what you could prove.

And now reporters had dug up proof by staking out Hart's home. This method was new and, to many other campaigns, frightening. Jesse Jackson's alleged sexual escapades had been mentioned in many profiles of him in 1987. But Jackson knew how to handle it. His wife launched a preemptive strike. She told reporters she didn't care about or want to see any stories about her husband's private life. "I don't believe in examining the sheets," she told reporters in the summer of 1987. "If my husband has committed adultery, he better not tell me. And you better not go digging into it, because I'm trying to raise a family and won't let you be the one to destroy my family."

Stories about George Bush's alleged extramarital affairs also had been circulating, though the public rarely heard about them. But the Bush campaign handled it with aplomb. George Bush, Jr., denied it publicly by saying: "The answer to the Big A question is N.O.," and the issue was defused. (Actually, rumors of adultery did not totally displease the Bush campaign at this early stage of the campaign. It made Bush seem less of a wimp.)

Hart believed, however, that it was he who had saved the other candidates from being stalked by reporters. "If my theory is correct, there was a conscious backing off of the personal investigation, surveillance, the staking-out excess," Hart said a month after the election. "Jesse benefited from that, as did a lot of others. I heard some—I mean there were some *outrageous* stories about him [Jackson], in his personal life—so it wasn't that everybody gave him a break. But I think he benefited to the degree that my experience *inoculated* everybody else in both parties from that kind of excess."

The night after Hart's press conference, Paul Taylor met with Kevin Sweeney and dropped the other shoe. He told Sweeney the Washington *Post* had obtained a surveillance report and photographs from a private detective showing Hart entering and leaving the house of a Washington woman in 1986. The detective had been hired by a man who thought his wife was having an affair with Hart and wanted the detective to follow him. As it turned out, the man's wife had not been seeing Hart, but the woman in the photographs had. The *Post* confirmed the story through an intermediary and the woman admitted to a long-term affair with Hart. As Hart knew, as his staff knew, as many reporters knew and as the public was beginning to suspect, there might be many such women out there.

That night, Sweeney passed along the *Post*'s information to Hart. "This is never going to end, is it?" Hart said. "Let's go home." Two days later, and nine months before any voter in America would get to cast a vote on whether he should become President, Gary Hart withdrew from the race.

At his news conference in Denver, Hart said he was "angry and defiant" in the face of political reporting that "reduces the press of this nation to hunters and the presidential candidates to being hunted." He withdrew to save his family, he said. Then he went to Ireland. He refused requests for interviews. He dropped off the front pages. Later, he said: "I didn't get out of the race because of the Miami *Herald* story. I got out of the race because I was then open season. And every newspaper in America was going to print . . . I mean, it was clear to us. Kevin Sweeney was getting calls from virtually all over the country saying, 'Did he have an affair with *this* woman or *that* woman?' and that would have been it for the rest of the whole campaign. It wouldn't have ended. And when I realized that, I realized I had no choice but to get out. But it was the *Post* incident that tilted it. Because it was just a signal that now I was total fair game to anything.

"I came along at the wrong time. And I became the test case for what the new boundaries of journalism are. And it hurt. Obviously it hurt me. I frankly think it hurt the country. But only history can decide that."

IN PELHAM HIGH this winter day, the kids look down at Gary Hart. They sit in tiers of seats rising amphitheater style toward the ceiling. Hart stands below them before a two-sided chalkboard on wheels. But when he writes on the board, when his scrawls begin to fill up one side and he threatens to go on to the other, a certain . . . tingle . . . goes through the room. A little electricity. A collectively held breath. Hart ignores it. Kids are his kind of audience. And he doesn't care that only about 10 to 15 percent of the kids at the school are old enough to vote in the primary.

"It's a great pleasure to be back at Pelham High. I was here almost four years ago today," Hart begins over the noise from the cafeteria next door. "This is my wife, Lee." Lee waves a small wave from her seat. "She's a former English teacher," Hart says. "She'll be grading your questions and my answers." Titters from the kids.

Hart drags the chalkboard forward as its wheels squeak in protest. "If you don't mind," he says, "I'll relax and be nonpresidential." In one graceful movement he strips off his herringbone jacket to reveal the tight-fitting Western shirt beneath, the one with the pearl buttons on the flap pockets. Hart likes Western gear. Cowboy boots and big belt buckles with his initials, GWH. With quick, sure movements he rolls his sleeves up over his tanned forearms. The girls go dreamy-eyed and giggle and nudge each other and whisper. Hart doesn't seem to notice. His gestures are not studied, but natural. The natural act of a natural performer.

He takes up a piece of chalk and begins his lecture, his chalk talk. It lasts about forty minutes—a long time for a campaign speech, though it really is not a campaign speech at all. He no longer believes in campaign speeches. His job is to elevate the state of American politics. And so while other candidates are out gathering votes, he is delivering civics lectures.

"I think this country is facing three major challenges and I would like to talk about them, using the chalkboard, if I can, to illustrate some of my ideas and positions," he says. "Now, the President of the United States, as those of you studying political science or social studies know, has at least three jobs. Can anybody tell me what one of those jobs is?"

There is a silence. And then a girl says: "Commander in chief?"

"Commander in chief," Hart says, writing on the board, and then looks up at the student who got it right. "What's your name? . . . Gallico?" He writes on the board: "Secretary of Defense Gallico."

Giggles from the kids.

"What about other jobs?" he goes on. "It's a little more complicated. Chief of staff? Let me say: head of government. The President of the United States runs the government. He is the chief executive officer. Does anybody know the third job? Head of state."

He goes on. Lee's eyes look like they are about to turn up into her head. It is difficult to listen to this lecture once; it is almost physically painful to listen to it day after day. Which is why I find I am the only reporter in the room. The others—there are only three and one photographer, and all had heard and seen the lecture many times—sit outside in the lunchroom, wondering when they will be assigned to a real candidate.

I leave my tape recorder behind and go out into the lunchroom. There, sitting at a table, are Paul Dugan, a Hart volunteer, and Andrea Hart, the Harts' twenty-three-year-old daughter. Today, they represent the entire campaign staff. I ask Andrea if I can speak to her father later in the day. Interviews are not normally given on the Hart campaign. He has announced that he will speak only to TV and to newspaper editorial boards. The press is the problem, not the solution. Andrea holds out little hope for an interview, but says she will ask.

Paul Dugan says he is happy with the day so far. "This is a good event," he says. "Visibility is the bottom line."

I don't have to ask what he means by visibility. It means Gary Hart having the nerve to show his face in public.

THE HART STAFF, such as it is, rarely makes arrangements for reporters. The Secret Service doesn't even bother to give them credentials as they do on the other campaigns. To follow Hart, one just rents a car and tries to keep up behind the caravan of Secret Service cars. Reporters call this "motorcading." New Hampshire police called it by different names. "High-speed chase" and "felony" are two of them.

It works this way: Hart finishes a speech at some event and then heads quickly for his waiting Secret Service car. The engine is always running. An agent holds the back door open for him. He folds himself inside. The agent slams the door, leaps into the front seat, and the car squeals off. The other cars, carrying whatever staff or Hart family members are there, follow, with a Secret Service car bringing up the rear. Sometimes Hart has local police escorts but that is rare. (Hart hates sirens and flashing lights and complains when local police use them.) His motorcade runs through stop signs and stoplights anyway, like a high-speed funeral cortege.

Reporters must take down the last words of his speech, do whatever interviewing of citizens they can find time for and then run for their cars. If they are blocked in by other cars or by people leaving the event, they must drive on sidewalks or on lawns. They can't allow themselves to get left behind, because only the Secret Service cars know where they are going. If the reporters lose the motorcade, they won't be able to find Hart for the rest of the day. So we all blast down the highway, weaving through traffic, cutting off semitrailers, passing on the shoulders, doing anything to catch up and keep up with the candidate. There is an undeniable exhilaration to it, the feeling that on a presidential campaign one is exempt from the laws governing normal people. You can see why it goes to the head.

AFTER HART'S TOUR of Kollsman Instruments and then a factory making airplane parts, the motorcade had headed for Main Street in Nashua. This is a ritual of campaigning in New Hampshire.

The idea is to "meet and greet." To go in and shake the hands of storekeepers and shoppers. So Hart gets out of his car and waits for Lee to join him before going into Rustic Accents, a flower shop. Because it is later in the day and warmer, about a dozen reporters and even a couple of camera crews are waiting for Hart on Main Street. Nobody expects Hart to make news, but there is always the chance something embarrassing may happen to him.

Hart sees that the camera crews and still photographers have run up ahead to set up a shot. The cameras are in the street facing a store and everyone is just waiting for Hart to walk into the place so they can grab a picture. Hart does not know what the store is, but he knows it is trouble. His pace slows, then quickens. The cameras wait eagerly as he draws closer, their lenses swiveling toward him like gun turrets on a battleship. He glances at them, he glances at the storefront and then, tightly clutching Lee's arm, walks on, staring straight ahead, chin thrust out as he passes Rice's Pharmacy.

But at Charles and James Panagoulias' shoe repair store, Hart has a good moment. Charles, seventy-five, motions him to a chair for a shine. "You'll do all right, you'll do all right," he says. "You're a fighter. In that chair there, four Presidents have sat. Carter. Eisenhower. Kennedy. And Nixon."

Hart looks at the chair. He walks over to it and sits down, trying it on for size. "Let's go after a fifth," he says with a grin. He lifts his pants legs for a shine and reveals a set of black, well-worn and undecorated cowboy boots. These are not what cowboys call "town" or "show" boots. These are the real thing, working boots.

"These are the third sets of soles on these," Hart says proudly. "I've got a pair that go back to 1973. And they're plain old calf from a plain old cow. I don't go in for exotic leathers." (Ronald Reagan favors ostrich skin, as does Pat Robertson, and Bush sometimes wears red, white and blue boots carved with a Texas flag.)

His shine finished, Hart fumbles in his pocket for a moment, whispers to Lee and then scans the room. He recognizes me as his lone "press corps" out at Kollsman Instruments. He walks up to me and drops his voice. "You got two dollars?" he asks.

I am so surprised that I just stare at him blankly.

"Lee only has a dollar and I want to give the guy more than that," he explains.

I take out my wallet and hand Hart two singles.

"Thanks," he says, glancing around to see if anyone has seen this. He walks over and gives the money to Charles, who protests and then takes it at Hart's insistence.

Hart plunges outside. A Chevy pickup truck pulls up on Main Street and stops for a light in front of him. The driver is wearing a Navy watch cap and buffalo-checked flannel shirt. He looks over at Hart and yells from the cab: "I had her, too!" His girlfriend reaches over and covers his mouth with her hand and they both tussle and laugh. Hart ignores them. He is within himself; nothing can touch him.

At an intersection outside Woolworth, Hart suddenly stops on the sidewalk for a red light while his Secret Service agents start across. "Wait, wait, wait, wait, wait," Hart says to them like a crossing guard. Hart wants their protection. He never talks about it, but he worries about assassination. And even though it seems unlikely that anyone would want to shoot a man who has already committed suicide, Hart has been getting tight coverage by the agents, who have been gently manhandling people and reporters out of the way. The agents know they probably cannot prevent a determined assassin from taking a shot, but they can deter the amateurs and catch anybody who tries. The agents keep the candidate in a protective triangle. But when you are a reporter trying to listen to what the candidate is saying to people and what they are saying to him, it is easy to accidentally invade that constantly shifting space. After repeatedly stumbling over agents and being nudged out of the way up and down Main Street, I finally give up near the end of the walk and keep out of their way. An agent comes over to me. "You've been really cooperative," he says, "and I appreciate that. Besides"—he grabs me and holds me in front of him—"I can always use you as a buffer." We both laugh.

Surprised to learn that agents really do speak, a local reporter comes up and asks the agent: "How many of you are here today?"

The agent peers down at her and then tugs his suit jacket around him until you can see the bulge of the .357 magnum on his hip. "Sorry," he says. "I could tell you that. But then I'd have to hurt you."

People are now stopping Hart and asking for autographs. Maybe it is the warmer weather, but everything begins to feel more relaxed or at least less grim. An older woman in a green Ford rolls down her window and shouts from her car: "We love you, Gary. We love you!"

Hart nods, waves, mouths: "Thank you." His sense of humor even begins to reassert itself. Seeing two nuns, Hart heads for them. "Sisters," he says to them, "I'm Gary Hart."

"Oh, how wonderful," one sister says, looking around at all the cameras. "Now we'll be on TV tonight!"

The Harts head into the Modern Restaurant on Pearl Street for lunch. Andrea Hart tells me I am invited to eat with her parents if I want. They are at a round table with a few supporters, and when I walk up, Hart immediately reaches into his wallet and hands me the two dollars he has borrowed. I tell him that the financial condition of his campaign must be improving.

"About seventy-five percent of what goes into a campaign is wasted," he says. "It is superstructure geared to pay for the superstructure." I take out a tape recorder and put it on the table in front of Hart and Lee where they both can see it. Tape recorders tend to intimidate ordinary people but candidates and their spouses are not ordinary people.

Hart now seems eager to talk. "We've had a lot of people say: 'This whole experience humanized you and your family. It made you people we could relate to. You went through some troubles. You had people peeking in your windows and all like that,' " he says. "And every family has troubles. Very few families have managed to get through life without some downside. To the degree that people *do* like us, they like us, maybe, even *more* in some ways than before."

Lee joins the conversation. "It's the national press people who *know* him who have treated him *worse* than anyone," she says. "What is all that anger really about? Nobody thought he could win the nomination for McGovern. Nobody thought he could win the Senate. Nobody ever thinks he will win. There is a similarity between Ronald Reagan and Gary. They both understand what they believe and why they believe it. That adds up to strength."

Gary looks down at his food as Lee talks. I ask Lee if she reads the stories about her husband. "I don't have the time to read or watch," she says.

You don't have the time or you don't want to read them?

"Both," she says. "Friends tell me what I need to know. Some of the things are so bad and so unfair, reading them is impossible."

I ask Hart how people are reacting to him on the street.

"It's beyond politics; there is more celebrity to it," he says. "I mean, you can't go through all the stuff we went through with *People* magazine and all that awful, awful stuff—and it still goes on—and

now, in some ways, I've become more of a figure of . . . I don't know
. . . a *dramatic* figure."

Some people, I say, think you're, uh, weird.

He looks at me blankly. Weird?

Have I chosen the wrong word? Let me see. A front-runner for
President, a man with a past who knows he is under extraordinary
scrutiny, goes to Bimini with a model just over half his age, then has
her over to his house when his wife is away, reacts angrily when
caught, withdraws from the race, reenters and runs by giving civics
lectures to high school kids. Yeah, weird. That's the word.

He considers it for a moment, chewing it over mentally. He takes
his napkin off his lap and lays it on the table. "No, I'm not weird,"
he says. "I'm . . . unconventional."

AFTER HE WITHDREW from the presidential race on May 8, 1987,
Gary Hart found himself in that one situation politicians never want
to be in: alone.

"Oh yeah, it was a very tough time," he said months later. "I got
out of the race on Friday, and Monday morning I was back at my
law office. So I didn't hide. It was hard, it was very hard to go back.
On Friday you're a candidate for President; on Monday you're a
lawyer in Denver. But I didn't take a week off or a month off. It was
very important for me to not run away. So I was back at the law
office the next day and I stayed there and then I went, well, I went
to Ireland in August, for two, three weeks."

Photographers caught sight of him there a few times. His hair
tousled, his face somber, he went "unrecognized," the captions said,
just Gary Hart, struggling with his soul, walking on the moors and
fens of the Auld Sod, grappling with himself each day before sitting
down before a peat fire to contemplate his future over a glass of
stout.

It was all nonsense, however. Hart had become a master at playing
the noncandidate candidate. Hart had started talking about reenter-
ing the race just *two days* after withdrawing from it. At home in
Troublesome Gulch, Hart talked with staff members about "a 'light
infantry' campaign," one aide told a reporter. "No gray eminences
from Washington, no press conferences, just Gary making speeches.
He had it all figured out. . . . I thought he might mean 1992 or
1996."

But he meant now, this time, 1988. And he knew some excuse had
to be found for his reentry. He couldn't just pop out of the race and
then pop in a few weeks later. People might think he was weird. So
Gary Hart went to Ireland and stood in the bogs and hatched a plan.

He would reenter the race because—surprise!—none of the other Democrats running were any damn good.

"When I got out of the race in spring of '87, I packaged up a bundle of positions, speeches on education reform, military reform, foreign policy," Hart said. "I said [to the other Democrats in the race], 'Look, these aren't just my ideas, these are the result of the work of dozens and dozens of people over the past five or 10 years, and this is what our party is going to do. It's not Hart's ideas; it's new ideas. Here they are. Use them.' Nobody did. And that's why— you know, I waited six months—and that's when I decided to get back in the race. To perpetuate those ideas."

It was an extraordinary act of ego, which is certainly not unknown in presidential politics. But it was also an act that damaged his own party. Hart was saying to the nation that he had taken a look at the rest of the Democrats and found them wanting. They were devoid of real ideas, and they could not lead, they could not win. So he, a discredited candidate, was forced—he had no real choice—to return to the race.

Jesse Jackson summarized the feelings of the other candidates. "Gary Hart has a superiority complex," he said, "without having the superiority."

On December 5, Hart breakfasted in Colorado with three former aides. "He had everything figured out pretty clearly," one said. "He said the media would give him a 'thirty-day bashing' and move on to another story." On December 8, Channel 9 in Denver asked Hart to come on the air and discuss the INF treaty, just signed by Reagan and Mikhail Gorbachev. Afterward, anchorman Ed Sardella asked him: "Are the media finally leaving you alone?"

"Oh yeah," Hart replied. "Maybe a little too much."

Seven days later, Hart flew to Boston, was driven up to Concord, New Hampshire, and reentered the race, paying the $1,000 ballot fee out of his own pocket. The media gave Hart the bashing he expected. The conservative and locally influential Manchester *Union Leader* labeled Hart's reentry: "The Revenge of the Nerd." The Washington *Post* printed (on page 31) the story it hadn't printed when Hart withdrew: that there was "documented evidence" of a "liaison" between Hart and a Washington woman. The name of the woman was not revealed.

(Hart never believed the *Post* story that this surveillance was initiated by a jealous husband who thought his wife was having an affair with Hart and hired private detectives to follow him. "I don't buy that," he said. "I don't believe it. Because you don't surveil the man, *you surveil the wife!*")

David Letterman presented "Gary Hart's Top Ten Christmas Wishes," which included:

—"Papers latch on to photos of Dukakis and bearded lady.

—"People start referring to sleazy womanizing as 'Kennedyesque.'

—"George Bush gets irresistible urge to fondle Jeane Kirkpatrick at press conference.

—"Miss September consents to be his running mate."

Letterman, Jay Leno, Johnny Carson and *Doonesbury* creator Garry Trudeau had real power. They did not have the power to make or break, but they had the power to humiliate, and the campaigns closely monitored their jokes. Lee Atwater said he paid attention to them "as a barometer of how the candidates play in the 'real' America . . ." Some felt that Letterman's Top Ten lists or Carson's monologues could mean a couple of points in the polls. And in a close race, a couple of points could be critical. By the 1988 presidential race, humor was no longer funny.

Within days it looked as if the people of America had made up their minds about Gary Hart. And they weren't laughing. A *USA Today* poll showed him in first place with 29 percent and Dukakis in second with 15 percent. A *New York Times*/CBS poll showed Hart in first with 21 percent, Jesse Jackson in second with 17 percent and the rest of the field in single digits. Three other polls concurred that Hart was once again the front-runner. Three days after his reentry, the Gallup Organization asked 707 adults: "What man that you heard or read about, living today, in any part of the world, do you admire most?" Ronald Reagan came in first. Pope John Paul II came in second. And Gary Hart tied Jesse Jackson for third.

Not everyone, however, felt Americans were really ready to usher a known womanizer into the Oval Office and the Lincoln Bedroom. Not everybody worshipped at the altar of polls. In the old days, polls were conducted door to door and the results were tabulated by hand and they took days or even weeks to complete. That meant that dramatic events had time to sink in. But now polls were done by telephone and tabulated by computer and the results were produced in days or even hours. So there was no time for people to think about how they felt. Thinking was not required of citizens by pollsters, only answering.

Further, a few pollsters were shocked at the small samples that other pollsters were using. After the amazing Hart polls were published, the Presidential Campaign Hotline asked some leading pollsters what sample size they felt was needed for reliable national polling data. Average answer: 950. Yet some of the Hart polls had sampled fewer than 400 Democratic voters. And the *New York Times*/

CBS poll had questioned only 218 voters for part of its data. The hotline quoted pollster Harrison Hickman as saying: "The only thing I've seen this week more reckless than Gary Hart's decision to get back in the race has been the national polling reports."

GARY HART PICKS UP the chalk and draws a house on the blackboard at Pelham High. "The reason this country is not a producing nation is that we have let the foundation of this house decline," he says. "We have to teach geography! We have to teach history! People have to know who's buried in Grant's Tomb! Where Africa is! We have a fifteen percent illiteracy rate in our work force; the Japanese have less than one percent. The next President has to change this country."

The blackboard is nearly filled and Hart reaches up to flip it over. The room falls suddenly silent.

AFTER HART REANNOUNCED for President in Concord, he got into a car and headed for the Pheasant Lane Mall in Nashua. Scores of cars containing reporters followed him there through heavily falling snow. It should have been a routine stop. Hart began working the crowds inside the mall, not paying much attention to where he was going, when he came upon a Victoria's Secret, a lingerie shop with lace teddies, silk camisoles and red garter belts in the window. Hart walked up to the display window, took one quick glance, did an immediate U-turn and practically burned rubber getting away. Nobody said anything, but nobody had to. George Bush going inside and buying a flannel nightgown would have gotten some nice press. And nobody would have questioned whether it was for Barbara. But Gary Hart going into a Victoria's Secret would have gotten him the next three monologues on Letterman.

The next morning, Hart greeted some workers at a plant gate and then went to Dover High School, where he spoke to about 700 kids. During the question-and-answer period that followed, a student asked him about politicians who "mislead the public."

"I don't think politicians have the right to mislead the public," Hart replied. "But on the other hand, the public does not have the right to know everything about everyone's personal life." The kids cheered.

Afterward, it was not so cheery. Hope King, seventeen, approached Hart as he was leaving the stage and tried to ask him about the "Donna Rice scam."

Hart would not answer her question. "He just gave me an ugly look and walked off," she said.

Hart went on to Portland, Maine, that day, trailing sixty cars of reporters. Then he and Lee flew off to South Dakota and Iowa. In some ways, it looked like a normal campaign. There was a candidate and reporters and crowds. But in other ways, it was not normal. It is not normal when a seventeen-year-old asks a candidate a question he cannot answer.

GARY HART PUTS DOWN the chalk and the students at Pelham High seem to let out a long, collective breath they all have been holding.

"I need your help," Hart says. "You can have an impact on changing this country. I believe we can't just change things on the edge. I believe we have to change the fundamental structure of this country and that's what my campaign is about. Thank you."

There is applause and Hart takes a few questions—nobody asks *the* question—and then a buzzer sounds and the kids grab their books and practically run from the room. Hart dusts the chalk off his hands and Lee gets up from her chair and the agents move out ahead of them as they leave the room.

I wait a moment and then walk up to the chalkboard. It is clear the kids had been worrying about it, worrying that Hart would flip it over. I walk behind it and look at the side Hart had not gotten to. There in a bold scrawl, written in large block letters, are the words: "I EAT RICE."

A photographer walks over to see what I am looking at and then he grins and unlimbers his camera and snaps a few pictures of the chalkboard. He knows no newspaper will run it, but it is the kind of thing that will be passed around in the newsroom until somebody has the guts to put it up on the bulletin board and somebody else has the guts to take it down.

BY THE TIME Gary Hart withdrew from the campaign for the final time, he was no longer news. By the time he pulled out of the race, few remembered he was still in it. Earlier, Hosni Mubarak, the President of Egypt, was giving an interview to an American reporter and wanted to make a point about the media and politics. But he could not come up with the example he wanted. "What was the name of that fellow with Donna Rice?" he asked.

Gary Hart would get 4,888 votes in New Hampshire out of more than 122,000 cast. Four years earlier, he had gotten almost eight times that number. When his 114-day campaign was over, his best showing turned out to be in Puerto Rico. He got 7.5 percent of the vote.

On March 11, 1988, at the Wellshire Inn in Denver, with Lee at his side, Hart called it quits. The people had decided, he said. There was no point in going on. Asked if he would run for President again, he said: "Not this year." And then he laughed.

Nine months later, Hart and I sat down over breakfast at the Embassy Row Hotel in Washington, D.C. He was wearing the same herringbone sports jacket he had been wearing at Kollsman Instruments that day in February. He had oatmeal with brown sugar and strawberries, bacon, wheat toast and coffee. Whatever else the campaign had done to him, it had not affected his appetite.

He had everything all worked out in his mind. Though he had previously admitted to making a mistake, he now did not believe he was responsible for what had happened to him. The media had done him in. "People say: 'You brought it on yourself,' " Hart said. "I *didn't* bring it on myself. I just have always insisted on my privacy. I never liked talking about myself. I hated it. I learned to do it, but I hated it. And I was getting a lot of questions [in the spring of 1987] about what my mother was like and what my father was like, and I just felt that people were on the boundary if not over the boundary of what a candidate had to do to run for national office. It was just too much.

"And I think it was that insistence on my retaining a small portion of my privacy that led to this 'what is he hiding?' kind of mentality. And then other candidates' campaigns were starting rumors about my personal life and so on. So reporters started saying: 'What about these rumors?' And then I was in the business of responding to rumors. And finally the rumor-rumor-rumor got to the point . . . In frustration, I said: 'Look, follow me around.' I obviously didn't mean into my house. I meant into restaurants, in public places and so on."

A lot of people felt your getting back in the race was an affront to public standards of behavior, I said to him.

"Well, let the public decide that," he said. "That's what the theme was: 'Let the people decide.' "

It's tempting to say they *did* decide.

"Yes, they did. Which is fine," Hart said. "But they made their decision in the teeth of sixty to ninety days of the nastiest press coverage anybody's ever gotten. The public didn't make its decision on me in a vacuum." He fiddled with his silverware for a moment.

"I told friends of mine that I seriously did not want to run for President," he said. "This is early '87, before I announced. I told Kathy Bushkin [his 1984 press secretary], I told Billy Shore [his senior adviser], I told my wife and I told Warren Beatty. I said: 'I don't like the feel of this, I don't like what I sense. Something bad is going to happen.' I knew it was being fed by other campaigns to a degree, who were saying to the reporters: focus on his personal life, focus on his personal life."

But if you had this ominous feeling and you knew other campaigns were urging reporters to focus on your personal life, why on earth did you have Donna Rice over at your house? I asked.

Hart's voice was firm and measured, with just the hint of frustration in it. "I felt I was *entitled* to have in my house, in our house, anybody I wanted to," he said. "It was *my* business. And I still feel that way, frankly. I don't think the press is justified in staking out or placing candidates under surveillance. I . . . don't know." There was a long pause. "I think the whole thing had less to do with bounds than it had to do with, in a curious way, *integrity*. For me, my independence was so much a part of who I was and my insistence on that independence was a condition of running. There was a part of my personal life that I was not willing to sacrifice."

Would you have won? I asked. If Donna Rice had never happened, would you have won the nomination and become the President?

"I think I would have won the nomination and I think I would have won the general," Gary Hart said. "But not by a landslide."

☆ **4** ☆

HART THROB

"Gary Hart said if he was elected he would not be the first
adulterer in the White House, but he would be the best."
—*Johnny Carson*

ONCE, AND THIS WAS WEEKS before they slept together, she
asked Gary Hart if he was the biggest womanizer in Washington.

"No," Hart replied. "Ted Kennedy is."

They dated about a year before Hart met Donna Rice. And this
woman was not exactly what you would call a party girl. She was
forty-seven, a mother, a divorcée, a businesswoman. She had little
interest in politics and even less interest, at first, in Gary Hart. To
her, he was a name out of newspaper headlines. Her life was occupied
by things like mortgage payments and college tuition and dentist
bills. She lived in that part of America that begins at the border of
Washington and is called the real world.

"He loved that I didn't know about politics," she said. "He said it
was so refreshing. He said he didn't have to debate with me and he
liked that. And he kept saying: 'You didn't really know who I was
when you met me? Really?' And I would tell him that I knew his
name, but that was all. He was impressed by that. He said he was
impressed that I was not impressed by who he was."

She had come to Washington, D.C., in the spring of 1986 for a
trade show. She was staying at the home of a girlfriend, who had
been invited to a party at the Greek Embassy.

"And Gary Hart is going to be there," her girlfriend told her.
"We've just got to go meet him."

She shrugged. "You go meet him," she said. "I'm really not that
interested." Cocktail talk with politicians was not her idea of a big
evening.

Her friend insisted and so they went. Hart, ruggedly handsome,
with craggy good looks, his full head of hair beginning to go gray at

the temples, was forty-eight then. He was already raising money for his presidential campaign. He stood in the center of the room as people swirled around him. "That's him," her friend whispered to her. "Let's go meet him."

"You go," she said.

Her friend tugged her along. They waited for their turn. They saw him greet people as only a professional politician can: a quick glance, a momentary squeeze of the hand and then the quick over-the-shoulder look to the next person in line. Keep those dogies movin'.

She took a deep breath, slapped a smile on her face and steeled herself for ten seconds of basking in his glow. She shook his hand, she mumbled a few words, and as she prepared to move on, she noticed something strange: he was still holding on to her hand.

He towered more than a foot above her. His gaze, she would later say, was "riveting."

"Why are you here?" Hart asked her. "In Washington, I mean."

She told him about the trade show.

"Where is it?" he asked. "The address. I want to come."

For a fleeting moment she thought he was making fun of her, being cruel, paying attention to her as some kind of joke. She looked around to see if he was clowning for his friends, but all she saw was the other people at the party looking at her goggle-eyed.

He continued to hold her in his gaze. "The show," he said. "I'd like to come and see you there."

She shook her head. Gary Hart was a famous man. A presidential candidate. And married. That much she knew about him. The thought of him sweeping into the trade show to see her was unimaginable. "It's just not . . . there would be too much commotion," she said to him. "You can't come."

"Give me the address," he said, smiling, the off-center dimple in his chin almost winking at her.

"I . . . I don't know it," she said. "I don't have it. The address. I don't really know Washington."

But such things do not put off a man of destiny. "Call me with the information," he said. "Call." He did not bother giving a number. If someone wanted to reach Senator Hart, a call to the United States Capitol would do it.

She murmured her goodbyes and he released her hand. She left his presence with a certain amount of relief. What was *that* all about? she wondered. She was blond and attractive, but she was hardly the kind of woman men swoon over on first meeting.

All the next day her friend urged her to call. "He won't answer his own phone, if that's what you're afraid of," she said. "He's a senator. Just call and leave a message."

"Look, this is crazy," she said. "If you want it done, you do it. You call."

Her friend grabbed the phone and called Hart's office. "This is ————," she said. "Senator Hart asked me to call." She left a number and hung up and both of them dissolved into giggles.

"He'll call in twenty minutes," her friend said.

She looked at her watch. It was 5 p.m. on a Friday. "No way," she said.

"Twenty minutes," her friend repeated. "I saw the way he looked at you."

At 5:25 p.m., Gary Hart called. "This is Senator Hart," he said.

She took the phone as her friend ran to the next room, where she proceeded to jump up and down and squeal.

"I want to go to that trade show," Hart said. "I want to see you."

Impossible, she repeated. Unthinkable. But Hart was insistent.

"It's just too visible," she said. What could he be thinking of? She was willing to do anything to keep him from coming to the show. "A drink," she said. "We could meet for a drink instead."

"Yeah," Hart said. "Yeah. We'll meet at the Jockey Club."

The Jockey Club is a fashionable restaurant patronized by the great and near-great and located in the Ritz-Carlton Hotel on Massachusetts Avenue above Dupont Circle. It is not the kind of place one goes for a clandestine drink.

"Are you sure you can be that visible?" she asked him when she heard the location.

He laughed. "You could be a reporter," he said. "You could be a contributor. A businesswoman. Anyone." After all, he was a public man. His very openness, he believed, was his best cover.

They met at the Jockey Club. She was nervous. She felt like she was in a play or a movie, standing outside herself and watching her say lines. They sat at a highly visible table and had a drink. There were no preliminaries.

"He said he had never felt this way before about anyone," she said. "He was perspiring. Nervous. But he treated me like I was a princess. Princess Diana. He wanted to be with me, he said. He was so taken with me, he could not wait. He would meet me anywhere I wanted. Here, there, in California, wherever."

"You have a home in California?" she asked him.

"I have two friends whose homes I have, uh, access to," Hart said.

"But I can't afford to fly to California," she said.

"Work it around your business," he said. "That way you can write it off your taxes."

And what did that tell you? I asked her later.

"It told me he wasn't going to pay to fly me to California," she said.

Trying to characterize him at that first Jockey Club meeting, she would later say: "He was not lecherous. Not macho. *Definitely* not macho. Boyish is what he was. Very boyish. Stumbling, bumbling. Not adept. I thought to myself: This must be the first time he has ever done this. I mean, there were beads of sweat on his forehead. He was that nervous.

"I have been divorced for some years and I have been out with a lot of men, but he wasn't like any of them. He was like a kid on his first date."

He told her how unhappy his marriage was. "He said he would not still be married if he was not in politics," she said. "Then he asked about my own divorce, my business, my children. Most men never ask you about yourself, you know. Gary Hart did. He was different. It wasn't just a sexual attraction, he said. He said he liked the way I dressed, the way I moved, the way my children had been raised. He went on and on."

And you thought he was being sincere? I asked her.

It is a question she has had much time to think about. "Either he was sincere," she said, "or he meant it at the time he was saying it. Because, I mean, he wouldn't have had to go through all the trouble if he just wanted to jump in bed with me. And if he just wanted somebody to go to bed with, well, why me?"

He told her he wanted to take her someplace special, someplace few people knew about. She agreed. She was more than eager to get out from under the stares of the other people at the Jockey Club. They left and got into his car. "It was a beater, a real mess, like one of my kids' cars," she remembered. "It looked like it had never been vacuumed inside. It was totally unpretentious."

By now, evening was coming on and the light was beginning to fade. Hart drove to the Lincoln Memorial and parked in front. The setting sun turned the white marble to a dusty rose. They sat in the car. Softly, Hart began talking about Abe Lincoln.

"Lincoln was his idol," she said. "He was what a man should be. He was for the people. Gary said this was his favorite place in the world." With one portion of her mind, she sat and listened to a monologue about America's Great Emancipator. With the other portion, she wondered when the guy behind the wheel was going to make his move.

He never did.

"There were no sexual overtures," she said. "What there was instead was a constant concern for me. Was I too hot? Too cold? Did I want the air conditioning on? The windows open? The windows closed? If I had to pick one word to describe him that night, I'd say: 'Gentleman.' And boyish. A boyish gentleman."

"I'm just a cowboy," Hart kept saying to her. "I'm not citified. I'm just a cowboy."

Yup.

He told her he was uncomplicated and unsophisticated. He told her he was a sincere man who believed in the goodness of Abe Lincoln and the American people. If she hadn't been sitting down, she would have been swept off her feet.

"I was flattered," she said of that night. "I was flattered he was sharing this with me. These were his most private moments, his most private thoughts."

As dusk faded into night, he drove her to her friend's home and dropped her off. There was no talk of sex. No double entendres. Not even single entendres. He was just a cowboy, leaving the girl at the doorway of the ranch house before riding into the sunset.

"He didn't even try to hold my hand," she said. "And I've been with men who are all over you on the first date. So I guess you can say I was charmed."

He didn't kiss you good night?

"I think we shook hands," she said. "I'm sure it wasn't a kiss. I would have *remembered* a kiss."

She began to keep a diary.

He called the next day. He wanted to see her again. She explained she was going to a ball at a downtown hotel and could not see him.

"What time?" he said. "I'm entertaining people from Colorado, but I'll get rid of them and join you."

Again, she could not imagine what he was thinking. "It was like he never believed anyone would know who he was," she said. "He believed he would never draw attention. In reality, he drew attention everywhere. I told him he was being ridiculous. I was not going to meet him at any ball."

He continued to call her while she was in Washington. "He would leave his name," she said. "Later, when he called me at my home, he would leave a message on the answering machine. He never tried to hide anything."

The trade show over, she flew back home. Hart called her there. No matter where he was, in the Senate, giving a speech, meeting people, laying the groundwork for his campaign, flying around the country, he would call her from wherever he was. "He was in San Antonio giving some kind of address when he called the first time from out of town," she said. "I told him I was shocked he had actually called. I said: 'I thought I'd never hear from you. I'm really surprised.' He said he was hurt that I felt that way. He could not believe I was surprised that he would call. He was totally, totally charming. He said he was taken with me. He would talk about how tiny I was and how delicate, but yet how strong. He asked my age, and when I told him, he said: 'But you look thirty-five! Whatever you have, you ought to have it bottled.' "

And what did you think of all this? I asked. A famous, attractive, powerful man calling you like a schoolboy from all over America? What did you think he wanted?

"All I can say is that it was not sexual," she said. "It was not lusty. All I knew was that he didn't have a happy marriage and was looking for something. But sex didn't seem to be it. I didn't know then about his escapades. When we met for drinks at the Jockey Club, he told me he had been publicly separated twice. And I even asked him: 'Have you had affairs?' "

He denied it. "I'm very visible and I have a lot of enemies, including in the press," he said. "And they will try to use this [rumors of affairs] against me. But it's not true. It only happened when I was separated. In the first place, even if I had the inclination, which I don't, I would not have the time. And I would never do anything in Washington. Not in my own backyard."

She asked if he had ever been in love. "Really-really in love," she asked.

"Really-really, no," Hart said. "Really, maybe."

Reporters and political insiders knew the rumors about Gary Hart. But the public had no reason to believe he was anything other than what he seemed to be: a twice-separated but now happily married man.

"Once, he asked me to come to his place in Colorado," she said. "And so I asked him: 'What about your wife?'

" 'She travels,' he said.

" 'I can't be in your wife's home,' I said. 'I could never do that.'

" 'That's *wonderful*,' he said. 'It's so *wonderful* that you would say that.' "

Weeks after their first meeting, he called to tell her he had arranged to give a speech in the town where she lived. "He was going to speak at some Democratic function and would be done at 6 p.m.," she said. "He said he would tell his aides he was through for the night and would get dinner on his own."

Again, she was worried about being seen with him. True, this meeting would be far from Washington, but it was still America. "Where could we go where you won't be recognized?" she asked him.

"It's not a problem," he said. "It's not a real problem. Just pick a place. Book a table and we'll go. Don't worry."

She booked a table at a small, upscale suburban restaurant not far from Hart's hotel. It was a dark, romantic place far from the beaten track.

The day she was to meet Hart, he kept calling her, just to say a few words in between events. "Busy men don't do this," she said. "I've dated important men and (a) they are not telephone people and (b) they are not that considerate."

But Gary Hart was both. Though he could be somewhat strange. There were certain subjects he would not discuss on the phone. He was afraid his phones were tapped, but he never said by whom or why. And when she would answer the phone, he would always ask for her by her last name, as if this could be just a business call he was making.

Once, he called her from his Capitol Hill home in Washington.

"How can you call from home!" she asked, astonished that he would risk calling with his wife around.

No problem, he told her, it was a cordless phone.

"So I assumed he was in the backyard, out in the bushes somewhere," she said.

Other times, he didn't seem to care who might overhear him. "I miss you," he once told her tenderly. "But I have to get back to the Senate floor now. I have to vote."

When he came to her town, they met in his hotel room. This was the first time they had seen each other since that night at the Lincoln Memorial.

"It was a hot summer day and he had been running around all day and he said he wanted to take a shower," she said. "But before he went in to shower, he kept asking me if I was comfortable. Did I want to order something from room service? Did I want a book to read? I was in his hotel room but there was no ripping my clothes off. I kept thinking: What a gentleman."

As he headed for the bathroom, he handed her a biography of Thomas Jefferson. "Skim this," he said. "We'll discuss it when I get out."

And when he did get out there was another surprise.

"He came out of the bathroom fully dressed," she said. "There was no parading around in the nude. No nudity at all. And he didn't try to get me to stay in the room, to order dinner there instead of going out. He stuck to the plan."

As they rode the elevator down to the lobby, she turned to him just before the door opened. "I'll walk behind you," she said. "People won't know we're together."

He was offended. "You stand right next to me!" he ordered.

"By now, I was head over heels," she said. "He never made me feel that I was doing something wrong. It was like his wife did not exist. As we walked out of the hotel, people came up and said: 'Senator! Senator Hart!' Heads would turn as we walked by. I turned to him and said: 'Are you crazy? You think nobody will recognize you?' It made no impression on him. He drove my car to the restaurant and even the carhop recognized him! The maître d' welcomed us as 'Senator and Mrs. Hart.' He naturally assumed I was Hart's wife. Why else would I be seen with him in public?"

Neither she nor Hart corrected the maître d's mistake. And throughout the dinner, other diners made pilgrimages to their table. "We could not eat," she said. "People would come up and say hello, want to shake his hand. A man, he was a college professor, came up and asked for an autograph for his daughter to be signed: 'From the next President.' But Gary believed that most people would not recognize him, that he could move about like an ordinary person. When the bill came, he even paid with a credit card. Most married men pay cash so there is no trace. But he did not care."

They drove back to the hotel and, as soon as they got in the lobby, she tried one more time to snap him back to reality.

"You go up first," she told him, "and then I'll join you."

"No way," Hart said. "You're coming along with me."

"It's going to look like we're going to your room," she pleaded. "There is no way I could be a reporter or a business acquaintance and heading for your room at a hotel at night!"

Hart did not care. They went up to the room together.

"In the room, *I* was a nervous wreck; *he* was a nervous wreck," she said. "It was like two kids on a first date. He didn't want to make the first move. I didn't want to be aggressive." Neither was a kid, of course. They were both in their late forties (Donna Rice could just about have been their daughter) and both had dated before. They had just had dinner in a romantic restaurant and had gone back to his hotel room. And they both knew they had not ended up there to discuss Thomas Jefferson and the Louisiana Purchase.

"We talked and talked and talked," she said. "We talked for about three hours. Finally something happened. *That* happened."

And?

"Total consideration," she said. "He showed total consideration. It was wonderful. He said it was everything he thought it would be. He wanted to know if I was O.K. He used terms of endearment.

"He could tell I was not slick or experienced. He took no precautions for AIDS. And I remember thinking: What if he was running for President and got AIDS? Why is he so trusting of me?"

It is testimony to the mesmerizing effects of power that there, in bed with him that night, she was worried solely about the possibility of his *getting* AIDS and not the possibility of his *giving* AIDS to her.

"How do you know I'm not a spy?" she playfully asked him afterward. "How do you know I won't sell a story about this?"

He smiled. "I know you," he said. "I take great pride in being a good judge of character."

"I think we must have been soul mates in a previous life," she told him. "Lovers in a different century. How else could we feel so intensely in so short a time?"

"Whales," Gary Hart said to her, "mate for life."

He had to make a speech the next day at 9 a.m., but did not set the alarm. He overslept and jumped out of bed at 8:45. "You use the shower first," she told him.

"No, no, you first," he said. Then he said he felt terrible that he had to leave so quickly.

It was the last time she would see him.

"The fact that he trusted me so much made me trust him," she said. "When [a year later] I heard about Donna Rice, I was amazed. From me to her? This was no ladies' man. Never. He was unexperienced, not suave. He acted like it was all new to him. Even in the sexual aspect there was nothing . . . unusual. Nothing. It was almost like it was his first time. It was not like he wanted to do all sorts of strange things to be turned on. There was no acting out fantasies, no weird things, no weird positions. He is very masculine. He wants a woman in his life. That's what I think he keeps searching for."

Couldn't that have been part of his act? I asked her.

"I don't know," she said. "Maybe he is the kind for whom the excitement is in the pursuit and then he loses interest."

For a while, they continued to talk by phone.

"He said he felt destined to become President," she said. " 'This is my destiny,' he would say. It wasn't like he was the Messiah or anything. He just really thought he could do something. He could do good. But he said that if he had a choice, he would escape to Ireland and live in a little house and write books instead. But he said he was at a crossroads in his life. He told me: 'If I win, I have to stay married.' "

She had asked only one thing of him. "If, for whatever reason, you stop calling, promise you'll tell me," she said. "Promise you just won't stop calling."

And did he promise?

She thought for a moment. "No," she said. "He said: 'Why ask such a dumb thing?' But he never promised. I think he took some pains to never lie."

He called two or three more times and then the calls stopped. "I was concerned it was me," she said. "I thought I must have been, well, less than perfect. So I called him. When I would call his office in the past, they would say: 'What is this regarding?' and I would say he'll know. And he would always call back."

Now, he didn't return her calls. She flew to Washington. She called three times. He did not call back. She did not call again.

"I felt bad," she said. "Disappointed. I was crazy about him. I was cutting out his pictures from the newspapers. I was like a schoolgirl. I thought: Either he'll leave her for me or he'll be the President and I'll be his girlfriend on the side. I was willing to be the President's mistress. I can see how any woman would fall for him. You feel you are the only woman who means something to him and that he has never felt that way before.

"And, well, he was so lost. He needed to have his head patted. He needed to have somebody to love him. Maybe that's why he searches with so many different women. But I'll say it again: It isn't sex. That's not what drives him. It is warmth and comfort and nurturing. And I feel sorry if he hasn't found it yet. Because he deserves it. He is so sad, so alone.

"You know, he was always afraid somebody would assassinate him. But, in the end, he assassinated himself."

Well, not really. Today, Gary Hart practices law, goes to seminars on politics, travels the world and is sought after by the media. On April 20, 1989, he appeared on *Nightline* to discuss the USS *Iowa* disaster, in which forty-seven men died in a gun turret explosion, and Ted Koppel identified Hart only as "a former U.S. senator and Democratic candidate for President."

There are no more scarlet letters. No one, as Richard Nixon has proven, is ever permanently damaged. Andy Warhol was only partially correct. In an era when our attention span has been shortened if not shattered, you can be famous for fifteen minutes, wait fifteen minutes and be famous again. In the age of television, resurrection is not only possible, it is an ongoing process.

She lives a somewhat more anonymous life. Only her friends and her children know about what happened between her and Hart. And they all find her attitude generous, to say the least. "Even today, I find no fault with him," she said. "He never wanted the woman to feel like she was being used. He would never force you to do anything you didn't want. Remember this: No one has exposed Gary Hart. Nobody came forward. If he was supposed to have had affairs with millions of women, then we all must have nothing against him. After Donna Rice, why didn't a woman come forward and make money off her story or take revenge on him? Nobody did. Most spurned women are vengeful. We are not. It says a lot for him. Either he's the victim of a bum rap or he's very clever.

"And I am not sorry. It was a beautiful experience. Unless, of course, I get AIDS from it."

HE ONCE TOLD HER: "I am a juggler walking a tightrope juggling a thousand balls."

"The Greeks have a motto," she said. "Everything in moderation."

"Cowboys have a motto, too," he replied. "Live fast, die hard and have pleasant memories."

This was not the man the public saw. Not the man who could stand at a blackboard and give civics lectures on the structure of democracy. Not the man who believed in a new America. Not the man who wanted to reinspire a nation.

This was a man desperately seeking something.

Maybe cuddling, like she thought. Or sex, as she does not believe. Or something nobody, not even he, can put a name to.

"Nobody knows who I am," he told her. "On the one hand, I am running for President. And on the other hand, nobody knows who I am."

☆ **5** ☆

NINETY SECONDS
OVER AMERICA

"If you screw this one up, you're in big, big trouble."
—Lee Atwater to George Bush before
the first Republican debate

WARREN STEIBEL lumbered up the slate walk to Al Haig's house
thinking that maybe the whole thing had not been worth lying about.
"Presidential candidates," Steibel said. "I'm sick of candidates and
I'm sick of candidates' wives." It was a hot, muggy day, and Steibel,
a large man, was sweating. "Some don't even offer you a glass of
water," he said. "Running for President and you can't get a glass of
water out of them."

Steibel, the producer and director of William F. Buckley, Jr.'s
Firing Line for twenty-three years, had come to Haig's house bearing
a gift, even if he wasn't going to get any water in return. *Firing Line*
was hosting a debate among the Republican candidates for President.
It would be the first time the six Republicans would share a stage.
All the Democrats had debated for the first time on *Firing Line* in
July 1987, but George Bush kept putting off the debate until finally
Steibel had wrestled him—duped him, really—into a late October
date.

Bush's reluctance to debate was understandable. His name recognition and his office made him the front-runner. Yet he had faced
no major test. This debate would be the first. And debates always
favored underdogs. They provided underdogs with free publicity
they could never have afforded on their own. And expectations were
always so low for underdogs (and so high for front-runners) that
upsets were very possible.

Bush knew he couldn't say no forever, but he could say it for a good long time. So it fell to Warren Steibel to persuade Bush that now was the time for the debate process to begin and that *Firing Line* was the perfect format for him. To do it, Steibel used a time-tested technique, popular in both media and politics: he lied.

"How did I get them all to agree? Well, see, you start with the easiest one," Steibel said. "You start with the guy most dying to get on the air. A guy who would *kill* to get on. So I called du Pont first. Do you want to debate? I ask him. Yes? Fine. Then what I did after that was lie. Yes, producers lie. I said to the next guy I called that I've got *four* of the Republicans lined up. Then to the next guy I said I've got *five* lined up."

Which worked up until the point George Bush said he didn't care how many had been lined up, he wasn't going to debate. But Steibel was ready for that. "Bob Strauss [former chairman of the Democratic Party], my mentor, told me to tell the press that Dole and Bush had a gentleman's agreement not to debate and just keep it to a two-man race," Steibel said. "I told everybody I knew. Nobody asked where I got it. Maybe they really did have such an agreement, I don't know." This would stir things up enough, Steibel figured, to force Bush to debate.

"Then it started falling apart," he went on. "We set a date and Bush didn't want to debate and he refused twice and then he said he would debate—but only if the date were changed to November 18. Then *I* refused. I could have changed it, but I refused. Why should I change it for Bush? So Bush says no, he won't debate.

"So then Bill Buckley calls me and says: 'The press is going to call and find out you didn't really have all those other Republicans lined up. Why did you say you had them lined up when you didn't have them lined up?' "

"Because I *lied!*" Steibel told Buckley. "This is a difficult enterprise and you have to lie."

"But what will I say?" Buckley asked Steibel. "What will I tell people?"

"Tell people your producer is a *fucking liar!*" Steibel roared. Steibel is a bearlike man, to whom roaring comes naturally. His outbursts are almost always strategic, however. In reality, he is a man of good nature and self-deprecating humor. The other quality that marks Steibel is tenacity. To sponsor the first full-scale debates for both parties would be a giant coup for *Firing Line*. So Steibel decided to employ an even more daring tactic than lying: he decided to tell the truth.

On August 14, he announced that the first Republican debate would be held in Houston on October 15, that Bush had declined and that the debate would be held without him. True, a debate without Bush would not be a real debate. But the other candidates would get two hours of free national TV. And could Bush really pass that up, especially with the Iowa caucuses just a few months away?

Eleven days after Steibel's announcement, George Bush's schedulers found out they had made a terrible mistake. The Vice President was *not* going to be washing his hair on the night of October 15 after all, and he would be delighted to come to Houston and debate. Texas, after all, was one of his several home states.

Bush was nervous, but his handlers were ready. "We *wanted* him to get hit in that first debate," Lee Atwater said. "We wanted somebody to punch him, so he would punch back." And to make Bush pay attention and take the first debate seriously, Atwater had a method all ready. "We went to him," Atwater said, "and we said: 'If you screw this one up, you're in big, big trouble.' "

Which is why many people watch debates. They certainly don't all watch them to learn about issues or further the cause of democracy. They watch them for the same reason people watch the Indy 500: to see who crashes and burns.

The possibility of seeing a presidential candidate burst into flames was entertainment in its purest form. And George Bush seemed likely to oblige. He was always saying these incredible things. Having lost a straw poll vote in Iowa to both Pat Robertson and Bob Dole, Bush explained it this way: "A lot of people that support me—they were off at the air show, they were off at their daughter's coming-out party, or they were off teeing up on the golf course for that all-important last round . . ."

Which was not exactly the image his handlers were going for. While they are busy trying to sell Bush's down-home qualities, Bush opens his mouth and starts talking about coming-out parties and golf courses. Jesus, who still actually *had* coming-out parties? The Vanderbilts? And when was the last time *they* voted in Sioux City, Council Bluffs or Dubuque?

So during a live debate, Bush almost could be counted on to say something incredibly inappropriate. (After a visit to Auschwitz, Bush had said: "Boy, they were big on crematoriums, weren't they?") That alone made the debate worth watching. And Dole might employ his famous slashing sarcasm. (His finest line was about a meeting of the three living ex-Presidents: Ford, Carter and Nixon. Dole described it as a meeting of: "Hear no evil. See no evil. And evil.") With Haig, du Pont, and Kemp, there was always a chance to see a kamikaze attack. And Robertson might try to turn everyone into a pillar of salt.

PRESIDENTIAL DEBATES are a recent invention. The famed Lincoln-Douglas debates of 1858 were for a Senate seat, though they did have one quality that modern presidential debates have. As debate historian Joel Swerdlow has noted: ". . . the Lincoln-Douglas encounters were popular mostly because they were excellent theater, and not because what was said was particularly wise or revealing."

Debates did not begin because of issues anyway. They began because of body heat. In America's first congressional elections, James Madison and James Monroe were running against each other for a seat in Virginia. "Both men suffered terribly from the cold as they toured the district," Swerdlow wrote. "As long-standing friends, they decided to travel together—not to better inform the public—but to keep one another warm in the coach."

Debates did not become a major part of political life in America until well into the twentieth century. The power of the broadcast media increased as the power of the political machines declined. Public opinion had replaced party loyalty in determining the outcome of elections. And the candidate who could use radio and television to shape that opinion could be well on his way to the White House.

It became harder, as the years went by, for presidential candidates to refuse to debate. That's because debates were seen as gut checks, tests of macho. It was easy to go around the country and insult people—Al Haig had already called Bush a "political hemophiliac," and wondered openly about President Reagan's mental health, saying people continually asked him if the President "had gone gaga." But to make—and face—those accusations across a small stage was another thing. For George Bush to refuse to debate would be to prove what his opponents had said all along: he was a wimp. So, in the end, he had to debate.

AS A TV PRODUCER and director, Warren Steibel had a keen sense of theater. He didn't care if the other primary debates that would follow turned out to be teeth-grindingly dull (they did). He wanted these first full-scale debates to be interesting. And he knew that words were not what made TV interesting. He knew that six guys, even bolstered by Bill Buckley and Bob Strauss as co-moderators, could not just jabber at each other for two hours. It might be good for the country, but it would not be good for TV. TV needed pictures. Pacing. Pizzazz.

"You know how I got the idea?" Steibel said. "I was sitting around

with friends and I said: 'I want a debate that looks like a pageant.'
Like the pageant in Atlantic City. The Miss America Pageant. If I
could have gotten these guys to walk down a runway, I would have
had them walk down a runway."

Which is why we were at the home of Al Haig with a TV crew.
Steibel had decided that if he, an educated person with an interest
in public affairs, had little idea what most of the candidates were like
as human beings, then the average American had no idea. So Steibel
decided to provide each candidate with ninety seconds of free airtime
at the beginning of the debate to tell the American public about
themselves. He would bring a camera crew wherever the candidates
wanted and tape them. It would not be edited.

For the candidates, it was an extraordinary opportunity to begin
the debate, not with a tough question, but with a free ninety-second
commercial. And they didn't even have to give Steibel a glass of water
in return.

"When we shot Robertson, we were there for two hours and didn't
get offered a glass of water," Steibel says, trudging up the walkway
to stand before Haig's front door. "Or sometimes they'll give you a
glass of water, but not the crew. Nancy Reagan is like that. I was
there one day, hot day, with a crew, and she offered *me* a glass of
punch, but not the crew. Sometimes, I have to say: 'Please, could the
crew have some?' It's like they don't think the crew are people."

Haig was living in McLean, Virginia, not far from CIA headquarters
in Langley. The quiet streets here have no names. The posh homes
have no numbers. The neighborhood seems to say: If you haven't
been here before, you have no business being here now.

The house has two wings made of white brick and four small
columns in front facing a circular drive. Inside, there is a formal
dining room with a crystal chandelier over an oval table. A stone
fireplace. Wood beams running overhead. Pegged oak floors. Oriental
rugs. Not a cushion is out of place, not a magazine askew.

We enter, are greeted by Haig staff members and sit down. After
about ten minutes, Steibel finally asks: "Can I have a glass of water?"
He gives me a knowing look.

Haig comes out and greets us warmly. He has a weathered, craggy
face, with deep-set eyes and bushy eyebrows that sometimes give him
an almost Tartar-like look. He has a high forehead topped by white
wavy hair that has grown somewhat darker over the last few years.
Not surprisingly, because he is a retired four-star general, he has a
commanding presence. His campaign staff always calls him "General."

Naturally, Steibel is unimpressed by Haig. Having worked with
Buckley so long, Steibel has met all the candidates before, and

virtually all the world's leaders to boot. Their power, their offices, their fame mean nothing to him. This is one reason Steibel dresses the way he does. He never wears ties, his shirts are often borderline disreputable and one of his shirttails invariably is flapping outside his baggy pants. This day it is the right shirttail. The shirt button over his belly has popped open and will go uncorrected for the rest of the day. It is a kind of statement that Steibel makes: I didn't dress up for you because you are nobody who needs to be dressed up for.

Haig is parade-ground sharp in a blue blazer, gray slacks and a rep tie (no medals). He is smiling, affable, eager. In a sense, this will be his national debut. A ninety-second chance to persuade the American people he is not a madman. It's a tough sell. Haig's chief problem is that he is a military man in an era without military heroes. He has the wrong kind of name recognition. Those who know him at all know him as the guy who tried to take over the country after Reagan was shot.

That day still haunts him. March 30, 1981. Reagan is shot by John Hinckley. Bush is in Texas. And Haig, then Secretary of State, bursts into the White House pressroom, sweat beading up on his face, and goes on TV to say: "As of now, I am in control . . ."

The U.S. Constitution had a different view. And Haig barely seemed in control of himself, let alone a nation. A few hours later, Bush arrived and democracy was reestablished in the land. But the damage had been done. At his fund-raisers, Haig would show a videotape of the entire news conference to try to put his awful moment into context and show what he was doing: he was trying to calm our allies and show the nation that the ship of state was not rudderless. But each time he showed the tape, there he would be, drenched with sweat and looking like he was mounting a palace coup. (One lasting side effect of that day is that now Haig is extremely conscious of his sweat glands. For the entire thirteen months of his campaign he insists that he have time to relax and cool off before any public appearance. He will not climb stairs or rush in any way before going on TV. Men may sweat, women may perspire and ladies may glow. But Al Haig does none of these things.)

Haig has raised $955,589 in campaign funds so far. In almost any other endeavor, this would be a sizable amount of money. To a presidential campaign, it is chicken feed. George Bush has raised $12.7 million and Pat Robertson $11.7 million. But if Haig is short of funds, he has no shortage of strategy.

Daniel Mariaschin, Haig's communications director, is in the kitchen outlining it for me. "Our ticket to Super Tuesday [a grouping of largely Southern primaries] is a strong New Hampshire finish," he says, as if that were a realizable goal. (As it turns out, Haig's ticket will be punched in Iowa and he will pull out before primary day in New Hampshire. He will throw his support to Bob Dole in a dramatic joint news conference. From Bush's point of view, this is the first time in history a rat has swum *toward* a sinking ship.)

But for Haig everything begins here, today. He has ninety seconds to present his warm, human, casual side. Naturally, he wants to use a TelePrompTer.

All of the candidates have asked to use TelePrompTers. Technically simple, though expensive, these machines reflect printed words off a one-way mirror that stands in front of the camera lens at a 45-degree angle. In effect, the camera lens shoots through the words, allowing the performer to look straight into the camera and read at the same time.

Steibel tells the candidates to forget about using TelePrompTers. The candidates insist. Steibel refuses. The candidates demand. Steibel stands firm. Only an expert can disguise the fact he is using a TelePrompTer (take a look at any TV editorial reply) and these guys are no experts. Steibel has envisioned a relaxed chat to the American people. He wants them to actually try to speak off the cuff for ninety seconds.

They are horrified. They are terrified. "Du Pont disappeared for a half hour to memorize his thing, because he didn't know it by heart and I wouldn't give him a TelePrompTer," Steibel says. "They all called the night before and demanded TelePrompTers. Demanded. I told them it kills spontaneity. They didn't care. 'Then try this,' I told them, 'I refuse.'

"The other day, I get a call from a guy who says he just wrote Dole's ninety seconds and it's very good and he wants it on the TelePrompTer. I say no. I say I'll do what ABC and CBS and NBC won't do: I'll show it to you and you can do it again if you don't like it. You can pick the take you want.

"They said: 'But we've rented our *own* TelePrompTer.'

"I said: 'No.'

"They said: 'We cut the check! We paid for it already!' "

Steibel shook his head. "These staffs are so *organized*. There's no spontaneity left. Who is running these campaigns, them or him? This isn't his inaugural address; it's ninety seconds! These guys, they're so . . . prepared. I know they don't want gaffes, like Ford and Poland. [During a debate with Jimmy Carter in 1976, Gerald Ford had said Poland was not under Soviet domination.] But none of them are good enough to be prepared and look spontaneous. You know what

I would tell them if I were working for them? I'd say: 'Stumble on a word.' As long as you're going to use artifice, use a lot of artifice."

(As it turns out, George Bush—who else?—will stumble on a word. And Roger Ailes, his media wizard, will insist on using that take. Ailes and Steibel understand that looking natural is much more difficult than looking prepared.)

Haig's media consultant, Jay Bryant, actually agrees with Steibel. "I prefer no TelePrompTer," he says. "You can be an expert at reading lines—like some Presidents we can think of—but unless you're a real expert, you don't project, you don't emote. You read. I'll take less polish and sincerity any day. After twenty years in political advertising, we deal with a double level of cynicism: people don't trust commercials and they don't trust politicians, so political commercials face a double hurdle. So anything a person looks at and says: 'That's real!' that wins.

"But it is important to get the candidate to agree to do multiple takes," Bryant continues. "Ninety seconds is a long time. But we don't have a script; the general didn't want it. He hasn't been a candidate all his life. So unlike a lot of candidates, he doesn't think he knows everything about being a candidate."

He takes me into Haig's den. It's like something out of an English manor house. A leather couch with brass studs. An antique desk. Crossed swords on the wall. Elephant tusks framing the fireplace. Flintlock pistols and oil paintings of sailing ships. A four-star general's flag. Autographed pictures of Reagan, Johnson, Ford, Rockefeller, the King of Belgium, Prince Philip, Prince Charles, Queen Elizabeth and King Hussein. A picture of Henry Kissinger and Haig, both asleep, across the aisle from each other on Air Force One.

"You see this and you know he's not some penny-ante pol," Bryant says proudly. Which makes it even more strange when Bryant decides to shoot the ninety-second spot, not in the den, but in the very nice, but very ordinary living room. Steibel shrugs. It's their ninety seconds.

Mrs. Haig, Pat, now comes in and greets us. She will appear by Haig's side during the spot. Normally, Steibel would refuse, but now he can't. That's because Pat Robertson earlier had insisted that his wife, Dede, be in his spot.

"We get to Robertson's house and he insists his wife speak in the spot," Steibel says. "Insists! I refuse. Robertson doesn't care. So I finally give up and say O.K. And then we have to wait because Dede is at the beauty parlor."

Dede (for Adelia) will end up saying twenty-seven words: "Well, I'm very concerned about the plight of women, both in this country and throughout the hemisphere. But probably my main concern is about the single parent."

The trouble is they're not the twenty-seven words Robertson wants her to say. He would rather she not bring up the whole "single parent" issue, especially because it has been recently revealed that he and Dede conceived their first child without benefit of Holy Matrimony.

So maybe Dede can find some other plight in this hemisphere to be concerned about. But while Robertson is huddling with his staff to come up with one, Steibel shuffles up to Dede. "That thing about single women was very good, very good," he tells her, just to get back at Robertson. "I'm not trying to influence anything, but I thought it was very, very good."

Naturally, Dede is pleased. An expert likes her line. And so she insists to Pat that it stay in.

"After all," Steibel tells me, "she almost *was* a single mother."

Pat Haig is in a blue-gray blouse with a pin at the throat and gray slacks. She is attractive and in her youth was a great beauty. Haig's people set up the shot. They have Haig perch on the arm of the living-room couch, while Pat sits on the cushion looking up at him.

"Just tell me when to start," Haig says.

Steibel checks with his crew, Bill South and Joe Sauvion, and tells Haig to start.

"Hello," Haig says, "I'm Al Haig. And this is my wife, Pat, who's been at my side for the past thirty-seven years. I've been asked why I want to be your President and the answer is simple: I've served seven Presidents in my lifetime, four at intimately close range. I think I know the job, its challenges, its rewards and the limitations of presidential power. Will we continue on with the renewal of the American spirit? Most importantly, however, I think Americans worry about world peace . . ."

Steibel then gives him a sign indicating he has thirty seconds to go. Haig assumes he is being told to shut up and he stops.

"You have another thirty seconds," Steibel says. "That was the thirty-second cue."

"Oh," Haig says. "Let's just skip the cue next time."

Steibel tells him to begin again.

"Hello, I'm Al Haig and this is my wife, Pat, who has been by my side for the last thirty-seven years . . ." he says, repeating everything nearly flawlessly, a considerable feat considering Bryant has said there was no script. (At the end of the day, I go into the guest bathroom, right off the den. On the sink is an open compact of

Natural Wonder powder and a legal pad. Carefully written out in longhand on the pad in black ink is Haig's "unscripted" script. "Hello," it begins. "I am Al Haig and this is my wife, Pat, who has been by my side for the last thirty-seven years . . .")

"As a military man," Haig is continuing, "I know that American mothers worry that such an individual might reach for a military solution in our efforts to preserve the peace. Let me tell you that precisely the opposite is true. Only a man who has seen battle firsthand, its frustrations and sacrifices, has seen our young people shipped home in bodybags, knows how critical it is to avoid armed conflict except in the most extreme of circumstances. These are the reasons I hope you will look carefully at my candidacy."

He stops. Steibel's heart sinks. Yet another candidate has used the ninety seconds to make a campaign commercial instead of presenting himself as a human being. Steibel smiles bravely. "You won't believe it, General," Steibel says, "but that was eighty-eight seconds. You're getting better than Bill Buckley."

"Well, there's not time to say very much," Haig says.

"I thought it was very good," says Steibel, lying through his teeth. "But I want to ask you one thing. We don't get anything about your education, where you were born. That was the idea of this, a personal look. Not a sales pitch."

Haig bristles. "The idea is we talk about *experience* and that I'm not a *warmonger*," Haig says. "*That* is the message."

"I understand," Steibel explains, "but I'd love to know whether you were born in South Dakota or Philadelphia or whatever."

"I could say: 'I'm Al Haig from Philadelphia, Pennsylvania,'" Haig says sarcastically. "Is that what you want?"

Steibel laughs, shrugs.

"'I was born in a humble shack in Philadelphia,'" Haig goes on. "But, you know, that sounds *exactly* like Bob Dole. All that humble stuff. And it makes me want to *vomit*."

Well, now. No need to get testy. Steibel decides a little humor might be called for. "All the Democrats said their fathers had milk routes and that's how they went to college," he says. "So when we taped Pete du Pont the other day, I said: 'Why don't you say you couldn't get into college and so your father *bought* the college.'"

Haig laughs. "I just don't want to be too . . . schmaltzy," he says, making everyone in the room wonder where on earth General Alexander Meigs Haig, Jr., ever picked up such a word. Surely not at West Point.

Steibel assures him that no decent American would ever associate schmaltz and Al Haig in the same thought. "O.K., let's do it one more time," Steibel says. "I want you to be happy with it."

Haig and Pat resume their positions on the couch. He is on the arm; she on the cushion. Because she has no lines, it is her duty to stare at him adoringly for eighty-eight seconds.

"Hello, I'm Al Haig and this is my wife . . . I've seen combat firsthand . . . The sacrifices, the bloodshed . . . I've seen our boys shipped home in bodybags . . . That's why I hope you'll consider me in nineteen hundred and eighty-eight."

He finishes and then strides over to the TV monitor. "Fellas, let's take a look at this," Haig says.

The tape rewinds with a high-pitched garbling sound and Haig does a Donald Duck imitation. Then he falls silent as he watches himself on the small screen. "Was I too emotional?" he asks when the tape is finished, again voicing his biggest fear.

"No, I like it," Mariaschin says. "But on 'bodybags,' I want two words. 'Body . . . bags.' Like that. Not just one, 'bodybags.' Let's see it again."

We see it again.

Finally, Steibel intervenes. "May I make a suggestion?" he says, and doesn't wait for an answer. "I think the living room is horrible for you."

"I agree," Haig says instantly.

"And you've got me so low down on the couch," Pat says. "It looks like I'm down on the floor."

Haig grabs a cigarette. "When I'm perched like that, the camera gets my shiny dome," he says. "I think we can get a more flattering shot if we're both at the same level. I remember also the irritation I felt at Gary Hart's announcement, where he starts out in front of Mount Rushmore [actually Red Rocks Park, outside Denver] with his family down at a lower level. I thought: That arrogant son of a bitch! Excuse my language."

We excuse his language.

"That's it," Steibel says. "If you've been happily married for thirty-seven years, how come you can't sit together?"

"Right!" says Pat. "That other looked like a tintype. Man standing, woman sitting. Let's get rid of that."

On Steibel's suggestion we troop into the den. The Haigs sit down on the leather couch and the crew sets up the camera. Directly behind the Haigs and clearly visible in the shot is a picture of the King of Belgium. Pat notices it and quickly replaces it with pictures of the four Haig grandchildren.

"Those are your grandchildren?" Steibel asks just to make sure the pictures weren't rented or something. "That's nice. O.K., so we'll do another take. Get comfortable and look natural. If you sit awkward, it will sound awkward."

"Let's make this a hundred percent!" Haig says in his best let's-hit-the-beaches voice.

Jay Bryant, who has been keeping silent, now steps forward. There is one word in Haig's speech that is troubling him. And Bryant is looking for a way to say it diplomatically.

"You're such a mythic figure, General. I think Steibel is right, people would like to know you're from Philadelphia and you have grandchildren," Bryant says, gingerly edging toward his real point. "And I am not sure, given the very dramatic appeal that we're making, that the 'bodybags' thing is going to be appropriate in the context. Strong as it is, I just worry that it's going to raise questions people hadn't thought to ask yet."

Like how many American boys Al Haig shipped home from Vietnam in said bodybags, for instance.

"Remember," Bryant goes on, "you're going to be in a context, unless I miss my guess, of a bunch of warm-and-fuzzies being laid out by these other guys during the debate. You know, they're going to try to be nice and likable. And I'm just worried that you'll once again—in attempting to defuse what we're talking about—be the person who suddenly in this nice warm, sort of friendly thing . . ."

"That means I keep the bodybags out?" Haig interrupts.

"You'll get plenty of chance to talk about *that* during the debate," Bryant says, hoping Haig never gets a chance to talk about it.

"Well, then can I use it in the opening?" Haig asks.

Bryant decides subtlety is not working here. Haig does not seem to grasp the effect the word "bodybags" will have on the viewers. To Haig, a bodybag was just an appurtenance of war. You had to ship the kids home in something, didn't you? So what's the big deal?

But Bryant appreciates the visceral impact the word is going to have. After the debate is over, the viewers might not remember Kemp's position on the gold standard or du Pont's plan for Social Security, but they sure as hell are going to remember Al Haig's bodybags.

"I would rather have the opening *not* have the horrors of war quite so graphically depicted," Bryant says as bluntly as he can.

"Well, it worried me," Haig says. "That's why I asked."

"Our problem," Bryant goes on, trying to sweeten the medicine for Haig, "is that we have a longer and more distinguished biography than anybody else and it can't be said in ninety seconds. Jack Kemp has no problem: 'I played quarterback; I was in Congress.' That's easy. So let's condense, General. I've seen you do that."

"Why don't I say this," Haig says. " 'I've served seven Presidents. I'm proud of the accomplishments of my party.' "

"Don't leave out 'I think I know the job,' " Mariaschin prods.

"What?" Haig asks.

" 'I've served seven Presidents; I think I know the job,' " Mariaschin repeats.

"Oh yeah, oh yeah," Haig says. " 'I think I know the job.' "

"That's a keeper," says Mariaschin.

"Oh yeah," says Haig.

"And keep the little—it's not a laugh, not a smile, not a guffaw," says Bryant. "But you say: 'I think . . . I know the job.' And you do a little thing with your expression."

The word Bryant is looking for is "smirk."

"All right," Haig says, and then walks back over to the couch, mumbling his new buzzwords. "Challenges, rewards, limitations, powers. Executive in government. In private sector. Professor. Strengths and weaknesses. Vision."

" 'And I have four grandsons, whose future means a great deal to me,' " Bryant suggests. "That's got vision of America in it."

"That's every candidate on the stump," Haig says, screwing up his face.

"Well . . ." says Bryant.

"That's every candidate on the stump!" says Haig. "I'm trying to get *away* from that. They're all going to say that. All of them. I'm trying to be *unique*."

He walks over to where Pat sits waiting patiently. "I've gone away from bodybags," he tells her. "And I need a new ending." He lights another cigarette.

As Haig goes over his new lines, I talk with Mariaschin about his dilemma: Bush and Dole are both known for their wartime exploits. Dole is not shy about talking about his terrible war wounds and how he got them. And Bush has a commercial using actual footage of him being pulled out of the sea after his plane was shot down in World War II. ("I don't care about them shooting *his* plane down," Haig will say of this commercial. "I want to know how many of *their* planes *he* shot down.") Both men had records as war heroes, yet neither man was thought of as a warmonger.

"That's because they were veterans, but not generals," Mariaschin says a little bitterly. "That's the difference. That's the punishment you get when you're a general."

"Anytime you're ready," Steibel says to Haig.

Haig begins. "Hel-lo!" he says, and his voice breaks like a teenager's. He laughs. "Let's do it again," he says. "Hello, I'm Al Haig and this is my wife, Pat, who has been by my side for the last thirty-seven years . . ."

He ends eighty-two seconds later, omitting all references to body-bags.

"Very good," Steibel says.

"Let's do one more," Bryant says.

Steibel stifles a sigh. "O.K., and then you pick the one you want," Steibel says. "But once we leave here, that's it. You don't get to see it again. We don't edit it, but you don't get to see it again."

Haig takes his cue and goes through the whole thing again. When he is finished, he walks over to the monitor and asks to see the last two takes.

"And can we do one more?" Mariaschin asks.

"Sure. Fine," Steibel says in a resigned voice. "I'm not rushing you."

"O.K., shoot it again, shoot it again," Haig says, and turns to Pat. "One more time, dear." They sit back down. "Hello, I'm . . ."

He finishes and Steibel bursts out coughing. "I've held my cough for the last thirty-four seconds!" he says. "I think that's the best one. It's eighty-seven seconds. You were a little slower. Dan, what do you think?"

"Well, it was a little more self-serving," Mariaschin says.

That settles it: it's a keeper.

EARLY ON AN OCTOBER MORNING in the dining room of the Hay-Adams Hotel in Washington, D.C., Warren Steibel is dribbling eggs down his copious shirtfront. "I always do that," he says, dabbing hopelessly at himself. "I got another shirt upstairs. I may change before we go."

His cameraman comes up to him. "We wear ties this morning, Warren?" he asks.

"Naw," Steibel says. "What for?"

Yeah, what for? We're just going to the Capitol to tape the Minority Leader of the U.S. Senate. No reason to get dressed up.

Steibel and his crew pack six huge cases of equipment into rental cars and drive to the Capitol. The dome shines a pristine white in the bright fall sunshine. It is going to be a good morning; Steibel can feel it. Bob Dole is no jerkwater candidate. He is a seasoned professional who has run for President before and now seems well-positioned for victory.

Steibel ambles inside the entrance to the Senate wing of the Capitol and asks the guard by the metal detector if there is somebody who can help with the equipment. Some Capitol maintenance people are rounded up and Steibel begins handing out bills as if he were tipping bellhops at the Trump Plaza in Atlantic City.

Everything is packed into the tiny elevators, which wheeze up to the second floor. We get off and wander past statues of men whose names and achievements are long forgotten, going down corridors rarely seen by the public to get to S-230, the outermost office of the Minority Leader's lavish enclave of seven rooms.

The rooms reek of history: the ceilings have murals that feature such symbols of power and wisdom as eagles, owls and maces; there are frescoes, detailed marble panels, friezes, gilded mirrors, five-tiered crystal chandeliers that date back to 1870 and a large, working marble fireplace.

It is in front of the fireplace, sitting in two salmon-colored silk-brocade wing chairs, that Bob Dole and Elizabeth Dole have decided to cut their ninety-second spot. We clamber into Dole's office, dragging the boxes of equipment behind us. Walt Riker, Dole's press aide, welcomes us, and tells us that neither Senator Dole nor Mrs. Dole is available for the taping. The nomination of Robert Bork to the U.S. Supreme Court is in disarray and Dole must meet with the President. Mrs. Dole is changing her dress. Nobody knows which will take longer.

Steibel sighs and settles into a chair. "I was at a little dinner party for Dan Rather," he says to Riker, "and Rather predicted the two tickets would be Nunn and Cuomo or Cuomo and Nunn for the Democrats and Bush and Elizabeth Dole for the Republicans."

Riker looks at Steibel to see if he is kidding. He is not.

"Dan Rather is wrong once again," Riker says. Then he goes off to see if he can find out what has happened to the candidate and his wife.

We are offered coffee. Even the crew. The minutes tick by as we sit and sip. "If I were Bill Buckley, I'd walk out, because that's what he would do," Steibel says. "But I'm not Bill Buckley."

To kill time, Steibel locates a videotape machine and decides to view the old tapes of *Firing Line* that feature appearances by each of the current Republican candidates. A few seconds of each appearance will be shown during the debate, just to give the show a little more pizzazz. Riker comes back into the office and asks what we are doing. We tell him, and he is immediately wary. "Isn't it unfair to show people ten or fifteen years ago?" he asks.

After seeing the first tape, however, Riker decides it is not unfair at all. Because the first tape is of George Bush defending Richard Nixon.

It is 1974 and Bush's hair is darker and longer, his sideburns extending almost to the bottom of his earlobes. His gestures are the same, however, his hands still sawing the air when he talks. He is the chairman of the Republican National Committee and he is wearing a business suit with a very preppy striped belt. The show was taped May 3, 1974, and aired May 5. On it, Buckley asks Bush if Richard Nixon, who is already in disgrace, will resign.

"The President isn't going to do it," Bush says with boyish enthusiasm and great finality. "I don't profess to be the world's closest person to the President in understanding his instincts and everything else, but I am close enough to feel that [resignation] will not happen *under any circumstances. . . .* I don't think it's in the *makeup of the man.* I've seen the President a good deal lately and I just *don't feel that's an option.*"

After the taping, as Bush walked off the set, Steibel had stopped him. "I'll bet you fifty dollars Nixon resigns," Steibel said.

"That's a bet!" said Bush. "And let's put it in writing!"

They did. And ninety-nine days later, Richard Nixon became the first President in U.S. history to resign his office. Two years later, cleaning out a desk drawer, George Bush found the piece of paper on which the bet was written. He immediately sent Steibel a hundred dollars by way of apology. All of which is pure George Bush.

(As an act of mercy, this Bush clip will never be shown during the debate. Another, somewhat less embarrassing one is substituted. In this one, Bush talks about how he was once at a news conference about Watergate where reporters were "goosing me from the back" with their microphones.)

Riker begins setting up a huge white pad of paper at least four feet high. Because Steibel has banned TelePrompTers, the Dole staff has decided to strike back with idiot cards. Printed on the sheets are Dole's buzzwords: "Leader's office. Better America. Voted 10,000 times. Made the tough calls. Been tested on the firing line. Small-town values. Freedom from government spending. Strong and compassionate. Mrs. Dole. Public service. Thank you."

Steibel is more amused than offended by this subterfuge. "O.K., use it," he says. "I didn't want a whole speech read, but if you want notes, fine."

"We don't want it to look like he's reading either," Riker says. "His eyes would go up and down. And we don't want that. We want him to have notes, but we don't want him to read notes."

Steibel's cameraman leans over to me and whispers: "If you can't talk about yourself for ninety seconds without notes, do you deserve to be President?"

Stan Wellborn, a Dole speechwriter, and Mari Maseng, Dole's communications director, walk into the office discussing the idiot cards. "Please don't give him anything written down, because he's a thousand times better spontaneous," Steibel begs Maseng.

"Right," Maseng says wearily. "But it's ninety seconds and you want to have him say the *right* things."

"What time will we really be doing this?" Steibel asks.

"Eleven-fifteen," she says.

Eleven-fifteen comes and goes.

"We're going to get shots of him picking his nose and we're going to use them if this goes past eleven-thirty!" Steibel shouts.

The Dole staff members practice flipping over the pages of the idiot pad, until Steibel's sound man tells them it won't work. As each giant page is turned it creates a swishing noise that is being picked up by the microphones. It will sound as if Dole is rubbing his thighs together like a cricket. Undaunted, Dole's staff quickly transfers the phrases from the large sheets of paper to three large pieces of cardboard, each of which will be held by a different member of the staff.

Steibel is now on his feet. "This is the longest we've had to wait for any candidate!" he shouts.

"He's the only candidate who has a real job," Maseng says to him sweetly.

Mrs. Dole walks in, smiling briskly. She is wearing a red dress with black polka dots. She greets us pleasantly, makes sure we have coffee and immediately departs.

Steibel shakes his head. While we continue to wait, he decides to make one last stab at making these ninety-second spots warm and personal.

"Have you got anything about where he's from, what college he went to, anything like that?" Steibel asks. "Human. Which is what this spot was supposed to be about."

No, there is nothing like that. Human is not on Dole's agenda today. He wants to look presidential instead.

"Uh-huh," Steibel says, and starts scanning Dole's idiot cards. " 'Strong and compassionate.' Now *there's* a new line."

We wait.

"Mari," Steibel says, "I want you to remember that in Houston it's a live show. It goes on at eight. So if Dole gets there at eight-thirty or nine or ten, he won't be on."

"I'm *sorry!*" Maseng says. "He has been meeting with the *President!*"

Steibel shrugs. Big deal. The President. Tall guy that used to be an actor, right? Steibel has taped the President. And the President was never this late.

At eleven-fifty Dole enters the room with Elizabeth. He carries a script in his left hand, the words having been typed on a large-type typewriter. As always, a black felt-tip pen pokes out between the fingers of his war-damaged right hand. This is to keep people from trying to shake it. He is wearing a black pinstripe suit and a red foulard tie with black dots. It takes Dole a very long time to tie his tie one-handed every morning (he also buttons his shirt himself, using a button hook) and that is why he hates it when, during TV appearances, sound men grab his tie to attach their microphones. If they loosen the knot, he must excuse himself and go through the agonizing process of retying it. He does not accept help.

Dole is immediately businesslike. "Tell Pat not to let anyone in," he says, "and cut the phones." He turns to Steibel. "What have we got? Ninety seconds?"

"Yeah," Steibel says, "but you want to go eighty-five seconds, that's fine. You want to look at the monitor after you do one or two, that's fine. Unless you think it will make you more self-conscious."

"He probably doesn't want to look at the monitor," Maseng says, answering for Dole.

Dole takes his seat in front of the fireplace, on the left side. Mrs. Dole takes her seat on the right side. They are color-coordinated, he mainly in black with a touch of red, she mainly in red with a touch of black. It has kind of a checkerboard effect. The setting, however, is stiff and formal, precisely what Steibel did not want.

Dole crosses his legs. "Does my knee show?" he asks.

"Yessir," the cameraman says.

He uncrosses his legs.

"Go up a little," Steibel tells the cameraman. "Now it doesn't show, Senator."

Dole recrosses his legs.

"We're ready. Anytime," Steibel says.

Dole remains silent.

"You can start anytime," Steibel tells him.

Dole grimaces slightly and begins following the notes on the idiot cards.

"Hello, I'm Bob Dole," he says.

"And I'm Elizabeth Dole," she says, "and we appreciate the opportunity to visit with you tonight."

"We're seated right now in the Republican leader's office," Dole says. "We're about a hundred feet from the Senate floor, where I've been working for the past nineteen years to make America a nation that's strong, compassionate and fiscally responsible and, of course, second to none.

"That's what I fought for in the Senate and earlier in the House. That's what I fought for in World War II. I've had about three decades of service in the Congress of the United States and I voted, oh, over ten thousand times in those twenty-seven years. And some were tough votes. But that's what leadership is really all about."

Dole, in this first take, is loose, relaxed and not at all bad. He is talking not just about what he has done but, by implication, what George Bush has not done: Dole has voted and has been tough. Bush has left no footprints behind him.

"I grew up in the small town of Russell, Kansas," Dole continues in the very manner that makes Al Haig want to vomit, "and we were concerned about each other, concerned about our neighbors, concerned about a strong America. I really believe as I travel around the country that what America is looking for is a leader who is concerned about their families, concerned about this country, and somebody who knows Washington and knows how to get results and how to work with Congress. And I believe I'm uniquely qualified to do that."

Elizabeth says: "Bob and I have devoted our entire lives to public service. Now it's my privilege to tell the American people why I believe in Bob Dole—with strong leadership, America's potential is unlimited."

Dole concludes with: "Thank you very much."

"One minute and forty-five seconds," Steibel says. "That's O.K." In fact, it is very long, but Steibel would like to get out of here sometime before sundown.

Dole gets up, feeling that it is all over. He begins to clown a little, suggesting we just take a picture of the idiot cards instead of him. Then he turns serious and asks: "Somebody going to be signing this for the deaf?"

"Uh, I don't know," Steibel says, caught off guard. "I don't think we did for the Democrats, though it would probably be a good idea."

"It would be good," Dole says. "You would be the first debate to do it. It would set an example. I know it's a little disconcerting. But it's very important to a lot of people who can't hear."

"I'll look into it," Steibel says. "They should have something for the 'near-deaf,' that's myself. But the deaf should have something also."

Maseng tells Dole he should do another take. He sits back down and she reaches over and tugs his suit into place.

"O.K., we're rolling," Steibel says.

"Hello, I'm Bob Dole."

"And I'm Elizabeth Dole."

And then the quorum buzzer, which tells senators they must come to the Senate floor and vote, goes off loudly.

"Keep rolling," Steibel says. "Keep rolling."

"Do I start over?" Dole asks.

"Oh yes," Steibel says.

"Hello, I'm Bob Dole."

This time it comes in at ninety-three seconds, mainly because both Dole and Elizabeth talk faster. Again, Dole ends on "thank you very much." But there is a problem. The camera must pull back from the close-up of Elizabeth to a shot of both of them in order to catch Dole's final "thank you."

"I missed it," the cameraman says. "He went too fast."

"Why do we need it?" Dole says, itching to end this. "I already said hello. Why do I need to say goodbye?"

"I think it's better without it," says Elizabeth.

"I don't think the senator wants to do it many more times," Steibel says to the room at large. "He's got that Bill Buckley 'no more' look on his face."

Dole does not dispute this.

"But could you do it once more?" Steibel asks. "Just so you'll be happy?"

They do it a fourth time. And now, without Dole's goodbye, the spot ends on Elizabeth. This is not good. It makes her look more important than the candidate.

Dole does not notice or does not care. He gets up from the chair. "Good enough for me. That's it. See you later," he says. "I got to vote . . . No, I don't want to see it on the monitor. So long." He leaves the room.

Mrs. Dole shakes hands with the entire crew, thanking each one personally. Then she decides to look at the last take. She sits down in front of the monitor on the floor of the outer office with her legs tucked under her, the staff around her in a semicircle.

She sees the ending and immediately grasps what is wrong with it. "It should have panned to him," she says. "The camera should have panned to him."

Mari Maseng isn't happy with the last take either, but for different reasons. "He looks *comatose* at the end," she says.

Dole comes back from voting. The problem is explained to him, though not the part about him being comatose. "When things are done, they're done," Dole says, his voice tight. "I want the last one. My message was better."

The staff digs in its heels. This ninety seconds is incredibly important. And they explain to him the message *doesn't matter*, the message is *inconsequential* if Dole *looks bad* at the end. This is not about words, which is a difficult concept to get through to men who have lived their lives by words. The camera must pull back and show both Doles, they tell him. There are already enough problems with talk of Elizabeth overshadowing Bob. They can't have this spot reinforce that.

Dole listens, nods and sits down in the chair once more. "Got those three sheets, Walt?" he asks Riker, talking about the idiot cards. "Let's do it one more time."

They do it again, this time with the camera pulling back and capturing both of them in the last shot.

Dole feels something is wrong, however. "One more time," he says. Then, inexplicably, he changes his line about having voted "ten thousand" times, which has been good enough in the previous five takes, to "ten thousand five hundred" times. There, that was it. That's what had been bothering him. He had been cheating himself out of five hundred votes.

"O.K.," Dole says at the end. "Wrap it up."

While the equipment is being packed up, he chats about the debate format with us. "Boy, that was a goofball question the Democrats had at their debate," he says. "The one about what pictures they would hang in the White House?" He laughs, shaking his head.

"Uh, it's the same goofball question for the Republicans," I tell him. "You're all going to be asked the same thing."

"Oh," Dole says, immediately switching gears. "Well, I think I'll say I'll put up the pictures of all the guys who ran against me and lost."

That Dole might have tried to convey some of his dry wit, his true personality, in his ninety-second spot was never seriously considered. Instead, his personality was hammered into a mold, a mold his advisers believe will sell to the American public.

Mrs. Dole, who had gone off to change, comes back in a green dress. She looks at herself on the monitor. "I don't think television does anything for me," she says. "I remember one time I was testifying before the Senate and C-SPAN had it on and I watched it for two minutes and I said: 'That's *grotesque*.'"

"Now," she says, brightening, "who wants a cheeseburger?"

We leave the Capitol four hours after we arrived. Outside, Steibel stops on the steps for a moment, looks over toward the Washington Monument and takes a deep breath of the autumn air. "You know, this whole thing has disenfranchised me," he says with great weariness. "I can no longer vote."

I ask him what he means.

He sighs. He shakes his head. "What did Dole do, six takes?" Steibel asks. "And that's not too bad. Some took nine takes. *Nine.* So now I have lost my vote. I am a disenfranchised American. Because how can I possibly stand on line to vote for some guy who had to read a ninety-second statement *nine fucking times!*"

☆ 6 ☆

GUT CHECK

"One of the most extraordinary things about debates is that tens of millions of voters have watched them and then decided not to vote."

—*Joel Swerdlow*, The History of
Presidential Debates in America

THE REAL SLUGFEST at the first Republican debate would not be between the six men running for President, but between Warren Steibel and the Secret Service.

Steibel is touring the debate site in Houston, maneuvering himself around hammering workers and yards of snaking cables. The air is filled with the smell of freshly sawed plywood and there is the constant whine of power drills and circular saws in the background. Luther Villagomez, who is assisting Steibel, is the unfortunate messenger.

"We have to take out the seats," Villagomez says, pointing to the rows of seats closest to the stage, the ones that would be virtually on top of the debaters. "The Secret Service says people can be no closer than twelve feet. So we have to take out some rows."

"No," Steibel says in a bored voice. "Tell the Secret Service no." He flops down into one of the plush blue folding chairs near the stage. He has arthritis and walking is difficult. The distances in the George R. Brown Convention Center are vast, and though Steibel has been offered a golf cart, he does not want to look like an invalid. So he trudges around on foot. Typically, this day he is dressed as if for a picnic—a picnic in a bad part of the forest: a bluish-green sports shirt, gray pants, black shoes. His shirttail is, of course, out.

"No," he says, shaking his head. "If we don't give the underwriters good seats, they'll never give to anybody again. The seats stay where they are." The underwriters are the corporate bigwigs who have put up the dough for the debate: the American General Corporation, NCR, Oppenheimer Funds and PPG Industries. Money may not be able to buy you happiness in America, but it ought to be able to buy you a good seat at a presidential debate. If Warren Steibel has anything to say about it, that is.

And the seats for the underwriters are not only good, they are fantastic. The makeshift stage upon which the debate will take place is only about two feet off the ground. And the front row of audience seats is less than an arm's length away.

Which is what is driving the Secret Service crazy. At this early stage of the campaign, candidates are not being given Secret Service protection. But George Bush is more than a candidate. He is the Vice President of the United States and for that reason alone he must be kept alive. Somebody wants to stick a knife in Dole, throw a rope around Kemp, frag Haig? Fine. That's not the Secret Service's worry. But nobody is going to get close enough to touch a hair on George Bush's head.

Given the size of the hall, you would think ripping out a few rows of seats would not matter. Inside the unromantically named General Assembly Hall there are four thousand seats, which start at ground level and rise stratospherically to the ceiling, a distance so far away that to anybody sitting there the debate is going to be a rumor. From Warren Steibel's perspective, it is a space more suited to the docking of dirigibles than a political debate.

The Brown Center had been built for trade shows and conventions and has a post-modernist, high-tech look: a large rectangle, it is colored red, white and blue and festooned with red ship's smokestacks. It looks like a giant Lego building block. It would have been perfect for a political convention and was in hot contention right down to the end for the Democrats. But Paul Kirk, the Democratic National Committee chairman, and the other Easterners running the party decided Houston wasn't "Southern" enough and chose Atlanta instead. Besides, Kirk said, the Brown Center couldn't possibly be ready by August 1988. It opened in October 1987.

"But the Secret Service agent is coming down to *talk* to you," Villagomez tells Steibel.

Steibel passes a hand across his face. It's not enough he has to worry about making a debate into a lively TV show. It's not enough he has to get the candidates here and on time (the possibility that Bob Dole might actually walk in a half hour late is very much on Steibel's mind), but he has to get them their hotel rooms, make arrangements for their staffs and fend off their zillion and one demands. And then there is the mechanical side of things. Because the hall is so vast, huge projection TV screens must be hung above the stage so those sitting a few hundred yards away will be able to see the show. Two screens have been arranged, but now a third is being contemplated. "I need to know costs," Steibel says, ignoring the Secret Service issue for a moment. "Is the screen going to be $4.14 or $2.14? I have to know things like that."

"It's $4,500," Jim McQuinn, another assistant, tells him.

"Forget it!" Steibel screams.

Workers in baseball caps look up momentarily from their drilling and hammering. A gray carpet is being laid on the floor and a thick layer of sawdust covers everything. Next to us, the stage is still being built.

"And nothing for the deaf! Nothing!" Steibel yells. Steibel had taken Dole's request to heart and had arranged for a closed-caption transmission of the debate. "They want $2,700 to do it for the deaf and now I say forget it!" He does not mean it. This is merely one of Steibel's tantrums that, like summer storms, blow over within moments. Steibel is actually a softie. A third screen will be purchased so the audience can see and the $2,700 will be found for the deaf. (As it turns out, a satellite problem makes it impossible to do the closed-captioning. Steibel, this time, is genuinely upset. "If we had done closed-caption, all the debates would have had to do it," he said morosely backstage. "It would have been a good thing. We could have done a good thing." Steibel may work for Bill Buckley, but he has a liberal heart that bleeds easily.)

Steibel struggles up from his seat and begins walking around the hall, stepping over cables and around workers. Backstage, he pokes his head into a large, bare room. "How much is this costing us?" he asks.

"Twelve hundred," an assistant tells him.

"Get rid of it!" Steibel bellows.

"Uh, Warren, it's the pressroom," the assistant explains.

"So what!" Steibel says. "*I'm* the press. *Bill* is the press. When Ted Koppel has a good show, does *he* invite thirty reporters in and pay $1,200 for the room?"

Eventually, the Houston *Chronicle* will pick up the bill for the pressroom, just so the four hundred reporters who show up will not have to wander the streets. Jody Powell, Jimmy Carter's press secretary, had attended the Democratic debate in July and was astonished by the number of reporters on hand. "I would have given my right arm for something like this in July 1975," he said. "In July 1975 we were reaching people three at a time."

The press does not get a totally free ride at these debates. Reporters are charged for things like phone lines (only the lines, not the phones, are rentable. Reporters running through airports carrying pink

Trimlines hastily snatched from their teenagers' bedrooms will become a common sight on the campaign trail), but the charges don't approach the true cost. While the phone company gets $115 from the press for each phone hookup, the phone company is also charging *Firing Line* $3,000 to bring the phone lines in. Everybody is looking for an angle, a chance to make a buck.

The Democrats had debated in the Gus Wortham Center, a $72 million neo-Romanesque box only a few blocks from the Brown Center, in an auditorium that sat 2,200 people. Each candidate was given 130 tickets and the remaining seats were given to dignitaries and to the program's corporate underwriters. There were, however, no seats for the press. Reporters were forbidden to enter the auditorium to view the debate in the flesh. "Reporters will have access to a press area set up at the Wortham in order to cover *Firing Line*," the letter of invitation that went to reporters had said. "Arrangements are being made for TV monitors and access to telephone hookups."

The press area turned out to be two rooms in the basement. But the basement of a $72 million building can be rather nice. One room was a ballet rehearsal hall with a twenty-five-foot ceiling and walls covered with large sound baffles. The other room had long wooden tables, two TV monitors, and phone jacks. Everything looked normal, but upon reflection it was really very odd. Hundreds of reporters had flown thousands of miles to watch an event on TV.

What's more, we could have watched exactly the same event at exactly the same time on our TVs at home or on the TVs that are in every newspaper office. And some reporters who flew to Houston decided that as long as they couldn't watch the event in person, they might as well watch it from their hotel rooms, which had the advantage of room service.

But why, then, did we come at all?

Well, the press is supposed to go out and cover things. If we all stayed at home and watched it on TV, we couldn't put a "Houston" dateline on our stories. And we would have missed the camaraderie and partylike atmosphere that always prevails among reporters at these events.

As it turned out, a violent thunderstorm kept many ticket holders away, and at the last minute reporters were told they could come into the hall and watch the debate in person. By my count, only about a half dozen abandoned the TV screens for reality. One reason was that it was easier to watch the debate from the pressroom. You had a table for your portable computer and a phone at your elbow. Besides, many reporters felt that watching it on television was the only way a debate *should* be watched, because that is the way most voters would see it. Everyone knew that the small group of reporters who watched the first Kennedy-Nixon debate live at WBBM-TV studios in Chicago in 1960 thought Nixon had won. They had not seen how pasty-faced and shifty-eyed Nixon had looked on TV.

(In about a year, at the end of the first presidential debate between Bush and Dukakis, Peter Jennings, who had been on the panel of questioners, will rush from the stage to the ABC booth to participate in a post-debate broadcast. David Brinkley will ask him what he thought of the debate. "I don't know," Jennings will say, "I haven't seen it on television.")

By 1987, campaigning had become a largely *in vitro* process, a campaign confined within the glass tube of the TV set.

But how could reporters justify the expense of flying to events only to watch them on TV? Well, one justification was spin. Before, during and after debates, campaign aides and elected officials would come to the pressroom and give their impressions, their own "spin" on the ball. But spin had limited value. The spinners were highly partisan and said predictable things. They were mobbed by reporters trying to find quotes for their stories. And as the campaign went on, the mob scenes got larger and more raucous and many stories were done making fun of spin and spinners. "The spin thing is humiliating and degrading and the media insisted on it," Lee Atwater said after the campaign. "And when you did it, the media ridiculed you for it. I was on the first spin patrol at the Reagan-Mondale debate and I'd be very happy to call it all off."

But spin was unlikely to be called off as long as reporters needed it to justify the cost of their plane tickets.

So at the Republican debate in Houston, reporters did not care that they were excluded from the hall. When you considered that many of the people actually inside the hall would be watching the debate on giant TV screens anyway, the point seemed not worth fighting over.

The big shots, however, the five hundred corporate underwriters and other VIPs, would not have to worry about TV screens. They would be close enough to the stage to see things up close and personal. Which was still the problem.

"Uh, the Secret Service is going to be here soon," Jim McQuinn reminds Steibel.

"I am not going to push the audience back," Steibel says grimly. "Once I did a show with Spiro Agnew and the Secret Service told me I had to push the audience back. I guess they didn't want anybody handing him money. But now I'm not doing it. I've given the Social Security numbers of all five hundred people who are going to be near the stage and that's enough. Enough. They want twelve feet of space? Then I'm going to everyone who loses a seat and I'm going to say to each one of them: 'George Bush threw you out!'

"You know," he says, turning to me, "I *want* the audience on top of the candidates. When you have people who are not actors, the more audience response they get, the more lively it makes them."

Steibel turns back to his assistants. "And no food and beverages for the candidates!" he shouts, his anger warming up again. "A glass of water. A Coke. That's it. No twenty Cokes apiece. Get a central supply, like fifty Cokes for all six of them. And a pot of coffee."

Eric Jones, the Brown Center's manager, asks Steibel if he wants bars set up outside the auditorium for the audience before and after the debate.

"Absolutely not," Steibel says. "Ab-so-lutely not! And the Cokes are just for the candidates. Not for the campaign workers. I'm not running a catering service here!"

A man in a blue blazer, charcoal slacks, a striped tie, a white button-down shirt and black loafers makes his way down the aisle toward us. He has a military haircut and is either a Secret Service agent, a Marine or both.

He introduces himself as Keith Steele. "I understand I'm going to have 4,700 people in here," he says in a calm, authoritative voice. "And some of them will be within hand's reach from the stage. We'll have agents in the crowd, but if the Vice President gets the end seat . . . well, I just don't know."

The seating on the stage will be an inverted V. At the apex upstage will be Bill Buckley and Bob Strauss, the co-moderators. The candidates will be on each side of them, their chairs stretching downstage toward the audience. Seating positions will be determined by lots drawn by the mayor of Houston. If Bush gets one of the seats nearest the audience, however, the Secret Service is going to be very upset.

"I also understand, with so many people in here, you have to worry about the fire marshal," Steele says, flexing a little subtle muscle.

"I've been told I can bribe him," Steibel replies coolly.

A millimeter or so of smile plays on Steele's lips. "Well, maybe in *New York* you could," he says. "But I wouldn't try that in *Texas*." He eyes the stage once more and then walks back up the aisle a few feet and stops. "Look," he says, "even five rows back, if I . . ." He sticks his hand under his jacket, whips it out and shouts: "Boom!"

We all jump.

"See? That's it. That's how easy it would be," he says.

Steibel sags in his seat. "We'll give you the names," he says. "You don't like one, we move the guy."

But there is a legal technicality here. It is called the Constitution of the United States. Though the Secret Service's mission is beyond question, it is not a national police force and America is not a police state. Should John Hinckley be released from his mental hospital and show up with a ticket in row five of the General Assembly Hall of the George R. Brown Convention Center on debate night, there would be no legal means to throw him out.

Steele shrugs. "I just don't know," he says.

"O.K., O.K.," Steibel says. "So what if Bush gets the first seat? The seat farthest away from the stage?"

"I understand that is to be the luck of the draw," Steele says.

Steibel sighs. Where is this guy from? Wichita? "It can be . . . arranged," Steibel says. "Certain things can be . . . arranged."

"Well," Steele says, "I wouldn't want to be in the position of saying later that we had . . . arranged . . . things. So just give me three feet. Three feet between the first row and the stage and give me a man up front on each side of the stage."

"What can I say?" Steibel says, getting up and sticking out his hand. "Since I've been fucked, I have to accept it and enjoy it."

THE NEXT MORNING, dressed in a tan golf shirt and faded blue pants, Steibel is back in the auditorium talking about the concept of the debate. "These candidates are coming to compete and I can't wait to get them onstage," he says. "I keep telling them the same thing and they won't listen: Forget about the cameras. Relate to the audience. If you relate to the audience here, it will look better to the audience at home. But they don't believe it. They've got these media consultants. And so they think they can relate directly to the home audience." He shakes his head. "Who do they think they are? Bob Hope?

"The Pete du Pont guy keeps asking me if there's going to be red lights on the cameras so the candidates will know when they are on. 'Stop telling du Pont about the camera!' I told the guy. The camera is my problem. Let du Pont worry about what he is saying."

Naturally, the first thing the campaign aides wanted months ago was a meeting on the format of the debate. Six hired guns in a room with Steibel to hammer out the details. "They wanted to discuss ground rules, the format, the people who would ask the questions," Steibel says. "It was very simple. I said: 'No. This is the Imperial Debate. None of your shenanigans.'"

Eight years before, I had seen what Steibel was trying to avoid. In February 1980, the aides to the Republican presidential candidates met in a high school auditorium in Manchester, New Hampshire, to hammer out the shenanigans. No press or public were allowed. The aide to one of the more hopeless candidates had sneaked me in and let me observe on condition that I didn't use names. "The public deserves to know it is done," he said. "They won't believe it anyway."

The debate had been sponsored by the League of Women Voters and was to be televised nationally by both CBS and PBS. It was the first time all seven Republicans—Reagan, Bush, Dole, John Connally, Philip Crane, John Anderson and Howard Baker—would be on the same stage.

In the auditorium, TV technicians were setting up cameras on platforms atop metal scaffolding and snaking out yard after yard of thick black cable. Very serious women were walking around carrying very serious clipboards.

"Will the audience be allowed to cheer and clap?" the Philip Crane aide asked first. Crane was an ultraconservative congressman from Illinois and did not want cheering and clapping. He figured most of the audience would be members of the League and most League members would not be cheering and clapping for ultraconservatives.

"Yeah, how about yelling?" asked the John Connally aide. "We going to allow yelling?"

"How about laughing?" the John Anderson aide said, laughing herself.

"And sighing," said the Bob Dole aide.

"And crying," said the Ronald Reagan aide.

Lee Hanna, the League's director for the debates, calmed everyone down. He told them there would be no laughing, sighing or crying allowed. Then Hanna ran through the schedule, outlining when each candidate would be brought in for makeup. "We'd like to start alphabetically with John Anderson," he said to the Anderson aide.

"No," she said firmly. "Let's draw lots for who gets made up first."

"Well, our man never uses makeup," the Reagan aide said.

Everyone burst out laughing. "And we don't use hair dye," the Crane aide hooted.

The Dole aide spoke up. "We want fifteen minutes beforehand just to let the candidates stumble around the stage," she said. "You know, let them look at the door they have to walk through, let them sit in the chair, let them see the microphone."

The other aides strenuously seconded the motion. "We gotta find out where all the cans are," one said.

While they were being told where all the cans were, I asked an aide what they really wanted—to go first in the speaking order?

"That and something else," he said. "But you didn't hear it from me."

I agreed.

"It's Dole," he said. "Nobody wants to sit next to Dole. He's got such a sharp tongue that the son of a bitch might turn it on whoever is sitting next to him."

The rest of the ground rules were discussed one by one. "Are notes permitted?" the Reagan aide asked.

Hanna said the League had no objection to notes.

"What about interruptions?" the Connally man asked. "Can the candidates interrupt each other?"

Hanna said no, that didn't seem like a good idea.

"Let's black out the audience," an aide suggested. "I want them sitting in the dark."

"Wait a second," said the Crane aide, "that's going a little far."

If the audience members were in darkness, the TV cameras could not take pictures of their reactions.

"We can't control that," Hanna said. "This is a news event and we can't control what television does. We can't control reaction shots." (Steibel would have no such problem. He not only controlled the debate, he controlled the cameras, too.)

An NBC producer and director were then summoned to answer questions about the TV coverage. Even though CBS and PBS were carrying the debate live, NBC was the "pool" camera crew, the one that provided the pictures.

The aides were extremely worried about camera placement, wanting to know the exact angles from which their candidates would be shot.

"Will each camera have a red light when it is on?" the Connally aide asked.

"All except the minicam, which will be roving," he was told. "Otherwise each candidate will know when the camera is on him."

Hanna decided it was time to draw lots for stage positions, which would also determine the speaking order of the candidates. A League worker brought out a Styrofoam coffee cup with seven folded pieces of paper inside.

"Let's pick alphabetically," Hanna said. The Anderson aide stood up to pick.

"Hold it," said the Reagan aide. "That means I go last. I get what everyone leaves over. Why does she go first?"

Hanna asked what method he would prefer.

"Let's pick to pick," he said. "We pick a number to determine what order we pick the numbers in."

Everyone groaned. "Look," the Anderson aide said, "you want to pick for me?"

"I want to pick for *me*," the Reagan aide said.

"O.K., O.K., you pick first," she said, and sat down. "We'll go in reverse."

The Reagan aide plucked the piece of paper from the cup. He slowly unfolded his number. It was No. 7. Dead last.

The others couldn't stop laughing. Finally, they continued picking in reverse order until there was only one slip left for the Anderson aide. It was No. 1.

Once again, the laughter showered down upon the Reagan aide. Not only was Reagan last and Anderson first, but Reagan would have to sit next to Bob Dole!

The Reagan aide tried to take it in stride. He looked up at the stage and ran over the seating order in his mind.

"Oh, well," he said with a shrug, "at least we're on the extreme right."

TO SATISFY the Secret Service, the chairs in the hall at the Brown Convention Center have been pushed back three feet from the stage. This involves moving hundreds of chairs and takes several hours. When it is completed, those sitting in the front row can still easily leap on the stage and throttle the candidate of their choice.

But Keith Steele is pleased. "This is excellent," he says, walking up and down the three-foot gap between the first row and the stage. "I thought we'd be right on the edge, but now we have a few feet. We have a *psychological* barrier and we have enough room for the agents to stand and not be on camera."

"I've got some kooks," Steibel says. "I've got some guy running for President and he says he's going to run up on the stage. He wrote me a letter."

"You have the letter?" Steele asks.

"Yeah, at the hotel," Steibel says.

"I want the letter," says Steele.

"And then I guess we always have to worry about Iranian terrorists," says Steibel.

"To name a few," says Steele.

While Steele is worrying about keeping the Vice President alive, Steibel is still worrying about keeping the show lively. He has added his pizzazz—the opening ninety-second spots and the videotapes from past shows—but he's still worried about keeping his audience awake.

So it seems like a good time to ask him what purpose these debates really serve, considering that governing is nothing like debating. At least it shouldn't be. Debating is about instant response, projecting to the audience and regurgitating memorized positions. Once in office, instant response can often be a disaster. Instead, the President assembles his team of experts, weighs data, considers options. And he does it without a TV camera peering at him. So what do debates really tell us about how these men would function as President?

"As an American, I get a chance to see these candidates and see whether they are plastic," Steibel says. "Are they real? Are they fake? You also get an opinion of them in a truly competitive situation. How well do they do on their feet? Nothing is as good as reading a book, but sometimes TV can get you so interested that you go home and read the book. It's the same way with a political debate. The people know it's a competition, so they tune in for a look. And in subsequent months, they read newspapers and concentrate more to form an opinion."

And, ideally, that is what happens. Debates hook people into the political process. But considering the vast amount of time the candidates spend on preparing for the performance aspects of the debate, aren't we really just seeing how well they can put together a TV act?

"That's a credible judgment," Steibel says. "But people are the sum of their experiences and their lives. You look in their eyes and you see their sum. You see their character. And TV displays their character and personality. It is not the best medium for analyzing substantive issues. But all of politics is gladiatorial. A competition. And to be President, you have to be competitive. To be a President in our times, you have to have some television magic to get elected."

(As Roger Ailes once put it: "If Abraham Lincoln had run in the time of television, he never would have been President. He was a modest, gentle, low-key guy who slumped down in pictures. He had an interesting face and high-pitched voice and awkward body movements. And just think what America would be like if we'd never had Abe Lincoln.")

But what happens once we elect the guy who has television magic and then he has to take office? I ask Steibel.

"Then you hope he has the intelligence to have good people on his staff to run the country," he says.

WE HAVE BEEN in Houston for nearly a week now and I have yet to see Bill Buckley. I ask about this. Steibel laughs. "He shows up about five minutes before airtime," Steibel says. "He doesn't want to know about projection screens and how close to the stage people get to sit and how much the Cokes cost."

I mention that he and Buckley seem an unlikely match-up.

"Yes, as people we're quite different," he says. "We have a warm and rich relationship, but I have to gag on some of his positions. And he probably thinks I'm a moron politically."

(Asked later about Steibel's politics, Buckley says: "I pray for him.")

So how did you get the job?

"I needed one," Steibel says. "I had worked with Harry Reasoner, but Bill was totally unimpressed by that. Later, after I was hired, he told me he had never before seen anyone come into a job interview with his shoelaces untied."

Unlike that of his patrician boss, Steibel's class consciousness is geared to making sure nobody feels class conscious. Not only does he eat every meal with his crew, but in Houston he invites the driver of his rented limousine, Bob Manning, to eat with him at every lunch and dinner. And just hours before the debate, with a thousand other things on his mind, Steibel stops to make sure that Manning gets a screen credit as "Driver."

Buckley has ultimate responsibility for everything, but refuses to exercise it on anything. And so Steibel is in charge. He is even in charge of Buckley. Before the Democratic debate, Buckley had been ill for a week and called Steibel to tell him he might not be able to go on. "You'll go on if we have to hook you to a fucking IV onstage!" Steibel yelled at him. Later he said: "We took Bill to the doctor in Houston and they filled him with $105 worth of antibiotics. He looked dissolute that night, but what the hell, he always looks dissolute anyway."

Buckley lent the debates star quality, not a small consideration in a field where so few of the candidates were stars. "Bill is not arrogant," Steibel says, correcting what he believes is a popular misconception. "He's terribly nice and I've never had an argument with him. But if, on a show, he ever said: 'I'm wrong' or 'I don't know,' I think I'd faint. If that happened, I'd know he was *really* sick."

THE MORNING of the debate, dressed in a huge yellow shirt he calls his muumuu, Steibel prepares for his final run-through, a dress rehearsal. He is tense and unsmiling. This is where small technical problems that were supposed to have been worked out turn into massive technical problems that have to be worked around.

An assistant tells Steibel that a White House aide has just called saying the President of the United States wishes to know the debate questions for the evening. Just for his own personal information. As a favor.

Steibel is delighted. "That's Bush! That's Bush!" he yelps. "That aide worked for Bush in the '80 campaign and now he's trying to get the questions in advance." Steibel is not the least bit offended by this low-level dirty-trickery. He seems pleased that the Bush campaign would go to the trouble.

The assistant asks what he should tell the President.

"Oh," Steibel says. "No. Naturally. No. Not a chance."

Steibel walks outside the hall to where a large trailer is parked in the baking heat. Inside, the trailer is outfitted with thirty small TV monitors and jammed floor to ceiling with electronic gear. The ceiling is covered with yellow foam sound baffles and the walls and floor are carpeted. The gloomy interior is pierced by overhead spotlights. It is air-conditioned to a fault. This will be Steibel's control booth for the broadcast.

When he walks inside, he finds every monitor turned to *Donahue* and the crew watching intently. He settles into a chair, puts on a headset and talks into the mouthpiece. He is linked to the cameramen on the debate floor. Some know him and some do not. "Try to pay attention to me," he tells them now. "I'm very important."

He goes through the Chyrons, which are the little labels that float beneath the faces on the TV screen, telling the viewers who each person is. "Why does it say 'Vice President' George Bush?" Steibel asks. "Let's just have names. No Vice President, no governor, no senator. And why 'Alexander Haig'? Doesn't he want 'Al' Haig?"

He asks a cameraman to give him a wide shot of the debate set and immediately discovers that the tall white pitchers of water on the tables in front of the candidates block the shot. "Throw out the pitchers!" he yells into his headset. "One glass of water apiece. That's it. That's all they get." In a choice between a dry throat for two hours and a good shot, there is no choice.

Steibel begins calling out camera positions: "Give me three. Give me six. Give me seven." As he calls each camera's number, its picture is transferred to the main monitor. Throughout the debate, he will look at what each camera is viewing and then decide which picture to transmit, cutting between them quickly, cleanly and dramatically. He hopes. He squirms in his seat and looks up. "I get excited calling out the numbers," he says. "My power is infinite."

Mistakes, however, are common. They are almost inevitable on live TV, especially when you have eight people onstage. Somebody will start talking, and you switch to cover that person. Someone interrupts and you instantly must locate him, get the shot and shift to him. But by the time you do that, he may have already shut up and the first guy is answering.

And there is no possibility of a real rehearsal. None of the eight people—Buckley, Strauss and the six candidates—will gather together until the show begins. Steibel also has to worry about running out of time. The show will start at 8 p.m. and end at 10 p.m. no matter what. Which means that if the candidates go long in their responses—which they always do—the show will never conclude on time. The Democrats talked so long, an entire segment of the debate had to be cut.

So for the Republicans, Steibel is ready. On the floor of the stage, where the candidates can't avoid seeing them, are monitors. The monitors will not broadcast a TV picture, however. They will broadcast time cues.

Steibel calls up the first time cue, which says: "Your time is up!" He calls up the second time cue, which says, "You're a bad boy!" On the third time cue, the word "bad" begins to flash.

"Beautiful," Steibel says. "Calling a presidential candidate a bad boy. I love it."

The door to the control trailer opens and the light bursts in. It is Jerry Wyatt, a Secret Service agent. Even in the heat, he is wearing a gray pinstripe suit (the agents know guns make the public nervous and they conceal them under suit jackets whenever they can). He has with him the letter the kook candidate wrote to Steibel.

"Are you prepared for the eventuality of this person getting a ticket and coming up onstage?" Wyatt asks.

"What?" Steibel says. "Look, if he gets onstage and makes a ruckus, I'll broadcast it. That's all I can do." It might even be good TV.

Which is not exactly what the Secret Service had in mind. Showmanship is not its goal.

"We'd have a problem with that," Wyatt says. "We're camera shy. If we have to go up and stop him, we don't like to be on television."

"Can't you stop him before he gets onstage?" Steibel asks. Christ, he is thinking, what do these guys have guns for?

"Well, first, we don't have a picture of the guy," Wyatt says, "and then there's the legal question. What if he has a ticket?" Translation: We can't just blow him out of his socks.

Steibel sighs. He shifts in his chair. "If this were New York," he says, "I'd get two big guys to throw him out."

Wyatt settles on a plan of action: if the guy gets inside and makes a move for the stage, the Secret Service will grab him and charges will be pressed by someone associated with the show.

"See, if he's man enough to walk up onstage on national TV, he may be capable of anything," Wyatt says.

(As it turns out, the guy is at home in New York and promises, via a phone call, not to fly down and try to get onstage. He seems astonished that he and his letter were taken seriously.)

Steibel now extracts himself from his chair and makes the long walk back to the hall to check things out in person. At the door to the hall, however, he is stopped by yet another Secret Service agent. George Bush has shown up for his pre-debate run-through. Each campaign staff still wants to be sure its candidate is comfortable onstage and knows where the can is.

Steibel has declared that the press may witness these run-throughs, but Bush, on the advice of Roger Ailes, refuses. And he alone among the candidates has the means to make the refusal stick: he has the Secret Service.

The agent blocks Steibel's path. If Steibel were wearing the little lapel button the chief Secret Service agent had given him, there would be no problem. But Steibel is not one to keep track of lapel buttons (or any buttons, for that matter). And besides, Steibel now looks upon the entire George R. Brown Convention Center as his property.

"I am going inside now!" he bellows at the agent. "And if I don't go inside *now*, George Bush will not go inside *tonight!*"

The agent lifts his hand to his mouth and talks into the microphone that dangles from his shirt cuff. He listens through his earpiece and then steps away from the door. Steibel is not dressed well enough to be an assassin.

Inside, George Bush stands on the stage. Typically, those who have never seen him in the flesh before are amazed he is taller than most of the people around him. He often talks about this. "People think I'm *shorter* than Ronald Reagan," he will say in his gee-whiz tone, "but really, I'm *taller* than he is."

Bush is wearing a dark pinstripe suit. He strides across the stage, shaking the hands of the crew and the center's security guards. The press is kept outside (I am allowed in because I am wearing a "Firing Line Staff" credential). A gaggle of vice presidential and campaign aides stay within hailing distance of their chief.

"I was here for the christening," Bush says, meaning the dedication of the center. "But gee, how many seats does this have? Look at it. Wow."

At his side, Roger Ailes prowls the stage. He hears Bush's gosh-and-geeing and whirls around. He points a finger at him. "Your mike is on!" he tells him.

Bush is immediately chastened, like a small boy who has been caught blowing bubbles in his milk. "I'll watch what I say," Bush promises.

It is something only a pro would catch. But Ailes knows that Bush's mike can be heard in the control trailer and who knows who is in the trailer. Any dumb comment that Bush innocently makes to what he assumes is a secured room could end up in print or on television.

Ailes tells Bush to take his seat and then walks over to a monitor and hunkers down and looks at it. He does not like what he sees. He is seeing Bush squinting into the lights.

"The lights are too hot!" Ailes shouts into the vast hall. "You're burning out the right side of his face! He's going to squint tonight! Can you come down a point?"

It is not within Ailes's authority to order Steibel's technicians to lower the lights. But Steibel and Ailes have come to respect each other. "I think Bush's ninety-second spot was the best and that's because of Roger Ailes," Steibel says later. "I would have done the same thing: have Bush sit outside on the steps of his house. Very informal. He was the only candidate who didn't wear a tie. It was very relaxed."

Bush sat on his steps (you couldn't tell they were the steps to the vice presidential mansion) surrounded by his family. The wind rustled his hair and he even squinted a little into the sun. (Here, Ailes allowed the squint. That's what people do outside in the sun. They squint.) Ailes was trying for a nice outdoorsy image. And as a sign of Ailes's true expertise, the take that he selected for broadcast was one in which Bush stumbled on a word. When Steibel and the crew had shown up, Ailes had a TelePrompTer ready and waiting, but Steibel nixed it. So Ailes had Bush's words written down on large sheets of butcher paper. As each one was flipped (just as when Dole's staff first tried it) you could hear the rustle of the paper.

"That's O.K.," Ailes said. "It sounds like the trees rustling. It's perfect."

"And even though Bush was reading it off that butcher paper, he still flubbed a word," Steibel says. "And after, Ailes says: 'O.K., that's the one we use.' Bush wanted to do it again, but Ailes says: 'No, it sounds spontaneous. It works.' See? That's the difference. The dumb media consultants say do it again, do it again until it's *perfect*. But the smart ones know."

The lights in the hall are lowered a fraction so that Bush will not squint, but they are still very bright. "Sitting here for ninety minutes is really going to be hot," Bush says to Steibel.

"Umm," Steibel says to him, not knowing quite how to put this, "it's going to be two hours."

Bush looks at him blankly.

"Not ninety minutes," Steibel says. "Two hours."

"Jeez," Bush says.

Jeez, indeed. And it could be a tough two hours for Bush. A great deal is riding on this first debate. Bush must protect his carefully crafted image for 120 minutes. His campaign is based on a combination of a carefully devised strategy (a concentration on Southern and Western states) and a meticulously prepared public image (George Bush as a good old boy, nonwimp, tough-when-he-needs-to-be regular guy). Everyone in his campaign works to support that image. And the only one who can destroy it in a second is the candidate himself. If the scrupulously crafted campaign image of the candidate does not match up with the image people see on the TV screen for two hours, it will be immediately noticeable. The candidate will look like a fraud.

"The debate was coming just after the *Newsweek* wimp cover," Atwater said later. "And I went to Bush and I said: 'O.K., they have put the ball on the tee and now you are going to hit it out of the stadium.' A mixed metaphor, but he understood.

"I wanted to convince him the wimp cover was a *positive*. It gave us the chance to crush the issue. And now he had two hours to prove he was not a wimp. I remember the morning of the debate, I went jogging with him in Houston. He was very relaxed, very upbeat. He knew the stakes were high. We knew the others were waiting for him to make a gaffe. That's exactly what they were waiting for in 1980 to defeat Reagan. People said Reagan was a bleeder and once he went down, he'd never get up. Well, as a campaign strategist, you can't base your campaign on the behavior of your opponent. Once you do that, you've lost."

Roger Ailes had even more concrete plans. He knew that the best way to prove you are not a wimp is to attack. "But Bush didn't want to do it," Ailes said. "He's not that kind of guy. But I said hey, it's going to be pile on Bush. O.K., so you don't come out swinging. O.K., so you're not an attack kind of guy. But if they hit you first, you knock the shit out of them." And so Ailes and the others wrote some knock-the-shit-out-of-them lines for Bush. Nothing important could be unscripted.

In the hall, Ailes is again peering into the monitor. There is a tiny bright spot on Bush's forehead. "We can put a little powder up there," he says to Bush. "No problem."

Bush, meanwhile, is worried about a different problem. Under the bright lights, his notes to himself on his yellow legal pad are hard to read. "I'll need a fat pen under these lights," he says to an aide.

The aide immediately produces a pen from an inside pocket.

"No, a *fat* one," Bush says in a frustrated voice. Where do they *get* these people? The civil service?

The aide runs out and a moment later runs back in from somewhere and hands Bush the required fat pen.

Jack Rains, the secretary of state of Texas, a man who drives a maroon Porsche because it matches the color of his alma mater, Texas A&M, enters the hall and walks down the long aisle to where he is shown his special seat at the foot of the stage. Rains, a Republican, will act as timekeeper for the debate and bang a gavel if the candidates go too long. Steibel wants a timekeeper as well as the electronic time cues in order to intimidate the candidates.

"This gentleman I believe you know," Steibel says to Bush, pointing to Rains.

"Yeah," Bush says, "but I've never heard him called a gentleman before."

Rains looks at the gavel that has been provided for him, a thin, toylike thing. "Pretty wimpy gavel," he says. Then he looks up at Bush and freezes in horror. Oh-muh-God. He's done it. He's used the w-word.

Bush smiles down at him. "I noticed you waited until you were around me to use that word," he says.

There is a terrible moment when nobody knows for sure if Bush is joking, and then when they realize he is, everybody bursts into long, too hearty laughter.

Ailes is pleased. If Bush can joke about it, that's a good sign. The first rule of taking a punch is never to show how much it hurts. It's like a baseball player getting hit by a pitch. He never rubs the spot.

Steibel clambers up on the stage and walks over to Ailes. He tells him that keeping the press out of this run-through is one thing, but immediately after the actual debate, the press will be allowed to run up to the stage and pepper the candidates with questions. Steibel allowed this after the Democratic debate and it worked nicely: reporters madly jumping up on the stage, surrounding the candidates, taking down their quotations. It made a great background shot for the closing credits. It looked so real. So Steibel wants to do it again for the Republicans.

"No," Ailes says.

Steibel has been expecting this. He isn't going to argue with Ailes—protecting Bush from the press is one of Ailes's chief jobs—but Steibel isn't going to give any ground either.

"O.K.," Steibel says, "but you'll have to get Bush out of the hall four minutes after the debate ends. That's when I'm letting the press in."

"He'll be out," Ailes says. "We don't want him trapped in here by the press."

"Four minutes," says Steibel.

"Four minutes," says Ailes. (When the time comes, Bush will make it out of the hall in two.)

Ailes scoops up his candidate, and in a great flurry of agents and staff, they sweep out of the hall.

Fifteen minutes later, Pete du Pont arrives. Now, however, reporters are allowed inside the hall and they are all waiting for him. Du Pont is dressed casually, but he is carrying two suits with him in clear plastic bags so he can hold them up to the cameras and see how they look on TV. One is blue-gray and one is gray.

It makes sense to see how one's suit will look on TV, but it also looks a little prissy. Yes, candidates care what they wear on TV. But they are not supposed to be seen caring what they wear on TV. And unfortunately for du Pont, he is not the Vice President with Secret Service agents to keep the reporters out. So fifty or so reporters, photographers and cameramen are gathered around the stage and immediately begin nudging each other and snickering at du Pont and his suits.

Du Pont struggles with an embarrassed smile. "Just want to see which looks best under the lights," he says weakly. (In the old days, his people could have had this rabble *shot*.)

The other candidates troop in one by one and face a flurry of pre-debate questions. When it is all over and the reporters have run back to the pressroom to file their stories, I ask Steibel why he let the reporters in this time, considering he did not do it with the Democrats.

"I let the press in so the candidates wouldn't give me a hard time," Steibel replies with a broad smile. "Nobody wants to give you a hard time with the press around to take it all down."

BOB STRAUSS walks into the control trailer, where Steibel is now finishing his technical checks. Strauss starts watching the pretaped ninety-second spots on a monitor. He gets through Dole, Kemp and du Pont and says to Steibel: "After this, there won't be any audience left."

Steibel grimaces. What can he do? He had only so much to work with.

After Strauss sees Haig and his wife finish their spot, he says: "Boy, how'd you like to spend thirty-seven years with that son of a bitch? No wonder she looks bored." Then he watches the Bush spot, him and his grandchildren on the steps, but will not give an inch to a Republican. "George Bush looks as tough as that little baby in front," he says.

At 7:20 p.m., just forty minutes before airtime, Buckley arrives at the center. He is unrushed and unruffled. He stands in the wings, about to take his place on the set. On the other side of the curtain, you can hear the loud burble of 4,000 people taking their seats.

I chat briefly with Buckley and then notice a terrible thing. It is one of those moments when, as a reporter, you don't know whether or not to cross the line and alter the outcome of events. The rules say you should report the event and not interfere with it, but there are always exceptions.

"Uh, Mr. Buckley, I've got to tell you something," I say to him. "Your fly is unzipped."

Buckley looks slowly down. "Oh," he says. "Sure." Then, but only after a moment, he slowly zips it up.

I feel like a fool. If I had left him alone it might have been like the King of England who accidentally left his last vest button undone and set a fashion trend that exists to this day.

At 7:56, four minutes before airtime, Buckley is still not in his chair onstage.

"Where's Buckley?" Steibel screams from the control trailer. "Get Buckley! Hurry up! Put Buckley in his chair. Put him in his chair!"

At 7:57, Steibel is still screaming. "Find Buckley! Find Strauss! Mike them! Put them in their chairs and put their microphones on!"

The two are found, put in their chairs and miked.

"Thirty seconds," Steibel says. "I'm in black. Roll tape. Roll the tape! Make sure they see it in the hall. If we get a lot of applause, I want to see it. Gimme five. Four, move in slowly."

On most debates, the lights come up to find the candidates already seated onstage. But Steibel can't stop thinking of his Miss America metaphor, a debate as pageant. And so he has insisted that the candidates walk out from the wings in darkness and then dramatically mount the brilliantly lit stage and take their seats.

Naturally, it goes wrong. Instead of heading for his chair, Pete du Pont walks over to shake hands with Buckley and then all the candidates want to shake hands with Buckley and there is a flurry of crisscrossing hands as Steibel madly screams out camera numbers to catch it all. (On the Miss America show they get to rehearse.)

"Cue Bill," Steibel says into his headset. "C'mon, cue Bill. I told you four times to cue Bill!"

Bill is cued. "We're here," he says, "to get the *flavor* of six candidates . . ."

As it turns out, the flavor is mainly vanilla. As in the many debates still ahead, much is spoken and little is said. Yet two moments will stand out:

Much of the debate centers on Bush's defense of the INF treaty, a nuclear arms reduction treaty backed by Ronald Reagan. Al Haig attacks the treaty, but Bush responds that Haig had earlier supported it.

Haig snaps back: "And if you'll recall, I fought it like the bloody devil at the cabinet table and we never heard a *wimp* out of you—not a word."

Bush ignores him and the w-word. But here the press will play what Tom Wolfe has called its "Victorian Gentleman" role. Even though *Newsweek* has used the word on its cover, commentators decide that they are outraged by Haig's use of it to Bush's face. They say it is in bad taste and they savage Haig for using it. (Although Haig later explains he meant to say "whimper," this is one grudge Bush will carry. After Bush's victory, he will meet with all of his primary opponents—except Al Haig. Just as James Baker will meet with all the living Secretaries of State—except Al Haig.)

Then the big moment of the debate. The moment that is later looked upon as pivotal. Pete du Pont begins by bashing Bush for being a follower and not a leader: "George Bush heroically followed America into war. And he skillfully followed Richard Nixon into China. And he somewhat less enthusiastically followed Ronald Reagan into the modern economics of tax cuts and job creation. But the question is: In a Bush presidency, where would he lead America?"

Backstage, watching on TV monitors, Ailes and Atwater hold their breath. It is the moment they have been waiting for. The moment for Bush to knock the shit out of somebody.

"Pierre . . ." Bush begins, and pauses, and everywhere you can hear the same thing. In his handlers' room, in the pressroom, in the audience, the same thing: giggles. Pierre. How perfect. Now that you mention it, "Pete" du Pont does look more like a "Pierre."

"My friend . . . *Pierre*," Bush goes on, "let me help you on some of this."

In the audience there are open hoots of laughter now and du Pont writhes beneath his skin, a rock-hard smile fixed on his face. George Bush has gotten him good.

"Sure, we had lines ready for him," Ailes told me later. "We had that line ready about du Pont, about Bush calling him Pierre. We knew that would work."

Atwater added: "Before the debate we told [Bush]: 'Your survival depends on this.' That took care of one point. And then we sat back and prayed he'd get hit first. That was critical. Our whole strategy—the Pierre line was an example—was based on the premise somebody would attack Bush."

The debate ends with Steibel still barking out camera positions in the trailer and George Bush getting to his feet, shaking a few hands and rushing off the stage before the press is allowed in. As he hurries down the aisle, his face is flushed and the sweat is beginning to bead up through his makeup. "Did we do O.K.?" he asks his people in a low, nervous whisper. "Did we do O.K.?"

It is not the imperial "we" he is using. He knows he has not been alone on that stage. He knows all his coaches and all his wizards have been flying with him as copilots. Barbara Bush stands by the backstage exit. The pressure is finally off, and like a dam that has burst, she says: "Oh, George, oh, George." She clutches at his arm. "Oh, George, we won, George. Oh, we won, we won."

And she is correct. George Bush has won. Two days after the debate, the Bush campaign will grow dizzy with delight over a David Broder column in the Washington *Post* that appears under the headline: "Round 1 Goes to George Bush."

It begins: "Houston — George Bush answered one of the key questions about his presidential candidacy just by calling one of his opponents by his rightful name in the first GOP debate here Wednesday night."

Broder goes on to say that Bush's use of "Pierre" signals that there is "no more Mr. Nice Guy" for the Vice President. "A better way to bury the 'wimp' image which has plagued Bush . . . could not be found," he writes. "Many of us reporters who have watched Bush over the years have wondered if he possessed the primal political instinct it takes to survive high-stakes presidential competition: the street smarts to protect himself when under attack and the instinct for the jugular to dispatch an opponent. . . .

"[Bush] was rough when he needed to be and skillful in evading punches, so he was the clear winner in pressroom evaluations and in the first round of interviews with voters who watched the debate. . . .

". . . this night belonged to Bush—the man who dared to call a Pierre a Pierre."

Broder is not alone in his assessment. Commentary in the Los Angeles *Times*, the Baltimore *Sun*, the *Arizona Republic*, the *Christian Science Monitor*, the Houston *Chronicle* and others agrees.

Issues? An exchange of ideas? Comparing and contrasting positions on matters of importance? Is that what you thought debates were about? C'mon. Grow up. Debates are about performance: the ability to deliver a devastating line—in this case just one word, "Pierre"—at the right moment. Nor did it matter that the line had been written by somebody else.

Far from decrying it, the press delighted in it.

And the lesson was not lost on the pupil. George Bush learned something about attacking. He learned something about knocking the shit out of the other guy.

It worked.

☆ 7 ☆

MIRACLE MAN

"You have to be eighteen, warm and breathing. You don't have to know anything."
　　　　　　　　　—*Pat Robertson explaining what*
　　　　　　　　　qualifications people need
　　　　　　　　　to vote for him, January 18, 1988

THEY HAVE JUST FINISHED their fried pork chop lunch out at the Iowans for Life convention at the Best Western Starlight Village in Des Moines and there is no time to clear the plates because the entertainment is about to begin. Pat Robertson is about to speak.

The display tables are brimming with the womb posters and the "Sex Clinics and Other Social Diseases" pamphlets and there is a wicker basket filled with what look like pink bonbons. Upon closer examination they turn out to be tiny plastic fetuses.

Eight teenage girls in maroon-and-white sweaters run up to the front of the room. They are the Right to Life Cheerleaders and they chant: "Abortion! Must! Stop! Fight! For! Life!" They wave pompons.

Robertson mounts the podium, applauding the cheerleaders. He is solidly built with short, graying hair, swept back from his forehead. There is a fine network of lines around his eyes and, at fifty-seven, his throat is just beginning to go crepey. He has a face like a full moon and when he smiles it splits almost in half. Even so, you get the feeling he could turn bread to toast with one glance. He begins to speak in soft, slow cadences.

"We had a boy on *The 700 Club*," he says, speaking of his popular religious show, "who, when born, could play the cello perfectly."

The audience is rapt with attention.

"I asked his mother: 'Did you play while pregnant?' 'Yes,' she said." Robertson grips the lectern with both hands and leans forward. *"That boy learned the cello perfectly in the womb!"*

"Yes!" come the shouts from the audience. "Tell it!" "Yes! Yes!"

"He was not a blob of flesh," Robertson intones. "Not a fetus! He was . . . He was . . ."

A what? A Yo-Yo Ma? A Mstislav Rostropovich? A Pablo Casals?

". . . a baby!" Robertson shouts.

Later, I call a music expert and he tells me that the existence of a child prodigy cellist, let alone an infant prodigy cellist, is highly unlikely. A cello, even scaled down, is just too large an instrument for a small child to play. This seems to be yet another example of what the reporters covering Robertson have taken to calling his "Funny Facts."

Robertson has said, for instance, he knows "an impotent man who gave his wife AIDS by kissing her" and also a man who got AIDS from standing in an elevator. He says children in Iowa are forbidden to say "Merry Christmas" in the public schools. The Soviets have nuclear missiles in Cuba. Planned Parenthood was started by Nazis. And he knows the location of the American hostages in Beirut.

"I talked to a woman who was told to have that 'tissue' removed," Robertson tells the audience. "And the nurse showed her a towel with blood and a 'substance.' And the woman said: "My God! *That's a rib cage!* I have killed my baby!"

Some in the audience look down at the remains of their fried pork chops and push their plates a few inches farther away.

"That woman had killed five babies! But her life was saved through Jesus Christ!" Robertson says.

Robertson rarely says "Jesus Christ" in public anymore, but this is a special audience, a pro-life group, many of whose members can be expected to have close religious ties. In front of more general audiences, Robertson is careful to say only "God." He is trying to convince people that he actually views the presidency as a secular office.

"Some twenty million babies have been slaughtered since *Roe* v. *Wade* and those hands and minds and hearts by 2020 would have produced three hundred billion dollars in taxes!" Robertson says, putting a "practical" spin on the issue. "It was not the intention of the Founding Fathers to have a five-member oligarchy of old men and women in black robes on the Supreme Court! Although they feel a certain omnipotence, *they do not live forever!*"

Whoops of "You tell it!" and "Yes! Yes!" come from the audience. The right to life apparently does not extend to liberal Supreme Court justices.

Robertson has little regard for the nation's highest court or for the judiciary branch of government as a whole. He believes, for instance, that "a Supreme Court ruling is not the law of the United States."

He knows this because he has counted the number of lines in the Constitution, just as he has counted the number of lines in the Bible.

"It's common sense," he has said. "You count the lines. There are, I think, 255 lines on the legislative, 130 on the presidency and 39 on the judiciary. Now, that tells you something. They are not equal."

INSIDE THE HILTON ARENA at Iowa State University in Ames, a toy plane glides down from the upper rows of the balcony, circles once, makes a swooping turn past my ear and skids to a halt on the basketball floor. I walk over and pick it up. It is made out of heavy Styrofoam and has "Robertson '88" printed on the fuselage.

We are at the Presidential Cavalcade of Stars, which, aside from the name, is a serious event. The Republican candidates for President will speak, but more importantly a straw poll will be conducted. The members of the audience will get to vote on their choice for President. All it takes is a twenty-five-dollar ticket and an Iowa driver's license.

To the campaigns, this is an important early test. And if all they had to do was buy a bunch of tickets, stuffing the ballot box would be easy. All the campaigns except for Pete du Pont's have purchased hundreds of tickets in advance. The tricky part, however, is getting actual human beings to shlep out to Ames on a Saturday when both the Iowa State University and the University of Iowa football teams are on TV.

So the Cavalcade of Stars is a test of organizational skill: who can line up the bodies, distribute the tickets, get the buses rented, get the people to the arena. The candidates themselves are superfluous. This is made clear when it is announced that the voting will begin *before* the candidates speak. What programs, plans or inspiration the candidates might convey in their fifteen-minute speeches will have nothing to do with the outcome of the straw vote. This is an exercise in muscle, not mind.

The inside of the basketball arena—Home of the Cyclones—is decorated like a national political convention. There is red, white and blue bunting. People are waving signs and wearing straw hats. The Jack Kemp forces are madly throwing little white footballs from the basketball floor up into the balconies. The Robertson campaign has handed out air horns that are now lashing the crowd.

I take the toy airplane back to the press table and look at it more closely. In the dead air of the arena, the light little plane could not fly well. And so with great care a penny has been taped to each side of the nose to give it added weight and better aerodynamics. Imagine the effort the night before: heaps of toy planes, stacks of pennies, rolls of masking tape. And smiling, fresh-faced volunteers working away into the wee hours while humming "Onward, Christian Soldiers."

Before it is Robertson's turn to speak, a very serious child of about eight or nine walks down the long rows of press tables and hands a fortune cookie to each reporter. I take mine and thank him.

"You're s'posed to *open* it," he says solemnly.

I open it. Inside, on a small strip of paper printed in red ink, it says: "Don't let country crumble. Vote Pat Robertson '88." I take a bite of the cookie. It is fresh.

In the stands above me, hundreds of Robertson supporters are dressed in white T-shirts and white sweatshirts with Robertson's name printed on them. Other supporters are still waiting to get inside, long lines of them snaking down the arena's concrete ramps. Every few moments, they began to chant, lifting their straw hats high into the air in unison: "Hats . . . off . . . for Pat! Hats . . . off . . . for Pat!"

As Robertson bounds across the stage, supporters wearing revolving lights on their heads, like the ones you see atop police cars, stand up in their seats and begin to shout wildly. The theme to *Rocky* blares through the arena's speakers. (The Robertson campaign plays this tune so much, it is later asked to pay royalties and so drops it.)

Robertson looks out at the screaming crowd, which seems to be in an advanced state of rapture. "Who *are* these people?" he asks rhetorically, the exact question that is going through many of our minds. Who are these people supporting this man; who are the three million of them?

In 1986, Robertson had announced that though God had told him to run for the presidency, he required the signatures of "three million registered" voters on a petition as a further sign. About a year later, standing next to a towering stack of petitions, Robertson announced he had gotten 3.3 million signatures and was beginning his campaign.

That figure was used in almost every story written about Robertson and it was taken as a sign of his national appeal. After his campaign ended, however, this turned out to be another Funny Fact. Robertson's campaign offered to sell a computerized list of the signatures to the Republican National Committee for $90,000. When the computer tapes arrived at the RNC, they contained only about 1.8 million names, however. When similar discrepancies were brought up by reporters during the campaign, they were told they were showing signs of atheism.

Robertson will use only eleven of his allotted fifteen minutes to speak at the Cavalcade of Stars. ("Did you say fifteen minutes?" Jack Kemp had wailed before his speech. "It takes me an hour and a half to watch *60 Minutes*!") Robertson does not need much time to run down the checklist of what his supporters demand of the next President:

"Communism is tyranny and they want us to establish the ultimate downfall of communism throughout the world.

"They want little children to pray in the schools in America.

"If we can give a tax deduction for child care for working women, we can give a tax deduction for women who stay at home and *take care* of their children.

"The best answer to poverty is a job, not a handout.

"We want children in a drug-free, crime-free school environment."

When Robertson finishes, his supporters set off their air horns, turn on their spinning lights and toss their hats in the air. Signs pop up throughout the crowd. "Jesus Is Coming," says one. "Bush was appointed / Robertson was anointed," says another.

Supporters of the other candidates sit like corpses. They are buffeted by wave upon wave of raw noise. The George Bush demonstration was nothing like this.

When Bush spoke, he read from a prepared text. In the copy handed out to reporters, the second paragraph began: "For the last seven years I've stood side by side with one of the greatest Presidents this country has had—and I'm *damn* proud of it."

But when he delivers the line, Bush changes it to: "and I'm *very, very* proud of it."

His traveling press corps erupts into gales of laughter. "That's our guy!" one reporter says.

Robertson will go on to win the straw vote this day with 33.65 percent of the vote. Bush will come in third. It will be front-page news across America. And even though Robertson garners only 1,293 votes, this will be taken as one of the first signs there actually may be something to Robertson's campaign. Robertson calls his supporters the Invisible Army because they have not made their power known in previous elections.

Pollster George Gallup, Jr., himself an evangelical, says as many as one-third of all Americans call themselves evangelicals. R. Marc Nuttle, Robertson's political strategist, claims that 56 million voting adults are born-again Christians. "That's enough base to win the nomination," he says.

IT IS EARLY MORNING in Davenport and the God Bus stands idling by the curb, plumes of exhaust rising into the cold, damp air. The front seat of the bus across from the driver is heaped high with doughnuts and plastic containers of orange juice. At curbside, two Robertson aides cheerfully accept cash or checks (no credit cards, please!) from a long, straggly line of reporters: $80 to ride with Pat Robertson for one day, $160 for two days. Pat Robertson will cross and then recross the state of Iowa, moving from east to west and back again, making twenty-seven stops. And if you buy a ticket for the bus, you are guaranteed an interview with the candidate. I like the audacity of it, the strict cash-and-carry nature of the transaction, and I buy a one-day ticket.

As I climb aboard, I am handed a doughnut, a container of orange juice and an audio cassette, "Pat Robertson: What I Would Do as President." Robertson has made more than a million of these and hands them out free at every stop.

The bus is luxurious. There are airline-style luggage bins above the gray flannel seats and a washroom in the back. The God Bus is not officially called that, of course, but the jokes have already begun this morning:

Q: Why don't fundamentalists make love standing up?

A: Because it might lead to dancing.

I throw my suitcase into one of the bins, get out my bulging Robertson file and once again go through T. R. Reid's profile of Robertson that appeared in the Washington *Post*. The piece reveals:

• Marion "Pat" Robertson is running for President because, he says, "I have a direct call and leading from God" to do so. In addition, God has told him which street to live on, which call letters to use for his radio station, which brand of transmitter to buy for his TV studio, which people to hire and which securities to sell.

One has to be careful in listening to such direct guidance, however, because there is a "percentage of error," Robertson admits. Some advice that appears to come from God is actually coming from Satan in disguise.

God sometimes speaks to Robertson in "the silence of his inner thoughts," but Robertson also hears an actual voice, "level and conversational." Robertson realizes that ordinary voters may find this "spooky."

• Though Robertson has claimed to be a "Yale-educated tax lawyer," in fact he has never practiced law and cannot legally do so, having failed the bar exam.

• Robertson believes that the religious beliefs of Mormons "are, to put it simply, wrong" and in 1985 said only Jews and born-again Christians were entitled to government jobs. (When Robertson denies having said this, it is located on a videotape and he retracts the statement.)

• On his TV show, Robertson has prayed for miracles ranging

from "cures from scoliosis to the recovery of a viewer's lost diamond ring."

There is one fact that Reid has omitted from his profile, feeling it is not relevant: Robertson, a strong opponent of premarital sex, fathered his first child before marriage. And then Robertson altered his wedding date in his biographies to cover this up.

But three weeks after Reid's profile appears, David Shribman of *The Wall Street Journal* will reveal that the Robertsons "were married secretly on Aug. 27, 1954, in Elkton, Md., known as a venue for quick marriages. Their son was born 10 weeks later."

One of the most devastating profiles of Robertson is done by Lisa Myers of NBC News. It airs December 21, 1987, and is titled "Miracle Man." The power of the piece is seeing Robertson in action on videotape in the days before he knew he was going to run for President. Here is Robertson claiming to divert Hurricane Gloria from his television station in Virginia, and claiming to cure a woman of cancer of the womb through his prayers to God. There is also a former aide saying Robertson plans to broadcast the second coming of Christ on television.

Robertson labels the report "religiously bigoted, biased, untruthful and irresponsible journalism."

The biographical information Robertson has released is full of inaccuracies, reporters find out, including claims of schooling he did not have and positions on boards of directors he did not hold. For years, Robertson has also failed to attend the church of which he is a member even though he has told people it is "very important" to attend a local church.

To his followers, all this makes little difference. "Frankly, in a strange sort of way, the attacks on Pat Robertson do nothing but strengthen the existing base," Scott Hatch, a Robertson spokesman, says. "I think the media is out of touch with what's happening in America."

Robertson makes this point repeatedly: There are large, heretofore unseen forces waiting out there. The rest of us have been blind to it, but America is not the America we thought it was. It is inhabited by a powerful movement, an Invisible Army, that had been biding its time, waiting for the right moment to spring forth.

The other Republican candidates are not willing to criticize Robertson for any of this. Nobody knows if the Invisible Army is real or another Funny Fact. But nobody wants to be accused of religious bigotry. At the first Republican debate in Houston, George Bush had called Pete du Pont's plan to let people accept a pensionlike alternative to Social Security "nutty." But Robertson also had a Social Security plan: he wanted Americans to have more babies so they would grow up and increase the tax base. Bush did not call this plan nutty, even though Robertson was a far more serious opponent than du Pont.

The reporters covering Robertson were caught up in a dilemma. Robertson had followers. He had money. He had won a straw poll. He was in all the debates. And so he couldn't be treated like a nut or fringe candidate, could he? Even if he went around diverting hurricanes and curing cancer of the womb, he had to be treated seriously, didn't he?

But if we were to take him seriously, I had a question. If Robertson believed he diverted a hurricane through prayer, why did he now support the vastly expensive Star Wars defense system? Why didn't he just plan on diverting Soviet missiles through prayer?

We discuss all of this aboard the God Bus. Not only is Reid on board, but also Lee Bandy of Knight-Ridder newspapers, another Robertson expert, who spends as much time studying religious matters as political ones in order to understand the candidate.

A few of us are also lugging the Gideon Bibles from our hotel rooms in order to check whatever biblical references Robertson may drop into his speeches. This will be a wasted effort, however, because Robertson has decided that he no longer has anything to do with religion. He talks about morality, values and the American family. But he does not talk about religion. He does not want to be addressed as "Rev. Robertson" but as "Dr. Robertson," apparently for either his Juris Doctor law degree from Yale or his honorary doctor of divinity degree from Oral Roberts University. (Virtually nobody goes along with this on the air except Dan Rather.) And Robertson also rewrites his past. Though he was a Southern Baptist minister for more than twenty-five years, this becomes a nonfact. In his large, expensive, extremely slick campaign brochure, Robertson is listed as: "Author, lecturer, educator, broadcaster, news commentator and Republican Presidential Candidate." Minister? TV preacher? A man of God? Nope, nowhere to be found. The TV network Robertson founded was called the Christian Broadcasting Network. Now in Robertson literature it is always CBN Cable Network.

And when Tom Brokaw refers to Robertson on the air as a "former TV evangelist," Robertson denounces him for "religious bigotry." He is a "Christian broadcaster," Robertson insists, and to call him by any other term is "like calling a black man a nasty word that begins with an 'N.' "

None of this retooling has happened by accident. Constance Snapp,

Robertson's director of communications, has helped engineer the change. A fundamentalist Christian who was the director of marketing for a Madison Avenue ad agency and handled the CBN account, Snapp set up focus groups to find out what people really thought about Robertson. "They don't really know who Pat is," Snapp concluded. "They confuse him with other people, with Falwell and Swaggart." So she immediately began scheduling Robertson in appearances on nonreligious TV shows. And went about trying to convince people that the Robertson campaign had nothing to do with religion.

The problem, however, is that for the reshaping of a public image to work, it has to be at least somewhat anchored in reality. It cannot be used to hide major events of the past. It is a cosmetic device, a light gloss to take away the shine from the forehead, a little rouge to brighten up a feature. But Robertson was employing plastic surgery. He was excising, cutting away whole chapters of his past.

Kerry Moody and Ben Waldman, two Robertson aides, ride the God Bus to make sure the press corps gets things right. "We have not been treated fairly by the media," Waldman complains. "Robertson has been asked unfair questions."

What's an unfair question to a presidential candidate? I ask.

"Is it appropriate to ask if a candidate passes gas, does it smell and is it loud?" Waldman says.

There is a silence on the bus. It appears this will not be an ordinary trip.

Has somebody actually asked Robertson that? I say.

"*USA Today* asked what position he prayed in," Waldman replies. "It is inappropriate. It is private. And inappropriate."

Actually, the editors of *USA Today* asked the questions: "Do you pray?" and "How do you do it, physically?" I don't know why they asked. Maybe they suspected Robertson hung from a trapeze. But they asked and he refused to answer.

"And the video of him healing," Waldman says, referring to the Lisa Myers piece. "It was done in a mocking fashion."

But it was actual video, I say. NBC didn't alter it. It showed the video.

"It was *mocking*," Waldman says. "He prays. And God answers his prayers. So what?"

So nothing. So the American public has a right to see it. That's what running for President is all about, isn't it?

Moody takes over. He has worked in all three of Ronald Reagan's presidential campaigns and has spent the last three years in the White

House as liaison to the General Services Administration. "When I first heard about Robertson, I said you got to be kidding," he says. "I knew him as a TV evangelist. Then I ran the numbers."

Political operatives today believe only in numbers. Goodness, decency, honesty, competence, intelligence, none of it matters if you don't have the numbers to go with them.

"Robertson had a large grass-roots base," Moody says, ticking the points off his fingers. "He had an ability to raise money. And he had the ability to communicate over the media."

And that's all anyone needed, he felt, to become President of the United States.

ROBERTSON BELIEVED he had the people—"I don't have to broaden my base. My political base is seventy million people . . . the seventy million evangelical Christians in this country"—but he knew he did not have the press. He hated reporters. In 1982, on *The 700 Club*, he had called reporters "professed atheists." And he banned T. R. Reid from his campaign plane. The banning of a reporter is virtually unheard of in a presidential campaign. It is considered an open admission that the candidate can't stand the heat and so he is kicking the *reporter* out of the kitchen. But Reid patiently arranged to follow the campaign on commercial flights. "In a dozen years of covering politicians," Reid would write in a magazine article he later decided not to publish, "I've never been in a situation as personally nasty as the Robertson-for-President campaign of 1988. . . . The candidate loathed the reporters and didn't bother to hide it."

On the bus, reporters would refer to Robertson as "the Bhagwan" and make jokes about his healing powers. (Could he, for instance, heal Bob Dole's right arm? And would Robertson offer to do so in return for Dole's endorsement?) But such jokes bugged Reid, who took religion seriously, and he wrote in his magazine piece: "I'm a Roman Catholic, another branch of Christianity that has come in for its share of ridicule. I believe in miracles, so I could hardly find it strange when Robertson said that some of his prayers had been answered. I talk to God, so I couldn't make fun of a presidential contender who did the same. I have written some tough copy about Pat Robertson, but I never challenged his faith or the sincerity of his belief."

It was a distinction lost on Robertson, who despised Reid for the profile he had done and another story exposing how Robertson had "embellished his résumé, misstated his income and altered his autobiography to enhance his appeal as a candidate." Robertson ended up refusing to answer Reid's questions, even when they were asked at public news conferences. Robertson referred to Reid's stories as "bilge water" and "lies" and in speeches and news conferences began referring to Reid as an "anti-Christian bigot."

"It all added up to an unhappy—indeed, bitter—campaign," Reid concluded, "noticeably lacking in love or Christian charity."

THE GOD BUS has thirty-seven reporters and technicians on board and more follow behind in their own cars. These reporters are willing to trade an interview with Robertson for the freedom of being able to leave the trail whenever they want. In a few hours, we begin to envy them. This is going to be a long day. We board the God Bus at 8:30 a.m. in Davenport on the Mississippi River and leave it 330 miles and thirteen hours later in Sioux City on the Missouri River.

The day is highly organized. Robertson aides are in constant walkie-talkie communication between the different vehicles in the motorcade. At each stop, an aide will announce on the loudspeaker: "This is an inside event!" or "Outside event!" so we know whether to bring our parkas with us. Robertson believes that his organization at the Presidential Cavalcade of Stars is what really impressed the media and got them off writing about his miracle cures and onto his executive abilities.

So he wants to be impressive again today. And in order to make sure he is, he has "secret" buses, filled with traveling supporters— the reporters end up calling them the Mobile Faithful—to swell his smallish crowds at each stop. The secret does not last long, however, as reporters begin noticing the same faces in every crowd.

The motorcade is twenty cars long. At one point, the rear of the motorcade is cut off by a thundering freight train, but the front of the motorcade keeps going. There is a real mania with keeping on schedule. No presidential campaign is ever on time, but Robertson believes that keeping on time will be seen as another sign of his secular skills. So, as the day progresses and we inevitably lag behind, Robertson keeps on schedule by cutting his speeches down to five minutes or less. But he is rewarded. Our arrival in Sioux City, the last stop of the day, is scheduled for 9:37 p.m. And lo and behold, as we roar through the streets of Sioux City heading for the final rally, we pass a bank clock that clicks exactly to 9:37.

"The press didn't believe it possible to keep on schedule and be here at 9:37," he tells the crowd at the rally, "but we got here and it's 9:37!"

"Praise God!" a man in the crowd shouts. "Praise the Lord!"

Robertson beams.

At the beginning of the day, as we pull out of Davenport, there is fog among the rolling hills and the low gunmetal sky threatens snow. We will not take the fastest way across Iowa, Interstate 80. That would defeat the purpose. Instead, we take U.S. 30, the two-lane blacktop that cuts through the small towns and county seats. "We are showing that we will go where other candidates won't," Kerry Moody says. "Some of these towns have never been visited by a candidate."

There is also another reason for the route. Some of these rural areas have had cable TV for years and they look upon Robertson not as an evangelist or a politician but as a TV star. Still, the crowds are small. Forty people here, seventy-five there. But Robertson goes all out for every crowd. He smiles, waves, presses the flesh as the TV crews capture it all. "I've seen him walk off the plane and wave above and past the cameras to a nonexistent crowd," one reporter said. Robertson knows his business; he knows how to use the tube.

The fields are filled with the stumps of cornstalks. Horses, kneeling on the frozen ground, stare as we pass by. In Tipton (population 3,055), not far from the birthplace of Herbert Hoover, the Tipton State Bank sign reads 33 degrees when we step off the bus. Only about twenty people are waiting, but soon the Mobile Faithful swell their numbers. Robertson's portable sound system blares "The Washington Post March."

Elmer Geadelman, sixty-four, wearing black rubber boots and a plaid work shirt under a quilted jacket, stands and waits. He has a 180-acre crop and livestock farm and is wearing a green gimme cap from Feed Squealer Fresh Feeds. "Well, I think he'd be a good leader," Geadelman says of Robertson, "though I'm not really a religionist. Last time I didn't vote. I didn't like anybody running. Reagan said he'd balance the budget, but he didn't. Now, I'm not sure. Dole might be pretty good. Or Ron Paul the Libertarian. Bush? No, he's too much for the big boys and the big banks."

The Robertson rally is in the bank basement, where sixty people, mostly women, are gathered. Robertson speaks in a gentle, yet urgent tone, the "polished mahogany voice" of an Elmer Gantry. "I want to see a time in America when husbands love their wives, when wives love their husbands, when men and women bring up their children as law-abiding, God-fearing citizens of this land," Robertson says. "I want to see us return to the fundamental moral values that made this country great."

He speaks for exactly nine minutes and then takes a few questions. When he is through, he goes down the aisles of green folding chairs shaking hands. He passes a table where volunteers are selling "Robertson for President" T-shirts for seven dollars. Outside the bank, the sound system again blasts out "The Washington Post March." I ask an aide why Robertson is using a march dedicated to a newspaper he hates and I get a shrug. Apparently, the campaign had to come up with something when the theme to *Rocky* was dropped and nobody knew John Philip Sousa had dedicated the song to the newspaper in 1889.

Later, I ask Robertson about this song selection. "I play it so I can turn it off," he growls.

At the IBEW Local 405 Union Hall in Cedar Rapids, the second-largest city in Iowa, Robertson's advance team has sped ahead to count the crowd. There are only about a hundred people, which will be a good-sized crowd for Robertson this day, but the union hall can hold five times that number. Quickly, the aides order the folding chairs inside the hall put away and the speech moved outside into the cold and windy parking lot.

Gary Butz, the business manager for the union, is amused by the change in plans. "It's about an average crowd," he says. "I don't know why they didn't want it inside. I guess they thought the crowd was too small for the hall. But they paid the $350 anyway. That's what we charge everybody."

Butz is standing under a sign that says: "Please do not throw dancing powders on this floor. Additional charge!" I would not be a reporter if I did not ask him what dancing powders are.

"Well, it's like talcum," he says as if this were common knowledge. "It's used for ballroom dancing. But it's hard to clean up."

In the parking lot, there is another sign that reads: "Parking of Imported Vehicles Prohibited on IBEW Local 405 Premises." Luckily, the God Bus is made in the U.S. of A.

In a stiff wind, Robertson again speaks for nine minutes. "I want our children to learn American history the way it happened rather than how some social scientist thinks it happened!" he says.

Back on the bus, Kerry Moody says: "We are building a fire under our local supporters in these little towns. That is one purpose of this trip. The other is to get media attention. To show that Pat is concerned and interested enough to hit the smaller counties. We had only six days to get this all together."

They have done an impressive job. In each town, the same large blue banner always serves as a nice backdrop for TV when Robertson speaks (it is taken down and rushed ahead to the next stop after each speech), there are traveling cheerleaders with straw hats and there are always plenty of leaflets and free tapes.

In Toledo (population 2,445) Robertson lists the bottom line for his presidency. "At a minimum, I want to see us bring God back into the public schools of America," he says.

We leave town, past homes with fiberglass hogs in the front yards, and head back out into the countryside. Strips of white snow stretch down the furrows of the plowed fields like stripes on an awning. Ben Waldman leans over my seat and reminds me of something I need to know before I get my turn to interview Robertson. "Pat will sometimes say billions for millions," Waldman says. "And millions for billions."

Hey, no problem. Why would a President need to know the difference?

Before I get my turn in the barrel with Robertson, I am trying to think of a joke to tell him. This sometimes cuts the ice, and I have a theory that humorless men make bad Presidents. (If America ever elects a President with a real sense of humor, I will get to find out if humorous men make good Presidents.) Lee Bandy of Knight-Ridder has a joke, but I don't get it.

Q: What happens when cannibals eat charismatics?

A: They throw up their hands.

What does that mean? I ask him. I know Robertson is a charismatic, but why is it funny?

"Have you ever seen charismatics in church?" he says. "They throw up their hands into the air."

And you think I should tell that joke to Robertson?

"No," he says, "but I'd love to be there when you do."

Later, I try out the joke on Kerry Moody, who assures me that Robertson will not be offended by it. But then Moody has spent the whole day trying to convince us that Robertson is just one of the boys.

We pass through Boone, birthplace of Mamie Eisenhower, and then get to Jefferson (population 16,316), county seat of Greene County, where Robertson speaks in the courthouse. Just before he finishes, I am told to get on board his bus, it is my turn for an interview. I slap a fresh tape into my recorder and climb aboard.

It is a very nice bus, more like a mobile home. The front seats have been removed and couches and swivel chairs have been put in. There is a microwave oven, a refrigerator and a television. Behind a wall there are living quarters with a bed and shower. As Robertson is finishing his speech, an aide runs up the steps of the bus, grabs a carpet sweeper from behind one couch and begins sweeping the plum-colored carpeting, picking up crumbs and confetti. He whisks the sweeper out of sight just as Robertson's ostrich-skin boots hit the front steps of the bus.

Robertson climbs on board, pulls down his tie and opens his shirt collar. It is just after 5 p.m. and he has been campaigning for nearly eight hours. He sits down heavily in a swivel chair and waves to the crowd outside the bus windows. As he waves, he speaks sharply to Constance Snapp. "Did we drop some TV?" he asks. "I thought there were fewer cameras out there."

In the old days, candidates counted the house. Today, they count the cameras.

"Oh no, we didn't drop any TV," Snapp lies.

Robertson is wearing a gray herringbone sports jacket, a cream-colored shirt and a black-and-red-striped tie. A purple paisley handkerchief peeks out of his jacket pocket. He asks for a cup of tea, which on the bumping and swaying bus threatens to splash on him throughout the interview.

I sit across the aisle from him and next to me is a reporter from the Des Moines *Register*. Robertson has so many interview requests, we have to double up.

Because I don't know how much time we will have until the next stop, I start right in. "People read about you or they see on TV that Pat Robertson stopped hurricanes and heals the sick and talks in tongues," I begin, "and that scares them. Are you a scary person? Do they have any reason to be frightened of you?"

Robertson laughs. But it is that kind of laugh where the laughter is almost spoken: "Ha. Ha. Ha."

"Not really," he says. "When they get to know me, they realize I'm really somebody they want to vote for. In my estimation, I'm as knowledgeable as any candidate in either party on the major issues facing the world."

I want to get him back to the miracles, so I ask him about the Lisa Myers piece on NBC. "She dealt with a number of those issues I've raised," I say. "Would you mind just talking about it? Did you ever stop a hurricane?"

"Well, I will say with Lisa Myers, that [NBC] said on the air, you know, that I'd, that we were given an opportunity to reply. That is not true," he says.

Which wasn't exactly what I had asked. I try again. "The main things you've brought up are the hurricane and whether you, I guess, cured a woman of cancer. Let's deal with those."

Robertson's face hardens. "I am a man of prayer and our ministry at CBN focused on prayer," he says. "We have had tens of thousands of people who have had answers to their prayers, which have been documented and recorded, a number of which have medical foundation. None of these things are anything that I did. We had counseling. People who prayed. And I believe God answers prayers. Nothing more spectacular than that."

But it was more spectacular than that. When you see Robertson performing on videotape, he holds up one hand, bows his head and tells Hurricane Gloria: "In the name of God, I command you" to turn north.

"Well, it's just that candidates rarely talk about praying for such things . . ." I start to say.

"Ronald Reagan talks about it a lot," Robertson says. "Jimmy Carter was a big-time pray-er. And George Washington, we've got pictures of him leading troops in prayer at Valley Forge. And Abraham Lincoln prayed all night long during the Civil War. McKinley wrote about being on his knees to ask Jesus what to do about the Philippines. Garfield was an evangelist before he was elected. And Woodrow Wilson was a dedicated Christian and wrote about it. Even Harry Truman *claimed* to be a good Baptist."

The reporter from the Des Moines *Register* steps in: "I don't know that any of them has said in front of a large crowd of people that 'someone out here has cancer.' "

"None of them had television," Robertson begins.

But Constance Snapp does not like the way this is going. "We've only got five minutes," she barks. "You want to waste five minutes on this stuff?"

Robertson gets the signal.

"I'll tell you what, fellas," he says, the anger rising in his voice and making it grow thick. "I've got three weeks to go and I've played this one to and fro and backwards about the last two and a half years. And I ain't got time on this bus tour to go into this stuff again. I'm sorry, I just haven't.

"I mean, I've answered this stuff over and over and over again. I've been *ridiculed, laughed at, pilloried* and, and *pinioned*. Right now, I've got to talk about national issues. I'll talk to you about the budget, I'll talk to you about national defense, I'll talk to you about INF, I'll talk to you about welfare, education, you name it. Enough of this."

He sits in his chair, tightly clutching his tea, vibrating with anger.

Robertson believes that bringing up his past is unfair. And some reporters go along with this, sticking to "national" issues when they speak to him. But either Robertson did certain things in the past and wrote certain things and claimed certain things or he did not. Politicians live their lives building records. And once built, they are almost impossible to do away with. They can be explained. Put in context. Apologized for. But, as Robertson is finding out, they cannot be expunged.

Snapp turns on the TV to catch the national news. Dan Rather, doing a piece on Robertson and Jackson, calls them "preachers" and Robertson's face hardens even further. Then Bob Schieffer, reporting on the God Bus caravan, comes on and says: "These men should be taken seriously." Robertson brightens. But Schieffer goes on to say that Robertson's crowds "are respectable size, but sometimes fleshed out by the faithful who travel with him."

Whoops, cat's out of the bag on the Mobile Faithful. Next time they'll have to change clothes between stops or wear false beards.

I ask Robertson a few more questions, and when the bus is almost at the next town, I decide, what the hell, go for it.

I'd like to tell you a joke, I say to Robertson. I am told you won't be offended by it.

There is silence on the bus. Snapp looks stricken.

What happens when cannibals eat charismatics? I ask.

Robertson looks at me wordlessly.

They throw up their hands, I say.

There is a pause. One–one thousand. Two–one thousand. Three–one thousand.

"Ha," Pat Robertson says. "Ha. Ha."

THE WHEELS COME OFF the Pat Robertson campaign in Columbia, South Carolina, on February 23. That is the day Robertson holds a news conference accusing George Bush of triggering the Jimmy Swaggart sex scandal for the express purpose of hurting Robertson in the South Carolina primary.

Asked if he really believes George Bush would involve himself in such a thing, Robertson says: "It's like the piano player in the bawdy house who says he doesn't know what's going on upstairs. Of course he knows."

Then he goes down his laundry list of other accusations against the Bush campaign: prank phone calls in the middle of the night, slashed phone lines and bribe attempts. Robertson says Bush is also about to run ads attacking Robertson's religious beliefs. "Perhaps they aren't even prepared," Robertson says a moment later. "I want to call it before it happens, that's all."

In the back of the room, Robertson's chief aide, Patrick Caldwell, frantically runs a finger across his neck, trying to tell Robertson to cut it off, stop it, shut up.

Robertson would not. Robertson could not.

ABC, CBS and NBC led the news with it all: Robertson standing up there in front of the microphones, face flushed, going on and on with his wild allegations.

T. R. Reid said: "I'll never forget the look of sheer disbelief on the faces of my fellow reporters as we stood there watching this formidable presidential contender dig his own political grave."

The next day, Bush, having earlier declined to call him nutty, called Robertson "crazy."

And when it was all over, Robertson's Invisible Army was not only unseen but unheard. Robertson's assumption that evangelicals would automatically vote for him proved false.

"The born-again vote went with Bush this year, but so did everybody else in the party," Richard Pinsky, a top Robertson aide, said after the election. "Nobody knows if there really is a Pat Robertson vote."

In trying to be fair to Robertson, the press often made him seem more reasonable than he actually was. We never figured out quite how to handle him. Robertson had the poll figures, he had the buses, the walkie-talkies, the trail car and the trappings of a normal campaign. So he had to be a normal candidate, right?

But not everyone, including some very religious people, thought so. "Because a person is a devout Christian does not necessarily mean he or she is well equipped to lead the country," the Rev. Jerry Schmalenberger, senior pastor at St. John's Lutheran Church in Des Moines, said. "History tells of terrible decisions made by leaders who thought they were following God. It can happen again."

Pat Robertson had warned us himself. There is a certain "percentage of error" when you listen to what you think is the voice of God, he had said. Sometimes it is the voice of Satan.

God had told Pat Robertson to run for President. Or had he?

☆ 8 ☆

FEAR AND LOATHING
IN NEW YORK

*A gunman leaps from the shadows and confronts a frightened
New Yorker with a question.*
*"O.K., who's gonna win the primary? Dukakis, Jackson
or Gore?"*
*The voter thinks about it for a while, then shrugs his
shoulders and says: "Aww, go ahead and shoot me."*
                                        —Joke told by Al Gore
                                        during the New York primary

THE MOST DANGEROUS PLACE in America is not New York
City.

The most dangerous place in America is anywhere between Ed
Koch and a TV camera.

The mayor of New York, already rumpled-looking in his gray suit
though it is only 7:30 a.m., stands on the northwest corner of Seventy-
seventh and Lexington under a Te Amo Imported Cigars sign. A
fringe of white hair crowns his head like a laurel wreath upon a
Caesar.

"Good morning," he booms to the knot of reporters that surrounds
him, and then begins without preamble: "I don't make predictions.
I hope Al Gore does well; I put my trust in God. I don't know
whether God is watching or not."

But if God is not watching New York, He is the only one who isn't.

A few weeks earlier Jesse Jackson had won the Michigan caucuses
and now fear stalks the land. The fear that a black man might actually
be able to win the Democratic nomination. The fear that Michael
Dukakis, whose campaign seems to be flabby and floundering, will
not stop this guy. The fear that an overwhelmingly white country

could wake up and find itself, somehow, someway, with a black President.

The newsmagazines, which have been holding on to their Jesse Jackson cover stories until he did something really spectacular, now unleash them. *Newsweek* calls it "The Michigan Miracle." *Time*, whose memorable cover is a picture of the candidate with the single word: "Jackson!?" says: "The Democrats have an unexpected front-runner." Dan Rather agrees. Two days after the Michigan caucuses, he tells America: "Jesse Jackson has become the front-runner."

While Dukakis still leads in the delegate count with 604 delegates to Jackson's 598 (with 2,082 needed to win), Jackson has captured more popular votes than Dukakis in the thirty-one primaries and caucuses held so far. The total popular vote will not count at convention time, but you can't take it away from Jackson. So far more people have gone into polling places and voted for him than for any other Democratic candidate.

Jackson starts thinking about his cabinet, letting it be known that he wants to lure former President Jimmy Carter away from his peanuts and into a Jackson administration. That is how big everyone is treating Michigan. A major Northeastern industrial state, it was one that Dukakis had been depending on. But Jackson crushed him there 55 percent to 29 percent. The dominoes begin to tumble. Mario Cuomo, who was going to endorse Michael Dukakis, now hesitates. Dukakis can't believe what is happening.

Traveling around Michigan in a small, six-passenger plane on the day of the caucuses, he had been confident of a victory, but confident in his steady, low-key way. Kitty, excited and nervous, was just the opposite. At every stop, she demands that aides call to see how the voting is going. "Call, call," she says. "I want to know."

Dukakis places a restraining hand on her sleeve. "Katherine, Katherine, be calm," he tells her. "We have one of these every week."

Finally, an aide calls Dukakis headquarters to find out how things look. "It's in the toilet," he is told. The aide walks back to the plane. "It's fine," he tells Dukakis. "Everything is going to be fine."

That night, Dukakis goes on the national news shows and the network anchors congratulate him on his impending victory in Michigan. Dukakis exercises his customary caution. "If things continue," he says, "we will have won a significant victory in Michigan."

Up in his suite, he gets a call from Susan Estrich, his campaign manager. "We're not going to win," she tells him.

Dukakis puts down the phone and the first words out of his mouth are: "You know, it is really something that the son of a sharecropper and the son of a Greek immigrant will be the last two candidates in the race."

His staff is nearly catatonic with fear—Michigan raises for the first time the possibility they may actually lose this thing—but Dukakis is thinking about the sociological implications of it all.

Jackson is almost goofy with joy. There are not just cabinet jobs to hand out—he has already decided he wants House Speaker Jim Wright as his running mate—but ambassadorships to be assigned and domestic and world policy to be changed. He now believes he may be unstoppable. Unnoticed, however, is the tiny number of voters involved in Jackson's Michigan victory. Only about 213,000 people voted in a state with 5.8 million registered voters.

But who cares? That's for the nitpickers to worry about. Jackson now believes that, at the very worst, if he doesn't win the nomination outright, he can keep Dukakis from having enough delegates to win on the first ballot.

Which has a lot of people petrified. "A lot more Democrats are thinking seriously about Mario Cuomo now," Senator Alan Cranston of California said after hearing the Michigan results. A Great White Hope is needed. If Dukakis cannot stop Jackson, then somebody else will have to climb into the ring and deliver the knockout punch.

Three days after Michigan, Senator Al Gore of Tennessee weighs in. Back in December, just before an NBC debate, Gore had been urged to attack Jackson for his Middle East positions, but Gore had refused. Now speaking to Jewish leaders in New York, however, Gore discovers he cares about Jesse Jackson's Middle East positions after all.

"I am dismayed by his embrace of Arafat," Gore tells them, and "I categorically deny [Jackson's] notion that there's a moral equivalence between Israel and the PLO. In a Gore administration no one will have reason to doubt America's commitment to the survival and security of Israel."

This goes over very well. And afterward, Gore, a Southern Baptist whose favorite Shakespeare play is *The Merchant of Venice*, joins the Jewish leaders at a kosher deli for lunch.

The day before, speaking to the Association for a Better New York, Gore had said: "We're not choosing a preacher. We're choosing a President. The Oval Office is a whole lot more than a pulpit." The gloves are off. Jackson, Gore says, has a "complete and total lack of experience in national government . . ." And if Jackson is a dummy, Dukakis is a coward for not calling Jackson a dummy. Dukakis is "absurdly timid," Gore says, for not attacking Jackson. And the press is making a "big deal" of his attacks on Jackson "only because Mike Dukakis is afraid to say a single word about Jesse Jackson," which is "ludicrous." The next day, April 1, Ed Koch says Jews "would have to be crazy to vote for Jackson."

So the stage is set. After Michigan comes Wisconsin, which Dukakis wins handily, but Wisconsin is dismissed as an eccentric farm state, whereas the New York primary, which follows, will be the major battleground.

And New York resembles a war zone. New York City is still enmeshed in the multiple agonies of the Howard Beach incident, the Bernhard Goetz incident and the Tawana Brawley incident, while Mayor Koch seems oblivious to everything but the sound of his own voice. Although Michael Dukakis woos him, Koch endorses Gore.

Now, on the day before the New York primary, Koch goes to Seventy-seventh and Lexington to show Gore how it's done.

"I had a stroke," Koch, sixty-three, says apropos of nothing, standing on the corner as the sun burns off the early-morning haze, "and Mother Teresa prayed for me. *And I'm Jewish!*"

You're kidding. Jewish? Really? Have the newspapers been notified?

"I have no more words about Jesse Jackson," Koch says. "I've said them all. What he did was an insult to this city, not marching in the Salute to Israel Day parade. Can you imagine him avoiding the St. Patrick's Day parade or the Puerto Rican Day parade or the Martin Luther King Day parade? That's an insult. He thought he wouldn't get a hospitable meeting? You don't pick and choose, you go. You go!"

The words gush forth from his mouth. It is hard to believe while listening to him that there is even a nanosecond of delay between thought and speech. Thus far, he has not been asked a single question by reporters. But somehow the usual method of question and response seems unnecessary for Koch, who is willing to provide not only the answers but also the questions.

The previous day, Jesse Jackson had declined to walk down Fifth Avenue in the Salute to Israel Day parade. It was widely viewed as an insult to New York's large Jewish community. Gore and Dukakis, the only other Democrats still in the race, had separately walked down the center of the street in the balmy April weather, waving to the large crowds. But Jackson would not appear. At war with what he called the city's "Jewish leadership," he did not want to expose himself to the taunts of the crowd.

"I am most vociferous in my criticism of Jesse Jackson," Koch goes on, "but none of my attacks have been disputed. None. Nothing.

Some people don't want the truth. You criticize a black and you're called a racist." He shrugs. Go figure.

Koch is standing in front of the entrance to the IRT downtown subway stop on Lexington Avenue. As the sun travels higher in the sky, a steady stream of commuters, heads down and walking quickly but carefully (you do not want to jostle anybody, you do not want to make eye contact, you don't know who has a knife), fills the sidewalks, splits around Koch, then descends into the IRT station. Every now and then a blast of dank, cool air rumbles up from the subway. The streets are already crowded with honking cars, trucks and taxis that skitter across the lanes of traffic like yellow bugs on a pond. Koch raises his voice to be heard above the din.

"This is my lucky corner, you know," he says. "I've run twenty-four times, congressman and City Council, mayor. And I come here at 7 a.m. and stand here until 8 p.m. on election day. On this corner. I had a stroke, but I walk. I dance. I talk." He does a sprightly little walk, back and forth, pumping his elbows. "See? No paralysis."

Those who have seen him only on TV, behind a lectern or seated on some talk show, see the round face and bald head and imagine a small man. In fact, Koch is large and imposing, with a considerable physical presence. Presence enough, especially when surrounded by reporters and camera crews, to block the subway entrance on his lucky corner, something the voters of New York have had to put up with on twenty-four mornings.

"Let people go through," Koch says, finally noticing that they have begun to back up into Lexington Avenue. "Otherwise we'll lose money on the subway. You know, we've got 175 different ethnic groups and religious groups in this city. Ethnicity and diversity. There is no such thing as a melting pot."

The words, sentences and ideas seem to pour forth in no particular order. It is just a man talking, saying whatever comes into his head, confident that whatever he says can be and will be turned into news. During an uncharacteristic pause, I wedge in a question: Hasn't the New York primary been divisive and hate-filled?

Koch screws up his face as if he has bitten into something sour. He puts a hand to his chest. "Oh, please," he says. "Puh-leeze. I don't see that at all. You ask a person [that is, Jesse Jackson] about his record for twenty years, is that divisive?"

As he talks, a handsome, square-jawed man arrives on the scene in a limousine. He is wearing a blue suit, white shirt and red tie. His hair is full and neat and is parted on the right side with surgical precision. Secret Service agents emerge and set up a yellow rope supported by plastic stanchions just in case the crowd, which is hurrying past with practiced indifference, decides to stop and meet the man.

Koch looks at the yellow rope and shrugs. "They've never done this for me," he says. "But lemme tell you: Al Gore has the potential for greatness that Jack Kennedy had."

Al Gore? Who's he? Where's he? Oh, you mean the silent guy in the suit over there looking like the second wheel on a unicycle? RoboCandidate? The guy running for President but unable to get a word in edgewise because the mayor of New York will not shut up? Yeah, that guy.

Behind Koch and ignored by him, the commuters continue their descent into the subway. It might be nice if the mayor actually stopped one or two and urged them to vote for Al Gore, but to do so Koch would have to stop talking to reporters.

"Dukakis is . . . acceptable," the mayor says through pursed lips, again in response to no question. "Acceptable. But he . . ." Koch points. "*He* has the potential for greatness."

The "he," Gore, lights up at the mention and takes a half step forward like an actor who has been waiting in the wings and has finally heard his cue.

"Oh, hi, Al," Koch says to him. "Well, I got it all wrapped up for you."

A large black woman in a blue cloth coat walks past Koch and does a little double take as she recognizes him. "You gonna lose!" she says to him. "Last time for mayor for you! You out!"

"Ahhhhh," says Koch, dismissing her with the wave of a hand.

Has this become a referendum on your own reelection? a reporter asks.

Koch shrugs. "Yeah. Sure. Whatever."

A middle-aged man in a short black trench coat hesitates at the subway entrance and peers through his thick glasses at Koch. "You," he says. "Hey, you. What did you put taxes up for, you?"

"Ahhhhh," Koch says again, and turns his back on the man in order to address the reporters. "Actually we *lowered* them, but what do you expect?" Sure, what do you expect? What do you expect from these jerks, these numskulls, these, these . . . voters.

Gore takes another half step forward and tries to enter the conversation. "He took me to a deli on the Lower East Side," he begins in a tone of awe and wonder last used when Stanley met Livingstone. "And we had pickles. Different kinds of pickles. They were called, uh . . . uh . . ."

"Sours and half sours," Koch says, and then winks at the reporters as if to say: Goyim—you can't live with them and you can't live without them.

"Right, right," Gore says. "I liked the half sours better than the sours."

Koch stands and listens, like a teacher waiting for his pupil to say something bright. But when Gore finishes expounding on his pickle preferences and falls silent, Koch moves on to a much more interesting subject: what *he* likes to eat. Especially what he likes to eat when he travels to exotic locales like Tennessee, which is underneath and to the left of New York somewhere.

"Spareribs," Koch says, "and I don't mind grits. They're like farina. I eat them with butter and salt."

"There is no city like New York," Gore interjects, "anywhere in the world." He waits. But no reporter rushes to the phone to alert the city desk. The day before, Koch had taken Gore to the Casa Bella restaurant on Mulberry Street in Little Italy. "This is cappuccino, Al, and this is cannoli," Koch explained carefully to the candidate. It was like a culinary *Sesame Street*. In reality, Gore, the son of a U.S. senator, had grown up in the salons of Washington, D.C., not the hills of Tennessee. He traveled widely and could probably tell cappuccino from cannoli without a guide. But while in New York, Gore played along with the mayor. He spent his days before the TV cameras eating yellow rice, fried bananas, spaghetti with garlic and oil, hot bialys and pickles. He gosh-and-gee'd on cue. He played the rustic. Gore had little choice. Once you sign aboard with Ed Koch, you ride with him to the end of the line.

Myron Waldman, a political reporter for *Newsday*, decides it might be nice to encourage Al Gore to keep talking, the primary being just twenty-four hours away and all. So Waldman tries to solicit a "brite," newspaper lingo for anything upbeat or humorous. "If you become President," Waldman asks Gore, "will you have half sours at the White House?"

And there could be a cute little ethnic angle here, something nice for the headline writers to work with, like: "Gore Not Sour on New York" or "Gore in Pickle at White House."

The only trouble is that Gore has not heard Waldman's question. That's because Gore has made the mistake of actually trying to talk to some voters, to meet some people, to solicit an actual vote, and has turned his back to the press. Koch reaches over and hits Gore on the arm. "Hey," Koch says to him, "he's *asking* you something."

But before Gore can hear the pickle question repeated, Koch begins to speak. "His whole persona is of potential greatness," Koch says, again using the word "potential," which only emphasizes the fact that

Gore is not great now, even though he is running for President now and must be ready to lead the nation now. Suddenly, Koch throws both hands into the air and begins to holler. "Hi, everybody! It's us. Al and me!" The TV cameramen nudge each other and grin. You gotta love a guy like this, a guy who's always good for a nice visual. Koch turns to the cameras. "They don't do this in Tennessee," he says.

Gore nods in agreement. "I've never seen anything like it," he says.

"I love campaigning," Koch says. "I love it. I have been to 125 town meetings and that revives the spirit. I go to every group that asks—unlike Jesse Jackson. Some of them are boisterous, but I go— unlike Jesse Jackson. I face them all—unlike Jesse Jackson."

This being New York, where anything can happen and does on a daily basis, McGeorge Bundy, one of John Kennedy's best and brightest, one of the towering figures of the Vietnam era and now a professor of history at New York University, innocently walks by on his way down into the subway.

Koch grabs him and demands a vote for Gore.

"I'm from Massachusetts," Bundy says apologetically, apparently meaning he's for Dukakis.

Koch turns his back on Bundy. "So? We can lose one vote."

"Actually," Koch goes on, "I am more popular in the suburbs than in New York City." He pauses a beat. "They don't have to live with me." Sha-boom.

There are fewer commuters now and Koch surveys the scene with a practiced eye. "O.K.," he says. "Enough." He turns to go back to his waiting car.

Gore grabs his arm. "I'm going to see you later, right?" Gore asks. "We'll get more food, right?" There is a plaintive tone to these inquiries, as if Gore were afraid to campaign in New York alone. The hard fact is that Gore, who has not done really well outside of the South (and did well there by latching on to the populist strategy of Midwesterner Dick Gephardt), is not a comfortable fit for New York. Gore's victories in the South during the Super Tuesday primaries resulted from the votes of conservative Democrats, who saw him as the only alternative to the Dukakis-Jackson liberal wing of the party. But in New York, there aren't that many conservative Democrats. And without conservatives to depend on, Gore needed a replacement: Jews.

After Michigan, Jewish voters realized the danger in voting for Gore, however. It would serve only to take votes away from Dukakis and increase Jesse Jackson's chance of winning the New York primary.

And no matter how many times Gore said that a vote for Gore was not a vote for Jackson, logic dictated otherwise.

Before climbing into his car and leaving Gore, Koch tells one more story. He tells how when he ran against Mario Cuomo for governor, Cuomo had put a commercial on TV saying voters should keep Koch as mayor of New York. "So people would come up to me," Koch says, "right here on this corner on election day, and they'd say: 'I didn't vote for you, because I want to keep you mayor.'"

And what did you say to them? I asked.

"I said: 'You're lucky I don't beat the shit out of you,'" Ed Koch says. There is no smile on his face as he says this, only a glint in his eye.

Koch leaves and Al Gore stands on the street for a while, stretching out his hand to passing New Yorkers, who don't grab it. Most don't bother to break stride.

Just before Gore decides to give up and move on, a man walks past him, digs into his pocket and flips Gore a quarter. "Here," he says with a smart-ass grin, "this is for your campaign." At this moment, Gore is $1.6 million in debt. The quarter flashes through the air. Gore grabs at it, bobbles it and drops it onto the sidewalk. We all look away, pretending this is not a metaphor for the Gore campaign.

The reporters get on buses, Gore gets into his car and we all head for Brooklyn. A Gore aide stands in front of the press bus and previews the next event: "We are going to the Interfaith Medical Center on Atlantic Avenue to see babies with AIDS."

There is a groan. The week before, Gore had visited the Love Canal. It was all part of Gore's Politics of Gloom, his attempt to convince Americans that extremely grave problems need extremely daring solutions—such as making Al Gore President of the United States.

We drive past gutted homes and brownstones with broken windows that stare out at us like the carved faces on jack-o'-lanterns. Interfaith is a tall, old building in the Bedford-Stuyvesant section of Brooklyn. It is a troubled hospital, stuck with troubled patients. This is not where people come to get nose jobs. Unless their noses have been flattened with baseball bats. The hospital is millions of dollars in debt—doctors have been known to buy their own medicine and sutures—largely because many patients are poor and without medical insurance. The neighborhood is a cornucopia of medical miseries: AIDS, hepatitis, tuberculosis, drug addiction. While some floors of the hospital sparkle, others still have dingy brown walls and worn linoleum. We troop down long corridors where disoriented patients in hospital gowns wander aimlessly. That indefinable chemical smell common to all hospitals catches us in the back of our throats.

But the Neonatal Intensive Care Unit, where Gore will do his thing for the cameras, turns out to be light and airy. It is closed off behind glass doors to cut the risk of infection to the babies inside. We line up outside the doors and are handed yellow paper gowns that fasten in back with white, sticky closures and gather at the wrists with elastic. To put them on, you stick your arms through them as you would with straitjackets. The reporters struggle into them and then hold the minicams for the cameramen so they can climb into their gowns. An unexpected silence falls over us. Suddenly, this doesn't seem like politics anymore. Suddenly, dressed in our yellow gowns, this seems serious.

A nurse comes through the glass doors. "Don't take pictures of the babies' faces," she tells us. "We have a release for our AIDS baby, so you can take his picture. And don't touch anything."

Gore is handed a yellow gown and begins to put it on. "Goes on this way, right?" he asks, poking his arms into the sleeves. The photographers begin taking picture after picture. The president of the hospital, who has dropped by to shake hands with Gore, steps to his side to help him into his gown. "Hey!" a photographer yells at him. "Get outta the shot! Get outta there!" The president steps back quickly.

Since there are dozens of us, we are split into platoons to walk through the glass doors and enter the intensive care unit. Even so, space is extremely limited inside. We look around and see these babies, incredibly small, doll size, almost doll-like, until you see their little hearts beating against their chests or catch the wave of a tiny arm. All sorts of tubes and lines run out of them. Some are in little plastic boxes called Isolettes. Others are in specially warmed beds, hooked to respirators with tubes that snake into their mouths and down their throats.

All around us are heart-respiration monitors with wavy green lines and orange lights. There are also oxygen monitors with red digital readouts that are linked to the babies by little white bandages that wrap around their big toes and measure the oxygen density of their blood through infrared light.

IV stands loom over the babies, the plastic bags slowly dripping fluids down tubes and through needles into the veins in their arms or legs. Some of the infants have Broviac catheters inserted into a vein in their chests. These feed them nutrients and medicine.

We stand there. We stand there trying not to move. Trying not to bump into things. Trying not to jostle the Isolettes, slam into the babies or knock over the equipment. We stand there all thinking the same thing: What the hell are we doing here? Why is this necessary? And when will either the press or the candidates develop some sense of shame?

I had been in a neonatal intensive care unit just a few months before. That one was in Washington, D.C., though it looked much the same. The first child of two good friends of mine, Brian Kelly and Pat Wingert, both journalists, had been born three and a half months premature, just on the edge of what doctors call "viability." Daniel (who is now healthy and happy) spent the first five months of his life in intensive care. When visiting, my wife and I had to look at him through a window.

"The greatest fear, the thing which kills babies the most in intensive care, is infection," Brian told me. "So the hospital staff takes extraordinary precautions: limiting the number of people who come in, washing many times a day, wearing surgical gowns and filtering the air. And anyone with the slightest suggestion of a cold wears a surgical mask."

In the unit in the Interfaith Medical Center, however, neither Gore nor the reporters are wearing masks, even though all of us on the road for long periods of time have coughs, colds and sore throats.

"The risk to the babies," Brian said, "is that they have little or no immune system. So very few people are allowed in to see them. My own sister and brother-in-law were kept out once. Besides, it is crowded in those places. The Isolettes are often packed end to end. It is an incredibly fragile environment. It is tiny beings, clinging to the edge of life. Anything disruptive could be very bad news for them."

Gore is walking now among the babies, the camera crews in front of him walking backward, shooting their pictures and, inevitably, knocking into things. "Watch out!" we yell at them. "Watch out! Watch out!"

"Nothin' we can do, man," a cameraman mutters back. "Nothin' we can do. Candidate's moving."

The candidate is moving. And the cameramen have to get the pictures. Because that's what politics is all about, isn't it?

Gore walks through the unit, nodding and pointing, and then finally gets to the showstopper, the headline act: the AIDS baby. Releases all signed, so the photographers can snap away.

Gore picks up the very small boy, who is wrapped in a blue blanket, and holds him in front of the TV cameras. "This is Baby Robinson," Gore solemnly announces to the boom mikes. "And Baby Robinson has tested positive for AIDS."

Gore looks down at the child and begins talking in a goo-goo voice. "What do you think about all these lights, huh?" he asks. "Huh?"

Gore then smiles into the cameras. "I've had some experience holding babies," he says. Then, incredibly, he goes for a joke: "Baby Robinson is not ready to answer questions."

Our platoon of reporters and camera crews is ushered out and the next platoon is ushered in. "This is Baby Robinson," Gore solemnly announces to the new cameras. "And Baby Robinson has tested positive for AIDS."

When Gore is finally, mercifully, through with his repeat performances, he gives Baby Robinson back to the nurses and heads downstairs for a news conference.

In a small administrative office on the ground floor of the hospital, a stifling room packed with press, a thin, wasted man in a pink-polka-dot shirt buttoned to the neck sits next to Gore. His name is Brian Snow. He is thirty. And he is dying of AIDS.

"You ever see anything like this?" Gore asks Snow, grinning.

Snow shakes his head a little.

"Everybody got a statement?" one of Gore's press aides asks. "All the mikes up front? Let's get all the mikes up front." Gore's statement is nine paragraphs long and begins: "GORE SPELLS OUT AIDS PLAN. FOR IMMEDIATE RELEASE." It is a six-point plan for ridding America of AIDS. The press release could have been handed out anywhere. Gore could have held an AIDS news conference anywhere. But would it have gotten on the nightly news and in the papers without an AIDS baby and an AIDS patient to jazz it up a little? Probably not.

Before the news conference begins, Gore has a stroke of genius. He turns to Snow. "You have a button?" he asks. "They're going like hotcakes." Then he reaches over and pins a Gore button onto Snow. Not onto his pocket but onto his shirt collar. That way, the Gore button is sure to appear in all the TV shots and photographs.

When the cameras are in position, Gore begins talking: "This is Brian Snow, who is an AIDS patient at this hospital." Snow, glassy-eyed, stares straight ahead as Gore continues. "If the boroughs in New York City were counted as states, four of the boroughs would be in the top ten states in terms of numbers of AIDS cases, led by Manhattan, then Brooklyn, then the Bronx, then Queens."

Gore drones on and on and finally turns to Snow. "Brian," he asks, assuming an immediate familiarity (does Snow call him "Al"?), "do they treat you pretty well here?"

Snow stares at him as if to say: No, the hospital tortures me with ice picks. That's why I'm here today. Jeez, Louise, what a lunkhead.

"Yes," Snow says in a small voice. "The outpatient clinic is very good. But you get sick, you know, and there's no place to go."

"From the standpoint of an AIDS patient," Gore says as if he were taking testimony at a Senate hearing, "what hasn't been said that needs to be said?"

"I don't . . . I don't . . . I guess more help," Snow stutters. "Instead of a lot of this other stuff. People need help. I don't . . . I don't know how to say it."

But Al Gore knows how to say it. Because Al Gore knows exactly what the script holds next. "Do you feel like sometimes people are afraid of you?" Gore asks, setting up the stunt perfectly.

"Not me," Snow says. "My friends help me out a lot. But I've seen it, though, other people. How they talk. They don't want to get next to them. Don't want to touch them."

Gore now smiles broadly. "Some people feel they can still get AIDS by shakin' hands or somethin', like that," Gore says, suddenly dropping his *g*'s and assumin' his country voice. "That kind of misunderstandin' has to be dispelled."

And Gore reaches over and shakes hands with Brian Snow, holding it, so the cameras can get it. And we all see—get this!—that Gore has a bandage on his hand. "Candidate Risks Life! Shakes Hands Even With Open Wound!"

"We're about to open this to the press," Gore says to Snow when the handshake is over. "You want to stay for that?"

Snow shrugs. "Yeah."

There are a few questions about drugs and then the reporters get down to the good stuff. Does Gore think he is going to win the primary? Gore waves off the question as if it were, somehow, in bad taste. "I can see everybody wants to go into the horse race, and it's not for me to suggest," Gore says, "but does anyone have questions on AIDS?"

You're right, Al. Sorry. We should not have tried to inject politics into a serious event like this.

One or two AIDS questions follow and then a reporter decides to stop being a sap and asks: "Will you drop out of the race if you don't get 15 percent?"

"No, I intend to be in until the convention," Gore says and switches to his cheerleader voice. "There is a *surge* of support. We have *tremendous* momentum. There is a major *switch* underway in the undecided category to our campaign. Volunteers have been calling and walking into our headquarters. A *dramatic* increase. I'm very excited about what is going to happen."

The next day, Al Gore will get 10 percent of the vote in the New

York primary. Two days later, he will drop out of the presidential race.

ONE YEAR AFTER the New York primary, I call the Interfaith Medical Center and ask what became of Baby Robinson and Brian Snow. It takes the hospital only a few hours to check its records and call me back.

Brian Snow had become ill just moments after the Gore news conference and had been hospitalized. He was later released and lost contact with the hospital. Given the advanced state of his disease, a hospital spokesman said, he was now presumed to be dead.

Baby Robinson, the spokesman tells me, was not really a baby with AIDS. He just had tested positive for the HIV virus. Half of such babies never develop AIDS. And a month after the New York primary, Baby Robinson had been discharged from the hospital and had been placed in a foster home by a child placement agency. Now he was probably "perfectly normal."

I had just one other question: Since the primary, had Al Gore or anyone from Al Gore's staff ever inquired as to the health or welfare of either Brian Snow or Baby Robinson?

"Never," I was told. "They never have."

AFTER THE AIDS EVENT, we clamber back aboard the buses to rejoin Ed Koch at the South Street Seaport and the Fulton Market, a yuppified renovation project in lower Manhattan. As Gore emerges from his car, he doesn't have to ask where Koch is. An enormous media crush, truly huge, has surrounded the mayor. As Gore gets closer, he can hear Koch braying: "Can you imagine any white candidate not going to the Martin Luther King Day parade? Can you imagine?"

The camera crews spy Gore and their lenses lock on him. Reporters shout for his reaction. Is Jackson insulting the Jews as Koch says? Should Jackson have marched in the parade? What does Gore think? "The mayor is speaking for himself," Gore says. "I'm working very hard to get along with all the candidates."

And, by now, he is. Gore has finally realized the true horror of what has happened in New York: he has been doing Dukakis' dirty work for him. Gore and Koch have been raising fears about Jesse Jackson, but Gore and Koch will not be the beneficiaries of that. Dukakis will be.

So Gore is secretly calling Jackson at night and apologizing. Gore admits he has been a sheep in wolf's clothing. And Jackson forgives him. Gore has called. Gore has shown respect. Jackson likes that.

Now there are only twenty-four hours for Al Gore to get through, one more day of Ed Koch. Gore has let the genie out of the bottle and he knows it cannot be stuffed backed in.

Koch bursts out of the media pack and heads into the Fulton Market, which is full of unsuspecting tourists. They hear this incredible noise and see this roiling mass of bodies and cameras and microphones and lights come barreling toward them. Network TV crews, which are no slouches at protecting their space, are elbowed aside by the far more aggressive New York crews. Koch strides over to a counter and buys a salami and the crews bash into each other, fighting for camera angles. Koch bolts off in another direction—he makes no attempt to actually campaign, to shake a hand or make a pitch for Gore—and the tourists are now caught in the direct path of the media herd, which numbers about two hundred. A man is knocked backward. A woman is separated from her toddler, who becomes lost in a sea of legs and can be located only by his terrified wails. I concentrate on staying upright, clinging to the clothing of the people around me (you go down in this kind of mob and your teeth will be turned into Chiclets). I turn and see a tall, young guy, a local TV technician, give Roger Mudd a vicious shove. Mudd staggers, but does not go down. Mudd turns, looks at the kid and shoves him back. The kid can't believe it. How old is Mudd? The kid takes an aggressive step toward him and Mudd throws up his fists. "C'mon," Mudd says. "C'mon." A Secret Service agent steps between them and puts a hand on the kid's chest. The kid looks grateful and runs off after Koch.

"The last time I saw something like this," Mudd says, "was when Khrushchev came to the United States in 1959. It was a supermarket in San Francisco. Displays were knocked over and canned goods were stripped from the shelves so the TV crews could climb up on them and get an overall shot."

We finally burst outdoors, like a clot being blasted from a clogged pipe. We hesitate, catch sight of Koch's bald, bobbing pate far ahead and then plunge across numerous lanes of traffic under FDR Drive to get to Pier 17. There, at an outdoor café on the East River, Koch and Gore are supposed to sit and have a nice relaxing al fresco nosh. But the temperature has dropped to the thirties, a stiff wind has come up and it has begun to rain.

Still, the two men, now joined by Gore's wife, Tipper, sit outdoors pretending that rain is not being lashed into their eyes. Tipper has been spending the primary doing the "helpmeet" thing, going from interview to interview saying how if her husband is elected President, she will be an active partner and give advice but will not interfere, etc., etc. It is standard stuff, but Tipper, because of her past campaigning against dirty rock lyrics, has the added goal of trying to prove she is not an uptight prude who thinks if you play the Beatles' White Album backward, Paul says: "Communism is good."

"Who runs this joint?" Koch says, slapping the table for service. "Can I get some coffee?"

The wind blows more rain into their faces. Tipper, coatless, sits shivering in a short-sleeved red dress. All three smile bravely for the cameras. The media mob, now restrained behind a rope, keeps shouting questions at Gore. Have you split the party? Has New York been divisive?

"We're going to be more unified than ever," Gore says. "All three of us [Gore, Dukakis, Jackson] are absolutely determined to have a unified party."

You gonna win?

"*Big* shift on the way," Gore said. "*Momentum.* Big shift in *our* direction."

Small snowflakes are now mixed in with the rain.

Has Mayor Koch been getting more attention than you? a reporter yells.

"He's a very popular figure," Gore says in measured tones.

Jesse Jackson says that Mayor Koch has been divisive and provocative. What do you think?

"I'm not going to characterize it," Gore says. "I respect Jesse Jackson." Wasn't anybody going to ask him about his six-point AIDS plan? Or his five-point drug plan? Or the depletion of the ozone layer?

Why didn't Jesse Jackson march in the parade? comes the shout from a reporter. The questions are openly provocative now, attempting to get Gore to insult Jackson.

"That was a decision for him to make," Gore says. "He might not have known what to anticipate."

"Jesse showed contempt and arrogance!" Koch announces, as if those traits are to be found lacking in himself. "He is treating Jews with contempt and arrogance."

Gore winces. Doesn't Koch ever get enough of this? Gore stands up. He shakes hands with the mayor. He must go. Phone calls to make and all. And he has to appear on *Donahue.* He is sure the mayor understands. He shakes hands with Koch, gathers up Tipper and leaves.

The reporters can either go with him or stay with Koch. For most, it is an easy choice to make. They stay with Koch, where the good quotes come from.

"Who is Jesse Jackson?" Koch says. "Is he like an icon? It's arrogance. It's like Kennedy at Chappaquiddick, a character flaw. If I said all this about a white candidate, would you think me unfair?"

By this point in the campaign, Koch is fully out of control on the subject of Jackson. Even his friends, his closest advisers, have recognized it and have tried to get him to calm down. As often happens, their advice has the opposite effect. On the Sunday before the primary, Koch had appeared on *This Week with David Brinkley*, where he accused Jackson of "lying . . . under stress," charging that twenty years before, when Jackson had said he had cradled Martin Luther King, Jr.'s head in his arms after King had been shot by an assassin, he was lying.

"Why do you think that Coretta Scott King and Hosea Williams and Andy Young, as of last week, have not endorsed Reverend Jackson?" Koch said. "It was not truthful and his people, the closest people to him—and those who know how to judge him—say it was not truthful."

The day after King's assassination, Jackson, then twenty-six, went on TV still wearing the shirt he said was stained with King's blood. The incident has dogged him for years and some in King's Southern Christian Leadership Conference have, indeed, accused Jackson of faking it. Hosea Williams, now an Atlanta City Council member, says the blood on Jackson's shirt did not come from King, and the Reverend Ralph Abernathy, who succeeded King in the SCLC, said he, not Jackson, was the first to reach King and that Jackson could not have bloodied his shirt with King's blood.

Jackson's campaign manager, Gerald Austin, now says simply: "There seems to be a lot of debate about what actually took place."

But Koch goes on to accuse Jackson of lying about using the term "Hymie" in 1984. Again, there is basis for Koch's accusation. Jackson certainly did fudge the issue, denying at first that he had said anything "derogatory" about Jews, then later saying he had "no recollection" of using the term and then eventually admitting he had used it.

The question as to Koch's attacks, however, is one of timing. None of what Koch is saying is new, yet he feels the need to say it, bellow it again and again, every day leading up to the primary. Gore, who is supposed to be spending these final hours campaigning, instead is spending his time distancing himself from his chief supporter. "I have no personal basis for questioning the honesty of one of my opponents," Gore is forced to say after Koch's TV appearance. "I respect him and believe he's a man of integrity."

Koch understands what he is doing. His friends have been telling him he is outraging people not just in New York but across the nation. Primaries are supposed to be about emphasizing differences between the candidates, but they are never supposed to shatter the party unity that will be necessary to elect the nominee. And the bloody shirt thing twenty years later? C'mon, Ed, friends tell him, you're going too far.

Koch replies that he has no choice. Everyone else refuses to criticize Jackson, so he must be "Paul Revere," he says, warning the nation. And it is left to him to ride to every Middlesex village and farm to alert the populace that Jackson will "bankrupt the country in three weeks and leave it defenseless in six weeks" if he is elected President.

Stanley Hill, Jackson's New York campaign manager, vows to get even with Koch in the next mayoral election. "This is the beginning of the 1989 campaign," he says. And on primary day an NBC News exit poll shows that 62 percent of the voters think Koch should not run for a fourth term in 1989. (He will run anyway and lose to David Dinkins, who becomes the first black mayor of New York.)

In the end, it all hurts Gore. People who really like him and want him to run again in 1992 see him descend to a level they didn't know him capable of. In a televised debate, Gore says: "I haven't mentioned 'Hymietown' in this campaign. I haven't even brought up the Far- rakhan matter." Well, thanks, Al, thanks for not bringing them up.

Gore has time to think about all this as he is driven over to 30 Rock, NBC studios at 30 Rockefeller Plaza, to appear on *Donahue*. Dukakis declined the same invitation, and Jackson has already been on and, of course, wowed the audience. Though *Donahue* is seen on tape in most cities around the nation, it is live in New York City and this will be Gore's last chance to reach a mass audience here.

The audience is lined up in the lobby waiting to be allowed upstairs into the studio. They had been on a waiting list for five months, the tickets had finally arrived—you don't get to pick which day you want; you're just so grateful that you'll take any day—and they had come downtown on a Monday to see . . . well, the audience is never told in advance whom it will see. It could be anyone: Paul Newman, a bisexual sky diver, the author of *The Sensuous Massage Diet Book* or Phil in a dress.

The elevators transport the people up to the *Donahue* studio, where they run inside to grab the good seats. Pat McMillan, the executive producer, begins the warm-up. The first thing McMillan is interested in is finding guests for future shows. *Donahue* can't just take out a classified ad to find these people. "We need women who stay in troubled marriages," McMillan begins. "If we have to put you in shadows [to hide their faces], we will. We want men who have left their wives for older women. *Older*. We have two, we need more.

People who have slept their way to the top. We have more men calling in than women so far. We were amazed." And then, as if to deliver the bad news quickly, she says: "O.K., Albert Gore is the guest today."

Awww's bubble up from the audience. Albert who? What movie was he in? Does he wear lingerie? There is actual groaning now, either from those who don't recognize Gore's name or from those who do.

"C'mon!" Pat McMillan says. "Who do you want? Dukakis? How many for Gore? About five hands, hmmm? Well, he's a young and good-looking man. Will this help or hurt him? It will help him! If you like what they are saying during the show, go 'Yaayyyy!' If not, moan. React even if you're in semi-darkness. We want moans and groans or Phil won't come out into the audience."

The audience laughs. Phil always comes out into the audience. Phil would never let them down.

"Stand up when Phil comes into the audience, we get a good focus and it makes you look thin," McMillan goes on. "You sit down and we'll make you look fat and sloppy."

This is the second show of the day and the audience wants to know who the guest was for the first show. They want to know what they missed.

"At 1 p.m. we did civil disobedience," McMillan said. "You know, Brian Willson, the guy who sat down in front of the train and got his legs run over? So you didn't miss male strippers."

The audience murmurs its satisfaction. Al Gore may not be much, but at least he's got two legs.

Donahue now enters carrying his blue pinstripe suit jacket. He is wearing suspenders over a white shirt and a tie. He is incapable of dressing himself properly and so his staff puts labels on all his clothing, indicating which ties go with which shirts and which shirts go with which suits. His silver hair is perfectly in place.

He begins by telling the audience that yesterday Jesse Jackson was on the show. The audience groans again. They missed a superstar by one day.

Gore enters wearing the same blue suit, white shirt and red tie he has worn all day. He sits down on the set and crosses his legs, ankle on knee. Tipper takes a seat in the audience. Paul Risley, Gore's press aide, stands up along the side of the studio casing the joint with a practiced eye. He points to a spotlight that is making Gore's forehead look shiny and asks that it be adjusted.

The director starts a countdown, cues Donahue, and the show begins. Donahue starts surprisingly tough. He hammers Gore with questions on foreign policy, armed conflict with Iran and the ethics of sending American boys to die in foreign wars. He mentions that Gore's father lost his seat in the Senate by having the courage to oppose the Vietnam War. The audience applauds Donahue's questions. Donahue has made no secret of his own political ambitions ("The House looks like more fun," he has said. "It's like *Donahue*. The Senate is like one of those Sunday-morning public service programs") and is showing he is no cream puff.

Gore responds calmly at first, coolly, defending the use of U.S. troops in the Persian Gulf. "When we have a vital American interest at stake, when . . . force can be used *successfully*, when we do have help from our allies, we've got to get over this feeling that we can't ever stand up for American values and principles and interests in the world," he says.

There is applause.

"But according to that logic," Donahue responds instantly, "we've got to send troops *everywhere, every time* somebody pops off!"

"That's nonsense!" Gore says, his voice high and strained. "That's absolute nonsense!"

"You support aid to the contras!" Donahue says.

"I did *not* support aid to the contras!" Gore snaps back.

"I am corrected," Donahue says.

"You . . . you certainly are," Gore says, angry and flustered. He is enough of a pro, however, to realize that he needs to lighten things. So he calms down. He answers the rest of the questions easily. And then, during a commercial break, he asks Donahue: "Can I introduce my wife?"

The studio audience cheers for this. What is Donahue supposed to say, no? When the show resumes, Donahue introduces Tipper and the audience cheers again.

The hour goes by quickly. There are no more angry exchanges and, at the end, Gore goes into his rehearsed wrap-up. He trots out the issue that will show everyone how warm and human and courageous and presidential he is.

"This morning I was at the Interfaith Hospital," he says. "I held a little baby, three months old, in my arms, who has AIDS."

The audience is moved. The *awww*'s break out again. This guy is no ordinary politician. This guy must really care.

"They had a whole ward full of them," Gore says. "It's just so *heartbreaking*."

9

UNDER THE VOLCANO

*"Because this is the only place in the country where a major
political leader, the mayor, has created a climate of violence."*
—*Jesse Jackson explaining why he is
wearing a bulletproof raincoat in New York*

JESSE JACKSON NEVER TIRED of telling the story. He was
campaigning in Beaumont, Texas, in February 1988 and shaking
hands onstage when he met a local union leader, Bruce Hill. "Back
in 1965 I was with you in Selma," Hill said.

Jackson welcomed him as an old comrade-in-arms. He began talking
about the great struggle there that day at the Edmund Pettus Bridge.
"So this is a reunion," Jackson said.

"No, no," Hill said. "I was there, but I was on the other side." Hill
had stood with the Ku Klux Klan that day.

Jackson looked at the man.

"But, Jesse," Hill said, "today I'm on your side!"

The two men embraced.

It was a very nice story. And even though it got a little better each
time Jackson told it, it was essentially true. It summed up the beauty
and the promise of the Jackson campaign: he was the candidate
willing to reach out to anyone. Even to those who had once despised
him or had shouted racial epithets at him or had tried to lynch him.

What's more, the very fact that a man who had marched with the
Klan would now vote for Jackson was a concrete sign of the healing
that Jackson could bring about. Jesse Jackson believed that he was
America's litmus test: a vote for him demonstrated not only that you
wanted a better America but also that America was better. In Jackson's
view, casting a vote for Jesse Jackson proved that America was a
decent nation.

(Jackson never quoted what Bruce Hill went on to say: "It's going to take years and years to change a lot of these black folks' minds. They're about as prejudiced as we are.")

In April 1987, Jackson had flown to Montgomery, Alabama, and taken a car to Fitzgerald Road, just off Zelda Road, to the home of George Wallace, the four-term former governor, the man who had stood in the schoolhouse door rather than integrate the schools. Did Jackson bring recrimination? Bad memories? Criticism? He did not. He brought love. Warmth. Compassion. Healing. "He closed some doors when he was on his feet," Jackson said that day. "He still has enough life to open some on his back." Then he praised Wallace for "challenging the rich to be fair" and led a prayer in Wallace's living room (the maid, Dolores Coleman, was summoned from the kitchen to join in) during which Jackson stood next to Wallace's wheelchair, clutched his gnarled white hand in his own strong black one and prayed to "the God of healing and health" to bring comfort to George Wallace.

Moved, almost tearful, Wallace said: "Jesse, thank you for coming—and I love you."

Healing. Jesse Jackson would also go to those who were hated and ignored like he was once hated and ignored, and he would talk with them and bring balm to their wounds: Arab-Americans. Striking workers. Gays and lesbians. Anyone.

Except Jews. Except in New York. Those people in that place, Jesse Jackson would not see.

It was perhaps the most astonishing decision of his campaign, a decision that called into question not only his political judgment but also his ethical underpinnings. Because if Jackson's Rainbow Coalition meant anything, if all the stripes of the rainbow were to come together, if America really was the varied quilt he talked about, then Jackson could not leave out one stripe or one piece of the patchwork no matter what that group had done to him in the past.

After all, if Jesse Jackson could embrace those who had marched with the Klan, he could certainly embrace Jews. But he wouldn't. That's how furious New York had made him. He avoided Jewish neighborhoods. He avoided Jewish groups. He refused even the symbolic act of marching in a parade to honor the state of Israel.

It made no political sense. It undercut his message and opened him up to charges of hypocrisy. But he did not care. To him New York was a volcano of hatred, spewing forth bitterness and anger like lava. The volcano had been set off by the mayor (who just happened to be a Jew) and the lava all flowed Jackson's way.

His campaign manager, Gerald Austin (a Jew, as Jackson rarely failed to point out), tried to explain why Jackson would not meet with Jewish leadership groups as the other candidates had done. "There is no reason for putting him on trial," Austin said. "We don't accept this as a one-issue campaign and the people who are angry at him and listen to Mayor Koch are not going to vote for him anyway."

But for Jackson to snub Jewish leaders and avoid Jewish voters made no sense to his future in politics. There were certain wounds that had to be healed. Certain incidents came up again and again whenever Jackson's relationship with Jews was discussed: Jackson's embrace of Yasir Arafat, chairman of the Palestine Liberation Organization. Jackson's reference to Jews as "Hymie" and New York as "Hymietown." Jackson's relationship to Louis Farrakhan, leader of the Nation of Islam, who had called Judaism a "gutter religion."

These issues had to be dealt with not just because Jews made up 25 percent of the New York primary vote or because they were politically active nationally (though they were only about 2.5 percent of the national population). Leaving the wounds unhealed meant that Jackson would have to face the same problem every time he ran.

The most Jackson would do in New York, however, was attempt to address the Jewish problem without addressing the Jews. A few days before the primary, he appeared on ABC's *20/20*. He said of his "Hymie" remark in 1984: "Any statement I may have made to offend or hurt anybody, I'm sorry. Because that's not good. And that's not my highest, truest and best self." He also said Louis Farrakhan had no role in his campaign and there had been no public dealings with him. But he would not repudiate Farrakhan's anti-Semitism. "It's not necessary," Jackson said.

Just eight months before, in a cable TV interview, Farrakhan had said his relationship with Jackson was "cool publicly" but "maybe at core, it is warm. I'm perceived in the American public . . . as an anti-Semite, so it's not politically expedient for the reverend to identify with his brother, although privately we have discussions and talks from time to time." The interview was rebroadcast in New York two weeks before the primary.

This did not help Jackson. Yet hostility, if handled correctly, can be turned into a political plus. If Jackson had accepted the invitation of the Conference of Presidents of Major Jewish Organizations, for instance, and had been assaulted by screaming Jewish leaders who rushed the stage and attempted to tear him limb from limb, that would have been enormously helpful to him. It would have been Jesse in the Lion's Den. The headlines would have been fantastic and the TV out of this world: Jesse standing there, arms crossed peacefully over his chest, as the audience members—yarmulkes flying through the air!—gang-tackle him. Jackson goes down in a flurry of fists while singing "We Shall Overcome." He could have made a heck of a political commercial out of it.

Even if Jackson had been attacked only verbally (which was much more likely), he would have been an object of sympathy to many voters, even Jewish voters, who would have been embarrassed by the treatment he had received. Playing the victim who accepted hatred and responded with love was something Jackson did routinely. It was part of his persona. But he would not do it in New York.

Refusing to march in the Salute to Israel Day parade was equally senseless. Those who felt Jackson avoided it out of fear of assassination didn't understand Jackson. Yes, Jackson felt Ed Koch had placed his life in danger by his personal attacks. And yes, the Jackson campaign said Jackson had received three hundred death threats in New York (a number subject to the usual exaggeration). But Jackson was used to death threats, had handled them before and almost never let them change his plans.

"You can't push it aside," he said of the possibility of his own assassination. "My mission is a high-risk mission. I am aware of it and so is my family. Pain goes with it. I hear about it. My family lives braced for the danger. We pray. We continue to have faith. There is always a chance *I* may get hurt. But there is a chance *they* [that is, his potential assassins] may get healed."

His campaign plans were usually chaotic, which made protecting him even more difficult. When, after a speech in Jackson, Mississippi, in 1984 he asked how many in the audience were registered to vote and he saw too few hands, he led the crowd outside the building and down the street, a street crisscrossed by viaducts, in search of a voter registration office. The Secret Service had no time to prepare, no time to secure the route. "Suddenly, the agents started grouping the reporters right around Jackson," Linda Wertheimer of National Public Radio, who was covering him that day, said. "And they kept us very close to him, which was unusual. It occurred to me that they wanted us there to block a bullet for him if one came. I guess it was the only thing they could do, but it was creepy."

Jackson would wear bulletproof garments when the Secret Service asked him to, but he did not avoid the streets. That is not why he failed to march down Fifth Avenue in New York to salute Israel. He just didn't want to salute Israel. The day he refused to march, Ann Lewis, a senior adviser to Jackson and a former political director of the Democratic National Committee, sat in a coffee shop on Seventh Avenue and tried to explain it.

"Meeting with Jews was not going to be positive," Lewis said. (Lewis, too, is Jewish; to his credit, Jackson did try to create a rainbow of backgrounds within his own organization.) "They've made up their minds. Jackson is saddened by it. He said something I've never heard him say before. He said: 'Children in this city have been taught to fear. That's not right. Jewish children have been taught to fear me. That's not right.' "

But if Jackson was saddened that Jewish children had been taught to fear him, the logical reaction would have been for Jackson to go to a Jewish school and talk to the children there. It was the kind of campaign event he relished. It would have been meaningful and good TV.

Jackson, however, had decided he was not going to make any concessions to black-Jewish understanding by actually entering a room to meet with Jews. "If someone wants my head," he said with uncharacteristic bluntness, "why should I hand them a hatchet?"

There was something at work on Jackson in New York that bent all his thinking out of shape. It was not political. It was not strategic. It was personal. And it had to do with one of the most humiliating days of his life, the day in New Hampshire at the end of February 1984 when he had to go into a temple in Manchester and explain why he had made anti-Semitic remarks.

A few weeks before, on January 25, Jackson had been at National Airport in Washington, D.C., waiting to depart for a campaign swing through South Carolina. Sitting in a cafeteria, Jackson invited Milton Coleman, a black reporter with the Washington *Post*, to join him at his table. "Let's talk black talk," Jackson said.

Jackson apparently believed that "black talk" meant, among other things, that he would not be quoted. He had talked "black talk" with other black reporters before, using odd, ugly phrases in those conversations, and nothing had ever been written. That such sessions were not to be reported was never stated by Jackson, but he probably felt he had no need to state it. He probably felt that black reporters would not embarrass him. As it turned out, this was a bad assumption on Jackson's part (and one that underestimated and misjudged black reporters).

Coleman would later write: "He said something to the effect of the following: That's all Hymie wants to talk about is Israel; every time you go to Hymietown, that's all they want to talk about." Like most people, Coleman had never heard the expressions before, but he knew they were references to Jews and New York. Coleman didn't make much of it at the time, though he heard later from other reporters that Jackson had used "Hymie" to refer to Jews on other occasions. Jackson would later claim it was a common term where he grew up in South Carolina. Nobody knew exactly how it originated, but everyone agreed it was not meant to be a compliment. (Farrakhan would later claim, fantastically, that it was a common expression among Jews, who often referred to each other as Hyman and Hymie. This healed no wounds.)

Coleman never did a separate story about Jackson's use of the words. He told another *Post* reporter about it and the words appeared in print nineteen days after Jackson had said them, buried in the thirty-seventh paragraph of the story. But the *Post* did an editorial about it a few days later, calling it "degrading and disgusting." The editorial also asked: "What does Mr. Jackson have to say?"

Very little, as it turned out. At a news conference in Washington, Jackson said: "I deny the allegation" that he had spoken "in derogatory terms about people who happen to be Jewish." It did not become a big deal. Not until February 23 at a televised debate at St. Anselm College outside of Manchester, New Hampshire, when the story burst forth in its full ugly glory.

It was a major debate. Hundreds of political reporters were there and Barbara Walters of ABC was the moderator. She began by asking Gary Hart if he really had any new ideas (he said he did), then she asked George McGovern if he really was a viable candidate (he said he was) and then she turned to Jackson and dropped a piano on him.

First she brought up the use of "Hymie." Then she quoted Jackson as saying: "I'm sick and tired about hearing constantly about the Holocaust. The Jews don't have a monopoly on suffering." Then she brought up a *60 Minutes* interview in which Jackson said both Israel and the PLO practiced terrorism.

"Is it unreasonable to think," Walters asked Jackson, "that such statements might be interpreted as being anti-Israel and anti-Semitic?"

Jackson looked ill. You could almost hear what he was thinking: Hart gets a softball. McGovern gets a softball. But the black guy gets hit with a baseball bat. How come she didn't ask me what kind of tree I wanted to be?

Jackson said he wasn't an anti-Semite and said he had "no recollection" of using the word "Hymie." But after the debate came the deluge. Reporters who had never read the original Washington *Post* piece (at least not to the thirty-seventh paragraph) besieged Jackson as if this were a new story. And so it became a new story, a national story. After three days of media frenzy, Jackson said the "attacks" on him had become a "continuing struggle" for his campaign. His remarks about Jews were "out of context" and he still had "no recollection" of having made them. But this "constant confrontation does irreparable damage to both blacks and Jews."

Jackson was noticing one positive result, however. The angry reaction by Jews had led to a backlash in the black community, which was now circling its wagons around Jackson and supporting him even more fervently. But even that threatened to whirl out of control. On the Saturday after the St. Anselm debate, Jackson had proudly been introduced at a speech in Chicago by none other than Louis Farrakhan. In 1984, Jackson saw Farrakhan as a bridge to younger, more militant blacks. So Jackson stood with Farrakhan on the stage of the Richard R. Jones Armory at Fifty-second and Cottage Grove on the city's South Side as Farrakhan "warned" the Jews: "I say to the Jewish people who may not like our brother, it is not an individual you attack . . . You attack all of us. That's not an intelligent thing to do. That's not wise. If you harm this brother, I warn you in the name of Allah, this will be the last one you harm."

By now, even Jackson realized things were getting out of hand. Later, Farrakhan publicly warned Milton Coleman of the Washington *Post* that "one day soon we will punish you with death." Jackson did say, when asked, that Farrakhan's comments were "a bit inciting and distasteful," but added that "it does not fall on my shoulders" to repudiate Farrakhan. (By the 1988 campaign, when Jackson reminded people that he had flown to Syria to secure the release of Navy flier Robert O. Goodman, Jr., he would fail to mention that Farrakhan had accompanied him.)

The day after the Farrakhan speech, Sunday, Jackson was back in New Hampshire and his advisers were telling him he had to deal with the Hymie remarks. Turn a negative into a positive, they told him. Do a little apology, admit you're only human, gain a little sympathy.

Jackson was not happy with the strategy. It required him to admit to human frailty. But on Sunday afternoon after a forum at New Hampshire College, Jackson angrily announced to reporters that he would appear that night at Temple Adath Yeshurun in Manchester between 9 and 9:30 to make a major statement. (Actually, Jackson was lucky to find a temple: Jews made up less than 1 percent of New Hampshire's population, there were fewer than 7,000 in the entire state and only about 700 Jewish families in Manchester.)

Jews did not exactly flock to the temple to hear Jackson that night, but the place was packed. The press of the world comes to New Hampshire for its political primary every four years.

The temple was modern in design with long wooden pews that were now crowded with some Jewish families, some Jackson supporters and hundreds of reporters. Jackson entered the temple around 10 p.m. with a somber expression on his face—mea culpas were not in his usual repertoire—and went immediately to a holding room to work on his speech with aides. Finally, he emerged and walked swiftly to the front of the sanctuary. He stood stiffly at the lectern, arranging his notes. He looked unwell, but he spoke in a clear, strong voice. He admitted to the Hymie slurs and admitted that when first he had been confronted with them he had "hesitated." But, he said, "what disturbs me now is that something so small has become so large. Even as I affirm to you the term was used in a private conversation, the context and spirit of that remark must be appreciated. In private talks we sometimes let our guard down. I used it, it was thoughtless, but not in the spirit of meanness. However innocent and unintended, it was wrong. In part I am to blame and for that I am deeply distressed."

This was widely hailed in the media as an apology, though the fine points, such as what the "innocent" use of the word "Hymie" could be and why Jackson was only "in part" to blame, were never really explored. Although the Hymie comment would never be forgotten, it eventually died down as an issue. Jackson was applauded in the temple that night and applauded again at the Democratic National Convention that year when he reminded everyone that he was not perfect and that God was not finished with him yet.

But Jackson never forgot the pain of that night in Manchester. He never forgot what he believed was an orchestrated Jewish conspiracy to sink his campaign. And he never forgot the humiliation he had felt when he had been forced to admit to human error. Four years later in New York, nobody was going to make him go through it again. Nobody was going to make him bow down to meet with Jews or talk to Jews or march in their parade. He was beyond that now, bigger than that. His moral stance was beyond question and beyond criticism.

And so, to that extent, Jackson stopped reaching out. He campaigned largely in black areas in front of unquestioning crowds. And he retreated into pure showmanship like marching across the Williamsburg Bridge.

The bridge march was an odd thing for him. Jesse Jackson usually did not have to stage elaborate events. Jesse Jackson *was* the event. But the Williamsburg Bridge was a way to direct some humiliation toward Ed Koch.

The Williamsburg, a steel suspension bridge, carried 240,000 commuters a day between Brooklyn and Manhattan. Though it was eighty-five years old, with proper maintenance a bridge can last two, three or even four times as long. With proper maintenance, a bridge can last forever. But the words "proper maintenance" and "New York City" rarely go together.

In 1984, holes in the floor beams of the bridge were noticed. In August 1987, a six-foot section of the bridge's steel deck plunged into the East River, leaving a huge hole and scaring people half to death. In March 1988, engineers discovered a thirty-four-inch crack in one of the bridge's fifty-inch beams. First two, then four of the bridge's eight lanes of traffic were closed to relieve the stress and the entire bridge was closed on weekends for study.

The week before the New York primary, it was discovered that several beams had suffered a 70 percent loss of steel. The roadway, supported between two giant towers, had dropped half an inch. On Sunday, April 10, the city's chief transportation engineer closed the bridge to subway traffic. On April 11, more holes were found and Mayor Koch closed the bridge to all traffic.

It was a huge headache for commuters and a huge story. Even in a city where disaster is not merely commonplace but almost a point of pride, hurtling off a bridge and falling into the river was a bit much. "Not since Dec. 15, 1973, the day a truck carrying concrete to be used to repair the West Side Highway crashed through the highway's elevated roadbed," *The New York Times* reported, "has a single event so focused attention on the city's deteriorating infrastructure."

Infrastructure was one of the great buzzwords of the eighties. Everything seemed to be crumbling in America. Bridges, highways, sewers. But infrastructure was not exactly one of Jackson's big issues and had rarely been heard in his speeches. The Williamsburg Bridge, however, was an ideal way to hit Koch, an ideal way to rub the mayor's nose in the problems of his city.

And so on the day he could have been walking in the Salute to Israel Day parade, Jackson walked across the Williamsburg Bridge. His long black car, the windows darkened against the curious and the snipers, moved slowly across the Manhattan Bridge from Manhattan into Brooklyn. Behind Jackson were two press buses filled to the bursting point. Reporters and technicians, balancing portable computers and camera equipment, stood in the aisles and swayed and jolted over the rough roadway. As we got to the Williamsburg section of Brooklyn and bounced through a semi-industrial neighborhood of low buildings and past shops with signs in Hebrew, Hasidic Jews, wearing round black hats and vests and with the fringes of their prayer shawls peeking out from underneath their long black coats, stared at us. It would have been a nice touch for Jackson to actually hold a rally in Williamsburg, which coincidentally was a center of Orthodox Judaism in America. But Jews were not on his agenda. The rally would be saved for the other side of the bridge in the Hispanic Lower East Side of Manhattan, an easier crowd.

(Later, Jackson would set up a meeting with a few preselected, "safe" Jews in Rockefeller Center, a meeting from which the press was barred. The meeting accomplished little and was widely criticized.)

The bridge loomed before him. It had remained open to foot and bicycle traffic, but nobody was sure if permission would be granted for bringing hundreds of marchers across. So Jackson didn't ask permission. He just showed up, knowing that if anyone tried to stop him, it would be a bigger story than actually walking across the bridge.

About three hundred Jackson supporters had been bused over for the bridge walk and they joined the two hundred or so reporters, photographers and technicians. A large banner was unfurled that read: "Invest in People, Invest in America. New Yorkers for Jesse Jackson." As with all marches, getting it started was a swirl of confusion. Jackson himself picked who would get to stand next to him in front of the banner, and state legislators, union officials and even a Chicago alderman vied for places of honor.

"Let's go!" Jackson finally yelled and the marchers lurched forward up the bridge, which rose ominously in front of them. It was a towering mass of cables and utilitarian girders, looking exactly like a child's Erector Set. A very old, very beat-up Erector Set.

The Secret Service urged the press to go first. Photographers leapt up on the low restraining walls to get a better camera angle, even though a misstep of six inches would have meant plunging into the river.

"Win, Jesse, win!" the crowd chanted.

"Swim, Jesse, swim," a reporter muttered, looking at the angry waters below. The walkway across the bridge was an open grillwork, and the East River, whitecaps racing across the green-gray waters, was clearly visible below our feet.

With the exception of Jackson, who was beaming broadly, nobody seemed very happy with this particular stunt. "Move!" a Jackson aide kept bellowing into a megaphone at the reporters, who were picking their way carefully across the grillwork. "Move! Move! Move!" The Secret Service agents also felt it was essential to keep the crowd moving so that the tons of weight did not rest in any one place too long. Besides, snipers were always on their mind. Which is why Jackson was wearing his bulletproof raincoat.

"MOOOOOOOVE!" the aide kept bellowing. "We gotta MOOOOOOVE!"

Jackson stopped. Three hundred people behind him instantly began stopping and stumbling into each other. The mood was not right. As in all Jackson events, the mood was to be serious, but upbeat and hopeful. And somebody bellowing orders into a megaphone was too much like what the other side used to do in the South in the old days. Jackson motioned the aide over to him with the crook of a finger. "Be still," he told him. "Be still now." No problem was ever too small for Jesse Jackson to handle personally.

The bridge arched up higher and higher over the river. "Don't look down! Don't look down!" the reporters in front shouted. Naturally, everyone looked down.

The surprise came in the middle of the bridge. Hidden by the arch of the bridge until we came suddenly upon them was an almost extraterrestrial-looking group of men dressed in coveralls, goggles and breathing masks. They were bright orange from head to toe because that was the color of the oil-based paint they were spraying on the bridge. Much of the paint had already been sprayed on the grillwork walkway, making it wet and slippery.

One of the painters was asked why he was painting a bridge that was going to require massive repair or total replacement. He shrugged. "They tell me to paint, I paint," he said. "Maybe Ed Koch owes the painters' union a favor." "Or maybe," another painter said, "the Japanese won't take our scrap metal unless we paint it first." In New York, everyone was a comedian.

Jackson asked the three painters to pose with him, which they gladly did. But the photographers had a complaint. To get a picture of Jackson and the painters and the banner and the marchers, the photographers had to stand with their backs to Manhattan and shoot the unimpressive skyline of Brooklyn as their background. Jackson listened to the photographers' complaints. Then he nodded.

"Turn around," Jackson said to the hundreds of people around him. "Everybody turn around."

And there, on the crowded, slick grillwork of an unsafe bridge, Jesse Jackson turned around and got all those people he was now facing to move around behind him so the photographers could get their pictures. When the marchers got turned the right way around again and headed for Manhattan, they began singing a little ditty to the tune of "London Bridge Is Falling Down." It went: "Koch's bridge is falling down, falling down, falling down. Koch's bridge is falling down, long . . . live . . . Jesse!"

As the Manhattan high rises loomed nearer and people could be seen in the windows waving at Jackson, the Secret Service drew tighter around him. As usual, an agent who looked somewhat like Jackson moved away from him in order to draw sniper fire, should it come, in his own direction.

Under what was now bright sunshine, Jackson and the marchers began the descent toward Delancey and Clinton streets. The neighborhood, formerly Jewish, was now Hispanic and known in Spanglish as *Loisada*, the Lower East Side. Signs on streetlamps said: "*Vota por Jesse Jackson.*"

Jackson was handed a megaphone with a microphone attached to it and began an attempt to make bridges relevant to his message. "We must invest in people and stop the flow of drugs," he said. "Drugs are causing people to collapse. We must invest in our infrastructure to stop the erosion of the bridges that is causing our economy to collapse.

"Build bridges between races! Build bridges between religions. Build bridges between the blacks and the Jews. Build bridges! Build bridges between the Italians and the Irish. We must build bridges! We must heal. We must expand. This campaign is a campaign of hope. Invest in people! Reinvest in infrastructure! In that way, we keep America strong! Thank you very much."

Eugene Gluck, a Hasidic Jew, stood in his long black coat at the edge of the crowd and listened to Jackson's speech. Within seconds, he found himself surrounded by Secret Service agents. They demanded to see what was inside the brown paper bag he carried in his hand.

Slowly, carefully, making no sudden movements, Gluck opened the bag. And showed the agents his coffee and Danish. Both unloaded.

It was hard to fault the agents for being antsy. Gerald Austin, Jackson's campaign manager, had already accused Ed Koch of encouraging assassination. "Instead of being a healer, Ed Koch has been a divider, and that can cause irrational things to happen," Austin had said. "The message he sends is: 'If I can attack Jackson verbally, then others can attack him some other way.' Koch is a lunatic. He's a lunatic [even] by New York standards."

Uppermost in Jackson's own mind, however, was not his actual death but his political death. Things had looked so good after Michigan that campaign contributions had begun rolling in to the tune of $60,000 a day. Money goes to winners and Jackson had looked like one. But now Jackson was beginning to realize what his victory in Michigan had really meant.

And in a few days, it was clear: Dukakis won the New York primary with 51 percent of the vote to Jackson's 37 percent. Jackson had the satisfaction of winning New York City and of getting 94 percent of the black vote. But he got (according to exit polls, whose reliability can always be questioned) only 17 percent of the white vote.

In one sense, 17 percent was very good. It proved once more that Jackson was not just a candidate for blacks. But such percentages, Jackson knew, would never spell victory. And it dawned on him that it was more than the Jews who were the problem. It dawned on him that white people in general were now afraid that he might really get the nomination. And so once it looked like Jesse Jackson could win, he could not win.

Fear had become the engine that was now driving the campaign. Fear that Jackson might actually be the nominee. The real lesson of Michigan was now apparent: the guy with the best chance of beating Jesse Jackson was going to get the Democratic nomination.

"After Michigan, there was all this talk of Jackson becoming the nominee and that really locked it up for Mike," Senator Paul Simon said afterward. "Absolutely. The Michigan victory put the election on racial terms. Now, I have to say that a lot of people who were opposed to Jackson were not opposed on a racial basis. But still, after Michigan really it was all over."

Even a master campaigner, a master showman like Jesse Jackson, had run out of tricks. He still had his speeches and his poetic language and he still had his crowds and his excitement. But after New York, it would not be the same. The race would not be for the presidency anymore. It would be for history, or ego, or getting across a message. But it would not be to win the nomination.

"Can't get a headline about health care, can't get a headline about welfare hotels, can't get a headline about drugs, or affording AIDS or a falling bridge," Jackson said bitterly at a rally on the eve of the New York primary. "It's all about diversions, it's all about bright lights, and show time and deflection. It's all about jive."

After years of campaigning for President, Jesse Jackson had finally met some jive he did not like.

☆ **10** ☆

DUMBSTRUCK

"In case you . . . hadn't noticed, this is not Iowa. The natives are not friendly here."
—New York *columnist Joe Klein's advice to the presidential candidates*

MICHAEL DUKAKIS had come to woo the Jews. He stood before the Presidential Forum of the Conference of Presidents of Major Jewish Organizations and opened up his heart.

We all knew he had one somewhere.

The flags of the United States and Israel flanked the stage behind him. His wife, Kitty, a card-carrying Jew, was seated directly in front of him in the audience. There was a polite, eager, standing-room-only crowd in the large room. This was to be a major performance.

Dukakis had taken a rare day off the previous day, Sunday, because it was Greek Easter and it would not have looked good for him to campaign on such a day. So he went to see a movie and still had plenty of time to work on his speech. Advised to keep his hands out of sight as much as possible when he spoke—they tended to flutter like little birds tethered to the ends of his arms—he kept them down behind the lectern.

He smiled. He beamed. He was among friends. He rocked once on the heels of his shoes and began his speech. A speech of remembrance. He remembered, he told the audience, his first trip to Greece, visiting a synagogue in Salonika and hearing the story of the deportation and murder of the Greek Jews in World War II. "It was one of the most emotional moments in my life," he said. He remembered "standing and crying." And he would "never forget the extraordinary experience that we had over a year ago when we became personally involved in the case of a Soviet refusenik family" and when that family came to America and when the son was bar mitzvahed in Wellesley, Massachusetts, how Kitty took part in the ceremony and how "there wasn't a dry eye in the house." Including, of course, his own.

For a guy whose emotions usually ran the gamut from A to B, this seemed like an awful lot of tears. But wait, amid the tears there was also laughter. The schmaltz was really beginning to flow.

Dukakis had an anecdote to tell. Years before, he had been running for the state legislature in Brookline, a suburb of Boston with a large Jewish population, and he was an "inveterate door knocker." So he climbs up three flights of stairs in an apartment building, knocks on the door and hands a woman his card. (He hands her a *card*? What was he doing, campaigning or selling life insurance?) The woman looks at it and says: "So? How come you're Jewish with a name like that?"

"Don't worry," Dukakis tells the woman. "I'm married to a Jewish girl."

And the woman looks at him "in horror" and says: "You are?"

"And I figured I better get out of there before she asked me what we are doing about the kids!" Dukakis said, and waited for the roars of laughter and applause from the audience.

Which did not come. Because, now that you mention it, Michael, what did you do about the kids? Just what religion *were* they raised in? That is what is on the minds of a goodly number of the Presidents of Major Jewish Organizations.

Dukakis, of course, is oblivious to all of this. The undercurrents in the room just flow by unnoticed. Certain complicated, unspoken, but very real sensitivities, the stuff of which all politics, but especially New York politics, is made, are over his head. Sensitivities are not programs or positions. They are something too much akin to human emotion. Which Michael Dukakis simply does not get.

Over and over again you hear it from both his friends and his enemies: the guy is smart, smart as a whip, and an overachiever and all the rest, but he simply does not get it. And probably never will.

But all right already, by now his limitations are known to all. And not everybody in the room this day cares that much about the intricacies of religious dogma. Dukakis could raise his children as Druids for all they care. Some care much more about the intricacies of Middle Eastern politics. Which surely Michael Dukakis must understand. So let's get to the good stuff, Michael. Enough of the Georgie Jessel routine. Henny Youngman's livelihood is not in danger from Mr. Personality from Brookline up there on the stage. Let's find out what Dukakis thinks about the *intifada*, the Palestinian uprising in the Occupied Territories of Israel, the shootings, the killings, the stonings, all the rest. What is Dukakis' position on this?

Michael Dukakis is ready for this one. It has been discussed by his staff, worked on, written out. In order to beat back the challenge of Al Gore, who by now is wondering if he can convince anybody that Tipper is really a Jewish name, Dukakis has come to an important decision: he will dare to pander.

The government of Israel, he says in his speech, bears no blame, no responsibility whatsoever for the trouble on the West Bank and in Gaza and Jerusalem. None. That is Michael Dukakis' position.

Now comes the applause. Boy, does the applause come. A mensch, I told you all along, is this Michael Dukakis! Get him to stand up straight, buy him a decent suit and you could imagine him in the White House. (Where Kitty's father has been saying in speech after speech in New York that he intends to host the first seder.)

It is critically important, Dukakis tells the Conference of Presidents of Major Jewish Organizations, that the world understand "who is responsible for the turmoil and violence."

"It is not the generation of young Palestinians who have grown up in uncertainty and who have been taught by their elders to hate," Dukakis said. "It is not a government in Jerusalem that struggles to maintain order while seeking an opportunity to negotiate with responsible Arab leaders about the future of the territories. It is regrettably Arab leaders themselves, who have time and again rejected the chance to sit down with Israel and negotiate peace."

Well, there it is. There is the core of Michael Dukakis' strategy in New York: a little tears, a little laughter and a major grovel. He will tell the Jews exactly what they want to hear. He will hold them to his bosom and keep them away from Al Gore.

And if only Michael Dukakis had shut up right then, he might have pulled it off.

Because faces were beaming in the audience. Heads were nodding, chins were being stroked approvingly. But now we have a little Q&A just to prove the candidate can think on his feet. A man stood in the crowd. "What is the role of the United States in peace negotiations?" he asked. A softball.

Dukakis nodded at him. "We're not going to impose a Pax Americana on the Middle East," he said. The crowd nodded with him. Then he said in Greek and translated into English: "The sweetest honey is made only slowly." More nods. Sure, what's the big hurry with peace all of a sudden? Another thousand years couldn't hurt.

Dukakis was on a roll. These were his people now; he knew it. He took another question. What does Dukakis think about the "Three Noes?"

A flash of panic zipped across Dukakis' face. Wait, wait, give him a second. He has heard about them. Somebody was telling him just the other day. Don't tell him, don't tell him, he'll get it.

Sensing there might be a little trouble here, the questioner helped him out. He knows Dukakis knows what they are—what man running for President of the United States could not?—but just in case some reporters on the edges of the crowd don't know, the questioner will list them: "No return to the '67 borders [of Israel]. No recognition of the PLO without its acceptance of the United Nations resolutions. No Palestinian state."

But Dukakis still looked confused. The audience seemed to be speaking a language he didn't share. And language is very important in Middle Eastern affairs. You instantly reveal your politics by whether you call it "the West Bank" or "Judaea and Samaria." By whether you say the "Occupied Territories" or the "Israeli-administered" territories. Whether you say a "Palestinian state" or a "Palestinian homeland" or a "Palestinian entity."

These are the code words and phrases that everybody in the audience knew as well as they knew their own names. And in order to talk to these people, you had to talk their language. But Dukakis had a problem most governors have: a lack of foreign policy experience. And it is an open secret during the New York primary—Al Gore hammers him on it daily—that this is Dukakis' Achilles' heel.

Unfortunately for Dukakis, foreign policy takes on an exaggerated importance in New York. The ethnic stew that is New York City makes it important. People here care about such matters. And they care that their presidential candidates care. Which is why Dukakis must do well, here, right now, with this audience.

Now what was the question? Oh yes, the Three Noes. Especially the creation of a Palestinian state. O.K., Michael, deep breath now.

"It is unlikely for the foreseeable future . . ." Dukakis began and then stopped. "Uh, let me put it this way. It's for the parties themselves to the negotiations who have to make those judgments."

Whaaaaa? Heads snap upright in the audience. Features harden. Chins thrust forward. There are not only loud mutters of discontent from the presidents, but actual snorts of scorn from the press section, where more than a few reporters understand the deep doo-doo Dukakis has just stepped in.

Maybe you better tell another funny campaign story, Michael, before they grab the hook and drag you offstage.

The presidents of the Jewish organizations now wanted to know what the hell was going on. What was Dukakis saying? That he was not opposed to a Palestinian state? Or was he opposed? Al Gore was opposed. Jesse Jackson was in favor. Where was Dukakis? In the middle? And what was this "parties themselves should negotiate" business? What was that supposed to mean?

To Dukakis, phrases like this were the ones that reasonable men used. To him, it seemed so democratic. Who could argue with the parties deciding themselves?

Well, only just about everyone in the audience. The Three Noes are not called the Three Noes for nothing. They are supposed to be positions not subject to negotiation, not subject to the "parties themselves" deciding.

When Dukakis had walked into the room a half hour earlier, he felt he could not miss with this crowd. After Michigan, something very close to real panic had set in among the Dukakis forces. "We never believed Jesse could win the nomination," a Dukakis aide said, "but that didn't mean *we* would win. It meant the party might demand that a Cuomo or a Nunn step in to stop Jesse. That's what worried us." So Dukakis had only one real role in New York. To sell himself as the Jesse-stopper. And that's exactly what many Jewish voters in New York were looking for.

So the presidents in the crowd today were *ready* to support Dukakis. They *wanted* to support Dukakis. And they *would* support Dukakis, if only Dukakis would stop screwing things up.

Another man in the audience rose. "What do you see as the solution to the city of Jerusalem?" he asked Dukakis.

Jerusalem was a flash-point issue. The city possessed the holiest sites of Christianity, Judaism and Islam. From the war of Israeli independence in 1948, Jerusalem had been a divided city, ruled partly by Israel and partly by Jordan. But in 1967, after the Six-Day War, Israel had captured the entire city and had annexed it. The West Bank and Gaza, which had not been annexed, were controlled by Israel. But Jerusalem was part of Israel, its capital. A fact the United States, among other countries, refused to recognize. Yasir Arafat wanted to make Jerusalem the capital of Palestine, a state that did not exist. Not yet. There was probably no issue as emotional or knotty as the fate and future of Jerusalem. Jews who could imagine trading the West Bank and Gaza for peace could not imagine ever giving up Jerusalem. Many Palestinians felt the same way, however. And so Jerusalem was an issue inextricably bound to the emotions, feelings and aspirations of millions of people.

So what about the Israeli annexation of Jerusalem, Governor?

"I think," Dukakis said, "that issue has to be subject to negotiation."

The man just does . . . not . . . get . . . it.

A shock wave flashed through the audience. People whirled around in their seats to talk to each other. There was suddenly a violent, jabbering undertone in the room. Had Dukakis really said it? Had such words actually left his mouth? Some of the presidents half stood, as if on the verge of walking out. Dukakis backers in the audience shook their heads violently, trying to signal him to backtrack, extricate himself somehow.

By now, even Dukakis realized he had blown it. Which only increased his sense of panic. What did these people *want* from him? Hadn't they heard him say how he had cried, how he had shed actual tears in that synagogue? Don't they realize his wife is Jewish? How can anyone ask more than that?

"To Jews everywhere," Dukakis now said, trying to save things, "it [Jerusalem] is the capital and should remain the capital."

O.K., well, at least that's something. There was a smattering of applause, but the audience was now wary. The emperor might not be completely unclothed, but he was down to his BVDs. So enough screwing around, Michael. Let's get to the heart of it.

Rabbi Fabian Schonfeld of Young Israel of Kew Gardens stood up and invited Dukakis to present his bona fides, to make the leap that Gore had made: to attack Jesse Jackson and to declare that Jackson would be bad for Israel.

Dukakis' face hardened. Forget that. He was not going to smash Jackson to please these Jewish leaders. And, politically, it was the right choice. It was fine for Gore to attack Jackson. The only place Al Gore was headed was back to Carthage, Tennessee, and his Senate seat. But Michael Dukakis intended to be the nominee of his party. And he was going to need Jackson. Didn't these people realize that? His resolved stiffened, Dukakis said firmly to the crowd: "Jesse and I have differences, but I express them in as friendly a way as I can."

Rabbi Schonfeld was not pleased. "Jesse Jackson is obviously a racist in reverse and an anti-Semite!" he said. "Why has nothing been said?"

Dukakis shook his head. Maybe he didn't know that much about politics in the Middle East, but he knew about politics in America. "Each of us has to decide how to campaign. I can only be myself," he said. "I want to win the presidency and bring this country together, unite this country."

The meeting with the Jewish presidents came to a desultory end. Afterward, on the sidewalk outside, Paul Bograd, Dukakis' New York campaign coordinator, stated the obvious: "They [Jews] know who they're going to vote against. They want to know who they're going to vote for."

Dukakis got in his limo and was driven the few blocks to his next stop, the Il Vagabondo restaurant, which had a bocce ball court inside enclosed by cyclone fencing. Here he would throw a few balls and try on another ethnicity for size. But a hundred reporters were waiting to confront him outside. On the sidewalk, in blue chalk, camera positions for the networks had been marked off: Net 1, Net 2, Net 3, Net 4. People across the street in the brownstone building above Miranda's Dry Cleaners sat in their windows and watched placidly.

Dukakis, however, was not used to the kind of questions he was suddenly getting shouted at him. He was not used to damage control. He was not used to explaining what he meant as opposed to what he said. The reporters crowded closer and closer to him, spilling out into the street, stopping traffic and setting off the usual cacophony of honking horns. Microphones were thrust at Dukakis, who was all but swallowed up by the press. "Only direct negotiation will produce a permanent peace," he said, trying to explain what he really meant about a Palestinian state. "I'm for whatever environment will lead to direct negotiation."

But you don't rule out a Palestinian state? Dukakis was asked. (Gore had ruled out a Palestinian state, but not a Palestinian entity. Gore understood the code words.)

"My position is essentially Israel's position," Dukakis said. "Direct negotiation." Then he forced his way through the crowd and into the restaurant. He took off his jacket, rolled up his sleeves and put on a wireless mike for TV. He tried to put a pleasant expression on his face for the cameras. He picked up a bocce ball, flung it down the court and watched it slew off to the right.

Ever do this before? he was asked.

"No," he said without a hint of humor. "Obviously."

But bocce was only a temporary interruption to the questions on Israel. When Dukakis emerged, they continued: What did he mean about negotiations on Jerusalem? Is Jerusalem a subject for negotiation?

Finally, Dukakis' advisers had to explain it for him: Dukakis did not mean negotiations on the fate of Jerusalem. He meant negotiations for access to the religious sites in Jerusalem.

But he didn't say that! the reporters said.

But that's what he meant to say! the advisers said.

The day after his meeting with the Jewish presidents, Dukakis would awaken to read a headline in the New York *Daily News* that summed things up perfectly: "Duke is milk and honey, and waffle."

The story, written by Adam Nagourney, a regular on the Dukakis plane, didn't waste any words in pointing out what a disaster the event had been: "Gov. Michael Dukakis took a hard-line, pro-Israel position on the Middle East yesterday, blaming Arab leaders alone for violence that has wracked the region.

"But Dukakis stumbled on three litmus-test issues: refusing to criticize rival Jesse Jackson and saying that the status of Jerusalem and the question of an independent Palestinian state were open to negotiation.

"His equivocal responses even dismayed supporters . . ."

Which was the bad news. But there was some good news:

" 'I will still vote for him,' said Ruby Ruenbaum of the National Council of Young Israel, an Orthodox group. 'But I would vote for Gore if it were not for the Jackson presence.' "

So Dukakis was right after all. It did not matter if he didn't know the Three Noes from the Three Little Pigs. As long as Jackson was in the race, he would be the bogeyman who would scare voters into Michael Dukakis' arms.

But while Dukakis probably could not lose the New York primary, he could go a long way toward convincing the American people he didn't know what he was talking about when it came to foreign policy. And in the days before the primary, Dukakis had seemed intent on doing just that.

Dukakis had a meeting with the editors and reporters of the *Daily News*. There he made the statement that the current government of Israel would be willing to negotiate with the PLO if the PLO would just recognize Israel's right to exist. A *Daily News* reporter, flabbergasted at this misreading of Israeli politics, turned to Representative Stephen Solarz, who had accompanied Dukakis to the meeting, and said: "Steve, tell him."

"They're right," Solarz corrected Dukakis. Yitzhak Shamir, Prime Minister of Israel, was not about to sit down with Yasir Arafat, no matter what recognition Arafat gave.

But Dukakis would not hear of it. He would not be corrected on Middle East policy by Stephen Solarz, who just happened to be the fourth-ranking member of the House Foreign Affairs Committee and represented the most Jewish congressional district in America. So instead of admitting he had made a little mistake, Dukakis stonewalled. "I'd want to take a look myself at what Shamir said," Dukakis sniffed. "I want to take a look at what he said."

Naturally, in the stories and columns that followed the meeting, the press tore Dukakis' head off. And things got worse. At a TV debate hosted by Gabe Pressman of Channel 4 in New York, Dukakis was asked about U.S. relations with South Africa. He responded by advocating "very tough" economic sanctions and bragged about what Massachusetts had done.

"I am very proud of the fact that my state was the first state in the country to divest its pension investments in South Africa," Dukakis said.

Pressman: "On a personal level, you divested your own investments about two years ago, is that correct?"

Dukakis (hesitantly): "Well, I think it was about a year ago."

Pressman: "So, in a sense, that was too long? [Laughter from the audience.] Perhaps?"

Dukakis (weakly): "Well, I did it and . . . and . . . and . . . should have done it earlier. [Laughter from the audience.] To tell you the truth."

Even his carefully constructed displays of warmth and understanding, which his staff had to beg him to do, went wrong in New York. At a tour of an AIDS hospice, where Dukakis was supposed to show his depth of concern just as Al Gore had done with his AIDS event and just as Jesse Jackson had done with his AIDS event, Dukakis summoned up all the warmth of a 60-watt bug light.

He was asked if, as President, he would an invite an AIDS patient to the White House. It was not a big deal. Since 1.5 million people per year visit the public areas of the White House, no doubt some AIDS patients had already been there. But, astonishingly, Dukakis refused to commit himself. The reporters pressed him on the issue. Nobody could figure out why Dukakis would not say he'd invite someone with AIDS to the White House. Did he think he'd have to replace all the toilet seats? But even though Dukakis was standing at an AIDS hospice, an event chosen by his own campaign to show his deep concern, he would not make the commitment. Finally, he said: "I might." And then grumped: "I've been inviting everybody else."

At the candidate debates, Dukakis was equally reserved. Dukakis did not see these debates as a chance to be engaging. He saw them as a chance to give America yet another look at how controlled, calm and measured he could be.

At a debate at the Felt Forum in Madison Square Garden, Gore attacked Dukakis again and again but did no damage. Hitting Dukakis was like hitting a pillow. He absorbed the blow and then oozed back into place. Dukakis just stuck to his senior statesman role and waited for victory. The Riverdale *Press* captured it well the next day in its headline: "Voters Yawn and Back Duke."

After the debate, the press, supporters and the merely curious crowded up on stage. Naturally, the reporters wanted to ask Dukakis more questions about Israel. Day after day, they wanted to ask him more about Israel. Did Dukakis really believe that Israel bore no responsibility whatsoever for the current violence in the Occupied Territories? they asked. That the Israeli government had done nothing wrong?

"The Israelis themselves have objected to certain things," Dukakis said very slowly and very carefully. "I believe in maximum restraint. But if years ago, Arab leaders had done what Anwar Sadat had done, we wouldn't have this."

But what about the deportation of the Palestinians?

"I'm not going to get into details on what is or is not appropriate. It is a very difficult civil conflict," Dukakis said.

How do you feel about Israel blowing up the homes of the protesters? Dukakis was asked.

Dukakis lowered his massive eyebrows. He spoke even more slowly, as if speaking to a child. "I'm not going to get into details," he said.

Then he walked off the stage to go to a closed meeting of the Council of Jewish Organizations.

IT WAS IN NEW YORK that Michael Dukakis began to get a taste of what a real campaign might be like. It was here he began (or should have begun) to grow up, to realize that the previous primaries had been easy and that a general election campaign was going to be like New York—vigorous, dangerous, bruising.

It was also in New York that Dukakis got his first big campaign plane, one on which reporters were now in close proximity to him. On the plane one day, reporters began asking him about the United States attack on an Iranian oil platform in the Persian Gulf. Was he for it or against it? Dukakis was cautious, noncommittal, and said he wanted to think about it. Then he got up and walked to the washroom in the rear of the plane. On the way, a wire service reporter grabbed him and privately asked him the same question. Perhaps because he wasn't thinking—or perhaps because he really needed to get into the washroom—Dukakis now indicated mild approval for the U.S. attack.

At the next stop, the wire service reporter rushed off the plane and filed his story. By that evening it was big news and the other reporters on the plane were furious. "They went ballistic," a Dukakis press aide said. "They felt they had been deceived."

The aide took Dukakis aside and told him how he had to be more careful, how the campaign was becoming more complicated and how little things like this could hurt him later.

"You mean I can't go to the bathroom on my own plane?" Dukakis said.

"That's right," the aide said. "You can't go to the bathroom on your own plane."

MICHAEL DUKAKIS would win New York with 51 percent of the vote, having spent six months and $1.2 million ($800,000 of it on television commercials) organizing the state. And he would get an even bigger plane. With a bathroom of his own.

After the victory, Paul Bograd would say that one of the chief goals had been to "get him [Dukakis] into the texture and culture of the place; personalize him." And one of the great successes, Bograd said, one of the three or four key events in winning New York, was what happened when Olympia Dukakis won an Academy Award. "We got terrific press," he said.

And they did. Even though the event had to be faked.

From the very start of his presidential campaign, Dukakis had one "personalizer" line, one line that made him appear human. At each speech in each state, starting with Iowa, he would ask: "Has anybody here seen *Moonstruck*? Well, my cousin Olympia Dukakis is in it." Later he would add: "And she's been nominated for the Academy Award and I am convinced that 1988 is going to be the Year of the Dukaki!"

It always got a laugh. "Dukaki" sounded funny. (Professional comedians will tell you all words with k-sounds are funny: pickle, cockroach, Cleveland.) But in state after state, Michael Dukakis failed to mention one thing when he asked crowd after crowd whether they had seen *Moonstruck*.

He had never seen *Moonstruck*. Never had time; never really cared to, though his own cousin was in it. But as the New York primary drew near, somebody noticed a great coincidence: the Academy Awards would be announced just eight days before the primary. And wouldn't it be a great boost if Olympia actually won? Well, yes, it would. Unless she actually won and her dear, close cousin Michael, who had been invoking her name in speeches for months, had to admit he had never even seen the damn movie. So on Greek Easter Sunday, the day before the Academy Awards, Dukakis and Kitty went to the Cleveland Circle Theater in Brookline and saw it.

The next day was the meeting of Jewish presidents and the bocce ball event, which would be followed by a speech on Staten Island. To end the day, Dukakis would go to a dinner event at the Grand Ticino restaurant in Greenwich Village, the restaurant featured in *Moonstruck*. Here, Dukakis would watch the Oscar show as the TV cameras recorded his reaction to Olympia's victory or loss.

One problem, however. The Supporting Actress Oscar was to be the first one given, a little hors d'oeuvre served to the audience to encourage them to watch the whole dreary show. So Dukakis would not be able to see the Oscar presentation while at the Grand Ticino, as planned. Instead, he would have to see Olympia's moment of triumph—she did win—in a holding room on Staten Island.

Which was no good at all, his staff had realized early on in the evening. It didn't matter if Michael Dukakis felt unbounded joy watching his cousin win if the minicams weren't there to record that unbounded joy.

So his staff videotaped the Academy Awards show and played it back at the Grand Ticino restaurant. Dukakis, surrounded by TV news crews, watched it on the television set, behaving as if it were happening live. He sat in the Grand Ticino, watching the videotape, with emotions rippling across his face at the moment Olympia's name was announced as if he were watching it for the first time. As Bograd would later say, it made for "terrific press."

But an aide said later: "I felt Dukakis was definitely uncomfortable having to come up with this emotion as if he were seeing it for the first time. He got choked up at the right moment, of course. But he was uncomfortable with the fact that he had to get choked up."

How did the old joke go?

"The voters want sincerity?" asks the candidate. "Hell, I can fake that."

THOUGH DUKAKIS would win the New York primary and thereby assure his nomination, two things would be foreshadowed here that would prove cataclysmic to his presidential campaign. At the time, few noticed.

The first came during the Felt Forum debate when Al Gore delivered what was generally considered a low blow, a sucker punch, an attack unworthy of the dignity of the Democratic Party. Gore had the unmitigated gall to bring up Dukakis' policy of giving unsupervised prison furloughs to convicted murderers. Gore didn't mention the names of any of the criminals, but he said that eleven murderers had never returned from those furloughs and two others killed again while on furlough.

If Dukakis was elected President, Gore asked, would he install the same furlough system in federal prisons?

"Al," Dukakis said sourly, "the difference between you and me is that I have to run a criminal justice system. You never have. I'm very proud of my record when it comes to fighting crime."

Gore and Jackson supporters in the crowd began booing Dukakis loudly. "Answer the question!" a woman yelled at him from the audience.

"We have tough gun control," Dukakis went on. "We're tough on violent criminals . . . We have changed our program. We will not furlough lifers anymore."

And that was that. "It never went anywhere," a Dukakis aide said. "It never hurt us." Not with Democratic voters in the New York primary it didn't.

But there were a few Republicans who thought the issue was fascinating. Yes, indeed, the Republicans decided, furloughs and crime might play very well in this election campaign. If only they could personalize it somehow, remove it from the cold realm of statistics. If only they could find a . . . name. An . . . example. A . . . Willie Horton.

The second incident that previewed what would help doom Michael Dukakis also happened at a debate in New York. This one took place in Rochester on the Saturday before the primary. One of the two moderators was Bernard Shaw of CNN. And his questions, *Daily News* political editor Frank Lombardi would write, were "quirky."

"If you contracted AIDS, or your children did, would you reveal it to the public or keep it secret?" Shaw had asked Al Gore.

Gore ducked the question and nobody gave it a second thought. Shaw's other questions were equally odd, bordering on the combative. But it was a small thing, just a few strange questions during one debate in a long line of debates.

A really first-rate campaign, however, a really crackerjack campaign, might have been keeping track of what kinds of questions were asked by which journalists during the debates, the way baseball managers keep a book on what kinds of pitches are thrown by opposition hurlers.

And a really top-notch campaign might have had someone write in a notebook somewhere: "Bernard Shaw—Likes to ask quirky, very personal, highly embarrassing questions. Be careful of this guy."

A really first-rate campaign might have done it.

Nobody in the Dukakis campaign even thought of it.

☆ **11** ☆

MOST VALUABLE
PLAYER

"By the time we're finished, they're going to wonder whether
Willie Horton is Dukakis' running mate."

—Lee Atwater

HE WAS BIG. He was black. He was ugly. He was every guy you
ever crossed a street to avoid, every pair of smoldering eyes you ever
looked away from on the bus or subway.

He was every person you moved out of the city to escape, every
sound in the night that made you get up and check the locks on the
windows and grab the door handles and give them an extra tug.

Whether you were white or black or red or yellow, Willie Horton
was your worst nightmare. "I thought of all the late nights I had
ridden in terror on the F and A trains while living in New York
City," Anthony Walton, a black writer and filmmaker, would write in
The New York Times Magazine. "I thought Willie Horton must be what
the wolf packs I had often heard about, but never seen, must look
like. I said to myself, 'Something has got to be done about these
niggers.'"

Horton defied common sense, which dictated that criminals committed crimes for some reason, for some gain. Give them what they
wanted and they would leave you alone.

But Willie Horton did not care if you gave it to him or not. As he
would demonstrate at least twice, giving him what he asked for would
not make any difference. Horton liked crime. He did it for pleasure,
for power, for control.

Decent people had no defense against him. That was the most
terrifying thing of all. Capture him and take away his knife and

sentence him and put him behind bars—we pay taxes for these things!—and what would happen?

He would be given a weekend furlough. Ten times, Michael Dukakis opened up the prison doors in Massachusetts and said to Willie Horton: "Go and sin no more."

Nine times Horton followed instructions. But the tenth time, he went to Maryland and broke into a home and tied a man to a joist in the basement, slashed his chest and stomach with a knife, then beat and raped his fiancée while she screamed and screamed and screamed.

Willie Horton was a killer, a rapist, a torturer, a kidnapper, a brute.

In other words, he was perfect.

BY 1988, the average television viewer had the set on for 6 hours and 59 minutes per day. There was entertainment, sports, drama, adventure, comedy, sex, documentaries, anything. And it was free. All you had to do was put up with the commercials that paid for it all. Every week, the average viewer saw about 1,000 commercials. They became part of our lives. We could recognize the jingles, the catchphrases, the music. We could date ourselves by the time stamp that commercials placed on our memories: "You'll wonder where the yellow went, when you brush your teeth with Pepsodent." The Marlboro Man. "I can't believe I ate the whole thing!" The Gardol shield. "See the USA in your Chevrolet!" L.S.M.F.T.

We didn't "watch" commercials. They were just there. They entered into our subconscious. Which made them a very potent force in American politics.

"The [political] commercials make the American public captive in two respects," Curtis Gans, director of the Committee for the Study of the American Electorate, wrote. "Since they occur in the midst of regular programming, they cannot be readily shut off. And since their primary appeal is not to reason but rather to emotions, they are virtually unanswerable."

The first political video commercial preceded television. In 1934, Upton Sinclair, the great muckraker, ran for governor of California as a Democrat. His big issue was hardly surprising considering the country was in the depths of the Great Depression: he wanted to eliminate poverty.

To combat him, the Republicans hired an ad agency and the first political consulting firm in the country, Whitaker & Baxter, to paint Sinclair as a crazed Bolshevik.

"Whitaker & Baxter produced phony newsreels of staged events," wrote Edwin Diamond and Stephen Bates in *The Spot: The Rise of Political Advertising on Television.* "In one, dozens of bedraggled hoboes leap off a freight train. . . . Explains one bum: 'Sinclair says he'll take the property of the working people and give it to us.' In another commercial, a bearded man with a Russian accent explains why he'll vote for Sinclair: 'His system vorked vell in Russia, so vy can't it vork here?' "

The phony newsreels were shown in movie theaters all over California thanks to Louis B. Mayer, head of M-G-M and a power in the Republican Party. Though more than a half century has passed, the fundamentals of that first negative video commercial are the same that are used in negative TV ads today: fear, danger and stereotyping the enemy.

Thomas Rosser Reeves, Jr., the son of a Methodist minister, became a millionaire in the advertising business by inventing something he called the USP: unique selling proposition. If you had a candy-coated piece of chocolate, you didn't say it was "delicious" or the "best" candy in the world. You said it "melts in your mouth—not in your hand."

"We discovered that this was no tame kitten; we had a ferocious man-eating tiger," Reeves said. "We could take the same advertising campaign from print or radio and put it on TV, and, even when there were very few sets, sales would go through the roof."

Harry Truman saw the possibilities of the infant medium. At the 1948 Democratic convention in Philadelphia, Truman delivered his acceptance speech in a white suit and dark tie, which *The New York Times* noted was "the best masculine garb for the video cameras." When another speaker at the convention announced plans to dramatize high food prices by waving a piece of meat at the cameras, the publicity director of the convention insisted the speech be scheduled for something called "prime time." People were learning.

But it was Reeves who saw the real possibilities of political ads. If TV ads could sell M&Ms, they could also sell a President. So he went to Thomas E. Dewey, Truman's Republican opponent. "This could be a very close election," Reeves told him. "I can pretty much tell which states are going to be close. If you would start two or three weeks before election day and saturate those critical states with spots, it could swing the election."

Dewey wouldn't even consider it. "I don't think it would be dignified," he said.

Dewey lost. In 1948, there were fewer than 500,000 TV sets in America. Four years later, there were nearly 19 million.

And nobody ever said no to television again.

☆

WILLIE HORTON was already famous in Massachusetts by the time Michael Dukakis began his campaign for President. But in July 1988, *Reader's Digest* gave America its first in-depth look at Horton in an article the Bush campaign would reprint by the tens of thousands. The article was titled "Getting Away With Murder" and free-lance writer Robert James Bidinotto began by recounting Horton's first big-time crime.

It was October 26, 1974, and Joey Fournier, seventeen, was working alone at a gas station in Lawrence, Massachusetts. William Robert Horton, Jr., Alvin Wideman and Roosevelt Pickett entered the station, brandished knives and demanded money. Fournier gave them $276.37 and pleaded for his life.

They killed him anyway.

Minutes later one of Fournier's friends dropped by and found Fournier's lifeless body stuffed in a trash barrel. He had been stabbed nineteen times.

Horton and the two others were arrested and all confessed to the robbery, but none confessed to the murder. Horton had previously served three years in South Carolina for assault with intent to commit murder and prosecutors believed he had done the stabbing.

In May 1975, all three men were convicted of armed robbery and first-degree murder. (Just which of the three actually stabbed Fournier—or whether it was done by one or two or all three—was not established in court. Under the law, it was irrelevant who actually delivered the killing blow. Under the law, all three were guilty of murder.)

A few weeks before they were sentenced, Michael Dukakis had vetoed a bill that would have instituted the death penalty in Massachusetts. But the state had a very severe first-degree murder law, which mandated life without parole.

Under a furlough program begun by Republican Governor Francis Sargent in 1972, however, Horton and the others would be eligible for unguarded forty-eight-hour weekend furloughs. Horton was granted ten such furloughs. On the last one, from the Northeastern Correctional Center in Concord on June 7, 1986, Horton went to a movie, a church, a few stores in Lawrence, and then disappeared.

"I didn't plan to do that," he later said. "It was spontaneous. I was out of bounds in my conduct."

OVER THE DECADES, we have learned not to demand absolute, technical truth from TV commercials. The negative TV ads directed against Michael Dukakis and his furlough program never told the complete, absolute, technical truth. They were TV commercials; they didn't have to. Ads are not about facts anyway. They are about emotions. They are very often about fear. Psychoanalyst Erich Fromm was the first to note that fear was the basis for much of American advertising. The famous and long-running "ring around the collar" ads featured people embarrassed in front of their bosses or co-workers or friends by having dirty shirt collars. But they could be rescued from the future fear of humiliation by a laundry detergent.

"This general fear operates primarily on an unconscious level," wrote Hal Himmelstein in *Television Myth and the American Mind.* "The solution to our rejection comes in the form of miracles." In political ads, the miracle that will cure our problems, save our nation, reduce the deficit and eliminate our fears is a person who represents a particular way of life. Ronald Reagan understood it well. He continually promised miracles: he would build a great nation, lower taxes, spend more for defense and balance the budget all at the same time.

Eight years later, the fear was of crime and any atavistic terror that lay deep within the souls of the voters. George Bush was the miracle. He was the cure. He would keep us safe. Safe from crime, safe from harm, safe from Willie.

WILLIE HORTON left Massachusetts and went to Maryland by car. On April 3, 1987, he broke into a home in Oxon Hill, a working-class suburb of Washington, D.C. The home was owned by two people who came to be known to America as "the Maryland couple." They were Clifford Barnes and Angela Miller and they were engaged to be married.

Cliff was twenty-eight and a sales manager for a car dealership in Washington. Angi was twenty-seven and did accounting work for a development company in Virginia. They were both registered as independent voters.

At 7:20 p.m., Cliff came home from work. His wedding to Angi was two months off. She was spending the evening at a birthday party with friends.

Cliff started unbuttoning his shirt as he walked up the stairs. He stripped off his tie and went into the bathroom. While there, he heard noises from downstairs and figured Angi might have come home early.

"Angi?" he called out. There was no answer.

Willie Horton kicked in the bathroom door. He was wearing a stocking mask. Earlier in the day, he had broken into the house through the basement and had searched the place. He had found Cliff's handgun. Now he hit Cliff across the head with it, while screaming obscenities at him at the top of his lungs.

Horton pushed Cliff to the floor, tied his hands behind his back and went through his pockets. Then he led him to the basement and tied him to a two-by-four support, using telephone cord and Cliff's shirt and necktie. He blindfolded and gagged him.

Then the torture began. Horton told Cliff he was going to hang him by his neck in the basement and watch him strangle. Then he jammed the gun barrel into Cliff's eyes hard enough to blacken them. Then he rammed the gun into Cliff's mouth. Then he began slashing Cliff with a knife. He slashed him across the stomach in all directions.

"Do you know how scary it is to have somebody drag a knife across your body and never know when they're going to push it in?" Cliff said later.

Cliff told Horton where his credit cards and bank cards were. He told Horton everything Horton asked. But the torture did not stop.

About 2:30 a.m., Angi came home. She walked up to the bedroom, where she noticed a broken beer bottle and Cliff's eyeglasses. As she walked back out into the hall, Horton jumped her.

He rammed the gun into her face, grabbed her by the throat and dragged her into the bedroom. He tied her hands behind her back and blindfolded her. Then he tore open her shirt and camisole. He cut her jeans open with his knife, dragged the knife over her body and raped her.

"Total disbelief," Angi said later, describing her emotions during the rape. "Then fear. Constant fear. Constant survival mixed with fear. Do anything you can to just get out of it alive. And then if you get a chance to kill them, that's what you want. You just want to get a chance to get ahold of that gun."

After he was done, Angi tried to distract him. She asked him to get her a beer, which he did. She asked him to watch TV, which they did. All the while, Horton held the gun to the back of her neck.

Then Horton raped her again, in the living room this time with the stereo turned on. Angi tried to grab the gun, but failed. "He got really violent with me," Angi said.

She did not know if Cliff was dead or alive, but Cliff could hear her screams while she was being raped and beaten. When he heard the second attack starting, Cliff knew he might be able to escape.

"This is really terrible, but if he hadn't attacked her, raped her a second time, I wouldn't have tried to escape because the way he had me blindfolded, I couldn't really tell where he was at," Cliff said.

Cliff managed to get free. Bleeding from his many knife wounds, his clothes hanging from him in shreds, he fled the house and ran for help. He pounded on the doors of four neighbors before one let him in to call the police.

When Horton had finished with Angi, he discovered Cliff had escaped from the basement. Knowing the police would soon be there, he began loading up Cliff's Camaro with booty from the house. While he was doing this, Angi escaped through a bathroom window.

Horton took off in the car and led police on a chase northbound down the southbound lane of a nearby highway. After a shoot-out with officers in which he was wounded, Horton was captured. It was now about 7 a.m.

Horton was tried and convicted of multiple counts including rape, kidnapping and attempted murder. Prince George's County circuit judge Vincent J. Femia sentenced Horton to two consecutive life terms plus eighty-five years and refused to allow Horton to return to prison in Massachusetts until he was done serving his time in Maryland.

"I'm not going to take the chance you'll be on the streets again, because you're dangerous," Judge Femia told Horton. "You should never breathe a breath of fresh air again. You should be locked up until you die."

("I never did the rape," Horton indignantly told me. Horton was not the only person feeling sorry for Horton. The Bush campaign's use of Horton would make him into the one thing he was not: a victim. There would be stories sympathetic to him. "During this whole ordeal, nobody has cared about *me*," Horton said. "I was used. Nobody knows the truth of my innocence. Someday they will." Horton had no shortage of people wishing to tell his story. While he was in prison, he had an aide to help him screen media interview requests.)

Later, Cliff found out that while in prison in Massachusetts, Horton had been cited for eleven disciplinary violations, including possession of drugs and drug paraphernalia. Yet during that period, Massachusetts prison officials had given Horton evaluations of "excellent" and said "he projects a quiet sense of responsibility."

Dukakis eventually would call Horton's furlough a "terrible mistake." But he would never apologize to the Barneses. The Dukakis campaign said there was no need for Dukakis to apologize for something that was not his fault. The Barneses never forgave Dukakis for that.

Cliff and Angi did not return to their home (though they had to continue the mortgage payments on it). They rented a house for a while—and got five large guard dogs—before buying a new home. Cliff checks all the doors and windows each day. Angi doesn't like to go out after dark anymore and doesn't like to be anywhere alone. She is withdrawn. Cliff is angry. They don't mind admitting that their sex life suffered.

Cliff, Angi and Horton were all tested for AIDS. All tested negative, but the Barneses worry that it might show up later. They worry about that because Horton was using drugs in prison. "How many clean needles can you get in prison?" Cliff asks.

Cliff doesn't sleep well and Angi wants to sleep all the time. When she does, she keeps a knife on the nightstand. Sometimes she keeps one by the bathtub.

Every time Cliff and Angi saw Willie Horton's face on TV during the election campaign, they remembered how lucky they were to be alive.

"The last guy who met Horton wasn't so lucky," Cliff said.

WHEN ROGER AILES heard the story of Willie Horton, he immediately saw its potential as an ad campaign for George Bush.

"The only question," Ailes said, "is whether we depict Willie Horton with a knife in his hand or without it."

THE FURLOUGH of Willie Horton was a supremely rational decision. Prisons are expensive ($15,000 to keep a person in prison for a year; up to $75,000 for each new cell built) and crowded. Over the decades, many governors of Massachusetts had commuted the sentences of men sentenced to life without parole.

Some of these men were old. Some were sick. Some were of no further harm (the governors hoped) to the community. So a furlough was a way of helping a man adjust to the outside world, a world he might eventually enter even though sentenced to life without parole.

Besides, furloughs were a way of maintaining discipline. A man with no chance of getting out of prison had no reason to behave himself while in prison. He was a danger to the guards and other inmates. But the possibility of a weekend pass was an incentive for good behavior.

Nationally, first-degree murderers serve only eight years on average before they are paroled or have their sentences commuted. So Massachusetts was hardly out of step with the rest of the nation. Under Michael Dukakis, Massachusetts had one of the lowest crime and incarceration rates of any industrialized state in the country. Furloughs were cost-effective and progressive. They were sensible. Michael Dukakis understood that kind of thing. His life revolved around that kind of thing. Government was based on sense. And furloughs made sense. As do a lot of things. Until they go wrong.

LEE ATWATER always insisted he first learned about the furlough issue from the Democrats. It was one of the few things he ever gave the Democrats credit for. Al Gore had raised the furlough issue on April 12, 1988, in New York during a primary debate, though he did not name Willie Horton.

The Republicans already were looking for dirt, however. Atwater had already formed what he called his "Nerd Patrol."

"The only group that I was very interested in having report to me directly," Atwater said after the election, "was opposition research." Opposition research was headed by Jim Pinkerton, thirty, who had worked in the 1980 Reagan campaign, at the White House and at the Republican National Committee. "He had about thirty-five excellent nerds who were in the research division," Atwater said. "They came back with enough data to fill up this room."

The Nerd Patrol researched the Democratic candidates, every controversial thing they had ever said, every controversial position they had ever taken or policy they had carried out. Dukakis, as the likely nominee, soon became their chief target. In the end, the thirty-five excellent nerds produced 125,000 quotes from 436 different sources and put them all on a computer disk for instant recall.

But Jim Pinkerton, too, claimed he first heard about the furlough issue from the Democratic debate in New York. A light went off in his head. And he called one of his best Massachusetts sources, Andy Card, a former Republican legislator now working at the White House. Pinkerton asked Card about furloughs. Card filled him in on Willie Horton and more. "If you think that's bad, let me tell you about the Pledge," Card said to Pinkerton. Dukakis had vetoed a bill that would have required teachers to lead schoolchildren in the Pledge of Allegiance because the state supreme court and the attorney general had said it was unconstitutional and unenforceable. Now Pinkerton had two issues.

"It was sort of like looking for penicillin and discovering nylon instead," Pinkerton said.

So Pinkerton told Atwater about Willie Horton and a light went off in Atwater's head, too. "It's the single biggest negative Dukakis has got," Atwater said.

And that's the way the Bush campaign insisted it happened: the Democrats raised furloughs first. So go blame Al Gore for injecting Willie Horton into the campaign. Don't blame us.

But if Pinkerton really did first hear about the furlough issue from

Al Gore, he should have been fired for incompetence. (Instead, Pinkerton was sworn in as deputy assistant to the President for policy planning on January 23, 1989.)

Because Pinkerton didn't need a Nerd Patrol poring over news clippings and transcripts of Democratic debates to learn about furloughs and Willie Horton. All he had to do was read some national magazines or watch TV.

Newsweek not only wrote about furloughs three months before Al Gore mentioned them during the New York primary but also provided details about Horton. On January 25, 1988, *Newsweek*'s Boston bureau chief, Mark Starr, wrote a half-page story about a voter registration drive in Massachusetts prisons. (Massachusetts is one of the very few states where inmates can vote.) The prisoners were organizing into a voting bloc because they were worried that the furlough program would be curtailed because of the "William Horton, Jr." scandal.

"The Massachusetts program has been under attack since last April, when William Horton Jr., a convicted killer who fled while on furlough, was arrested in Maryland after raping a woman and stabbing her companion," Starr wrote.

The article did not mention Dukakis' name and was not treated as a political story. But Pinkerton could have been expected to know who the governor of Massachusetts was even without the Nerd Patrol.

And if nobody in the Bush campaign was reading *Newsweek*, that still left *Business Week*. In the March 28, 1988, issue at the end of an opinion column attacking Dukakis, there was this: "One escapee from a 'Dukakis furlough' dropped in on a Maryland couple last year, stabbing the man and raping the woman. Maryland Judge Vincent Femia locked the prisoner away for several lifetimes after refusing to return him to Massachusetts. The Boston *Herald* quoted Judge Femia: 'I am not going to take the chance that he will be furloughed or released there again.' "

Which brings up another point. The Massachusetts press had been writing about Willie Horton for months and months before Al Gore ever opened his mouth. The Lawrence *Eagle-Tribune* had done more than two hundred stories about the furlough program in 1987 and had won a Pulitzer Prize for them in March 1988. There had been public meetings, stormy debates, legislative maneuverings and a petition with 70,000 signatures to place the furlough issue on the ballot.

And even if nobody at the Bush campaign was reading any printed matter, all they had to do was watch the *CBS Evening News* on December 2, 1987, to hear all about Willie Horton and furloughs.

But Bush officials always insisted they first heard about furloughs from Al Gore. Once they heard, though, they knew what they had. "The Horton case is one of those gut issues that are value issues, particularly in the South," Atwater said. "And if we hammer at these over and over, we are going to win."

Nobody had to ask what Atwater meant by "particularly in the South." Everybody knew how the Bubba vote would react to a black man raping a white woman.

Dukakis was not especially worried about furloughs. It was a local issue. It was an old issue. He had handled it. Besides, he had all sorts of facts and figures in his defense. And on May 17, 1988, a *New York Times* / CBS poll showed Dukakis leading Bush by 10 points. On May 25, the furlough policy came up once more in the last Democratic debate in San Francisco, raised by one of the panelists. Dukakis brushed it off, and many papers, including the San Francisco *Chronicle* and *The New York Times*, didn't even mention it in their coverage. The furlough issue was not a big deal.

The next day, a Washington *Post* / ABC poll gave Dukakis a 13-point lead over Bush.

But on that same day, Bush's top handlers got together behind a two-way mirror in Paramus, New Jersey.

BY THE MEMORIAL DAY weekend the Bush campaign was in low gear. Bush had spent almost all the funds he legally could on the primaries and now, except for a few events, he had to coast until the Republican National Convention in August. It was not a good period for the campaign. Bush's negatives were high, up around 40 percent, and he was doing especially poorly with women, his so-called gender gap.

At the same time, the Democrats seemed to be sending out signals as to what kind of campaign they were planning for the general election. On May 20, Paul Kirk, chairman of the Democratic Party, had called Bush "a quintessential establishment elitist Republican" who had "neither the toughness to govern nor the compassion to care."

Bush had seethed when he heard it. This was "wimp" under a different label! But conventional campaign wisdom dictated that Bush would have to establish a strong positive image of himself before he could strike back at the Democrats.

Lee Atwater didn't care about the conventional wisdom. He believed in attack. Attack early, attack late, attack often. Attack was always good. Driving up the opponent's negatives had been his strategy in every campaign he had ever run. "I knew we had to go on the attack," he said. "If we waited until our convention to go on the attack, we would have been hopelessly behind. And I knew if we could pick the right three or four issues for a frontal attack we could shave off ten points from the polls."

Bush had retreated to his home in Kennebunkport, Maine, to powwow with his top advisers over the Memorial Day weekend. But few of his top advisers seemed to be around. Bush was around (he greeted reporters on Memorial Day with a cheery "Happy Veterans Day!" and nobody bothered to correct him), but where were the important people? "Where's Teeter?" David Hoffman, a ferociously tenacious reporter for the Washington *Post*, kept asking people. "Where's Lee? Where *is* everybody?"

EVERYBODY WAS HUDDLED at a modernistic white-sided, black-windowed office building off a shopping strip in Paramus, New Jersey, about a dozen miles from Manhattan. A marketing company hired by the Bush campaign had assembled two groups of people in a conference room. The people were being paid thirty dollars apiece to sit in comfortable blue-backed chairs around a round wooden conference table for ninety minutes. They had been carefully selected.

"They all had voted for Reagan last time," Roger Ailes explained later, "but they said they were going to vote for Dukakis this time. They were lower-white-collar, upper-blue-collar types. And they were not going to vote for George Bush. We were trying to determine why." The people were white, largely Catholic, over twenty-five years of age and making more than $40,000 per year.

They were swing voters, those people who swung back and forth between one party and another and determined the outcome of elections. (Some campaign strategists feel that each party has a base of 41 percent of the vote and the real election is a battle for the remaining 18 percent.) These particular swing voters were, in campaign terminology, "Joe Six-Pack" voters: white, urban and ethnic.

Republican consultant Stuart Spencer had identified a "Mediterranean tilt" among swing voters in general. Many swing voters were Catholic, many were Italians, and while they had supported Ronald Reagan in the past, they could be expected to feel a certain affinity for the "ethnic" Dukakis. So the Bush campaign wanted to know what it would take to swing these swing voters away from Dukakis and toward George Bush.

On one wall of the focus-group room was a huge two-way mirror. The participants were told they were being watched, but they could hardly have missed it anyway: the mirror was the size of a small movie screen. Behind it were Atwater and Ailes; Robert Teeter,

Bush's pollster; Craig Fuller, Bush's chief of staff; and Nicholas
Brady, Bush's senior adviser. They sat in upholstered white-backed
chairs and watched through the mirror as the moderator began to
tell the story of Willie Horton to the group. And then he told them
about Dukakis and his veto of the Pledge of Allegiance bill. And then
about his opposition to prayer in the schools and to capital punishment.

Some of the people reacted with outrage; almost all reacted with
surprise. They had not known these things about Dukakis. They
hadn't realized, until the moderator told them, how liberal Dukakis
really was. And they sure hadn't heard about furloughs and how he
let that guy out of jail.

At the beginning of the focus groups, all had been Dukakis
supporters. By the end of the evening, about half had switched to
Bush.

"Basically, their mouths fell open," Debra Vandenbussche, in
charge of interactive group research for Market Opinion Research,
said. "They were appalled that he would let first-degree murderers
out on furlough. There was some real strong reaction. In that hour
and a half we ended up switching as many as half the voters from
Dukakis voters to Bush voters."

Behind the mirror, just about all the Bush aides were impressed.
The reactions of the Paramus focus groups were taped and brought
back to Kennebunkport for Bush.

ROGER AILES was pretty much alone in his opposition to focus
groups. A focus group, he said, "is five professionals in a room who
say: 'We don't know what to do, so let's get twenty amateurs to tell
us what to do.' " Even so, the Bush campaign used focus groups for
everything, including testing Ailes's commercials.

But these focus groups were different from the one in Paramus.
For these later groups, citizens were gathered in Birmingham,
Alabama; Orange County, California; Livonia, Michigan; Toledo,
Ohio; Cleveland; and Chicago. These groups included Bush voters,
Dukakis voters and undecided voters and represented a broader
cross section of the public.

And no longer did the focus-group members just talk. Instead,
they were wired to a computer. Each had a device called a "perception
analyzer" that was about the size of transistor radio and had a dial
on it. You sat in a chair and watched, say, the first debate between
Bush and Dukakis. If something you saw on the screen made you
likely to vote for Dukakis, you turned the dial to the left. If it made
you more likely to vote for Bush, you turned it to the right. The

more you turned the knob in either direction, the stronger you felt. You could turn the knob for any reason. It could be a statement, but it could also be the way the candidate looked or sounded or gestured.

The focus groups were shown the primary debates, the convention acceptance speeches by each candidate and their TV commercials. Prospective one-liners for Bush to use in his first debate against Dukakis were also tested. But the Bush campaign didn't stop there. It also aired fake news broadcasts for focus groups. In these broadcasts a handsome (though somewhat beefy) actor, with dark curly hair and wearing a gray suit, white shirt and red tie, plays anchorman. As he speaks, a smiling picture of George Bush appears over his shoulder, just as it would in a real news show. "Bush said if his Democratic opponent, Mike Dukakis, was elected, Americans could expect more of the failed economic policies of the Carter-liberal Democrats," the anchorman says.

As the forty people in the focus group watched this "news" broadcast, they turned the dials on their perception analyzers. A computer instantly translated the information into a graph with three lines marching across it. The top line was the reaction of likely Bush voters, the middle line was the reaction of undecided voters and the bottom line was the reaction of likely Dukakis voters.

The graphs were then superimposed over the actual footage. Thus when Bush and his handlers wanted to see reaction to his convention speech, for instance, they could watch Bush deliver the actual speech and, ·while Bush is talking, see the graph lines travel up and down in reaction to his every word, glance and facial expression.

There on the screen was Bush delivering his line: "Read my lips— no new taxes!" and all three lines rose toward the top of the graph. But when Bush mentioned crime and furloughs, that's when he got real results.

"The graph could hardly cope," said Michael Crick, the Washington correspondent of Britain's Independent Television News, who obtained the focus-group tapes. "It convinced the Bush staff that crime was the major issue on which to attack Dukakis." And when Bush's furlough ad attacking Michael Dukakis later was screened for the focus groups, not only did the graph line of Bush voters head for the stratosphere, but so did the graph line of the undecided voters.

This was not the first time perception analyzers had been used. Comparable devices—sometimes called "people meters"—were used in 1984 by Republican pollster Richard Wirthlin, who tested reaction to the Reagan-Mondale debates. Wirthlin then used them during Reagan's second term to test reaction to his televised speeches and news conferences.

In July 1987, in a West Des Moines Holiday Inn, eighty-five Iowa Democrats, gathered by a Democratic polling firm, also had used such devices to measure reaction to the first Democratic debate in Houston. This was done mainly to show off the potential of the new technology. But not everybody was pleased.

"So you put people in a room and wire them and watch the needles go up and down," Joe Trippi, political director of the Gephardt campaign, had complained afterward. "It cost $25,000. Pretty soon, two weeks before a debate, we'll all put eighty people in a room and pay the $25,000 and find out what makes the needles go up and then we'll have the candidate say that."

Trippi talked about this with mild outrage. But the Bush campaign saw it as the next logical step in campaigning. Orwell's *1984* had come to 1988.

One of the things that made the perception analyzer groups so popular with the Bush team is that everybody loves data that confirm what they already believe. And the data from the focus groups told the Bush handlers that the furlough issue was especially potent with women. Home invasion and rape were subjects that could be expected to outrage women. And women were exactly the voters Bush needed; this could wipe out his gender gap.

Atwater could barely believe his good luck. If the Bush campaign needed Bubba and Joe Six-Pack and women, the furlough issue was one good way to get them all. Willie Horton was going to be 191 pounds of rompin', stompin' dynamite.

The Bush campaign had found its poster boy.

ON JUNE 9, at the Texas Republican state convention in Houston, Bush officially launched his negative campaign against Michael Dukakis. Though there were to be pauses in it, it would continue to election day.

Bush did not have to lead the attack himself. It could have been left to surrogates, so he could keep his own hands clean in order to lead the nation unsullied after being elected. But this idea was rejected. "We knew that if we left it to surrogates, it wouldn't have the impact," Atwater said. "Plus, Bush didn't have an image of personal meanness, so we knew he would be credible."

And George Bush did a very credible job.

"Declaring that 'today, it's a whole new ball game—spring training is over,' Vice President Bush ripped into Massachusetts Gov. Michael S. Dukakis . . . as a tax-raising liberal who let murderers out of jail and whose foreign policy views were 'born in Harvard Yard's boutique,' " David Hoffman wrote of Bush's June 9 speech. Attacking how Dukakis had given "unsupervised weekend furloughs to first-degree murderers," Bush said: "The question is: Is this who we want to put in charge of our drug program? Is this who's going to get tough with the kingpins and break the cartels?"

(Jack Katz, associate professor of sociology at the University of California, Los Angeles, would later identify an intriguing parallel between Willie Horton and George Bush: ". . . the politicians seem to be seduced by the symbolism of crime in much the same way as are street criminals, as a resource for showing themselves to be 'tough' when others might doubt it.")

"What it all comes down to," Bush said, "is two different visions."

Dukakis was not worried by Bush's speech when he read it the next day. He was even a little contemptuous of it. The presidential race, he knew, was not about "visions." It was about programs. Policies. Getting things done. It was about competency. Because, deep down, which was more important? Letting Willie Horton out of jail or creating 400,000 new jobs?

Dukakis' communications director Leslie Dach made the official response to Bush's speech: "The American people aren't interested in mudslinging and tearing down."

Yeah. Right. That would never work.

''WHO WAS THE WILLIE HORTON AD made for?" Murray Fishel, a political science professor at Kent State University, asked after the election. "It was made for the sixty-eight-year-old lifelong Democrat in Parma, Ohio, who saw it and said: 'If I vote for Mike Dukakis, Willie Horton will be my next-door neighbor.' "

ON JUNE 22, Bush used Willie Horton's name in a speech for the first time. He was speaking in Louisville to the National Sheriffs Association. "Horton applied for a furlough," Bush said. "He was given the furlough. He was released. And he fled—only to terrorize a family and repeatedly rape a woman!"

The Bush campaign knew what it was doing. Mention furloughs in a speech and that got reported. Keep mentioning it, give the press a name, and you set the press in motion. You started reporters looking into the Horton case on their own. And that would produce more stories in print and on TV. And both media liked pictures. Mention Willie Horton and you got Willie Horton's picture on TV. You never had to mention Willie Horton's race. The pictures would do it for you.

On June 27 *Time* magazine published an article about Willie Horton titled "The One That Got Away" and subtitled "Why an escaped murderer haunts Michael Dukakis." More importantly, however, *Time* did what *Newsweek* had not: it ran Horton's picture.

Menacing, evil, brooding, Willie Horton stared out from the page and into the homes of millions of Americans.

ON THE WALL above his desk at Bush campaign headquarters, Mark Goodin, deputy press secretary, pasted a mug shot of Horton. He was now a member of the team.

"I felt if we could keep the Democrats tied up until our convention," Atwater said, "we could open wounds and build their negatives up."

Building up their negatives was critical? "Some voters will go for you because of your positive message," he said. "But most of the swing voters are 'aginners'—they tend to vote according to who's on their side against the common enemy."

And everybody knew just who the "common enemy" was. Big guys who break into your home, tie you up, slash you and rape you are, generally speaking, the common enemy. And George Bush was "on your side" against those kinds of people.

Willie Horton was what the Bush people called a "wedge" issue. It was an issue that separated people. It was a "hot button" issue, one that drives people to instant anger.

"We can't worry about being too negative," GOP analyst Ed Mahe said. "If we don't get the anti-Dukakis message out, we can't win—period."

After the election, E. J. Dionne of *The New York Times* heard rumors of a Massachusetts furlough case similar to Willie Horton's, where the facts "were more devastating to Governor Dukakis, where somebody was pardoned and then murdered someone."

Dionne confronted Atwater with his suspicions at a seminar. "You never used that case, and it appears the guy is white," Dionne said.

"E.J., about what you just said, I learned about that case after the election," Atwater replied. "Frankly, had I known about it, we would have been smart to go with that and never mentioned Willie Horton. If the guy was white, there would have been zero question about our intent."

But Atwater didn't learn about that white guy until after the election. He had sources in Massachusetts, he had Pinkerton, he had the Nerd Patrol—thirty-five excellent guys tapping away at those computer keyboards!—but he didn't learn about a white example until *after* the election.

Gosh. Darn.

☆

MICHAEL DUKAKIS was still not worried. He felt he had already handled the issue. After Horton's arrest in Maryland in April 1987, Dukakis had halted further furloughs until the policy could be studied. And after outrage from both the public and the state legislature convinced him he could not really veto a bill ending furloughs, he signed it into law in April 1988. And that, he thought, was that.

Besides, the polls after the Democratic convention were very good. Oddly, the same polls that pleased Dukakis also pleased Atwater.

"I was pleased when we came out of the Democratic convention seventeen points down," Atwater said. "Being seventeen points down was a victory. Without the attacks we would have been twenty-seven points down. And I was pleased with their convention for being so ungracious and unwise in their personal attacks. It gave us all the room we wanted to be personal back."

The Democrats had been in high spirits at their convention in Atlanta. The keynote speaker said Bush had been "born with a silver foot in his mouth." And Jim Hightower, the Texas agriculture commissioner, had called him a "toothache of a man." Hightower was a genuinely funny man, in the Will Rogers mold. Humor to Hightower was the means of getting attention, of making a point.

"Mah friends," he would tell people during the campaign, "ah'll tell you, if ignorance ever goes to forty dollars a barrel, I want drilling rights on George Bush's head. Here comes George Bush, strapping on those Gucci boots he wears, got himself a little tweed farmer suit. His idea of a good farm program is *Hee Haw*. And check out his running mate, Dandy Dan Quayle. He thinks Cheerios are doughnut seeds. And as for George Herbert Walker Bush the second, he's just another Kennebunkport millionaire with four names, three home addresses, five presidential appointments and five weeks to go in his political career!"

Yep, that Hightower was one funny hombre. He believed in busting guts.

The Republicans believed in busting kneecaps.

AFTER the Republican convention in August, the polls were no longer so good for Dukakis. The negative campaign was hurting him. So Dukakis struck back. Speaking in Massachusetts on August 30, he said: "Here's a man who supported the sale of arms to a terrorist nation, one of the worst foreign policy disasters of this decade; was part of an administration that was doing business with drug-running Panamanian dictators, funneled aid to the contras through convicted drug dealers; went to the Philippines in the early '80s and commended

Marcos and his commitment to democracy—and he's talking about judgment?"

Afterward, Dukakis explained why he was now giving as good as he had gotten. "I came to a reluctant conclusion that if it continues, you have to respond," he said. "I think that's unfortunate, but I think it's very clear what kind of campaign the Republicans are running, and I think we're going to have to deal with it."

By Labor Day, the polls showed Dukakis and Bush running even. Now it was time for the Republicans to go nuclear.

Just after Labor Day, the National Security Political Action Committee (also known as "Americans for Bush") called a news conference to launch a thirty-second commercial featuring the face of Willie Horton.

Titled "Weekend Passes," it went like this:

VISUAL: Side-by-side photographs of Bush and Dukakis.
SOUND: "Bush and Dukakis on crime."

VISUAL: Picture of Bush.
SOUND: "Bush supports the death penalty for first-degree murderers."

VISUAL: Picture of Dukakis.
SOUND: "Dukakis not only opposes the death penalty, he allowed first-degree murderers to have weekend passes from prison."

VISUAL: Police photograph of a glowering Willie Horton.
SOUND: "One was Willie Horton, who murdered a boy in a robbery, stabbing him fourteen times."

VISUAL: Picture of Willie Horton towering over a police officer who has him in custody.
SOUND: "Despite a life sentence, Horton received ten weekend passes from prison. Horton fled, kidnapped a young couple, stabbing the man and repeatedly raping his girlfriend."

VISUAL: The words "Kidnapping," "Stabbing" and "Raping" appear on the screen.

VISUAL: Photo of Dukakis.
SOUND: "Weekend prison passes. Dukakis on crime."

"When we're through, people are going to think that Willie Horton is Michael Dukakis' *nephew*," Floyd Brown, a political consultant for the group, told reporters.

The group notified James Baker, the Bush campaign chairman,

that the commercial would run for twenty-eight days. It ran only on cable TV, but that didn't matter. The network news shows picked it up and used it as an example of how negative the campaign had become.

On the twenty-fifth day of the ad's run, and after considerable public criticism over the use of Horton's picture, Baker announced his official disapproval of the ad and sent a letter asking that the commercial be stopped.

Floyd Brown responded: "If they were really interested in stopping this, do you think they would have waited that long to send us a letter?"

The Bush campaign disavowed the ad and said it was made by an independent group and the campaign had nothing to do with it. But as *The New York Times* would point out in a front-page story, the ad was filmed by a former employee of Roger Ailes and the group claimed to have the tacit support of Bush officials. "Officially the [Bush] campaign has to disavow themselves from me," Elizabeth I. Fediay, the group's founder, said. "Unofficially, I hear that they're thrilled about what we're doing."

The Dukakis staff was pleased with the *New York Times* story, of course. But it couldn't help noticing that on the front page the *Times* had run a freeze frame from the commercial. It was the picture of Horton towering over his guard, with the words: "Horton Received 10 Weekend Passes From Prison."

So even when Dukakis won, he lost.

PRISONER NO. 189182 at the Maryland State Penitentiary was allowed a television set. "I had borrowed a set to keep up on the ads," Willie Horton told a reporter. "I had it in my cell. The first time I saw it was on the eleven, eleven-thirty news. With Mary Hartman. What's the name of that news? *E.T.* That's right. *Entertainment Tonight.* They had me on that.

"When I woke up in the morning, I saw the ad again. When I went to bed at night it was on again. On again the next morning. They even had it on at midnight. One night I watched a midnight show and they was making a joke of me."

Mark Gearan, Dukakis' deputy press secretary, now was beginning to see signs of Horton mania. "I knew the election was over," he said, "when I returned a phone call to a newspaper and I was told the reporter couldn't take my call because she was talking to Willie Horton."

☆

DUKAKIS UNLEASHED his own negative ads. ("I have the video-tapes of *nineteen* Dukakis negative ads," Ailes would fume after the election. "People just don't remember his because they weren't very good.") One ad showed black-and-white photos of padlocked factory gates. The announcer said: "Should there be a law to give you and your company sixty days' notice? George Bush says no."

Six days later, the Bush campaign responded with "Crime Quiz," the ad that asked: "Which candidate for President gave weekend passes to first-degree murderers who are not even eligible for parole?"

There were two pictures: Bush, brightly lit, looking handsome and clean and American. Dukakis, shrouded by a dark background, looking swarthy and foreign. Not quite as menacing as Willie Horton, but close.

Once again, the news media gave a huge boost to the Bush ad. Though "Crime Quiz" ran only in Texas and California, newspapers, newsmagazines and network TV picked it up and ran it everywhere. The three network newscasts were reaching into more than 25 million homes every night. A one-minute commercial on the nightly news cost about $90,000 and to get on all three network newscasts would cost more than a quarter of a million dollars. But the networks were running Willie Horton's picture for free.

The value to the Bush campaign was incalculable. By election day, there were few people in America who could not have picked Willie Horton out of a lineup.

THE DUKAKIS CAMPAIGN floundered for a fresh response. On September 21, it had released a five-page document titled "George Bush Distorts Mike Dukakis' Record." Within twenty-four hours, the Bush campaign responded with a 127-page refutation.

So on September 30, the Dukakis campaign aired "The Packaging of George Bush." The commercial featured actors playing the Bush handlers (one looked a little like Roger Ailes) sitting around a table and saying wry, cynical things:

"I think we need another TV commercial on this furlough thing."

"No way. They're beginning to write about Dukakis' real crime record."

"Nobody reads anymore."

"Let's hope not. First of all, Dukakis changed that furlough program. Look at this: more cops on the street, more drug offenders behind bars, crime down thirteen percent in Massachusetts."

"Just what I mean—how long do you expect to get away with this furlough thing?"

"How many more weeks to the election, Bernie?"

They laugh.

Then the announcer says: "They'd like to sell you a package. Wouldn't you rather choose a President?"

The Bush campaign conducted a focus group to test the effectiveness of the Dukakis ad. They found that people were confused. They didn't know if it was a Dukakis ad or a Bush ad.

"We didn't worry about it from then on," Ailes said.

Some Dukakis staff members were equally confused. They knew it was their commercial all right, but they couldn't figure out why Michael Dukakis was spending millions of dollars on a commercial that brought up the furlough issue.

In Texas, where the campaign was being especially hard fought, Ed Martin, executive director of the Texas Democratic Party, was near despair at how the Dukakis campaign was being run. And he didn't believe the "Packaging of George Bush" ad was the answer.

"Maybe if you tied Bubba in a chair and tortured him with cattle prods, you'd get him to pay attention through the whole thing," he said.

AILES UNVEILED the kind of ad Bubba would watch without a cattle prod. It was called "The Revolving Door." It was made by the Milwaukee ad agency of Dennis Frankenberry & Associates and it was a beaut.

It was in black and white. Grainy. Documentary style. (Marvin Baiman, a pollster who conducted a survey for *Adweek*, found that viewers frequently couldn't distinguish between ads and news. "People are confused as to what is advertising and what is not advertising," he said. This was no accident, of course. Some commercials were meant to look like news.)

Ailes might not know Erich Fromm from Erik Estrada, but he knew all about fear. In an interview with the *Gannett Center Journal*, Ailes said the Bush campaign's most effective commercials against Dukakis were "thematic" ones like "The Revolving Door." How did the commercials make people feel about Dukakis? "They're afraid of him," Ailes said.

"The Revolving Door" was a brilliant play to fear. It began with throbbing, ominous music in the background.

VISUAL: A security guard walking up the steps of a tower.

SOUND: "Governor Michael Dukakis vetoed mandatory sentences for drug dealers. He vetoed the death penalty."

VISUAL: A long line of prisoners walks slowly through a revolving door made of iron bars.

SOUND: "His revolving door prison policy gave weekend furloughs to first-degree murderers not eligible for parole."

VISUAL (on screen): "268 escaped. Many are still at large."

SOUND: "While out, many committed other crimes like kidnapping and rape and many are still at large. Now Michael Dukakis says he wants do for America what he has done for Massachusetts. America can't afford that risk."

Only a few of the men who streamed through the revolving door in the ad were black. Ailes said that he and Atwater had made sure that only "one or two" were black. But as *The New York Times* noted, the ad's "dull gray tones make it hard to identify the men by race."

Numerous stories were done about how "The Revolving Door" ranged from misleading to untruthful. The 268 escapes from Massachusetts prisons were over a ten-year period, and only four of them involved convicted murderers. And at least 72 of the 268 were not really escapees, but had returned from their furloughs more than two hours late. Only three were still at large, not "many," and none of them was a convicted murderer.

There were also long detailed stories about furlough policies across the country. On an average day around 800,000 people are in prison or jail in America and temporary releases from custody are granted to almost 10 percent of them.

But the absolute "truth" about furloughs was not the point of "The Revolving Door." Ailes wanted to create a feeling and he had. People were scared to death.

ON OCTOBER 18 Willie Horton was asked by the Gannett News Service whom he supported for President. "Obviously, I am for Dukakis," Horton said.

The next day, Dukakis was on a campaign bus, waving to supporters through an open window. Sam Donaldson came up the aisle with a camera crew and asked: "Did you know Willie Horton said he would vote for you?"

Dukakis didn't even turn around. "He can't vote, Sam," Dukakis said in a tired voice. "He can't vote."

CLIFFORD AND ANGELA BARNES went on a tour of seven California and Texas cities to speak against the furlough program.

Cliff said part of his motivation was that Dukakis had never apologized to them or shown the least bit of concern.

When he heard this, Roger Ailes went to see a psychiatrist. Not for himself. But to check out Dukakis.

"I talked to a psychiatrist about him, because I was worried Dukakis was going to turn around and start apologizing for the furloughs and everything and we'd be in trouble," Ailes said. "The psychiatrist said: 'Forget it. This is a classic narcissistic personality; he's right and everybody's wrong and he's smarter than everybody else. He'll never apologize.' "

GINGERLY AT FIRST and then more openly, the press began questioning whether the use of Willie Horton was racist. It was an obvious question and there seemed to be an obvious answer. But the Dukakis campaign didn't want any part of it. The Dukakis campaign didn't want to accuse Bush of racism. Only after the campaign did Susan Estrich, the campaign manager, explain why.

" 'We can't afford to alienate white voters,' I was told by many in my party and my campaign; whites might be put off if we 'whine' about racism," Estrich wrote. "I am not proud of our silence."

The Dukakis campaign needed Bubba and the Six-Pack vote as much as Bush did. So it kept silent about the racial aspect of the Horton attack. Which left it to Jesse Jackson to say that the Bush campaign's use of Willie Horton and "the furlough ad with black and brown faces rotating in and out of jail" was "designed to create the most horrible psychosexual fears."

Finally, when Dukakis' silence on the subject threatened to alienate his black supporters, Lloyd Bentsen, his running mate, was allowed to speak. In an October 23 appearance on *This Week with David Brinkley*, Bentsen was asked whether the Bush campaign's use of the furlough issue contained racial elements.

Bentsen paused and then said: "When you add it up, I think there is, and that's unfortunate."

After the campaign, Estrich, speaking as a white woman who had herself been raped by a black man, said: "There is no stronger metaphor for racial hatred in our country than the black man raping the white woman. If you were going to run a campaign of fear and smear and appeal to racial hatred you could not have picked a better case to use than this one."

THERE WERE MANY ATTACKS on Dukakis besides the furlough issue. He was attacked for his membership in the ACLU, his veto of the Pledge of Allegiance bill, phony reports that he had seen a psychiatrist, phony accusations that his wife, Kitty, had burned a flag while in college and even rumors that he supported bestiality.

But no issue was as potent as Willie Horton. In October pollster Lou Harris said the furlough ad and attacks on Dukakis' opposition to the death penalty had influenced voters more than anything else in the 1988 campaign. "Really more than the debates, more than anything else, they have determined the set of the election until now," he said. Some 63 percent of the voters now saw Dukakis as soft on crime as compared with 52 percent before the Bush attacks were aired. And 49 percent now termed Dukakis out of the political mainstream as compared with 34 percent before.

Time magazine declared in a headline that Willie Horton had become "Bush's Most Valuable Player."

So in the end, everybody wanted to know the same thing: why did Dukakis wait so long to respond to Bush's attacks?

But the real problem in responding to the Willie Horton ad and the furlough ad was that Dukakis had nothing to say. This was best demonstrated by a senior Dukakis aide who disgustedly pushed a piece of paper across a table at me and said: "O.K., *you* write our response to Willie Horton. You write the catchy phrase. You come up with the thirty-second spot. You come up with the jingle. What are we supposed to say? That Horton *wasn't* let out of prison and that he *didn't* rape that woman? What the hell are we supposed to say?"

The Willie Horton attack did not succeed against Dukakis because Dukakis responded to it too late. It succeeded because race and fear worked in America in 1988. And every time Dukakis responded by mentioning furloughs or Willie Horton, it only reminded people of how Dukakis had let this terrible man out of prison.

In desperation, Dukakis took another route. There is an old saying that you should never get down in the mud with a pig because you will get dirty and the pig will like it. But with his ad about Angel Medrano, Michael Dukakis got down in the mud with George Bush.

"George Bush talks a lot about prison furloughs," the Dukakis ad said. "But he won't tell you that the Massachusetts program was started by a Republican governor and stopped by Michael Dukakis. And Bush won't talk about the thousands of drug kingpins furloughed from federal prisons while he led the war on drugs."

Then the photo of Angel Medrano, a convicted heroin dealer, appeared on the screen.

"Bush won't talk about this drug pusher—one of his furloughed heroin dealers—who raped and murdered Patsy Pedrin, pregnant mother of two." Then the picture of Patsy Pedrin being carried away in a bodybag flashed on the screen.

"The real story about furloughs," the ad concluded, "is that George Bush has taken a furlough from the truth."

The Bush campaign felt that Dukakis had given up any moral superiority by running that ad. After all, the Bush campaign had never "officially" used a picture of a black man, while the Dukakis campaign had "officially" used the picture of a Hispanic.

"What about their ad about the halfway house?" George Bush asked reporters whenever they brought up his furlough ad. "Is that racism against Hispanics? That's what I think."

Michael Dukakis was sure that the voters would see through Bush's ads. "The American people can smell the garbage," Dukakis said.

But by the end of the campaign, neither side was exactly smelling like a rose.

THE BUSH HANDLERS recognized that Willie Horton had set off a hue and cry in the press. They read the analytical pieces saying they were making Dukakis look like a victim and gaining him sympathy. They read predictions that the public would become disgusted with their tactics and reward Dukakis with a victory.

They read these pieces and they shrugged them off. They were not going to change course now. By October 18, the Bush campaign had earmarked half of its remaining $30 million advertising budget for negative commercials. "We decided against changing our ad flow," a Bush aide said. "It would be foolish."

And they prepared a doomsday device just in case Dukakis turned things around in the final days of the campaign. They prepared a new negative commercial and they sent it to TV stations for safe-keeping so it could be released onto the air immediately if they needed it. It was a "Greatest Hits" commercial, one that contained snippets from all the previous attacks: furloughs, the Pledge, etc. There was no clearer sign of the Bush handlers' faith in negative ads. Let others question the ethics of negative ads. They never questioned how well they worked.

Not that the Horton campaign had no downside. It was dirty. It was vicious. It was racial. Many people were upset by it. But little of that rubbed off on George Bush.

That was no accident. The Bush campaign team knew the enormous value of compartmentalizing blame. The handlers had seen it work in the Reagan White House. The Iran-contra scandal? The Ed Meese scandal? The arms procurement scandal? All the other scandals? They all had happened on Ronald Reagan's watch, but the public did not blame Reagan for them.

Reagan was off to one side in his safe, attack-proof compartment while others took the fall. Nobody seemed to blame Reagan. The worst people said about him was that his "management style" was "detached."

The Bush campaign protected Bush in exactly the same way. It was rarely called the *Bush* furlough ad or the *Bush* attack, even if Bush was speaking the words. It was almost always the Ailes ad or the Atwater attack. Others, voters were assured, were making Bush do what he was doing. He was too nice a guy to *want* to do it.

(To make compartmentalizing work, the candidate had to yield power. The aides around him had to be credible as Svengalis. This is why the strategy worked so well for Reagan and Bush and could not work for Dukakis. Dukakis wouldn't yield power. He could barely delegate it. Which is why, both during and after the campaign, most of the criticism was directed at him.)

Bush's aides took pains to point out how Bush had to be dragged—kicking and screaming!—into going negative. Atwater told me he needed the data from Paramus not because he believed so much in focus groups—Atwater would have gone negative without focus groups—but in order to persuade Bush.

"I needed that [Paramus] to convince everyone on the staff so we could all go to the candidate united and convince him," Atwater said. "That was the purpose. When we went to Kennebunkport and explained it to him, he understood. If you have a valid point, you can make it to him."

So what was your valid point to Bush about going negative? I asked.

Atwater said: "I said to Bush: 'We're seventeen points back and they'll pick up ten more points at their convention and we won't win. Even with a good campaign we won't win. You can get so far behind that even a good campaign won't win it for you. That's what happened with Jerry Ford.' And that's what I told him."

And?

"And after that," Atwater said, "it was an easy sell."

As revealing as that anecdote is about Bush's character, it still covers up as much as it reveals. The fact is that Bush began attacking Dukakis *before* the Paramus focus groups and before the Memorial Day meeting at Kennebunkport. Weeks before Paramus, Bush had attacked Dukakis about his lack of foreign policy experience and his decision not to support the death penalty for drug dealers. And on May 25, the day before the Paramus focus groups were conducted, Bush attacked Dukakis for vetoing the Pledge of Allegiance bill.

Still, anecdotes his aides recounted always had the same point: you had to twist Bush's arm to get him to attack.

You had to twist his arm in Houston. You had to twist his arm with Dan Rather. You had to twist his arm with the Straddle ad in New Hampshire. And you had to twist his arm with the Paramus data on Willie Horton.

But viewed another way, George Bush appeared to be a man who went around with his arm stuck out saying: "Twist it! Twist it! Somebody twist it quick!"

George Bush saw early how going negative worked. A silly little put-down of Pete du Pont at the first Republican debate in Houston had won him huge accolades. And for each attack after that—against Rather, against Dole—the rewards seemed to be greater and greater. He looked more like a winner and less like a wimp each time.

George Bush wanted to win. That was his bottom line. The press would start writing about Good George and Bad George. How in the mornings Good George would tell crowds that he wanted to become the education President and how in the afternoons Bad George would attack Dukakis for being soft on crime.

But it was not a matter of Good George vs. Bad George, each struggling for the soul of the candidate. From virtually the first day of the campaign to the last, there was only Flexible George. Pliable George. Expedient George.

To him, the question was not whether it was the right thing. The question was whether it was the winning thing.

"I have no regrets," Bush told reporters shortly before election day. And he didn't.

Earlier in the campaign, on the same day Bush had first used Willie Horton's name in a speech—thus assuring Horton's picture would be on television that night—reporters had gathered around him shouting questions on the negative slant of the campaign and his use of Horton.

Bush said it wasn't a matter of being negative; it was a matter of his opponent's real record.

Then Bush raised both his arms to the sky and said: "God strike me down if I'm not telling the truth!"

All eyes followed his arms upward.

But the heavens did not open. No lightning bolt rent the sky. George Bush lowered his arms.

Some thought he looked relieved.

☆ **12** ☆

THE REDEEMER

"Dukakis called me [after the convention] and said: 'I really need to sharpen my message. You've got to help.'

"And I said: 'I'll try.'

"And he said: 'You're the best at that.'

"And that was the first non-Negro *thing Dukakis had ever said to me. The first time he recognized I could do something more than deliver him votes. The first time he recognized that I had more than* motor skills. . . .

"They go around saying Jesse has 'charisma.' Fuck charisma. . . .

"Had there been a three-man race—if Gephardt or Gore had not collapsed—I would have won *this time. . . .*

"By 1992, having me . . . on that ticket is like a reasonable expectation. That won't even be radical *by '92."*

—*Jesse Jackson to author*

Jesse Invictus. June 1988

It is the campaign that will not die. Nothing can stop it. Not losses in the primaries. Not plummeting polls. Not a stake through the heart.

In 1973, Jackson had said: "I would not run for President of the United States because white people are incapable of appreciating me." Now, in 1988, he is giving white people a chance to appreciate him. All they have to do is vote for him to wash away their sins and be saved.

In fact, Jackson has already taken their sins upon him. "I carry not only the burden of this campaign but the burden of history with me," Jackson now says. "By people concentrating on the blackness of Jesse Jackson, they do not concentrate on the Greekness of Dukakis or the Jewishness of his wife or the Italianness of Cuomo. Because of me, it is less an issue. See what I am saying? If I wasn't in the campaign, there would be much more focus on Greeks and Turks or what it means to have a Jewish wife. All that is off the table now. As it should be."

And just in case you need the image brought even more clearly into focus, try this:

"The more of a grudge you carry, the slower you run," Jackson says. "It is too heavy a burden. I beat Koch in New York by not fighting back. He kicked me and broke his foot. One of the hardest things to do is not dignify people with an attack. You always lose. Jesus on the cross. All his great works. Been in touch with his Father. On the cross dying. Some nameless, faceless person said, 'If you're the Son of God, come down.' It was a temptation to come off the cross. The blind he helped see didn't come to his rescue. The hungry he fed didn't come to defend him. And here was this guy ridiculing him. But if he had come down, he would have disproved himself. The leadership role is not to come down."

Got the image now?

"Now, after New York, Dukakis thinks we were supposed to concede," Jackson says, smiling at the thought. "I find that to be utterly unreasonable. I mean, that flies in the face of the rules of simple intelligence. Soon as I decide to act like a loser, that's what losers should do. Except I didn't lose."

Jackson is feeling better now that he is out of New York. The Jewish issue has evaporated. Now that it is clear to people that Jackson cannot get the nomination—that he is in the race to run but not to win—he excites much less anger.

Though Dukakis does not yet realize it, he is lucky that Jackson is remaining in the race. As long as Jackson hits him from the left, it makes Dukakis look like a man of the center. Lee Atwater is one of the first to see it. "Once Jackson is out of the race," he is already telling his people, "Dukakis is no longer going to look moderate. Then we've got him."

Jackson has no intention of getting out of the race. Aside from letting America down, it would cut Jackson off from the light: the light from the TV cameras and the Sunday talk shows, the light from the shining faces in the crowds. He is a man who lives for the light.

I sit talking with Jackson in Suite 819 of the Beverly Wilshire Hotel in Los Angeles on primary day in California, the last primary of 1988. The room is relentlessly gray. There are gray rugs and gray couches and gray blinds and gray walls and a long glass dining-room table on a gray marble base. Around the table sit Jesse Jackson's campaign staff, checking with him on the most picayune details: "One-on-one interviews. Eleven to noon, O.K.?"

Jackson nods, rises from the table and picks up a Stetson cowboy hat. It had been given to him Sunday at his fund-raiser at Spago. The celebrity restaurant had served $1,000-a-slice "nonviolent" pizza (the vegetables had been killed humanely).

"Now," an aide asks, reading from a long list, "should the press bus go along with us or go to the next event?"

Jackson plays idly with the hat, spinning it on his finger. He walks over and puts it on my head. It comes down to the tops of my ears. Jackson cocks his head and contemplates it. His photographer steps forward and takes a picture.

"Press bus should go along," he says. He takes the hat off my head.

Jesse Jr., twenty-three, is watching CNN on a large-screen TV. He is young, attractive and famous in a city that worships all three. But he has been working on the campaign every hour of every day, learning the family business, as it were. "I've been working on this campaign since August 9 [of 1987] and I'm sick of it," he says. "It'll take me ten years to recover."

His father gives him an unsympathetic look. The Jackson children are bright, personable and unfailingly polite. Jesse Jr. always calls people "Mr. Donaldson" or "Mr. Brokaw" and, when others are in the room, always refers to his father as "Reverend."

He now answers the door when Ted Koppel knocks.

Koppel walks in with a full entourage: an executive producer and three assistants. Jackson walks over slowly and sticks the cowboy hat on Koppel's head. It settles down around Koppel's nose. The photographer snaps a picture. Koppel whips off the hat, turns a bright red and swears. Jesse playfully grapples with him, trying to get the hat back on his head.

"Some people should not wear hats," Koppel says, laughing now, too. "I'm one of them."

Jackson has a playful nature, but much of his play is devoted to deflating the egos of those around him. When Koppel had walked in the suite it was Superstar Newsman makes his entrance. Now everybody has seen Koppel with a dumb hat on his head, wrestling around with Jackson. The chemistry in the room has changed.

Most of Jackson's aides are ushered out. Koppel does not want leaks about this meeting. Jackson sits down at the dining-room table and Koppel sits across from him. Jackson's lunch, a salad, at the insistence of his wife, has arrived from room service and he looks at it with distrust. "We're about to get a cucumber and all kinds of fruit shoved up us," Jackson says.

Jackson does not like vegetables and fruits. He likes fried chicken, fried fish, fried anything. (Jackson's press corps has printed up

T-shirts showing a chicken with a slash through it to protest their near-daily diet of fried chicken. But at least now they are being fed. In the South in March, I had traveled with Jackson for days when no food was provided at all. You would cover events from the early morning, when no restaurants were open, to late at night, when all the restaurants were closed, and so you would never eat. In desperation, reporters drew up a "Petition on Nutritional Violence" that began: "Red, black, brown, yellow, white—hunger knows no color." The reporters asked that food sufficient to sustain human life be provided the press corps each day. They would gladly pay. The petition was handed to Jackson. He read it, reached into his pocket for a pen, signed it and handed it back.)

As Jackson picks at his salad, Koppel makes his pitch. Aside from the highly acclaimed *Nightline*, Koppel now has his own show, *The Koppel Report*. And he wants to make a big splash with it. He wants to have his crews follow Jackson around twenty-four hours a day from now up until the Democratic National Convention in July.

Jackson, he knows, has no chance of being nominated. He knows Jackson has no chance even of winning California today. (Dukakis will stomp him 61 percent to 35 percent.) But Jackson is always good for a story. And in this particular story, Jackson is holding up the hoops and making Dukakis jump through them. Will Jackson demand the vice presidency? Secretary of State? Chairman of the Democratic Party? A fixed number of black seats in the cabinet and on the Supreme Court?

The day before, Dukakis and Jackson had met for ninety minutes while more than a hundred reporters milled around downstairs in the lobby waiting for news of some deal on the vice presidency. None came. Future meetings are planned.

"It's trust," Koppel says, ending his pitch. "We trust you to give us access. Starting with a debriefing on your meeting with Dukakis yesterday."

Jackson looks down at his salad. He pushes a radish a millimeter to the left and watches it roll back.

"Now, we don't expect to be there for *all* the meetings," Koppel says generously. "But we do expect you to tell us what went on. We want that kind of access."

Jesse Jr. sits at the end of the table. His father invites him to contribute to the discussion. Jesse Jr. now asks the key question. "What's the benefit, Mr. Koppel?" he says. "I mean, what's the benefit to Reverend Jackson?"

"Immediately, none," Koppel says frankly. "But five years, ten years from now, even six months, there will be a historical record of what went on."

Jesse Jackson nods. "We're going on to San Diego tomorrow," he says. Tomorrow, with the last primary over, he will go to the La Costa spa with his press corps. "We can talk in the car on the way down."

Koppel thanks him and he and his group depart.

Jesse Jr. is very unsure about the whole thing, but his father seems intrigued with the idea of a historical record. He likes the term. The sense that what he is doing is history is very strong in him.

"I wish we had it earlier," Jackson says. "There's been nothing like this in history. This has been the greatest social movement ever. It's gone beyond King. King tried to plow the ground, but the ground was too hard. This is the direction he was heading in." (Jackson is respectful of Martin Luther King, Jr.'s accomplishments, but has no problem comparing his own with them. "People are listening to me now," he said earlier. "King never had that.")

He gets up, stretches. "Rog-uh," he says, which is the way he has pronounced my name ever since I met him twenty years before, "gonna take a four- or five-minute nap."

He takes off his shirt and walks into the bedroom. There is no door between the bedroom and the living room of the suite. He takes off his pants and lies down on the bed and immediately is asleep.

Jesse Jr. tries on the cowboy hat. "Do you think I could make the cover of the *National Enquirer* with this?" he asks.

Bert Lance walks into the suite. He is now one of Jackson's most trusted advisers. Formerly he was Jimmy Carter's budget director and the man Walter Mondale had assigned in 1984 to "deal with" Jackson. Lance is a roly-poly man, resembling a large, tanned bowling pin. He is wearing a blue pinstripe suit and a white shirt. "I just came in a few days ago," he says. "I wasn't going to make five percentage points' difference in this race."

Lance, a Georgian, is Jackson's link not only to white Southerners but also to the party's power structure. A devout Methodist, he describes his relationship with Jackson as one of prayer. "I pray for him. He prays for me. And my wife, La Belle, prays for us both," he says.

Following Lance into the suite is John J. Hooker, Jr. I have seen him often during the campaign, dressed like a character from a Tennessee Williams play. This day he has on a dusty white three-piece suit and his gray hair curls out from beneath a white panama hat. Hooker always looks like he could benefit from being run through a car wash. He sits down at the table in the seat recently vacated by Jackson.

"This meal anybody's?" Hooker asks. "This yours?"

I tell him Jackson was eating it.

Hooker nods, picks up a spoon and begins shoveling the salad into his mouth. Lance looks at him and shakes his head. "We're going to have to tell people you're the Secret Service food taster," he says.

Hooker smiles through a piece of radicchio. Many assume Hooker is some kind of political camp follower, the kind that all campaigns attract. But in real life he is a millionaire Nashville lawyer, an unsuccessful candidate for Tennessee governor and senator, who made his money by founding the Hooker's Hamburgers chain. Now he is attacking the greenery on Jackson's plate as if he does not know where his next meal may come from.

Lance sits down heavily on the couch across from me and I ask him if Jackson is going to be able to get the vice presidential nomination.

He shrugs a massive shrug. "We're going to have to *finesse* that," he says. Many don't think it is worth finessing. Many can't figure out why Jackson even wants it. Benjamin L. Hooks, executive director of the NAACP, has advised Jackson not to take the post even if it is offered. "I do not believe that this nation is prepared to elect a black as Vice President," Hooks said.

Margot Kidder walks into the suite. She is wearing a pink jumpsuit and is chewing on a piece of red licorice. She looks into the bedroom and sees Jackson asleep and then sees the rest of us in the living room. "Oh!" she says. "I don't have my makeup on!"

Kidder likes to hang around the campaign, occasionally speaking at rallies and riding on the press bus. She always seems to be playing the Lee Remick role in *Anatomy of a Murder*. In their article "The Dweebs on the Bus" for *GQ* magazine, Alessandra Stanley and Maureen Dowd wrote: "In Oregon reporters got a kick out of observing actress Margot Kidder, a Jackson supporter who played Lois Lane in the *Superman* movies, as she traveled with the campaign. After she surprised Jackson offstage with what one alert Secret Service agent described as 'a huge swallow' of a kiss, reporters jokingly began humming the theme to *Superman* on the bus. But they always stopped before the candidate came within earshot."

Naturally, there is much speculation on what relationship Kidder might have with the candidate, but it is hard to believe anything is going on in a suite with no bedroom door.

And the next person to walk into the suite is Jackson's wife, Jacqueline. She is wearing a flowing robe. "Oh," she says, looking at the sleeping form of her husband and then over at us. "I'm so embarrassed. These rooms don't have doors."

None of this conversation seems to have any effect on Jackson.

"Gonna need a *crane* to get him up," Lance says.

Alan S. Bowser, a Jackson speechwriter, walks in next and introduces himself. I ask him what on earth a Jesse Jackson speechwriter does for a living. He laughs. "It's fun," he says. "We put 'talking points' on yellow pads and somehow they find their way into his speeches."

It is widely but wrongly believed that Jackson speaks extemporaneously, that somehow the words just flow from him like water from a spring. Actually, Jackson works carefully on his speeches and almost always uses notes.

We all sit and wait for Jackson to awaken. He has been sleeping about twenty minutes and we have to leave soon for a rally. But nobody wants to go in and get him up.

Bert Lance tries on the cowboy hat. It sits on his head like a derby. "Whaddyuh think?" he asks.

I tell him it looks better on him than it had on Ted Koppel.

"Well, Koppel's sort of a little fella," Lance says.

Jackson comes out of his bedroom, fully dressed and refreshed. But instead of getting ready to leave, he sits down on the couch and begins talking about the first time he stayed in this hotel.

It was in 1965 or 1966 and Jackson was in his mid-twenties. He was working for Operation Breadbasket and had come to Los Angeles on behalf of Martin Luther King, Jr., to organize a hotel boycott. "Came into town about 10 p.m. and saw one of those cheap steak houses on Wilshire," Jackson says. "Waited all night, waited until 7 a.m. for it to open, and then I went in and ordered the continental breakfast. They had a sign advertising their continental breakfast and I figured it would be a steak and grits and everything. So they bring this orange juice and roll and I ate it. And then I had me another orange juice and roll. And finally I said: 'When is *breakfast* coming?' And they told me that's what a continental breakfast is. I thought continental was like *Lincoln* Continental! What I had was a *Volkswagen* breakfast, a *Datsun* breakfast!"

Jackson laughs and laughs. "Next memorable moment in California was the McGovern campaign in 1972," he continues. "I was sitting by the pool and there were the famous reporters there: Mary McGrory, Teddy White. The blacks and the Hispanics were down at the pool. Had nothing to do. Upstairs, in the suite, the strategists were debating tactics. *We* weren't the strategists. They wanted us for our *motor skills*. So we sat around the pool for several days.

"But by 1984, I had my *own* suite. And there wasn't *anybody* at the pool. Blacks, whites, Arabs, Asians, Jews, they were all up in the suite. Everyone was involved in the process."

Jesse Jr. asks him what he is going to do about Koppel.

Jackson shakes his head. He has slept on it. There will be no TV crews haunting him these last few weeks before the convention. "It's a shame in a way," he says. "When I had much to say, there was no interest in me."

We go down to the lobby, where the tourists wait. There are always about twenty to thirty of them. They mostly are white and they have their IQ Zooms and Sure Shot auto-focus cameras hanging around their necks. They wait for a glimpse of Jackson like they wait for a glimpse of Robert Redford or Meryl Streep. With the exception of Ronald Reagan and possibly Ted Kennedy, Jesse Jackson is the only true political celebrity in America.

Jackson waves to the crowd and shakes hands and poses for a few pictures. He gets on the press bus and we head for Compton, to the last rally of his campaign. He sits in the back at a little table and goes over the talking points in his speech with a gold Cross pen. "You can't just throw information at people," he says.

The talking points say:

"Much has already been built across the country."

"Helping to expand the party and win in November."

"We have to show that economic violence can be challenged."

After one point he writes: "Quiet." A stage direction to himself. After another point he writes: "Rainbow is real."

His staff calls this process "Jesse-izing" the speeches.

"The message must be translated into the language of the masses," he says. "I had some facility with the language in high school and college. In college the issue was that if we demonstrated, the school could lose its accreditation. Some did not want to risk it. Others did. The phrases came to me: 'The issue is not about degrees but about dignity.' 'Demonstration without hesitation.' 'Jail without bail.' 'Forward march!' "

And you use phrases because they are memorable? Powerful? Quotable? I ask.

He leaned forward as if revealing a secret. "You speak in epigrams, in quotable phrases, *as a way of protecting yourself against the media*," he says.

You mean so the reporters can't change it? Misquote you?

He nods. "You protect the integrity of what you're saying. And, of course, this is a sound-bite generation. You have to say a lot in a hurry. So you develop a rhythm. 'Keep hope alive.' 'Put hope in your brains, not dope in your veins.'"

And you saw all that early on?

"As a quarterback I had to see things," he says. "I had to see the guard running a blocking pattern. The tackle running a fake. I had to see patterns. Now, I still must see patterns."

Jack Kemp was a quarterback, too, I say. Doesn't do much for his speeches.

Jackson gives me a sour smile. "There are good and bad quarterbacks," he says.

We roll through city streets. The buildings are sprayed with gang symbols and covered with "Jesse Jackson '88" posters. I ask Jackson what he would do as Vice President. He has not yet publicly stated he wants the job, but it is an open secret.

"It is not just presiding over the Senate," he says. "The office of Vice President is to be the President's No. 1 ambassador. An effective Vice President can carry out significant missions if he or she has the ability. No one stopped Bush from being the No. 1 fighter against drugs except his own lack of interest and abilities. What has stopped him from giving advice to the President? A Vice President can be involved in schools and party affairs and help interpret the party program. A creative, hard worker could help the President and help the country."

Just what Michael Dukakis needs: an activist Vice President to debate policy with him and compete with him for headlines.

If you became Vice President would it be a plus or minus for you toward later becoming President? I ask.

"In my case, probably a plus," Jackson says instantly. "The public would see me more and more in an official capacity. This country has seen me as a fighter, one who argues for the disinherited and does courageous things. But the country has not seen me operate in an official capacity."

But isn't being Vice President in some ways beneath your talents?

"Listen to this, everyone," Jackson says, raising his voice, laughing. "Listen. First it was: 'Is he presidential material?' Then it was: 'Is he electable?' Then it was: 'Why is he running?' And now, now it's: 'Is the vice presidency too small for him!'"

He grabs the armrests of the bus seat and rocks back and forth with laughter. "That's something. That's really something."

But what if you don't get the vice presidency. What if you get nothing? Don't you expect some reward?

"Certainly," he says, sobering up. "And in 1992 clearly the nomination will be in reach. I have to look at the total perspective. I am down on the five-yard line and it gets rough. But I look back at the ninety-five yards I have come. That puts everything in context."

In a few weeks, the context will become more clear. Jesse and Jacqueline will be invited to dine at the Brookline home of Michael and Kitty on July 4. Dukakis will soon have to announce his running mate and Jackson sees this as his job interview.

It is a disaster. Jackson is served a meal of white clam chowder and poached salmon. He is allergic to both. And afterward, when he has Dukakis alone and gets ready to make his pitch, Dukakis' daughters pop in the room and ask if anyone wants ice cream. Then they all go to the Boston Pops concert.

Though as they leave the Dukakis house Jackson pats his stomach for the waiting reporters and says, "Balanced meal, well cooked," after he gets to the concert he pointedly sends an aide to the concession stand for some food he can actually eat. He never gets to make his case for the vice presidency.

It is clear to those close to Dukakis that the vice presidency will never go to Jackson. But at least, they assume, Dukakis will be smart enough to "handle" Jackson, to inform him of his choice in advance and get him on board. But Dukakis doesn't. It is one of those bobbles that everybody ends up blaming on everybody else:

Somebody is supposed to call Jackson and tell him the choice is Lloyd Bentsen, senator from Texas, but nobody does. And so when Jackson lands at National Airport reporters are waiting, asking him what he thinks of Dukakis' choice for Vice President. "I'm too controlled, too mature to be angry," Jackson tells reporters. But he is furious. The phone call that never happened is something he will never forget. "They didn't call me by *design*," he tells me later. "It was designed as a public rebuke." It is a slight he will wait until election day to pay back.

The Democratic convention convenes in all its telegenic glory. And up until the very end, Jackson manages to dominate the news. There are summit meetings between him and Dukakis, this time with thousands, not hundreds, of reporters down in the lobby waiting for news.

But in the end, Dukakis holds the cards. Jackson may have the star power, but Dukakis has the delegate votes. Dukakis makes a few meaningless "concessions" to Jackson—a few Jackson aides will go on the payroll, a plane will be provided for Jackson to fly around and register voters—and that is that.

One by one, the cameras turn away. Jackson's press corps dissolves. There are other stories to pursue. The man who lives for light is now in the shadows. Jackson calls Bert Lance and asks for advice.

"I told him the time had come for him to be invisible," Lance says.

But it is the one thing Jesse Jackson cannot do, can never be.

On the Sunday before the convention convenes, Jackson preaches at the Salem Baptist Church in Atlanta. He is introduced by the Reverend Jasper Williams, who says: "In Jesse, we got hope, brothers and sisters. If Dukakis be President, what we got to hope for?"

Jackson then delivers one of the most forceful and lyrical speeches of his campaign. It is better than the one he will deliver on national TV in a few days. That speech is designed to lift the national spirit. This speech is designed to lift his own.

"It's not over till it's over," Jackson tells the cheering congregation. "And *then* it's not over!"

Jesse Agonistes. September 1988

It was over.

The eyes of the nation were turned to Wake Forest University in Winston-Salem, North Carolina, where Michael Dukakis and George Bush were about to have their first debate.

Jesse Jackson was giving a speech at the Los Angeles Trade Teachers College, a low, stucco factory-like building in a gritty industrial neighborhood south of downtown LA.

Gemma Green, Jackson's advance person, stares down the street, looking for his car. "When he had the Secret Service, it was so much different," she says. "They would radio and say: 'He's two minutes away.' Now, all I know is that if a Toyota shows up and he pops out, then he's here."

Officer Lane of the Los Angeles Police Department stands waiting at the curb. "We have no indication of any protection at all for him," he says when I ask.

When Jackson finally shows up, May Louie, his special assistant, says: "After the Democratic convention, we were given thirty days' notice by the Secret Service that we were losing our protection. We complained privately through the channels we had. But it takes an executive order from Reagan to keep it. So forget it. And we couldn't complain publicly or we would have made Jesse a target."

Jackson gets out of the car and looks around. He is accompanied by Frank Watkins, one of his closest advisers, who has been working with him since 1969. Jackson smooths his suit. It is blue with a faint blue pinstripe. He is wearing a white shirt with blue stripes and a blue tie. A pale blue handkerchief sticks out of his jacket pocket. He walks into the building and sits down behind the stage of the auditorium at a small table. He eats a chicken sandwich.

I ask him what he has been doing for the Dukakis-Bentsen ticket.

"Many people attempt to obligate me as if I was on the ticket," he says. " 'You *must* do this and you *must* do that. You *must* travel and you *must* register.' Many of the people who were hesitant"—he practically spits out the word—"who were hesitant about me being on the ticket are not hesitant about me acting as if I were on the ticket. They expect me to do more than Bentsen! Register more voters and get voter turnout. It's schizophrenia. Cultural schizophrenia. A double standard."

Jackson wants to register voters. Voter registration and the political empowerment it brings have been his big issues for years. But he also knows that the Dukakis campaign wants him only for the heavy lifting. "It is reasonable to expect me to register voters," he says, "but my contribution is in strategy and the sharpening of the message. Just to mobilize voters, but not plan strategy, is like picking cotton but not being invited to the big house."

While others had been summoned to Boston to help Dukakis prepare for the debate with Bush, the party's best debater, Jackson, was not invited. Nobody wanted to hear his strategy. They just wanted his voters.

Jackson's goal here in Los Angeles today is to get 1,000 volunteers to each register 100 voters. "They gonna bring me 100,000 new voters," he says. "Gonna do it here and in Illinois and Texas. The key is expansion."

But Jackson's expansion is a double-edged sword for the Democratic Party. Some party elders are afraid that the new voters Jackson registers are going to be the young, the radical and the black. People likely to vote for Jesse Jackson in the future, not for the white Southerner the elders yet dream of finding to lead them back to the White House someday.

Still, they need Jackson. These days, they need every voter they can get. The polls have turned around.

I ask Jackson if Dukakis' 17-point lead would have disappeared if Jackson had been on the ticket as Vice President.

"I know it would not have," Jackson says. "When you go to the championship, you get the best players from the playoff. But I was not put on the team. If they had asked me for my advice, I would have said urban mobilization was the answer."

This is the biggest substantive conflict between Jackson and Dukakis. After the election, John Sasso, Dukakis' campaign vice chairman (he came back to the campaign after the Democratic convention), would put it this way: "Jackson believed Dukakis was reaching way too far to attract the so-called Reagan Democrats, traditional Democrats who in the past couple of elections had voted Republican in large numbers. He was convinced we could not lure them back. Instead, he wanted us to concentrate on constituencies who had far more consistently and faithfully voted Democratic: blacks, Hispanics and those under economic stress. "He warned us we were slighting these constituencies, taking them for granted. We held a different view. We felt it was vital to reach out and broaden that base. This was an ongoing debate."

Jackson walks up behind the auditorium curtain and peeks out at the waiting audience. Many are wearing "Jackson 1992" T-shirts. "I have come to the top of Dr. King's mountain," he tells them later. "I may not get to the promised land. But we as a people will get there! I may not get to the White House. But we as a people will get to the White House!"

Afterward, he spends a long time making sure the people have their voter registration materials, gets their names on lists, gets people signed up. Speaking is not the point, he says as we leave, organizing is. Inspiration is not the point, using that inspiration is.

There is still no police escort outside. So we form a makeshift motorcade. It is not your usual, somber, dark-car-only Secret Service-type motorcade. There is a yellow Cadillac, a blue Cadillac, a blue van, a white van, my rented blue Toyota and a silver Corvette.

Only the lead yellow Cadillac knows where we are supposed to go and it takes off with a roar. The rest of us follow through the streets of Los Angeles, blasting through stop signs, running stoplights, drawing shouts and horns and single-finger salutes from other motorists. This is not New Hampshire, where traffic is relatively light and amateur motorcading is a common sight every four years. This is Los Angeles, where driving is a contact sport.

To keep up with the motorcade, I have to run a stoplight on Alvarado Street with my horn blaring and my lights on. The silver Corvette behind me slams on its brakes with a hideous squeal and fishtails to a stop as the cross traffic immediately fills the intersection behind me. I can see the driver throw up his hands in despair. Now he will never be able to find Jackson.

Serves him right. Chicken.

The rest of us manage to get to the United Teachers of Los Angeles building on West Third Street. There are only about a hundred people in the basement meeting room. The room has acoustic tiles in the ceiling and is lit by strips of harsh fluorescent lights. The walls are yellow and there is brown industrial-strength carpeting on the floor. A couch has been pulled up in front of a TV set. Somebody has put three small potted plants around the TV to try to rescue the room.

Jackson sits down on the couch. He scans the press area. It is not hard to scan. There is one crew from *USA Today: The Television Show*, one crew from the ABC network, one from the CBS local and one from the NBC local. There is one print reporter from *USA Today*. She is here to pick up maybe a line or two of what Jackson has to say about the debate. That's it. There is no *Time*. No *Newsweek*. No *U.S. News & World Report*. No LA *Times* or Washington *Post* or *New York Times* or *Wall Street Journal*. No AP or UPI. No radio. No buses full of reporters.

Which is what living in the shadows is like. Tonight, the lights are all in Winston-Salem.

Jackson sits with his left leg crossed over his right knee and watches the debate. He sits stony-faced with his suit jacket buttoned. He writes on a pad now and then and nods his head as the debate grinds on. He puts his hand on his chin. He leans over. "Bush is on the defensive and that was Dukakis' major challenge. Dukakis is coherent and offensive and Bush is defensive and he's getting incoherent. Dukakis has a command of the facts. This is Dukakis at his best, when he has command of the facts."

After the debate ends, Jackson does a stand-up interview with *USA Today* TV. "I chose to be here," he says. "I was invited to Winston-Salem, but I chose to be here."

Frank Watkins stands off to the side of the room. I ask him how hard the Jackson campaign is really working for a Dukakis victory.

"If we register the voters and deliver those votes, we get credit and a moral claim on the Dukakis administration," he says. "If Dukakis loses, he loses and we say: 'Hey, we told you so.' And we are in the driver's seat for the nomination in 1992.

"But if we don't register the voters, we get no credit and get no claim if Dukakis wins. And if Dukakis loses, we get blamed. So we are working hard. It's a win-win situation vs. a lose-lose situation."

If Bush wins, Jackson can run again in 1992. But if Dukakis wins, well, won't he have to wait until 1996?

"If Dukakis wins, I say on November 8 we form our exploratory committee for our run in 1992," Watkins says. "If nothing else, it gives us leverage. Dukakis doesn't want Jesse to run against him in '92. That's our leverage."

But what does Jackson want leverage for? To become chairman of the party? A place in the cabinet?

Watkins snorts at that last one. By now, Jackson knows that he is not going to get any big crumbs from the Dukakis table. "We're not going to be in the Dukakis administration," Watkins says. "Dukakis is not going to offer that."

So you're already planning to run against him in 1992 if he wins?

"Ted Kennedy ran against Carter in 1980 after endorsing him in 1976," Watkins says. "So we can do it."

Jackson does not linger at the union hall. As soon as the interview is over, he gets back in the car and the makeshift motorcade pulls out and heads for the Musicians Union Hall No. 47 on Vine. The inside of the building is done up in bunting and balloons and Dukakis posters. The crowd has been watching the debate on TV. It is getting late now and there are only seventy-five people and the ruins of a buffet. Jackson takes the stage and gives a brief speech, but he seems dispirited. The small crowd has reminded him of his new, reduced station in life.

"Even though we won a debate tonight, don't get happy," Jackson tells the crowd prophetically. "I won a few debates myself this year."

Now he glances over at the buffet table and tells the crowd what's really on his mind. "After here, I'm going to get me a serious meal," he says. "No hors d'oeuvres and beets and pickles and potato chips. Gonna get an ethnic meal. Lots of grease! Lots of sugar! Eat your hearts out!"

He comes down off the stage and talks to Watkins. "They could have put these two meetings together and made one *good* crowd," he says, shaking his head. "Why have one small crowd at one place and another small crowd at the other place?"

We get back in the cars. We drive and drive for miles through neighborhoods exactly alike. We finally arrive at Marla's Memory Lane restaurant on West King Boulevard. It is owned by actress Marla Gibbs, star of the TV show *227*. The restaurant, its walls covered with glossies of celebrities, has been reserved for Jackson. But the disco-bar next door is hopping and the noise comes through the connecting entranceway.

Jackson sits down in front of an empty buffet table that is covered by a white cloth. He waits like a patient bird of prey for the food to be brought out. But he wants to talk.

In 1984 I had written a column saying that the two candidates with the most similar campaigns were Jesse Jackson and Ronald Reagan because both eschewed "issues" and talked about values instead. This is what he wants to talk about.

"In a strange kind of way, Reagan and I represent the two wings of this country," he says. "We rose together. His has been a much more explosive rise. But that's because he's been so heavily backed, so heavily endowed. I've had to make bricks without straw.

"At this level of politics, we are the only two people in the country with identifiable followings and constituencies. People find in us the embodiment of what they feel. He's never been open to dialogue and he has a closed mind, of course. While I've striven to grow."

The first steam trays arrive from the kitchen, rich fragrances wafting out from beneath their stainless-steel lids. Jackson walks swiftly to the buffet table and takes a plate even though the waiters are still bringing out food.

"I talk to Dukakis every day," he says. "I urge him: Don't spend a lot of time in Massachusetts. Don't be reduced to a governor. Go on the offensive. Challenge Bush on Noriega! Punch and counterpunch." Jackson whirls and throws a punch that stops a half inch from my nose. "See?" he says.

"His approach to voter registration has not been smart," Jackson goes on. "His approach to the black community has not been smart."

Does he listen to you on anything? I ask.

Jackson considers this for a moment. Then says: "Dukakis called me and said: 'I really need to sharpen my message. You've got to help.'

"And I said: 'I'll try.'

"And he said: 'You're the best at that.'

"And that was the first *non-Negro* thing Dukakis had ever said to me. The first time he recognized I could do something more than deliver him votes. The first time he recognized that I had more than *motor skills*.

"I told Dukakis: 'Your position on drugs is indistinguishable from Bush's. You're both against drugs. So what? What you need to do is sharpen. Say: "You've been in charge of the war on drugs for seven years! What did you do? You dealt with Noriega!" Raise the whole arms-drugs issue. Counterpunch! Counterpunch!' "

Jackson holds his plate in one hand and punches the air with the other. Then he reaches into a steam tray filled with fried catfish and picks at one with his fingers.

If Dukakis wins, could you really run against him in 1992? I ask.

Jackson looks at me levelly. "I not only could run against him in '92, but I could make his life hell for four years," he says. "King did it to Johnson. I could do that to Dukakis."

And that is the leverage he holds. But leverage for what? He is not going to be in the cabinet. So what does he want?

"I want respect," Jackson says.

And he means it. People think it is a code word for something, but it is not. Respect is one of the most important words in Jesse Jackson's vocabulary. Respect means not sitting at the pool with the reporters while others are being invited up to the suite to plan strategy. Respect means being seriously considered for Vice President. Respect means being told about it before the press is told about it. Respect means being listened to about campaign strategy and not just being sent out into the fields to pick up votes.

"They go around saying Jesse has 'charisma.' *Fuck* charisma," Jackson says. "Charisma is of the spirit. What I do is concrete. Two plus two equals four. That's scientific. That has proof." Jackson is tired of picking up newspapers and reading about how "articulate" he is and how he "inspires" the crowds. He wants them to write about the concrete: that he registered the voters in the South that elected the Southern senators that gave a majority of the Senate to the Democrats in 1986. And those Democrats were able to keep Robert Bork off the Supreme Court. Jesse Jackson changed the course of history and why don't they write about that? he wonders. That is scientific. It has proof. Not like some bull about "charisma."

"They act like they're doing me a favor," Jackson says of the Dukakis campaign, but then shrugs. "But Dukakis has got pressure. White racist pressures. And Jews telling him that if he makes me Secretary of State, they'll never vote for him. I understand that. My relationship with the Dukakis campaign is . . . nonhostile. That is not the same as cooperation and friendship. But when it gets down to it, he got 9 million votes and I got 7 million. I got more first- and second-place finishes than he did. I got 46 out of 50."

This is Jackson's New Math, the thing that frustrates the Dukakis camp the most. Where is it written that you add up first- and second-place finishes and the total means something? Who wrote that rule? Jackson keeps wanting to change the rules as he goes along. The fact is, Dukakis won and Jackson lost and it would help everybody, they believe, if Jackson would wake up to that simple fact.

Jackson switches moods. He grows playful. The music from the disco is coming through the entranceway and Jackson bops a little to it as he stands in line for the food.

"This is the way we *Ne-groes* act at night, Rog-uh," he says. "You didn't know that, did you? Oh yes. We cut up at night." He smiles. Jackson knows I grew up on the South Side of Chicago, a few blocks from where he now lives, a place where the behavior of both Ne-groes and whites could be witnessed with some regularity.

May Louie, his assistant, sees him loosening up. "Does that mean we're going to dance later?" she asks.

"No," Jackson says, smiling and shaking his head. "Some Negroes also go to bed at night."

The buffet table is now full. A waiter in a white jacket comes up to Jackson. "Would you like a salad?" he asks.

It is the wrong question.

"Oh, man," Jackson says, "I don't want rabbit food. Let's get to the real stuff."

Jackson loads up his plate with fried chicken, corn swimming in butter, fried catfish, rice, hot buttered corn bread and peach cobbler. One steam tray remains empty and he reluctantly skips it. But as Jackson is about to exit the line, the waiter appears and fills the tray with fried potatoes. Jackson immediately returns. "Po-ta-toes," he says. "Ahhhh."

You must think cholesterol is a health food, I say to him.

He gives me a dirty look. And then tells me how he had recently been at a buffet and saw a woman eating a huge amount of food, tons of chicken and potatoes and rice—and then she put Sweet'n Low in her coffee.

"I leaned over to her," Jackson says, "and I said: 'You must think Sweet'n Low is a *laxative*.'" He laughs and laughs and wipes an imaginary tear from his eye. "I couldn't help myself. I just couldn't."

We sit down in a booth and Jackson looks over at my dessert: sweet potato cheesecake. He shakes his head. He can't believe a restaurant would ruin something as good as a sweet potato by making it into a cheesecake. "It's supposed to be pie," he says. "Sweet potato pie. Not cheesecake."

California. Go figure.

He listens to the music for a few moments, but something is still bothering him. He leans over the table.

"They are trying to pick their own cast of characters," he says. "They think blacks are fungible. 'We don't need Jesse's blacks; we got *our* blacks.' That's not smart. See what it translated to tonight? Two different meetings."

That is what has been bothering him. The small crowds at the two union halls. He can't help counting the audience wherever he goes. Jackson pushes back from the table.

"If Dukakis wins or loses, my responsibility is the same," he says. "I'm going to have to remind America there is hope."

Jesse Redux. March 1989

He sifts through the ashes and picks over the bones. He looks for signs. He mulls over the might-have-beens.

"Had there been a three-man race—if Gephardt or Gore had not collapsed—I would have *won* this time," Jesse Jackson says.

He is sitting in Maybell's Soul Queen Restaurant No. 2—"Quality Soul Food for All Souls"—on Stony Island Avenue on the South Side of Chicago. In few months Jackson will move from Chicago to Washington, D.C., where he can run for senator if Washington becomes a state, or, of course, for President. There is always that.

"We still beat everybody else in the race except Dukakis," Jackson says. "We still got more votes than any second-place finisher in history."

He still won the nomination and you did not.

"First of all, he didn't win on *merit*," Jackson says.

What is that supposed to mean?

"It means a lot of votes he inherited," Jackson says. "I earned mine. He got a lot of his because he was the other guy."

The white guy?

"Yeah. He inherited those votes."

And what does that tell us?

"I'll tell you what it tells us," he says. "In the last thirty years, those white male leaders who challenged racism properly were rewarded every time except for once." He ticks off the points: "Kennedy, a white, Catholic liberal from Boston, chose to attack Martin's being in jail. Nixon backed away. Kennedy won. Johnson took the race issue on head-on, said we've got to go another way. He beat Goldwater. Humphrey lost, but the party was split over the Vietnam War and even after that he lost only by 500,000 votes. Carter in 1976 took the race issue on frontally. He said I'm from the South, I can relate to Daddy King, and he just gave us the right ideas. And he won."

So what are you saying? I ask. That Dukakis didn't challenge racism? And that's why he lost?

"Dukakis went to Philadelphia, Mississippi, and he ducked the race issue! Just ducked it," Jackson says. He shakes his head. He still cannot believe it.

It was August 4, 1988, and Dukakis had spoken to a nearly all-white crowd at the Neshoba County Fair in Philadelphia, Mississippi. He spoke just nine miles from where James Chaney, Andrew Goodman and Michael Schwerner had been slain in the cause of civil rights twenty-four years earlier. But Dukakis' only reference to civil rights in his speech was: "Here in Mississippi, you know the importance of equal rights and civil rights. We've got to work together."

Jackson was flabbergasted, offended. Courting white Southerners was one thing, but, to Jackson, this was a desecration of history.

Now, in the restaurant, Jackson adds to the list: "Dukakis produced commercials and did not have black mayors or black congressmen in those commercials. And so he ended up appearing not to be decidedly better on the question of race than Bush."

Wait a second. Dukakis was no better on race than Bush?

"Not *decidedly* better," Jackson says. "Here Bush is playing these games and Dukakis says: 'I stand for racial justice and social whatever.'

I mean, you know, Dukakis was *different* than Bush on race. But not *decidedly* different.

"And Dukakis decided to campaign away from our base. Away from urban America. I mean, he left Atlanta with a seventeen-point lead! Michael said the night I was speaking that he saw all those black and brown faces in the audience and he knew the ticket was a shoo-in for victory. The night *I* spoke was the night of the highest TV ratings. America went for *that*. America went for *my* family.

"You know, take a look. There's a majority of Democrats in the Congress. There's a majority of Democrats in the Senate. There's a majority of Democratic governors. A majority of Democratic mayors. It takes some work to *lose* when you have that. Dukakis had to work *hard*." Jackson laughs. "Mike Dukakis had to work hard to lose!"

Had you had been on the ticket, would it have won?

"The party would have believed it could win," Jackson says. "Look: Bentsen didn't deliver Texas or the South. Miss Ferraro didn't deliver Queens, Catholics or women. But I would have delivered urban America! Blacks and Hispanics and a lot of workers. No doubt in my mind about that. So just think about that. The people who they did put on the ticket did not deliver their base constituency. I would have delivered my base constituency.

"And, you know, if I had made the vice presidency a showdown issue, I would have prevailed. Everybody knew I had earned it, that I had the popular votes, the delegate votes. But that would have split the party right down the middle based upon race. And it was a moment for me to be magnanimous."

And in the future? I ask.

"By 1992, having me, if I were to run again, or another African-American, on that ticket is like a reasonable expectation," Jackson says. "That won't even be *radical* by '92."

Jackson does see a bright side, however, in not being on the ticket in '88. It made Dukakis look even worse.

"Really, if I'd been on the ticket, Dukakis' inadequacies would never have been exposed," he says. "Everything that happened would have been blamed on me because I was on the ticket. So, really, my not being on the ticket gave him maximum options. They [the white Southerners in the Democratic Party] wanted Super Tuesday; they got it. They wanted a tight platform, not too many words; they got it. They wanted a guy for Vice President and they got the guy of their choice. He didn't carry his state, but they got it! He didn't carry the South, but they got it! And so now, look at me, I still remain. And they were obviously wrong. They got everything they asked for and failed!"

You talk like they deserved to fail.

Jackson mulls that over. "The Dukakis campaign could not deal with the Democrat who had registered the most other Democrats," he says. "They could not deal with the Democrat who fought the hardest for common ground. They could not deal with the Democrat who had put forth the issues that were adopted as the critical issues." He nods. "People like that," he says, "don't deserve to win."

But what about the future? If the future of the Democratic Party is getting white Southerners and white ethnics back in the party, how will Jesse Jackson ever help that?

Jackson makes an angry, dismissive gesture. "The future of the party is not in re-calling; it's in expanding. Our future is not the Reagan Democrats nor the Wallace Republicans. The issue is not who leads us, but who needs us."

I ask him to explain this particular piece of poetry.

"My point is, ya'll looking for the mythological white male? Well, I'll tell you what the white male is, since I'm the candidate who had a net gain of white males voting for him this time!" He laughs again. "It's true! And what did I do to get them? I went to the picket lines. I went to the family farm. I went to the hospital clinic. I went to the mortuary where their children were dead on drugs. How do you get the white male? You have him *need* you.

"I mean, people say, 'Jackson has an inside track with the black voters.' I wonder why! I wonder why! I registered them to vote. I defend them on television. I march with them. I write articles for them and preach in their churches. Shit, there ain't nothin' so *mystical* about that.

"You know, to assume that these white voters are going to leave the Republican Party while they are prospering means you don't understand organizing. You organize people where their *needs* are. I mean, that's just a basic organizing principle.

"You can't get these people unless you offer them what they need. You can't get them just because you're white. You get them because you service their *need*."

So how did Bush win them over? What needs did he fulfill?

Jackson spreads his hands flat on the table. "Bush got them on three basics:

"The perception of economic security—he sold people a bill of goods that things are well economically.

"The perception of national security—we've got somethin' going with the Russians.

"And titillating racial insecurity—we'll save you from Willie Horton.

And don't underestimate that one. Because that one does not have a price tag. That's the emotional one.

"What am I saying? I'm saying that for Goldwater, it was states' rights. It was a race thing. For Nixon, it was law and order. A race thing. For Reagan, the welfare queen. The race thing. For Bush, it was Willie Horton. The race thing. So the Republicans played the race thing once again."

But if the forces of race are so strong, how will you ever defeat them?

"I'll tell you what," Jackson says. "The same people who once said 'never' on slavery, now they say 'never again' on racial segregation. The slavemasters had the power, but the abolitionists now prevail. Those who don't have the back of the bus as a frame of reference may get discouraged. But not me. I mean, folks think we *lost* this time. Can you believe that?"

Well, yes. I mean you did lose, didn't you?

He shakes his head.

"Look," he says. "We had a net gain of voter registration. We had a net gain of knowledge. A net gain of experience. We won. We won in every conceivable way.

"I mean, if you think I lost, who is there a world demand for today? Who do people want to see? Who do people want to come out and hear? Who do people want to help them?

"Dukakis? Or me?"

SO WHAT DOES Jesse want? Respect. A place in history. And this:

It is a warm night in May 1988 in Southern California, a few weeks before the primary. The crickets are chirping on the quickly darkening streets.

The bus pulls up to the New Revelation Baptist Church in Pasadena. Jesse Jackson sits up straight in his seat. He stops talking and looks out the window.

The sidewalks are crowded with people. Some run through the streets to keep up with the bus.

"Look, Rog-uh," Jackson says, pointing out the window. "See? White. Hispanic. Black."

He gets up and stands in the aisle so the people can see him better. He smiles and makes a thumbs-up gesture.

"Despair abounds," he says. "But hope abounds more."

The bus comes to a stop. The people press against it, flattening their hands against the windows. They shout his name. We can hear them, muffled, through the glass.

The bus doors open with a sigh. Jackson steps out. The crowd surges toward him.

Jackson bends down and picks up a child. His name is Tony Loving. He is eight. His mother is Myrna Loving.

"Lord have mercy!" Jackson shouts, laughing, lifting Tony Loving high into the air.

Then he runs. He puts back his head and laughs and runs down the darkened streets carrying the boy with him. His face flashing in and out of the streetlights, he runs.

Myrna Loving runs after him, laughing. The Secret Service men run. The reporters run.

The TV cameras probe the darkness with their cones of light, catching Jackson in them and making him glow. He stands now surrounded by a sea of shining faces, a sea of people shouting his name and reaching out to him.

"Rog-uh, look," Jackson says, the child giggling in his hands. "Look? Do you see it? It's what I mean. Don't you see it? It's not politics. It's love, Rog-uh. It's *love!*"

☆ **13** ☆

BUSH LITE

"But our family is close. We're strong. And we came to the bottom line that first and obviously I'd be interested in being Vice President or President *someday. We had talked about it. . . .*

"Because, I'll be honest with you . . . I think Marilyn and I had a one-minute conversation one time whether I would even perhaps, maybe, sometime run myself [*for President*] *in 1988. And in this one-minute conversation, I . . . said* no, *not this time, George Bush is there,* [*and*] *we'd have to take two years away from the family."*

— Dan Quayle to author, emphasis added

THE MAN WAS spitting at Dan Quayle. They were only inches apart, both of them trapped in the crush of the crowd, and flecks of spit were flying from the man's mouth as he shrieked at the candidate.

"Barbecue the Quayle!" the man bleated.

Quayle looked away from the guy.

The man took a deep breath, filling his lungs for another, louder attack. Perhaps Quayle might not be grasping the cleverness of his bon mot, the play on words, as it were. And so, like someone shouting to a foreigner as if volume could make up for a lack of understanding, the man screamed again: "Barbecue the Quayle!"

Quayle looked around the guy.

The man was in his forties and neatly dressed in a blue windbreaker and chinos. His hair was wavy and lined with gray. Like many of Quayle's hecklers, he did not look like a heckler.

"Barbecue the Quayle," he croaked, weakening, hoarse now with effort.

Quayle looked through the guy.

The man's chest was heaving as he summoned up strength for one final assault. But now the Secret Service agents around Quayle moved, thrusting a hip here, throwing out a forearm there, opening up a narrow passage through the crowd. This was an elbow event, hated and feared by the candidates and the Secret Service alike. Elbow events are crowds that engulf the candidate, where walking space can be cleared only by the elbows and body checks of the agents. Protecting the candidate from assault is nearly impossible. "When you get to an event and the Secret Service comes out and says, 'We've had this warning or that,' " Quayle had said, "you say: 'Well, you do the best you can.' "

At elbow events the agents concentrate on trying to give the candidate a few inches in which he can have some space to himself. But even this can be difficult. The crowds tug at him and touch him, press on him and maul him. It is not always a sign of popularity. Sometimes the people do it to assure themselves that these men they are used to seeing only on TV are actually real, alive, breathing.

Here at the Mallard Creek Barbecue outside Charlotte, North Carolina, the crowd had been on top of Quayle ever since he emerged from his long blue limo. At first, it looked like a friendly and supportive crowd, the kind that would welcome a local prizefighter back to his old neighborhood after a bruising bout. "You're *better* than Kennedy," a man in overalls and a battered hat yelled at Quayle. "Better."

Quayle reacted with a small, tentative smile, glancing quickly at the man and then quickly away as if waiting for a blow to fall. Was this a supporter or a heckler in disguise? Was the Kennedy remark genuine or a prelude to an insult? You could see this look on Dan Quayle's face at event after event. It was the look of a battered child so abused that he no longer can accept affection without suspicion. So now he is always watchful, always waiting for the worst.

For Dan Quayle, the candy bar would always contain razor blades.

Nor was it simple paranoia. As the saying goes, even paranoids have enemies. The previous Sunday, Quayle had attended Mass at Transfiguration Roman Catholic Church in a Polish neighborhood of Cleveland. It was one of his rare joint appearances with George Bush and Quayle wanted to shine, to be at his best, to show that he was pulling his own weight and not dragging down the ticket. Quayle, his wife, Marilyn, Bush and Barbara sat in the front row of the church. And as "Ave Maria" played in the background, Samuel Scaffidi, a retired doctor and combat veteran of World War II, rose after having received Holy Communion, turned to Quayle and snarled: "You're a draft dodger."

Quayle was stunned speechless.

"He was shocked," Scaffidi said afterward. "He just looked at me.

He does not deserve to be Vice President. He is a draft dodger of the first class."

So now Quayle was always on guard, the look was always there. He may be insulted again, but he will never be shocked again.

The Mallard Creek Barbecue was not a fancy thing. A few low buildings on bumpy pastureland. Hickory smoke rising against a cloudless late October sky. People doing serious head-down eating at long wooden tables.

But when Quayle started moving down the dirt path between the buildings, many looked up, abandoned their food and began surging toward him. Contrary to the belief popular in some circles that women were offended that George Bush had chosen a "pretty boy" to be on the ticket ("Women Want the Beef, Not the Beefcake" was a popular anti-Quayle picket sign), some women liked his looks just fine. And at every event there were oohs and aahs, bouncing eyebrows, nudges and exchanged smiles when Quayle was first seen in the flesh. In Lexington, Kentucky, one young woman held up a sign that said simply: "Dan, Call Me." Below it was a phone number.

And while Quayle looks more like Pat Sajak than Robert Redford and while Gary Hart is more ruggedly handsome, Quayle possesses the boyish, rosy-cheeked, aw-shucks good looks that we associate with Norman Rockwell paintings and small-town America. He has the kind of inoffensive, all-purpose face you would see in a Coke or Burger King commercial. In other words, the kind of face some people would like to take a poke at.

The crowd was on him now, the Secret Service agents struggling to maintain even a semblance of order. Quayle was wearing a blue suit, white shirt, red-striped tie and shiny black business shoes. He moved over the packed-down earth, shaking the outstretched hands of the people on each side of him with both his left and right hands, moving hand over hand, like a swimmer moving through water.

"Give 'em hell!" a man shouted. "Weee-oooo, doggie!" Rebel yells echoed from the crowd. Quayle gave the man a wary look and a half smile and kept dog-paddling through the crowd.

Though it was only 11:30 a.m. and he didn't actually feel like having a plate of pork barbecue, Quayle knew he had to eat some for TV. Unable to get a clear shot of him through the swirl of people surrounding him, the camera crews got up on the tabletops to shoot down at Quayle. They moved along, stepping on plates of barbecue and knocking over soft drinks as people quickly snatched away their hands to avoid having them crushed. "Excuse us," the cameramen mumbled, eyes glued to the camera eyepieces. "Sorry. 'Scuse us."

Quayle was handed a plate of barbecue and applesauce and a slice of white bread. He sat down and ate a little barbecue and then a little applesauce and then took a bite of white bread. The cameras recorded it all for history. And then it began. The dark cloud that Quayle knew lurked just behind every silver lining.

A man tried to thrust a leaflet at him. It had a picture of George Bush and the Ayatollah Khomeini on its cover. It said: "George Bush sold arms to the Ayatollah. We all pledge allegiance to the American flag. But Democrats don't believe in selling arms to countries that burn it. It's time for a change!"

The man waved his leaflet in Quayle's face, but Quayle ignored him, eating another plastic forkful of barbecue, making pleasant, meaningless conversation with the people next to him at the table. ("Where you from? . . . Really? I hear that's a real nice place. And where you from? . . . Really?") The crowd was very tolerant of the protesters with their signs and their leaflets. A party atmosphere prevailed, not a political one, as if this were all a giant game and neither side was to be taken too seriously. Local candidates had been circulating through the crowd all morning, handing out their own literature. And by the side of one building was a large garbage can with a sign: "For Political Junk."

Quayle made no attempt to give a speech or even to talk to very many people. After a few more bites of barbecue, he got up and shook a few more hands, then pushed along through the crowd, edging as quickly as he could to the waiting limousine. When he got there, the door was already open and Quayle stood briefly on the rocker panel and waved as people took snapshots of him.

"Vote Republican and give my kid a future!" a man with a two-year-old on his shoulders shouted at Quayle. He got the same quick smile and wary look that the heckler had gotten and then Quayle ducked into the car and moved on.

"You have to judge the crowd, you've got—you look to find if there are any adversaries in the crowd," he said later. "You look around. You get a feel for it."

He had gotten a feel for it. All campaigns draw hecklers, protesters, members of the opposition. No candidate likes them (Richard Nixon wanted to have them arrested), but they are part of campaigning in a free and open society. Liberals carried picket signs linking Bush to the Iran-contra scandal. Right-to-lifers carried signs attacking Dukakis for being pro-choice.

But Quayle drew protest of a much different, much more personal kind. The picket signs said: "Sissy Little Rich Boy!" "800-Wah-Wah, Daddy's Private Line." "Keep Bimbos Out of Politics!" "Draft Dodgers for Quayle." "It Isn't the Skeletons in His Closet, But the Brain in

His Head." "What Is the Difference Between Dan Quayle and Jane Fonda? Jane Fonda Went to Vietnam!"

The signs didn't express opposition to Quayle's stands on issues, they attacked Quayle as a person. And the people holding the signs didn't try to maneuver them in front of TV cameras to get on the network news. They tried to maneuver the signs where Quayle would see them. The object was not to communicate their feelings to America, but to communicate their feelings to Dan Quayle.

Dan Quayle had escaped service in Vietnam by joining the National Guard. Certain calls were made on his behalf. And George Bush's defense of this, that at least Quayle "did not go to Canada," did not help much. Those going to Canada had to be prepared to live in exile for life. Going to a National Guard armory one weekend a month required somewhat less of a commitment.

Many of the people who picketed and yelled at Quayle were of his generation. This was the generation he was supposed to reach out and touch. That's why Bush put him on the ticket in the first place. And yet four days before election day, a Washington *Post* / ABC poll showed that Dan Quayle's negatives were four points *higher* among baby boomers (45 percent) than with the public at large.

The picketers were almost always neatly dressed and had a comfortable look about them. Many had opposed the Vietnam War and would have been only too happy—at the time—to see anyone get into the National Guard rather than serve in Vietnam. So why weren't they happy that Quayle had stayed home rather than killed Asians?

Part of it was Quayle's seeming hypocrisy. He was a hawk on defense matters and a supporter of the war in which he declined to serve. And part of it was privilege. Quayle and the rest of his class always seemed to get what they wanted. In the manner of the rich and powerful everywhere, he had it both ways. He could escape service in Vietnam and yet support the war. He could continue to coast through life while calling for the sacrifice of others. The path was always clear for him, the way always paved, the skids always greased. After a stint of writing press releases in the Guard, he worked in the Indiana attorney general's office, became associate publisher of one of his family's newspapers, was elected to the House of Representatives at age twenty-nine and the U.S. Senate at age thirty-three.

And yet, what was he? his opponents asked. A pretty face. An empty suit. A man, some said, who was so dumb that he could not count to twenty-one without taking his clothes off. The joke about his family motto, "Too dumb to pass; too rich to fail," seemed perfect.

Unlike Robert Dole and Jack Kemp, two leading candidates for the Republican vice presidential nomination, Quayle had no national name recognition, no national campaign staff and no national constituency. Instead, he was the "demographic" choice for running mate: he was young, enthusiastic, attractive. And considering the duties of the job he was running for (virtually none whatsoever), what else was needed?

But to many, Quayle was an affront to the process itself. After an election, Americans "rally 'round the flag" and support the winner. Personal deficiencies and campaign animosities are largely forgotten. A honeymoon period begins. Democracy works, we all know that. And democracy would not allow bad men (something must have happened to Richard Nixon after he was elected) or dumb men (sure, Ronald Reagan was detached and delegated a lot of authority, but you couldn't actually call him dumb) or wholly inadequate men to attain the highest offices in the land.

And if democracy did, something was seriously wrong.

So what Dan Quayle's election threatened was a loss of faith in the process itself. When a man who will be a "heartbeat away" from the presidency seems to be a national joke, some Americans felt a special kind of anger. They felt that democracy itself was being demeaned.

And as Michael Dukakis' campaign went on, floundering for some coherent theme, attacking Quayle seemed to be Dukakis' last, best hope of winning. So Dukakis split his time between defending himself against the attacks of George Bush and counterattacking against Dan Quayle.

It was called the Fear Factor. At stop after stop, Dukakis hit it hard: if J. Danforth Quayle were elected, the nation would be in actual peril from his stupidity, his youth, his dearth of qualifications. Even his name was unpresidential. (While Bush would attack Dukakis for calling Dan Quayle "J. Danforth Quayle," this was how Quayle's name appeared on the ballot. Besides, Dukakis had picked up the tactic from Bush, who had called Pete du Pont "Pierre.")

By the end of the campaign, Dukakis would spend $5 million on anti-Quayle commercials. And if Quayle had been running for President, they might have worked. But even though Quayle would be first in line of succession and even though in the last quarter century John Kennedy had been shot and killed, Gerald Ford had been attacked by would-be assassins and Ronald Reagan had been shot and wounded, Americans are not a people who take very seriously the possibility of assassination.

No, Dan Quayle would be Vice President if elected. That's all. And what, when you thought about it, did that take?

☆

"WE WERE LOOKING for someone more conservative than Bush, but that was not the driving factor," Lee Atwater said after the election, explaining how the Bush campaign came up with Quayle. "I had Elizabeth Dole, Kemp and Quayle on my list. Elizabeth Dole was good with baby boomers and would electrify women. We had a gender gap problem at the time. Kemp was good with baby boomers and conservatives and good in California."

And Quayle? Well, while all the other candidates drew knockout criticism from one or another of the Bush aides, Quayle seemed to draw no big negatives. People weren't crazy about him, but nobody was crazy against him. And that's how he ended up with the job.

"But it was a crucial mistake for Dukakis to focus on Quayle," Atwater said. "I told Quayle he was one of the great rabbits in the history of politics [that is, people chased him]. Had Dukakis not wasted his time and money attacking Quayle, he might have stumbled on his populist message earlier in the race and done us some damage."

But you couldn't know Quayle would be a rabbit when you picked him, I pointed out. You didn't know his negatives then.

Atwater paused. "A lot of Quayle's value was an *unintended consequence*," he said, choosing his words carefully.

In retrospect, could you have done better than Quayle?

"That's irrelevant," Atwater said. "George Bush is President now. So how could things have come out better?"

Did you ever consider dropping Quayle? And if so, did you decide not to because of political concerns or because there was nothing to drop him for?

"The politics was more important than the reality," Atwater said. "We could *not* drop him from the ticket. Politically it would have looked so bad that we never seriously considered it. And as it turned out, there was nothing to find out about Quayle. And there was no sense that he had kept anything from us. I knew about the Paula Parkinson stuff from a friend who was one of the guys there that weekend. [Parkinson was a lobbyist who spent a golf weekend with a number of politicians including Quayle.] They made fun of Quayle for being such a pussy that he didn't get laid.

"People do not make their decision based on who is second on the ticket. My simple notion was that a vice presidential candidate was not a consideration one way or another. I think you can get a plus out of a wise choice, but not much of a minus out of a bad choice."

SO, ACCORDING TO ATWATER, the old political axiom was still true: nobody votes for Vice President. When Americans went into the voting booth, they would decide how they felt about Bush and Dukakis, not Quayle and Bentsen.

Which is one reason Quayle spent all of his time attacking Dukakis and none of his time attacking Bentsen. It was called the "Lloyd the Void" strategy. The Bush-Quayle campaign would just forget about Bentsen. And it was because of that strategy that Quayle believed his greatest disaster, the vice presidential debate, was really not all that bad.

"Matter of fact, after that debate, you know, I was convinced that we came out on top," Quayle said. "And I still think that we did [win] and I'll tell you why: because Dukakis' negatives went up about four or five points after that debate. And so what if Bentsen's positives go up? When Bentsen's positives go up, that hurts Dukakis. I mean, what has happened is that they've allowed Bentsen just to really overshadow Dukakis. That doesn't help Dukakis."

And you knew that was going to be the strategy from the beginning?

"Well, I knew from the very beginning that Dukakis was the target and just ignore Bentsen," Quayle said. "I had known him in the Senate, we had had some disagreements, but on major issues, particularly on defense and things of that sort, there wasn't that much of a difference. Furthermore, it was my idea that if you talk about Bentsen, it showed that you had a moderate on there, so it gave some cover to Dukakis' liberalism. So from day one, I just ignored Bentsen and focused on Dukakis."

For the entire campaign Quayle and Bush would beat up on Dukakis while Dukakis and Bentsen would spend a lot of time beating up on Quayle. From a political standpoint, this helped the Republicans. They were attacking the top of the ticket, which is where voters were used to focusing. The Democrats were attacking the bottom of the ticket, which most people were not used to caring about.

But on a personal level, the Republicans had to pay a price. Dukakis could take a punch better than Quayle could. The icy demeanor that did not allow Dukakis surges of great joy also protected him from descents into great depression. Further, Dukakis was better armored against attack. He had gained experience from the primaries.

Quayle had been plucked like an apple from a tree. And his entire campaign amounted to on-the-job training. Which is why so many people felt superior to him: members of his own staff, who ostensibly worked for him but who really took their orders from Bush; many in the press, who had covered candidates of greater stature; and the protesters, who often mobbed his speeches. All put Quayle under a pedestal.

And on October 27, in Syracuse, New York, the Secret Service actually had to rescue the guy.

QUAYLE HAD ARRIVED two hours late. It was only 7 p.m. in Syracuse, but Quayle already had been campaigning for twelve hours in a day that had begun with the spitting man at the Mallard Creek Barbecue and had progressed to a semi-ugly crowd at the University of North Carolina at Charlotte and then to a crowd of hecklers at Morristown, New Jersey, where people held picket signs picturing a featherless little chicken with a red slash through it. Quayle had given the protesters a withering look and said: "Hey, you're real creative."

So he ended up in Syracuse after a full day of this and he got to the downtown Civic Center for a nice little set-piece speech: a stage crowded with hundreds of balloons and eighty-five American flags. The audience was not happy with the two-hour wait, but Quayle drew a nice round of applause when he was introduced.

He bounded onto the stage, looked out at the audience, cleared his throat . . . and saw these people in the balcony unfurl a banner that said: "You're no JFK!"

O.K., ignore them, he told himself. Don't even bother to waste a squelch line on them, just get going. "I've been to thirty-eight states in this campaign, but this is the first time I've been to upstate New York and, boy, do I love it!" Quayle said.

Which is when the guy in the second row stood up. He had arrived early and gotten a seat directly in front of the lectern. He was beefy and middle-aged, wearing a dark brown jacket and light brown pants. And he began shouting at Quayle. It was hard to hear what he was shouting, but he would not shut up.

Finally, it just got to Quayle. He'd been getting this all day, the shouts, the stupid signs, the attacks on his character and his manhood, and, hey, he had been a U.S. senator at age thirty-three, you know? In Indiana, he was somebody. Somebody a lot more important than some fat jerk in a brown coat and brown pants from Syracuse.

"Siddown!" Quayle yelled at the guy, his voice booming over the loudspeakers. "Siddown!"

Normally, this would have worked. It was not a dignified thing for a man running for the second-highest office in the land to do, but normally it would work. Hecklers like the anonymity of the crowd. And it was more than a little intimidating to have a national candidate single you out and start shouting back at you.

But Quayle hecklers were not normal hecklers. They felt intellectually superior to Dan Quayle. So the guy in brown kept standing. And yelling. Quayle had a few thousand watts of amplification behind his own voice and could easily have ignored the guy, but restraint was not always one of the arrows in Quayle's quiver.

As a last resort, he did try sweet reason, however. "We're glad to have you here," Quayle told the guy, leaning over the lectern, looking directly at him. "But despite what you may say, these people are going to hear what I have to say."

The audience cheered. But the man stayed on his feet, pointing his finger at Quayle now. And that's when the Secret Service moved on the guy. Two of Quayle's agents, who had been flanking him on the stage, came down into the audience to confront the guy in brown.

The agents walked down to the area between the first row and the stage and stood in front of the man, who by now was flapping his arms. The agents stood there with their hands folded nicely in front of them, staring at the guy and delivering a silent message: "Make one false move, wise guy, and we'll blow you out of your socks."

Now the rest of the audience was on its feet, straining for a look at all this. Meanwhile, back onstage, wasn't there a candidate trying to make a speech or something? "They have a right to their opinion," Quayle said, trying to rescue the event from chaos, "but I have a right to mine."

Working furiously behind the scenes, Quayle's staff organized some cavalry. A bunch of sign-carrying supporters burst down the aisles to surround the man in brown, ringing him with signs that said: "Save America's Ass—Keep Dukakis in Mass." Outnumbered, unable to see anything, the man finally sat down. And Quayle finished his speech, to the chant of "No more lies! No more lies!" from the back of the hall.

Afterward, I asked David Prosperi, Quayle's press secretary, if this was one of the worst moments of the campaign. "Well," he said, pausing as if examining a long catalogue of worst moments, "it ranks right up there with Albuquerque."

Albuquerque in September was the first time Quayle was heckled by people when it was hard to heckle back. As one press account noted: "He had silently suffered the taunts of steelworkers in Ohio, senior citizens in Wisconsin and students in Colorado," which was quite a list of accomplishments considering he had been the nominee for only about a month.

But in Albuquerque at the New Mexico State Fair, Quayle confronted the one set of people he didn't want to confront ever: Vietnam veterans. Some were in uniform and a lot were shouting at him. Quayle was visibly rocked. These guys *in green berets* are yelling at him. And they are yelling: "Chickenhawk! Chickenhawk!" *"El Pollo! El Pollo!"*

For a few horrifying moments, Quayle's handlers thought he might actually be driven from the stage. But, give him credit, he gutted it out. He stood up and gave his speech and even hit back a little, talking about all the "babble" he had to face on the campaign trail.

Quayle's people knew they couldn't let this go on forever. No candidate could take such brutal treatment on a daily basis. Quayle was beginning to see his campaign as a cauldron. The reporters were waiting to pounce on his every word while they dug into his past like skunks into a compost heap. He had a set of handlers whom he had to obey but whom he did not trust. And it seemed like every day he picked up the papers to see one more unnamed Bush aide saying what a drag on the ticket he was. All this and heckling, too. It couldn't go on. The campaign could not let it.

"It's going to get a little easier," Prosperi said after the speech in Syracuse. And he was right. Because the next day, Dan Quayle spoke to a crowd that gave him no trouble at all. He had seen them standing by a large mulberry tree in Neffsville, Pennsylvania, and had stopped his motorcade to go over and talk to them.

"Do you know who's going to be President?" Quayle asked the group.

They shook their heads.

"Do you know who's going to be Vice President?" Quayle asked.

They shook their heads again.

"Well, I guess I'll have to help out," he said, tapping a finger on his chest. "Me, I'm going to be Vice President."

Most of the crowd nodded. A few giggled. One ran after a squirrel.

"And I want you to talk to your mothers and fathers," Quayle said, "and tell them to vote for me."

"Yaaayyy!" the first-, second- and third-grade classes of the John Henry Neff Elementary School shouted. The kids, who had been assembled by the side of the road in the crisp fall weather, yelled and waved their arms, their mittens flapping up and down where they were clipped to the sleeves of their brightly colored parkas.

Dan Quayle liked kids. He especially liked how they never yelled at him or spat at him or wore green berets and shouted "*El Pollo!*" at him. "Think about your education," he told the kids, wind tugging at his tan trench coat. "But have fun. I want you to take the weekend off." He waited for a laugh, but the kids just stood staring at him. "And when you come back to school, if the election goes the right way, you can say: 'I know those two. They were right here!' "

The kids looked at each other for a moment and then shouted "Yaaayyy" again, and Quayle smiled and walked back to the waiting cars.

Next, he motored up to the Milton J. Brecht Elementary School, where the kids had been assembled on the lawn under an increasingly blustery sky to meet him. (There was something definitely bizarre about watching Secret Service agents holding back eight-year-olds.) Quayle was handed a pumpkin and then addressed the crowd about the approach of Halloween. "Make sure you get a lot of treating and not tricking in," he told the kids. Then he wrapped up his speech and waited for the cheers. There weren't any.

"Yell his name," a Secret Service agent stage-whispered to the kids. "Yell his name."

The kids didn't do it. Maybe they didn't know it. Maybe they were Democrats. Anyway, it had started to rain and Quayle went quickly down the line of kids, shook hands with a few teachers and then turned to an aide. "O.K.," he said, "back to the bus."

On the press bus, Kathy Layfield, a Quayle aide, informed reporters that there would be a filing center at the next stop, from which they could send in their stories.

"What do we file?" B. Drummond Ayres of *The New York Times* drawled from the back of the bus. "My paper doesn't have a children's page."

But that was not Dan Quayle's concern. He went from school to school, meeting and greeting people who wouldn't be able to vote for nearly a decade, but that didn't matter. His campaign was not designed to reach voters. His campaign was designed to keep voters from reaching him.

Quayle's speeches rarely changed no matter what the age of the audience. He would misquote a little Victor Hugo—"There is nothing so powerful as a new idea whose time has come"—throw in a little Chevrolet commercial—"The Midwest is the heart of America"—and even borrow a little Jerry Brown, who no doubt borrowed it from somebody else—"Land is not inherited from our parents; it is borrowed from our children."

He would, on occasion, attempt humor: "The governor of Massachusetts, he just lost his top naval adviser last week. The rubber duck drowned in his bathtub."

And while all candidates repeat the same stump speech over and over, Quayle's efforts did not resemble speeches so much as a string of one-liners. It became common practice for some regulars in the Quayle press corps to turn on their tape recorders and nap during his speeches, confident that later they would not even have to play back the tape.

But when Quayle was off the leash and away from the protection of his prepared speeches, he could turn even the simplest replies into great explorations of the English language. He sometimes entered into a sentence like a spelunker entering into a cavern and had to search for a way out with just as much difficulty.

The morning after the Syracuse speech, the sheer dreary weight of the campaign hung heavy on the press corps that was gathered in the lobby of the Syracuse Marriott. As we slouched on the chairs and couches waiting for the bus to arrive, a radio reporter kept playing her taped interview with Quayle over and over as if she could not quite believe it. She had come upon Quayle as he returned from his morning jog and had asked him what she thought was an easy question: where was he going to campaign this day?

Easy answer: Pennsylvania.

Quayle answer: "The western part of Pennsylvania is very, uh, Midwestern. Midwestern. And the eastern part is more [pause] East. Uh, the Midwest, uh, Pennsylvania is a very important state, a big state, we've done well there in the past. The western part is— Pennsylvania is a divided state, like Tennessee is divided into three parts, Pennsylvania is divided into two parts. You have western Pennsylvania and then you have eastern Pennsylvania. And that's the way you campaign there. And we're going to, I think we're going mostly to the eastern part.

"I have to check my schedule."

We all agreed it was fortunate she had not asked him about our balance of trade with Japan.

Quayle's handlers tried to arrange local press interviews for him rather than national ones, on the theory that the locals would ask easier questions and would be more awed and intimidated by actually meeting a man running for national office. This is an old and increasingly untrue theory, however. And as it turned out, local reporters often were not awed or intimidated by Quayle in the least.

A few hours after delivering his lesson on Pennsylvania geography, Quayle headed out to the Syracuse airport to board his plane. But before he boarded, he stopped at the edge of the tarmac to field a few questions from a local (that is, supposedly harmless) TV reporter.

"How ya doin' this morning?" she began disarmingly, the wind-whipped rain tearing at both their hairdos. "Last night, when I said to you the voters here would rather vote for Lloyd Bentsen, you said that's because they don't know the real Dan Quayle. So I'd like you to tell me: who is the real Dan Quayle?"

Quayle got ready to deliver his stock response to this stock question, but the reporter was ready for him. "And don't tell me I'm lookin' at him, because you told me that yesterday," she said. "What's the *real* Dan Quayle like?"

O.K., so the stock response was out. So Quayle mentally had to switch gears. But some gears switch easier than others. "You are looking at him," he began, then realized that this is what she told him he could not say. "Right here. Here. In person." There, he had changed the answer a little, hadn't he? He had added "in person."

The reporter tried a different tack. "Do you get a bad rap, Senator?" she asked. "Are you smarter than people think you are? Are you better than people think you are?"

"I'm a heck of a lot better than what the news media said I am," Quayle replied.

"How much better?" the reporter prompted. "In what way?"

"In every way," Quayle said. Ha, got her there.

But all this was really a warm-up for the hardball the reporter had been saving. "There is a rumor running rampant that somebody took your law boards for you," she said. "Is that ridiculous or what?"

Quayle looked shocked, then affronted. Who did this twerp think she was? Lesley Stahl? She was local press, for cripe's sake. She wasn't supposed to ask stuff like this.

"You got it," Quayle said in a knife-edged voice. "It is absolutely ridiculous."

"You took 'em, right?" the reporter said.

Quayle, really angry now, said: "Of course."

"Thank you, Senator," the reporter said.

Quayle turned away and loudly muttered his favorite post-interview mutter: "Jee-*zus!*"

Which is exactly what the reporters felt like muttering sometimes, but for different reasons. Being on the Quayle plane looked like a pretty good assignment right after the Republican convention. Quayle seemed capable of making any mistake, and the rumors about him seemed ready to become scandals. It looked like covering Quayle would provide exactly what the reporters wanted: a good story. Which translated to airtime for the TV and radio reporters and the front page for the pencil press.

But the "Quayle Factor" never really became what some had expected it would. The rumors never burgeoned into anything. And this, coupled with Quayle's strategy of keeping out of the national news, turned the Boys on the Bus into the Lost Boys. Quayle's press corps was out there somewhere, but you couldn't prove it by reading their newspapers or tuning in to their network news programs.

So Quayle was protected by the boredom level of his own campaign. And by the fact that he had become such a punching bag, such a victim, that to attack him further looked like piling on. He made all sorts of slips and gaffes, but they were just small blips on the radar screen.

"Bobby Knight told me this," Quayle said at the City Club of Chicago in early September. "He said: 'There is nothing that a good defense cannot beat a better offense.' "

As the audience sat in a somewhat stunned silence, Quayle provided simultaneous translation: "In other words," he said, "a good offense wins."

After the speech, Quayle's aides told the press that from now on they could either quote Quayle's actual words or the prepared texts since "both reflected his thinking." But the aides also began demanding of Quayle that he stick to his prepared texts.

There was no way to save him from questions, however.

About two weeks before election day, in an especially grisly interview with a young girl from the Children's Express, Quayle advised her against getting an abortion even if she became pregnant through incest. A week later, Quayle was asked what Willie Horton's victim should have done if she had become pregnant by him. Have the baby or have an abortion?

Quayle said it wasn't a problem. Rape victims didn't have to worry about abortions, he said, because they can "have a D and C. At that time that is before the forming of life. That is not anything to do with abortion."

Wrong answer. Dilation and curettage is a type of abortion, doctors said.

Quayle was later asked what he would do if his wife were raped (the press by now had an unquenchable fascination with "red meat" questions) and became pregnant by the rapist. What would he advise?

An interesting question, because few could imagine Quayle advising his wife, Marilyn, about much of anything. In college Quayle had shown what his poly sci professor had called "an ostentatious indifference" to academics, while Marilyn had labor induced in July 1974 so she could have her first child and be sure the birth would not interfere with her bar exam, which she took while seated on a special cushion. Reporters noted that when Quayle was asked a question in her presence, she would rub his back when he gave a good answer, tug at his suit jacket when he gave a bad one and link his arm with hers and lead him away saying "Thank you very much" when he gave a really bad one.

So what would Quayle do if Marilyn became pregnant by a rapist? Quayle replied the only way he could think to reply: with the truth. He would leave it up to her, he said.

But that was also the wrong answer. Wrong if you are pro-life, as

Quayle was supposed to be. Leaving it "up to her" is a pro-choice answer and the press jumped all over it.

That night, Quayle called his ultimate handler, the only one he really trusted, and asked for advice.

"Don't answer any more hypothetical questions," Marilyn told him.

ON THE SUNDAY MORNING after the election, Dan Quayle's son, Tucker, fourteen, came downstairs and saw his father. "They're still making fun of you on *Saturday Night Live*," Tucker said. Then he began to repeat some of the jokes.

"Those aren't funny," Quayle replied.

They weren't? Then why was America laughing? Why were people calling him "Bush Lite"? And saying:

Q: What's the scariest sentence in the English language?

A: "Dan, I don't feel very well."

Jay Leno summed it up best: "A lot of people feel he's just too inexperienced for a do-nothing job."

Sitting with Quayle in the front of his plane a few weeks before election day, I asked him if the jokes, the bumper stickers ("Honk If You're Smarter Than Dan Quayle") and the picket signs ("D-D-D-D. The Sound That Quayle's Grades Would Make If They Were Released") ever got to him.

He sipped a scotch on the rocks and then looked into the glass for a while, swirling the ice around. "Actually, it's the personal ones that sort of . . . you just tend to ignore them," he said. "Some you sort of laugh at. The one I got to sort of laugh at was: 'Hi, Jack, I'm Elvis.' I don't think I'll ever forget that sign. It was funny. Another one I remember was: 'Can you type?'

"So you look at those things and—I know what they're saying— and it's all from the media. And also I think the Dukakis campaign has been pretty good at organizing against me. They've spent a lot of time going after me. Which is fine with me. But obviously, in some respects, it's pretty rude, to speak honestly."

And then he laughed a small laugh to indicate, well, hell, none of it *really* hurts, none of it *really* reaches him. Why should jokes attacking his courage and morals and intelligence hurt him? "But some of it, as I said, some of it is for fun," Quayle said, making sure I knew he was not stung, making sure I knew that Dan Quayle could take it. Then he took another drink.

We were on board the *Hoosier Pride*, Quayle's Boeing 727. It was the end of a long day of campaigning, of stop after stop at school after school in small town after small town. He had made nine speeches. The first-class cabin of the plane was his sanctuary. On

Lloyd Bentsen's plane, Bentsen was never out of sight of the press. There was no partition, no curtains. On Quayle's plane, there were two partitions between him and the press and he was never in sight except when he chose to be. (Dukakis, too, was partitioned from the press, and Bush had the best deal of all: he flew on a separate plane, Air Force Two.)

Quayle's personal cabin had been reconfigured for comfort. The seats on the port side had been taken out and replaced with a long couch. And on the starboard side, four seats had been turned to face each other with a table between them. Quayle flew facing forward in the seat by the window. His aides sat facing him. By this point in the campaign, the cabin was crowded with the baseball caps and T-shirts and other mementos candidates are given at each stop. On one wall was a framed, autographed picture of George Bush lifting Quayle's hand in victory at the Republican convention in New Orleans.

There was an open bottle of Dewar's and one of Chivas Regal. After boarding the plane, Quayle had headed for the washroom, and when he got out, an aide had a drink ready to put in his hand. He sat down in his window seat and motioned me to sit next to him. His youthful features and perpetual tan made him look always vigorous, but as soon as he was away from the crowds, his face sagged. He flopped back into his seat with a sigh and ran his fingers through his hair. The locks fell back perfectly into place. He might not be Jack Kennedy, but he sure had his hair.

On the table in front of him were faxed copies of newspaper clippings, what the press had been saying about him. All candidates read their reviews. David Prosperi, Quayle's press secretary, sat across from us, which is not unusual during an interview. There was a fourth person, however, seated next to Prosperi, in the seat across from and facing Quayle. He was a young press aide and he clutched a boom mike, which is a microphone attached to a pole. It is used by TV sound technicians to record from a distance and for reaching over crowds. Quayle's boom mike was attached to a tape recorder, which sat on the table. While many candidates tape-record interviews (it can be their only protection against being misquoted), using a large boom mike, especially when the participants are only inches apart, not only was unusual but looked ludicrous.

I took out my own tape recorder (a reporter's only protection against a candidate who denies saying what he said) and put it on the armrest between Quayle and me. As Quayle began to answer my questions, his aide moved the microphone back and forth between us. And I got the impression that the conspicuousness of the mike, its intrusive size, was Quayle's handlers' way of constantly reminding him that his every word was important, that he should never let down his guard and that every interview, even a relaxed one over scotch at the end of the day, was a potential minefield.

Do you ever wish you hadn't brought up John Kennedy in your debate with Lloyd Bentsen? I asked Quayle.

He shook his head emphatically. "No, not really," he said, "'cause he was going to use that line anyway, even if I hadn't made that reference to the experience [Quayle's experience vs. JFK's]. At some time during the debate, he was going to say: 'Senator Quayle over here has tried to compare himself to Jack Kennedy.' I'm convinced of that."

Quayle was correct. Bentsen had the line ready. On August 25 at the Missouri State Fair, Quayle had said: "I'm very close to the same age of Kennedy when he was elected, not Vice President, but President." That line, and every other word he uttered, was recorded by Bentsen's campaign staff. They knew Quayle would be heavily briefed and heavily rehearsed before the debate, but they felt that under pressure he would fall back on familiar defenses and familiar lines.

In Bentsen's debate rehearsals in Austin, Texas, a mock stage had been set up in a vacant bar near the Four Seasons Hotel. The stand-in playing Quayle, Ohio congressman Dennis Eckart, stood with a golf tee stuck behind one ear, and, in one rehearsal, had made a Kennedy comparison. When he did, Bentsen had responded with: "You're no more like Jack Kennedy than George Bush is like Ronald Reagan!"

Bentsen was hoping to use the line whether Quayle raised the Kennedy issue or not. And when Bentsen delivered his "You're no Jack Kennedy" in the real debate, the applause and laughter told him he had scored such a hit that he didn't need the Bush-Reagan part.

"At that debate was where they were going to come at Dan Quayle," Quayle said, "and they were going to try to, you know, break it or make it."

OMAHA, NEBRASKA, had been picked for the site of the vice presidential debate because it was in the heart of the heartland. Quayle was delighted. Here, in the Midwest, people would understand him.

In the bowels of City Auditorium, the press had gathered and was waiting. Nearly 1,500 had shown up, 500 phone lines had been installed and scores of TV satellite trucks waited outside. As in most cities when they play host to a national audience, the homeless had been driven off the downtown streets so that the visitors would not be offended by reality.

Corporate debate sponsor Philip Morris had done its best to create a mini-city for the press in the basement of the auditorium. It set up tables with red-checkered tablecloths and put out cold cuts, soft drinks and beer as well as hundreds of packs of Parliaments, Marlboros, Benson & Hedges, Virginia Slims and Merits. And if the press wanted some red-and-white plastic Marlboro ashtrays or a very nice silver-and-gold Philip Morris pen in its own little red felt sack, they were available for the taking. And they got taken. The pens disappeared as fast as the public relations people could put them out.

Next to Philip Morris Village were utilitarian tables set up in long rows where the press could work. In front of the tables was a long stretch of maroon carpeting—Spin Alley—where partisans from both parties would give their impressions before, during and after the debate.

Upstairs in the auditorium, 400 feet of blue carpet had been laid out on the basketball court for the debate set. That's how everyone looked at it: a TV set. That morning, Roger Ailes had taken Quayle onto the set. Quayle was tense and unhappy. At one point, he asked Ailes if he could use a certain hand gesture. "Hey, Roger . . . does . . . on, on this, you know, if I'm gonna, if I, if I decide on my gesture over there . . . is that all right? . . . You don't mind?"

Ailes said he didn't mind.

Many of the reporters who had flown to Omaha for the debate were scheduled to depart with Quayle on his campaign jaunt the next morning—but only if he screwed up during the debate. Only if he screwed up would he be news.

As the debate began upstairs, the reporters stared intently at the TV screens in the basement. Bentsen, sixty-seven and looking every year of it, stood with almost military uprightness behind his lectern. Quayle, forty-one, and looking even younger, had one foot up on the base of his lectern.

The audience was enthusiastic, demonstrative and at times even raucous, which was not surprising considering that almost two-thirds of the seats in the hall had been given to campaign partisans.

The questioning of the candidates began. The first big moment came when Brit Hume of ABC asked Quayle: ". . . let us assume . . . that you have become Vice President and the President is incapacitated for one reason or another, and you have to take the reins of power. When that moment came, what would be the first steps that you'd take and why?"

Quayle was rocked. It was a basic question, but not one he had been briefed on. Looking like he wanted nothing so much as to call a time-out so he could huddle with his handlers, he stumbled his way through an answer: "First . . . first, I'd say a prayer for myself and for the country I'm about to lead. And then I would assemble his people and talk."

While much fun would be made of this answer later—who wouldn't pray if Dan Quayle were President?—author Leslie Southwick wrote in *The Wall Street Journal*: "Spending a few minutes of silence with the late President's widow, then summoning the cabinet were exactly what Harry Truman in his memoirs said he did in 1945 at the death of FDR."

But Quayle remained nervous as he plunged on through the rest of his answer. When it was over, he visibly relaxed, confident that he had muddled through.

But a few questions later, Hume hit Quayle again: "Senator, I want to take you back to the question that I asked you earlier . . . You said you would say a prayer and you said something about a meeting. What would you do next?"

The audience burst into laughter. And an unnerved Quayle now proceeded to blow it. "I don't believe that it's proper for me to get into the specifics of a hypothetical situation like that," Quayle said.

This was even weaker than his first response. Worse, what Quayle did not know was that the reporters on the panel had decided before the debate that they would try to follow up not only on their own questions but also on each other's in order to prevent the candidates from slip-sliding away.

And a few minutes later, Tom Brokaw picked up Hume's ball and advanced it a few yards: "Senator Quayle, I don't mean to beat this drum until it has no more sound in it. But to follow up on Brit Hume's question: when you said that it was a hypothetical situation, it is, sir, after all, the reason that we're here tonight, because you are not just running for Vice President . . ." Here Brokaw was interrupted by tumultuous applause. "Surely you must have some plan in mind about what you would do if it fell to you to become President of the United States, as it has to so many Vice Presidents just in the last twenty-five years or so."

Quayle stalled for time. "Let me try to answer the question one more time. I think this is the fourth time that I've had this question," he said.

"The third time," Brokaw said.

That pissed Quayle off. Now, forced onto the defensive, he retreated to a safe answer from the past and thereby gave Bentsen the greatest straight line of the campaign.

"Three times that I've had this question," Quayle said, "and I will try to answer it again for you, as clearly as I can, because the question you are asking is what kind of qualifications does Dan Quayle have to be President . . . I will be prepared not only because of my service in the Congress, but because of my ability to communicate and to lead. . . . I have far more experience than many others that sought the office of Vice President of this country. I have as much experience in the Congress as Jack Kennedy did when he sought the presidency . . ." (Which was not really true. Kennedy had served fourteen years in Congress to Quayle's twelve.)

Bentsen could hardly believe his good fortune. It was just like the rehearsal in Austin. Quayle had actually brought up Kennedy, the icon of a whole generation of Americans. And now Bentsen spoke the words that immediately became political history: "Senator, I served with Jack Kennedy, I knew Jack Kennedy, Jack Kennedy was a friend of mine. Senator, you are no Jack Kennedy."

The auditorium erupted. There were shouts, applause, hoots and hollers. It went on for what seemed like minutes.

Quayle, a hurt-puppy look on his face, interrupted the hubbub to say: "That was uncalled for, Senator."

The rest of the debate proceeded without incident. And in the wild spinning that immediately followed the debate, the partisans played their predictable roles: the Republicans saying Bentsen could not defend Dukakis and the Democrats saying Quayle was not prepared to be President.

Susan Estrich, Dukakis' campaign manager, stood in the crush of reporters wearing one of the first blue "President Quayle?" buttons that would become so popular among Democrats. Another, much more grisly button also surfaced this night. It was red and showed an EKG blip with the words: "Quayle—A Heartbeat Away."

But while the debate was certainly Bentsen's highest point and Quayle's lowest, I wrote the next day that Bentsen had failed in his main purpose: to make America really afraid of Dan Quayle. True, Quayle had looked unprepared to become President and overly ambitious. But George Bush could take care of the unprepared part by not dying. And as to overambition, well, accusing a politician of that is like accusing a ballerina of dancing on her toes.

But what Quayle did not understand and could not accept following the debate was members of his own party bashing him. He never quite grasped that members of George Bush's staff looked upon him at best as a problem they had to handle and at worst as a hapless goof who had concealed the National Guard issue in order to worm his way onto the ticket.

So after the debate, Quayle had to read front-page quotes from "one Bush aide" saying: "We are wringing our hands as we get through the next forty-eight hours." And another unidentified Bush aide saying Quayle looked "like a wounded fawn" during the debate and how he was a "drag" on the ticket and how the Bush staff had to "potty-train" him.

Nor did it help when Bush failed to appear with Quayle on the day after the debate and made no mention of the debate in the next half dozen campaign stops over the next two days. Immediately after the debate, Bush had said that Quayle was "outstanding, commanding, assured." But this was before the polls appeared showing Quayle as the overwhelming loser. Now Bush seemed to be distancing himself from Quayle.

And while Bush would eventually mutter mild praise for Quayle, the first for-attribution responses from the Bush camp were entirely underwhelming. "When you think about what might have happened," Jim Baker said, "we have to be pretty happy."

After two days of this, Quayle had been pushed to the brink. He knew he had not done great, but he didn't expect the Republicans to be the ones to rub it in. So on the Friday after the Wednesday debate, Quayle called Baker. Quayle, who made sure the call was later leaked to the media, "raised the roof" with Baker and said the sniping from Bush aides had to stop.

Though Quayle was acting out of personal pique and embarrassment, he was right politically. A wounded Quayle flopping around on the ground did not help the Republican ticket. Before the debate, Quayle could have continued as a mild national joke, an unimportant adjunct to the Bush campaign. But after the debate, it was clear that Quayle could hurt the ticket if Republicans joined in the attack with the Democrats.

Besides, Quayle was a loose cannon. A loyal Quayle was something the ticket could survive. But nobody was quite sure what an angry Quayle would be like, an angry Quayle who might want to hit back at his own party in the middle of a presidential election campaign. The only solution: Republicans would have to rally around him. The Quayle hunt would have to stop.

And after a few days of despondency, Quayle began to bounce back as he realized the party could not desert him. His old self-confidence returned. "The big change is access to the media," Quayle said of the post-debate period. "For a couple of weeks, I'd always look around and say: 'How's the quickest way I can get in the car without having to talk to anybody.' Now, I'm sort of back to the way I used to be in the Senate. I see a camera and it's flying elbows to get over there and answer questions."

And while Quayle's words could not be taken completely seriously—from his nomination to his election he did not appear on a single network interview show—he did begin to take center stage in his own campaign, something most candidates do from day one. A week after the debate, Quayle summoned reporters and made his breakaway speech. "I'm Dr. Spin," he told them. "I don't want you to ask some aides. You ask me and I'll give you the answer. There's not going to be any more handler stories, because I'm the handler."

It was not literally true. The speeches, the issues, even the itinerary would all continue to be determined by Bush-selected aides. But no longer would Quayle be portrayed by his own campaign people as a puppet. And no longer would Bush aides be allowed to say nasty things about him to reporters.

It was such a good idea that reporters had a question: was the breakaway a phony, yet another example of masterful handling? Lloyd Bentsen's press secretary, Mike McCurry, instantly branded it as such, saying that Quayle's handlers were "brilliant" in "letting him" break away.

But Quayle talked about his liberation with such passion and conviction that reporters became convinced of his own sincerity. Which led to the triple-cross theory: Yes, Quayle was sincere in thinking the breakaway was his own idea and not that of sneaky handlers—that is, a double cross. But in reality, his handlers were so clever that they maneuvered him into the breakaway without his knowing it. In other words, they had fooled not only the press but also him. They had pulled off a triple cross.

Quayle, needless to say, did not believe in the triple-cross theory. But then, for it to work, he would be the last person who would.

He believed that the aftermath of the debate and his liberation from the spinners really made the difference in his campaign. And it might have helped. But far more important was that America began focusing back on center stage, where the real show was occurring: the presidential race. Dan Quayle was an interesting sideshow for a few weeks, but he got old fast.

"So that debate, and aftermath right after that, was a very major turning point for me and for the campaign in a positive context," Quayle told me aboard the *Hoosier Pride*. "And then, you know, George picked up the . . . remember the great job in that second [presidential] debate—that certainly was helpful."

Well, yes, it was. George certainly was doing his part to help out the ticket. Dan Quayle had showed the way and now George was being "helpful."

It was a jarring phrase. Jarring when I first heard it from Quayle and every time I played the tape back. Here was Dan Quayle relaxed, jacket off, sipping his scotch at the end of a campaign day, flying on his own jet, and being . . . generous. Being . . . expansive. Giving George credit where George deserved it.

While many people might look upon Quayle as a drag on the ticket, that wasn't the way Quayle saw it. No, he saw himself as a major player, a coequal. He had done his part in his debate, and while Quayle had nothing to say about Bush's performance in the *first* presidential debate, George certainly did a "great" job in the *second* one and that was "helpful."

The Bush staff would have found Quayle's statement not only patronizing but also ridiculous. Quayle was an anchor around their necks, but he was too thick to know he was an anchor.

"Many things have just turned—they've really turned around," said a happy Dan Quayle. "And the way you can tell that is that, as my wife pointed out last week, when she was in California all week, she said, well, how are things going with you? And I said fine. She said, well, I know you're doing a great job. I said, how's that? She said, you must be giving great speeches, drawing big crowds, and doing all the right things *because I haven't read one word about you!*"

Quayle laughed, an easy, genuine laugh. He was not laughing at himself. He was laughing at the truth: that the whole philosophy of Dan Quayle's campaign was for him to be the Invisible Man.

As his aide moved the boom back and forth between us like a brontosaurus searching for a juicy tree branch, I asked Quayle if he felt he would have anything special to prove if he was elected.

"I don't know if it's something special to prove, and I'm really not going to be concerned about that," he said. "I'm just going to go in and sit down with George Bush and figure out what we need to do and go about doing it."

Right. Like a couple of partners figuring out what "we" need to do, not George Bush telling him what he was going to do. Quayle seemed to have no real sense of just what role the Bush people saw him playing. He really believed all that guff about being a heartbeat away from the presidency. And he actually believed that Bush picked him because he thought he could lead America should the worst happen.

In Gail Sheehy's *Vanity Fair* article on Quayle, she concluded that Quayle's mind is a "closed book" and "if he is aware of his own limitations, it is not apparent." She meant it as a criticism, but actually it was Quayle's most powerful weapon: he was unaware of any limitations. How else do you get to the House at twenty-nine and the Senate at thirty-three and your own office at the White House at forty-one? Self-doubt slows you down. Those who go far, fast, jettison it as excess baggage.

"I have complete confidence that whatever I want to do, I can do," Quayle once said. "I am confident that things will turn out right for me. And they always have."

People who saw Quayle on the stump saw him as halting and unsure, unsure of the material he had been given to read and unsure of how to handle the national press, which seemed to jump on his every word. But there was one thing he was never unsure of: Dan Quayle was never unsure of Dan Quayle. Call it confidence or call it ego, it worked for him. Whatever doubts others had about him, Dan Quayle never suffered from self-doubt.

And while most thought he was very lucky to be chosen to run for Vice President, in Dan Quayle's mind running for Vice President was somewhat of a sacrifice on his part. Because he had already thought of running for *President* in 1988.

"When George first called, I said I was flattered and honored. And when he gave me all the papers and everything, I sat down that week, probably that night or the next day, with Marilyn. We had a very long discussion about it," Quayle said, sipping on his drink. "The only concern we had was the impact on the family. Because it was—it will be a change. But our family is close. We're strong. And we came to the bottom line that first and obviously I'd be interested in being Vice President or President someday. We had talked about it. And if George Bush wanted me to be Vice President, we were ready to do it."

I asked Quayle if one of the reasons he hesitated to run for Vice President was having to play second banana.

"No, that really wasn't the factor," he said. "The only factor was the family. And the children. And the timing of it. Because, I'll be honest with you, I mean, I had made, I think Marilyn and I had a one-minute conversation one time whether I would even perhaps, maybe, sometime run myself in 1988. And in this one-minute conversation, I just dismissed it, said no, not this time. George Bush is there, we'd have to take two years away from the family."

So here was Dan Quayle, unknown senator from Indiana, young, no national experience, staff or following, his National Guard service, his grades and a golf weekend with Paula Parkinson rattling around in his closet, and he is giving brief consideration to running for President, when George Bush calls and offers him No. 2. And he figures, well, why not scale back his plans, because, after all, George "is there" already. Not that George would have kicked hell out of Quayle in a presidential primary campaign. Not that such a campaign would have been a hopeless endeavor ranking well below that of Al Haig's and Pete du Pont's. No, Quayle abandons his idea to run for President "this time" because George "is there" in the White House already, so heck, why not let him stay?

Rarely has there been such a gap between self-image and public image. To much of America, Quayle was the puppy that followed George Bush to the White House.

"Gee, Barbara, can I keep him, can I, Bar, can I?"

"Well, O.K., George. But you'll have to feed him and take care of him and get him his shots. He'll be your responsibility."

"Oh, I will, I will, I promise."

"And what are you going to call him, George?"

"Uh . . . the Vice President of the United States?"

"That's nice, George. Now make sure he goes on the paper."

While the Bush campaign thought Quayle should be grateful for being offered the job—thought he should get down on his knees and thank God every night—Quayle was conscious of the *sacrifice* he had made by taking the No. 2 job. Because he could have given George Bush a run for his money if he had wanted to.

So let the Democrats print up buttons and joke about "President Quayle?" Because he can erase that question mark and insert an exclamation point.

In 1996, Dan Quayle will be forty-nine.

He will be tanned. He will be fit. And he will be ready to run.

SAY GOOD NIGHT,
MIKE

*"Governor, if Kitty Dukakis were raped and murdered,
would you favor an irrevocable death penalty for the killer?"*
—The Eighteen Words That Ate Michael Dukakis,
asked by Bernard Shaw, CNN, October 13, 1988

BERNARD SHAW liked to see them sweat. He liked to see the panic
in the candidates' eyes. Reporters were too easy on the candidates.
In the words of Bill Moyers, reporters "ask bumper sticker questions
to get fortune cookie answers." But not Bernard Shaw. He liked to
zip in a high, hard question right from the get go and see these men
who run for President gulp and gape and search their memories for
the answer they had read in their briefing books.

Except that the answers to Shaw's questions were almost never in
the briefing books. He had asked Al Gore what he would do if he or
one of his children got AIDS. He asked Dan Quayle if it was "fear
of being killed in Vietnam" that caused him to join the National
Guard. He had asked Al Haig, flat out: "Do you think Bush is a
wimp?"

And to Jesse Jackson, well, let others be deferential to Jesse Jackson.
He was just another chunk of meat to Shaw. "Mr. Jackson," Shaw
had asked in a New York primary debate, "you've *fawned* over farmers
in Iowa, Texas and elsewhere. Why have you *ignored* New York State
farmers?"

Bernard Shaw was one tough customer.

"As reporters, we are not doing our jobs if we don't ask the toughest
questions possible," Shaw said. "I couldn't *not* do that. I'm from the
Chicago school of journalism. I believe in asking tough questions.
This whole process is too *easy* on politicians. They fly up and down

the country asking for votes and they ought to be forced to stand up and say what they really feel. Otherwise the voters are being jilted.

"The American voters endured so many insults to their intelligence in Campaign '88 that if they ever rebel, the politicians are going to be in deep shit."

Shaw, forty-eight, anchorman for CNN, grew up on the South Side of Chicago, went to a tough high school and at age thirteen had seen how Edward R. Murrow had stood up to Joe McCarthy. While others had cowered, Murrow had taken McCarthy on. A lot of people had told him he was being too tough, he was committing professional suicide, but Edward R. Murrow was a tough man who did not care what others said.

"He was," Shaw said, "my idol."

Now it is 2 a.m. and Bernard Shaw is smoking menthol cigarette after menthol cigarette in a cheesy Holiday Inn room in Los Angeles not far from the UCLA campus, where George Bush and Michael Dukakis will have their final debate. Shaw stares at the ceiling. As the moderator of the second and last presidential debate, he was allowed just one question of each candidate. After that, he was reduced to a glorified timekeeper. So his questions had to be good. No, scratch that. They had to be fantastic.

Coming up with a question for Bush had been easy. He had come up with that one on the way to the airport. Shaw was in Washington and had gotten the call at 1:45 p.m. on a Tuesday that he was going to be the moderator for the Thursday-night debate. So as he rushed out the door to catch a limo to Dulles Airport for the flight to Los Angeles, he grabbed a book on the Constitution. On the ride to Dulles, he flipped through it and came upon the Twentieth Amendment, ratified in 1933, which declared that on Inauguration Day, if "the President elect shall have died, the Vice President elect shall become President."

That would be his question to Bush. What if he were elected and died before Inauguration Day? How would he feel about Dan Quayle's becoming President?

It was perfect. It hit at Bush's greatest vulnerability—the selection of Dan Quayle—and it asked Bush about his own death in front of 62 million people! It was an archetypal Shaw question: daring, offbeat and just a little grotesque.

But what would he ask Dukakis? What would skewer him? What would shake him up? Shaw didn't know. It didn't come to him on the plane flight and it didn't come to him in Los Angeles. And now the debate was hours away.

"I finally came up with the question at 2 a.m. in the Holiday Inn on the morning of the debate," Shaw said. He would ask Dukakis a crime question, a capital punishment question, a Willie Horton question, but also a personal question. One that nobody in the world would dare to ask: What if some criminal had raped and murdered Kitty? Would Dukakis still oppose capital punishment?

There. He had it. "But as I went to bed at 2:30 a.m.," Shaw said, "my worry was: What if you ask him and he hits it out of the park? People will look back and say: 'Look at Shaw, what a softball!' I also had the same concern with Bush, that he knocks it out of the park. Finally, I just resolved it by saying: Reporter, do your job; don't worry about the consequences. I just shut off my self-doubt and went to bed."

But Shaw could not sleep. Because another thought occurred to him. "I thought: What if Dukakis attacks me for asking the question? And then I thought: Well, there's nothing I can do. If he does that, he won't be answering the question."

When it was all over, some thought Dukakis would have been better off attacking than answering.

BY OCTOBER 1988, passion was no longer a subject just for the bedroom. It had now entered the public arena. At the first presidential debate in September, Peter Jennings had said to Dukakis: "The theme that keeps coming up about the way you govern is passionless, technocratic, the smartest clerk in the world . . . Given the fact that a President must sometimes lead by sheer inspiration, and passion, we need to know if this is a fair portrait of your governing or is it a stereotype."

"Peter," Dukakis said, "I care deeply about people . . ."

Yeah, tell us about it. Dukakis seemed to care about people as a *concept.*

Which he was sick of hearing. To Dukakis, the presidency was not about passion. Passion is what got us in trouble. Passion is what caused us to launch the Bay of Pigs invasion and send Marines to Beirut. Passion was for ideologues like Ollie North, who would trample on the Constitution to fulfill his own burning desires in Central America. Passion and ideology were not what America needed in the last decade of the century.

"This election is not about ideology," Dukakis had said in his acceptance speech at the Democratic convention, "it's about competence."

A line that didn't exactly trip off the tongue and resonate through the hall. And a tactical mistake to boot. Not only did an emphasis on competence feed Dukakis' image as cold and robotic; it also left him especially vulnerable to attacks on his competence. Any little chink in his record—like letting Willie Horton out of prison or not cleaning up Boston Harbor—could be blown up into a major issue.

"You know, I read that line in his acceptance speech and it did not jump out at me," a Dukakis aide who read the speech in advance said. "And later, Mark Goodin [Bush's deputy press secretary] said he had not noticed anything special about it either, but that Atwater came in the day after the speech and repeated that line and slapped the desk and said: 'Now we're gonna get him! We're gonna get him!' "

It's the kind of thing Lee Atwater would notice.

Ice Man, that's what Bush had called Dukakis in the first debate. Computer Heart is what Ailes now called him. And so the Bush team tried to frame the latter part of the campaign as the battle between the Ice Man and the Nice Man.

It began to take its toll. And as the poll numbers began to slide and then plummet, Dukakis tried to explain it to Larry King. "I think it's important to have an administration that's competent, that's able, that knows what it's doing," Dukakis said. "It's also important to have an administration that cares very deeply about the concerns of average Americans . . . and passionately deals with these problems. And that's the kind of person I am."

"So you can be passionately competent?" King asked.

"You can be passionately competent," Dukakis said.

WHEN BERNARD SHAW joined CNN as its principal Washington anchor in 1980, the infant network reached into only 1.7 million American homes and was referred to as Chicken Noodle News. By 1988 it reached into more than 50 million TV households, and now its anchorpeople were being invited to moderate presidential debates just like the big guys.

It was a coup for Shaw to be asked. (Jennings had been on the first presidential debate panel, Brokaw had been on the vice presidential debate panel and Rather had refused to be on the second debate panel.) And it was a big deal for CNN to have Bernard Shaw up there, seen live on all four networks. When Bill Moyers of PBS had moderated a Democratic primary debate in New York in December 1987, he had said: "A moderator is like a body at an Irish wake. You need it to have the party, but it doesn't say much."

Bernard Shaw wouldn't get to say much at the last presidential debate, but he knew it was what you said and not how much you said that made people remember you.

Shaw loved his question for Dukakis. But he was the only one. The three reporters on the panel, Ann Compton of ABC, Andrea Mitchell of NBC and Margaret Warner of *Newsweek*, listened to it, shuddered and asked him to change it.

"On the morning of the debate we met in Ann Compton's suite at the Westwood Marquis," Shaw said. "I was surprised that she was staying at the same hotel as Dukakis. To avoid duplicating questions, it was decided we would share questions. But I didn't want to share my question. But they pressed me and so I told them it was: 'Governor, if Kitty were raped and murdered' etc.

"They went: 'Unnnhhhhhhh!' " Shaw imitated a huge intake of breath. "That was their reaction. They didn't like it. So we went through the meeting and we agreed it would all be secret. There was also a rehearsal later onstage at UCLA, and afterwards in the chancellor's office they came to me, the three of them collectively, and said: 'Really, Bernie, we think you should change the wording.'

"I said: 'I disagree with each of you and I'm not changing anything.' But I was petrified that the question would become known to Dukakis in advance."

You mean you thought one of the three reporters would leak it to Dukakis to punish you or out of sympathy for him?

"I thought it might become known," Shaw said carefully. "I mean, a couple of them were *covering* Dukakis. Compton was staying *at the same hotel*. But I don't want to impugn motives."

The secrecy of the questions was the last privilege the press held on to in the debates. Everything else had been taken over by the campaigns. The rules of the debate, agreed on after much negotiation between Dukakis aides and Bush aides, ran sixteen pages. And even though the debate was to be broadcast live as a news event, no newsperson was present at the negotiations or had anything to say about them.

The moderator and panelists were picked by the campaigns and the Commission on Presidential Debates, which had been formed by the Republican and Democratic parties. The two sides agreed that the podiums would be 48 inches high and that "neither candidate's height will exceed 74 inches above the stage floor when the candidates are standing at their podiums." There would be no audience reaction shots by the TV cameras and "there will be no cutaways to the candidate who is not responding to a question while his opponent is answering a question."

Only the questions themselves had not been taken over by the campaign aides. As Shaw would proudly announce at the beginning of the debate, ". . . there are no restrictions on the questions that my colleagues and I can ask this evening, and the candidates have no prior knowledge of our questions."

In reality, however, Shaw was not so sure. He was deathly afraid someone had leaked his first question to Dukakis.

Before the debate, Andrea Mitchell had come to Shaw, he recalled, and said: "It's clear your question has impact, you saw our reaction. And I know you can take the heat. But how about substituting the words 'your wife' instead of 'Kitty'?"

Shaw refused.

MAUREEN DOWD of *The New York Times* may have been the first to write about likability as an issue. In April 26, 1987, well before most Americans even realized a campaign was going on, Dowd wrote: "Everywhere you look, the men who would be President are, as the poet Rod McKuen once put it, 'listening to the warm.' "

Dowd quoted pollsters and consultants and academics. "The question isn't 'Where's the beef?' anymore," Robert Shrum, a media consultant said. "It's 'Where's the heart?' "

Geoffrey Garin, a Democratic pollster, said that while in 1984 both Reagan and Mondale strove to project a "masculine leadership" style, this time the key issue would be "mechanical vs. warm, technocrat vs. soul."

It was an impressive prediction coming more than a year before either party even had a nominee, but Garin was wrong on one point. Americans hadn't changed from wanting a "masculine leadership" style into wanting someone warm and friendly. Americans wanted both. We always wanted both. We wanted Presidents who were wise but not intellectual, tough but warm, on a pedestal but not aloof.

Dowd quoted experts who tried to explain our desire for a warm leader. Some said cynical TV advertising and fancy electronic campaigns had made us want leaders who were "real." Others said the popularity of "sensitive but masculine men" such as those on *L.A. Law* and *Moonlighting* had created a new market for sensitivity. And some said Americans were reacting to the new ability of men to show feelings.

But really it was neither new nor dramatic. Americans had always wanted Presidents who were of the people and not just for the people. We always wanted to like our Presidents.

"The campaign was not about platforms or issues," said Stephen Studdert, the man who staged Bush's events for him, the man who made sure the balloons, the flags and the apple-cheeked cheerleaders were always in place. "The Republican candidates for the Senate who lost and the Republican President who won ran on the same platform. So the campaign was about individuals and the way we felt about those individuals."

And you created how America felt? I asked him.

"I crystallized it," he said. "You don't vote just because of what's in your mind. You vote because of what's in your heart. A campaign communicates the message of the heart. And what I do is pull a heartstring."

Roger Ailes believed the Democrats never caught on to that. "The Democrats didn't understand that Americans are electing a guy whose finger is on the trigger and we don't want a nut, but also we want to *like* and be *proud* of him," he said after the election. "It's that simple. And they never understood it."

What led Dowd to explore likability as an issue, however, was Dukakis himself.

"I had traveled with Dukakis really early, maybe his first campaign trip to Iowa," she recalled, "and I asked him what I always ask people: 'What do you do for fun?'

"And he said: 'Black mulch.'

"And I said: 'Black mulch?'

"And he said: 'I like to put black mulch on my tomato plants.'

"And I thought to myself right then: This man will never be President."

Dowd said she always got the impression that if Michael Dukakis ran a city, all the lights would go off at 8 p.m.

''I MEANT MY QUESTIONS to Bush and Dukakis to be as personal as possible," Shaw said, "and I just recently took my asbestos drawers off." It was five months after the debate and Shaw was still being criticized for his question to Dukakis.

"The debate was seen on all four networks and I got an inordinate amount of mail," he said. "It ran five to two critical against me, not that I operate by opinion poll. I have become known as the asker of The Question. I got a call from a friend in Chicago, and he said: 'What you asked in that debate in 1988 will be the hallmark of your career.' And I said: 'I hope not.' I had become part of the story. I didn't want to be. And I resented people flippantly telling me: 'You really killed Dukakis.'

"Bullshit. *I* didn't kill Dukakis."

MICHAEL DUKAKIS believed in control. Control had always gotten him through. While other candidates had self-destructed during the primaries, he had been Mr. Cool, waiting for the others to make the big mistakes, to drop by the wayside. Emotions were something for one's private life, not one's public life.

He knew the public wanted to see a little warmth and he gave in now and then, but when it came right down to it, he would play the game only so far. He would perform only so much.

Dukakis would kiss a baby here and a cheerleader there. He would grow misty-eyed seeing (for the second time) his cousin Olympia win an Academy Award. He would, if forced, talk about his feelings. But he would not throw himself into it. He would not give himself over to the campaign. He knew TV thrived on emotion, but he would go only so far in feeding it. Like Gary Hart, also accused of being icy, Dukakis believed his campaign was an opportunity to redefine and reform politics, not give in to its worst excesses.

"I express my emotion through my commitment to public service," Dukakis had said on *MacNeil/Lehrer*.

Kitty would, with a mixture of admiration and amusement, tell stories about how Michael could actually open a can of peanuts, eat just one and then reseal the can. And on his first cross-country trip at age twenty-six in 1960 to see John Kennedy be nominated in Los Angeles, Dukakis had stopped off in Las Vegas, put one coin in a slot machine—won—and then never played again. And over the past thirty-three years, Dukakis had kept his weight within one pound of his goal of 155 pounds.

But sometimes Dukakis' own control amounted to insensitivity to the feelings of others. After he won his first term as governor, he invited his campaign staff of Young Turks into the governor's office for a victory lunch. They had labored, slaved, worked and won. And now, victorious and elated, they would enjoy the fruits of victory. Dukakis turned to his secretary and ordered one cheese sandwich for each person. His staff was somewhat underwhelmed.

Everyone also told the story about how he had once invited two labor leaders to his house and offered them a drink. They asked for a beer. Dukakis brought one can and two glasses.

And on the day of his nomination at the Democratic National Convention in Atlanta, he went to the Conyers and Gwinnett County Boys Club outside Atlanta. The kids were excited to meet this famous man, who was now at the crest of his popularity. And one kid shyly came forward and presented Dukakis with a T-shirt.

Dukakis took it. He held it up. He peered inside at the label, which said extra-large. "You got a large, maybe?" he asked the kid. "Or even a medium?"

Mr. Warmth.

Some of the reporters who covered Dukakis would play a game. If you were sixteen and wrecked the car, they asked each other, who would you want as your father: Bush or Dukakis?

Bush always won.

"Bush would yell at you and he might even hit you," one reporter said, "but in a few weeks, he'd forget about it. Dukakis wouldn't yell; he wouldn't hit you. But he'd tell you how *disappointed* he was with you. And he'd *never, ever* forget it. And he'd make your life hell for as long as you lived."

It was immaterial that Dukakis' kids seemed to dote on him and love him deeply. Or that the Dukakis family seemed to have the true "family values" that the Ronald Reagan family only professed. What was in question was Dukakis' public image, not his private reality.

And his finest moment came in public when he seemed to choke up for a moment during his acceptance speech at the convention, his one ad-lib, when he said he thought his late father would be proud of him.

But that was a rarity. He guarded against such moments. The Democrats seemed to have picked a cold fish once again. As Jay Leno put it: "Dukakis is Greek for Mondale."

It became an issue. Maybe it was silly (Dukakis thought it was), but it was not unimportant. "The notion that there is, on the one hand, a set of 'real' issues and, on the other hand, lots of 'symbolic' or 'emotional stuff' is . . . based on a false set of assumptions," wrote Jean Bethke Elshtain, centennial professor of political science at Vanderbilt University. "In fact, there are no clear criteria that allow voters or political analysts to separate 'real' from 'symbolic' or 'rhetorical' issues."

After opinion polls showed that voters thought Dukakis had won the first presidential debate but they still *liked* Bush better, the Dukakis aides realized they had to thaw their candidate a little.

So when Dukakis flew from Massachusetts to Los Angeles for the second debate and stopped in Fargo, North Dakota, for refueling—his plane, *Sky Pig*, a twenty-year-old Boeing 737-300, could not fly cross-country without refueling—a large crowd had been assembled so the new Dukakis could be shown off.

There were some local cheerleaders there, and Dukakis unexpectedly kissed two of them. Then he led the crowd in singing "Happy Birthday" to Ted Mondale, the former Vice President's son, who was traveling with him.

"Hey," a pleased John Sasso said to the press corps afterward, "you want warm?"

And back on the plane, George Kevarian held forth. Kevarian, the speaker of the Massachusetts House and a huge guy, maybe 350 pounds, was the comic relief of the campaign. "Michael Dukakis is one of the friendliest, happiest people I know," Kevarian said. "Of course, I'm a manic-depressive."

A reporter asked Kevarian if Dukakis had a sense of humor.

"Yes!" Kevarian said. "Of course, I've never seen it."

Everybody laughed, and Kevarian went on: "Michael Dukakis is one of my closest, personal friends. Which tells you something about my life."

Soon, however, reality set in. Soon, reporters would learn just how warm the new warm Dukakis was. Soon, there would be the incident of the porcelain pig.

The traveling press corps sometimes get little gifts for the candidates. Some Bush reporters, for instance, had done this on the day of Bush's victory in the South Carolina primary. Bush was overnighting in North Carolina, having dinner with some major Republican contributors in Charlotte. And in the same hotel restaurant, at a table about twenty-five feet away, was a group of his traveling reporters. They wanted Bush to come over and talk to them about his victory, but they didn't want to go over and interrupt the Vice President.

Then one of the reporters noticed Dom Pérignon on the wine list. "How do you get Bush to respond?" the reporter said. "You give him something!" After all, he was a man famous for his thank-you notes. Bush even sent thank-you notes in response to thank-you notes.

So the reporters ordered a bottle of Dom, composed a funny note and sent the note to Bush.

Bush read it, gave them a quizzical look from his table and kept eating. Then the chilled bottle of Dom Pérignon arrived at his table. Bush gave the reporters a huge grin. He and his party drank the champagne and afterward Bush walked over to the reporters' table and chatted with them for ten minutes. They got all the quotes they needed for their stories.

It is not exactly what they teach you in journalism school, but it was a simple way of getting the story. It all depended, however, on Bush's reacting the way a normal human being would react to a nice gesture. Which is why the porcelain pig and Michael Dukakis was such a disaster.

Before flying west for the second presidential debate, a few Dukakis reporters were eating at a restaurant in Boston. The restaurant had different knickknacks on each table and on their table was a large porcelain pig. The reporters liked it because it reminded them of *Sky Pig* (which was called that because the plane was so slow, not because it was dirty. Dukakis never would have tolerated a dirty plane). So they bought the pig for forty dollars and they tied a red bandanna around it and pinned a Dukakis button to the bandanna so they could present it to Dukakis.

"Those of us who were prone to vote for Dukakis wanted to like him," one of the pig-buying reporters said. "So we would desperately search for a human side of him."

They should have used a road map.

So the reporters climb on board *Sky Pig* with their porcelain pig, they all land in Fargo, where Dukakis does his "warmth" thing for the cameras, and they all climb back on board to fly to California. Now the reporters figure Dukakis is in good spirits and so they ask Kevarian to take the pig up front and give it to Dukakis and ask Dukakis if he will come back and chat with the press.

Kevarian says sure and puts the pig under his arm and disappears up front. He goes into the screened-off area in first class, holds the pig out to Dukakis and explains it is from the press, it is a gift, a joke, and they'd love to spend a few minutes schmoozing with him.

Dukakis looks up at the pig. "Get rid of it," he says. Then he looks back out the window.

Kevarian doesn't know what to do. He can't take it back to the reporters. That would really be an insult. So he sticks the pig in the luggage rack and it sits there for a few days until finally Kevarian takes it home with him, a memento of the short-lived Warmth Campaign.

EARLY ON, the Bush handlers had realized the importance of warmth. Even Bush's goofy statements—announcing that September 7 was Pearl Harbor Day, for instance—were portrayed as a sign of what a regular, ordinary guy he was. Sheila Tate, his press secretary, put it this way: "He came to the realization himself that he needs to be more open about sharing his family and private existence with people so they have a better sense of what, as he said, his heartbeat is. Tabasco. Horseshoes. Speedboats."

AS DUKAKIS was answering your question, I asked Shaw, what was your reaction?

"I was surprised that he took no time for reflection; he began an immediate reply," Shaw said. "That was first. And second, I thought: Governor, that is not the right response.

"I read later that Sasso and Estrich were ready to drive stakes through their hearts when they heard Dukakis' answer. And I think Bush smelled blood."

But was there any good answer to your question? How could a person really answer a question about what he would do to the rapist and killer of his own wife?

"I think Dukakis could have helped himself by saying: 'I would have killed. Even though I oppose the death penalty, I would kill him,' " Shaw said.

In other words, the only good answer, the only emotional and human answer, at least according to Shaw, would have been for Dukakis to betray his principles.

In fact, however, there was nothing wrong with Michael Dukakis' answer to Bernard Shaw's question. It might have been Dukakis' finest moment. Though nobody would ever believe it.

THE REPORTERS SAT at long blue tables in the pressroom, waiting for the debate to begin. TV sets had been set up on carts every few yards. Onstage, Bush entered from the left and Dukakis from the right. Dukakis stuck out his hand about fifteen feet away from Bush and had to carry it across the stage like a spear before Bush got near enough to shake it.

They stood behind their podiums. By agreement, Dukakis got to stand on a small sloping platform that was hidden behind his. Also by agreement, neither candidate was allowed notes. This was supposed to be a test. A test of how well they had memorized their briefing books.

The panel of reporters was introduced. Everybody looked appropriately stiff. Shaw, looking commanding and stern, said: "By agreement between the candidates, the first question goes to Governor Dukakis. You have two minutes to respond:

"Governor, if Kitty Dukakis were raped and murdered, would you favor an irrevocable death penalty for the killer?"

There were gasps from the reporters in the pressroom. Then a few murmurs. "Whaaaa?" "Did he really say that?" "Un-*believ*-able."

Any TV director worth his headphones would have immediately ordered a camera to get a reaction shot from Kitty, who was sitting in the audience. After all, it was her rape and murder being talked about. But reaction shots of the candidates' families were expressly forbidden by the debate agreement. So the camera stayed locked on Dukakis.

He answered instantly and smoothly. "No, I don't, Bernard," he said. "And I think you know that I've opposed the death penalty during all of my life."

He had been on the record for years and years on that subject. Massachusetts had no death penalty and also had one of the lowest crime rates of any industrialized state in the country. Dukakis didn't believe in capital punishment. He had seen all the studies and he didn't believe it deterred crime.

So should he throw out that principle because the hypothetical victim was now his wife? Is that what principles were all about? They were good when others' loved ones were involved but not good when your own were involved?

In the pressroom, the murmurs over Shaw's question now turned to mutters over Dukakis' answer. "He's through." "That's all she wrote." "Get the hook!"

The reporters sensed it instantly. Even though the ninety-minute debate was only seconds old, they felt it was already over for Dukakis. He had not been warm. He had not been likable. He had not shown emotion. He had merely shown principle.

Afterward, his aides would try to explain that he had been sick. He had seen two doctors before the debate. He had a fever, a virus. He wasn't himself.

But while he may have been sick, he was himself. That was the problem.

Susan Estrich was in despair. "It was a question about Dukakis' values and emotions," she said later. "It was a question that was very much on the table by that point in the campaign. When he answered by talking policy, I knew we had lost the election."

Democratic consultant Greg Schneiders would come up with the line of the evening: "Bernie Shaw asked him the wrong question. He should have asked him how he would feel if his favorite regional planner was raped and murdered."

People across the country would express outrage over Dukakis' calm and cool answer. Yet was Dukakis' position that outrageous? (Ted Kennedy does not favor the death penalty for Sirhan Sirhan, the slayer of his brother Robert, and would not have favored it for Lee Harvey Oswald, the slayer of his brother John.) Dukakis believed that people of principle make principled decisions. And they stick to them. That is what integrity is about.

O.K., the critics said, but even if Dukakis didn't favor the death penalty, couldn't he have shown a little emotion in answering the question? After all, Dukakis' handlers had said before the debate that they were preparing him for a "Willie Horton type" question. And they had written an "emotional" answer for Dukakis. It was one in which he talked about his father, a doctor for fifty-two years, who, at age seventy-seven, had been beaten, bound and gagged by an intruder looking for drugs. And then he would talk about his elder brother, Stelian, who had been killed by a hit-and-run driver in 1973. It was an answer in which Dukakis said he knew what it was like to be a victim of crime.

But when the time came to give the answer, Dukakis did not.

Instead, he told the truth. Dispassionately, he expressed his true feelings. And he was savaged for it. He was savaged for giving a sincere and unemotional answer instead of giving an insincere and emotional one.

But if he had given the prepared answer, would that really have made him any more warm? Or would it have just made him a better performer, a better actor? If he had given his prepared response, the people, press included, would have praised him. He would have been congratulated for delivering his lines as written, just as George Bush did.

By the final presidential debate, we were demanding the road show. Fool us, we were saying. Trick us. Fake a little sincerity for us.

Another candidate might have survived that first question and answer. But not Dukakis. It devastated him because his coldness was already an issue. Afterward, *Time* magazine would run the headline: "Bush Scores a Warm Win: The debate in Los Angeles illuminates the power of personality as well as Dukakis' real Frostbelt problem."

Only in an accompanying story would the irony of that criticism be revealed by a line from *Death of a Salesman*:

". . . And that's the wonder, the wonder of this country, that a man can end with diamonds here on the basis of being liked!"

"WHEN IT WAS OVER, an eerie thing happened," Bernard Shaw said. "I had to walk off the stage to get back to the CNN anchor booth. And when I walked down through the audience, the people parted. They just stepped back in silence."

Shaw got up from where he was sitting at the table across from me and stepped back, pinning himself against the wall, to imitate it.

"Nobody said 'thanks' or 'good debate' or anything like that," he said. "And then I realized I had walked through the Dukakis side of the hall, through his supporters. And that's when it struck me what impact my question must have had."

LATER IN THE DEBATE, both candidates would get a moment to show how emotional they could be. And Dukakis would not blow this one.

Margaret Warner had asked George Bush about his stand on abortion. (Warner's byline had been on the *Newsweek* wimp article, but the Bush people knew she had opposed the use of the word. Otherwise they never would have allowed her on the panel.) Warner asked why a woman who discovered that her baby would be born with an incurable disease that would doom that child to "two years of incredible pain" should be forced to carry the fetus to term, "and yet a woman who becomes pregnant through incest would be allowed to abort her fetus?"

Bush's answer was masterful: "Let me answer your question—and I hope it doesn't get too personal or maudlin. Barbara and I lost a child, you know that—we lost a daughter, Robin [who died at age three] . . . the doctor said, beautiful child, your child has a few weeks to live. And I said, what can we do about it. He said, no, she has leukemia, acute leukemia, a few weeks to live. We took the child to New York. Thanks to the miraculous sacrifice of doctors and nurses, the child had stayed alive for six months and died . . . And so I just feel this is where I'm coming from. And it is personal."

A touching and warm answer. The kind of answer that presidential politics demanded in 1988. But here is the account from *U.S. News & World Report* of what George Bush had to say about the same incident when he had been asked by an interviewer about Robin in 1980:

" 'I'm just not going to do it,' he said with real anger. 'I will never, ever trade on her memory to gain sympathy or to show that I've suffered. So help me God.' "

But eight whole years had passed. And in politics, eight years is as good as "never, ever." So help him God.

By this point in the debate, Dukakis had finally awakened to the fact that he was losing on likability points. So when he was given one minute to respond to Bush's answer, Dukakis did not falter.

"Margaret," he replied, "Kitty and I had very much the same kind of experience that the Bushes had: we lost a baby, lived about twenty minutes after it was born."

Attaboy, Michael! See his three-year-old child and raise him a twenty-minute one!

AFTER THE DEBATE, the spinners were unleashed by the two sides to make their points. But few reporters really needed the spin. The mood in the pressroom was pretty well set: Dukakis was out of it. He was down for the count.

"Jesus," a reporter next to me said, "it was like watching Mike Tyson fight Cicely Tyson."

Lee Atwater came into the pressroom looking like a 600-pound gorilla that had just swallowed a 300-pound canary. "Dukakis did not achieve the goal of showing that he was a warm man," Atwater said. "I think he showed he was mean-spirited."

All the reporters scribbled this into their notebooks and nobody made the obvious joke: Being called mean-spirited by Lee Atwater was like being called ugly by a frog.

Mark Gearan, deputy press secretary, did his best for Dukakis. "Likability and warmth was not a major thing," he said. "We're electing a leader here. We have time left on the warmth thing."

Susan Estrich greeted reporters with a smile that looked like she had to have it tattooed on. She had some papers rolled up tightly in her fist and she kept twisting them back and forth.

Was Dukakis likable? she was asked. Did he seem warm?

"He did to me," she said. "We needed a conversation about our future, not a conversation about who is warm and cuddly. We're not looking for a neighbor. We're looking for someone to lead the world."

In Baltimore, at least one other observer liked Michael Dukakis' answer about the rape and murder of his wife.

Willie Horton, watching from his cell at the Maryland State Penitentiary, said: "What could the man do if that happened? He has to wait for the police. You can't take the law into your own hands."

"AFTERWARDS," Shaw said, "I shook hands with Dukakis and Kitty [Kitty would later say of Shaw's question: "It was inappropriate. It was pure theater"] and then I shook hands with Bush and he lingered with me for two or three minutes.

"Then Bush said to me: 'When are we going to have dinner? What are you doing tonight? Have dinner with Bar and me tonight.'

"And I thought to myself: There is no way in *hell* that I'm going to be seen having dinner with him tonight!"

Three weeks after his election, the President-elect called Shaw.

"Bernie," Bush said, "how does Peking duck sound?"

They met at the Vice President's residence and then went to a restaurant in Falls Church, Virginia. "People heard about it later and said: 'Now the payoff is apparent,' " Shaw said. "Then there were rumors that Bush wanted me for director of the USIA [United States Information Agency] or press secretary."

And did he offer you either of those? I asked.

"There was a desire to have me in the government," Shaw said. "But I told the President-elect I had three reasons not to. One, I believe once you cross the line into government you can never come back to journalism. Two, a pay cut is not progress to me. Three, I value my wife and children and the privacy of my family."

And if you had taken a job with Bush?

"It clearly would have been seen as a payoff," Shaw said. "And your credibility is all you have in this business."

Shaw's question to Bush about Quayle taking over as President posed no problems for Bush. His handlers had foreseen it and Bush had practiced his answer many times. Bush even felt comfortable enough to add a little humor by saying "Bernie!" in mock horror when Shaw mentioned his hypothetical death.

"Bush played that answer like a violin," Shaw said. "But all you can do is ask the question. And leave the rest to the intelligence of the voter."

AFTER THE DEBATE, the Dukakis people felt massive damage control was necessary. Not only was Dukakis the clear loser, but everybody kept harping on the same point: why hadn't he given his prepared answer about his family being crime victims?

This appeared in so many stories that finally Sasso decided that Dukakis had to go on the air and *repeat* the damn story just to satisfy people.

"A week and a half after the debate, we got a curious series of calls at CNN from the Dukakis people, suggesting an interview," Shaw said. "We said: 'Fine.'

"They asked: 'Who will do the interview?'

"We said: 'Either Shaw or Mary Alice Williams.'

"They said: 'We think it should be Shaw.'

"Well, that was a red flag, immediately making us suspicious, alarmed and resentful," Shaw said.

But Shaw and CNN went ahead with it anyway. "The interview took place in the airport manager's office at the Youngstown, Ohio, airport on November 1," Shaw said. "It was about 11 a.m. and Dukakis came in and we shook hands and he went immediately to a holding room. He came out with Sasso. We talked, but I was determined not to mention the debate. In the news, Bush had been hitting Dukakis for finally using the l-word. It was a two-camera interview, we were ready, rolling, and I said: 'Governor, Bush says that he has smoked you out of a liberal closet.' "

Dukakis decided to give his prepared answer no matter what Shaw asked. (And now, he no longer called him "Bernard," as he had in the debate. Dukakis was warmer now.)

DUKAKIS: "Well, Bernie, let me begin by saying thank you to you for coming out and doing this interview. And can I say something at the beginning? Lots of people have asked me about that question you asked me at the debate and let me say that I thought it was a fair question, a reasonable one.

"I think it took me aback a little bit, and in thinking about and [if] I had a chance to answer again, let me say this. Kitty is probably the most, *is* the most precious thing, she and my family, that I have in this world, and obviously, if what happened to her was the kind of thing that you described, I would have the same feelings as any loving husband and father."

SHAW: "Would you kill him?"

DUKAKIS: "I think I would have that kind of emotion. On the other hand, this is not a country where we glorify vengeance . . . but I'm a member of a family that has been victimized by crime . . . [Dukakis goes on to tell the story of his father and brother.]

"And I guess had I had to do it over again, that's the kind of answer I would have given."

Shaw said later: "As Dukakis was giving his answer Sasso was on one knee, out of camera range, and had made a fist with one hand and was going: 'Yeah! Yeah!' as Dukakis answered. It was like he was cheering on the team on the one-yard line. At that moment, I was vindicated. I knew that Dukakis' original response had haunted him for seventeen days. The press and his staff had been chewing his butt off for seventeen days. And Rather and Jennings led with my interview on the news that night."

But what did you think of Dukakis' new answer?

"I was embarrassed for him and appalled," Shaw said. "This was an attempt to revise history. He was trying to undo what he had done, change the public record."

Dukakis had been persuaded. He did a little tap dance this time because he was persuaded that it was how the game was played. This is what campaigning had come down to. Anyone who wanted to be the leader of a great nation and do great things first had to deal with furloughs and flags and bodybags. He had to show emotion. And in order to be likable, he had to tell people that yes, he would want to take a human life.

TWO DAYS AFTER the debate, George Bush was asked how he thought he had done.

"Read my smile," he said.

Two weeks after the debate, George Bush was asked if he would accept Dukakis' challenge to a third debate.

Bush pointed both his thumbs down.

"Read my fingers," he said.

☆

"I WAS JUST DOING my job, asking that question," Shaw said. "I thought of Murrow taking on McCarthy. That was the essence of what I wanted to be. And H. L. Mencken. People who were fearless, not afraid of the scorching bite of public criticism.

"I'm not afraid of being disliked. I'm not afraid of being criticized. In that debate, I did the right thing. I know I did. I know it."

☆ **15** ☆

THE PROMPTERS

"Can't act. Just have to be me."
—*George Bush, August 7, 1988*

ROGER AILES and Lee Atwater were the perfect Good Cop/Bad Cop team, but with one twist: there was no Good Cop.

There was no guy to hold your hand and comfort you after the other guy hit you with the rubber truncheon. There was only another guy with a bigger truncheon.

"I *hate* those people," Ailes was once overheard saying of the Dukakis staff. And nobody doubted that he meant it.

"He has two speeds," Atwater once proudly said of him. "Attack and destroy."

Ailes knew he and Atwater would be disliked by the opposition and the press throughout the campaign, but when things were over, well, he expected that people would realize that none of it had been personal. "You do what you're forced to do to win," Ailes said.

But as the campaign ground along, Ailes also realized that his and Atwater's role had become much too high-profile. Stories on handlers started making magazine covers. Which really was inevitable. As the candidates retreated farther and farther away from the press, the role of the handlers became more visible. The handlers were the guys who talked to the reporters. And reporters write about the people they talk to.

A few felt the power of the handlers was vastly overrated. Fred Barnes wrote a persuasive piece in *The New Republic* in June 1986 saying: "Consultants can help, but not much. If all goes extraordinarily well, they might add one or two percentage points." And for every consultant on the winning side, Barnes pointed out, there was one on the losing side that you rarely heard about. ("Hey, Babe Ruth struck out 1,300 times," Ailes said. "So what?")

Barnes may have been right, but those who studied Ailes and those who came up against Ailes were impressed by Ailes. And they thought he was worth more than one or two percentage points. "If Roger Ailes was working for Dukakis, he would be the front-runner," Kathleen Hall Jamieson, the oft-quoted political scientist, had written during the campaign.

"We didn't have a Roger Ailes," Susan Estrich said after the campaign. "I wish we had."

Ailes knew what they were really saying. They were giving the devil his due. They were really saying that Ailes was loathsome, but effective.

But only after the campaign did Ailes fully realize what had happened to him and Atwater: by compartmentalizing Bush, by keeping the blame away from him, they made themselves into the devils. And it could hurt.

"Underneath that exterior, he's really soft inside," Ailes's mother, Donna, seventy-two, once said of him.

"Yeah, that's what Mrs. Manson said," Ailes replied.

The criticism was O.K. while the campaign was going on. It was even kind of fun in a way. But after the election, it did not stop. And Ailes and Atwater were not, like President Bush or Secretary of State Baker, living high above the fray.

They were still down in the mud.

SPY MAGAZINE, which specializes in acid description, once described Roger Ailes, forty-nine, as "a dark, downright Satanic-looking character" (and Atwater as a "nervous little devil's helper . . . a bug-eyed gnome with a perpetual smirk and an uncanny ability to patronize blacks").

The adjectives most often found in the profiles written about Ailes are "plump," "balding," "burly," "hefty," "portly," "protean" and "wily." He is sometimes compared to Hemingway and sometimes to Orson Welles. His nickname for himself, "the Old Fox," does not seem to have caught on.

I see him coming toward me through the lobby of the Marriott in Crystal City, Virginia, across the Potomac from Washington. He is a rotund, but not a particularly large man. Say five feet ten and about 240 pounds. But not soft-looking.

He is wearing a blue suit, which looks expensive, but not elegant. A blue shirt, open at the collar, and a tie with geometric designs that places it either in the Eisenhower era or in the height of current fashion. His salt-and-pepper goatee is neatly trimmed.

It is months after the election, but Ailes is still an issue. Clients who hire him are accused of sending the signal that they are "going negative" and that there will be no holds barred. And Ailes knows that the easiest way for George Bush to signal that he wants to take the high road and be more presidential in his 1992 campaign is to dump Ailes.

On the other hand, Bush might want to win.

Ailes has recently had his name in the newspapers for attending a state dinner at the White House for Hosni Mubarak, the President of Egypt. "It was the *first* state dinner," Ailes points out. "I had to sit next to Cheryl Ladd." He laughs. "I told George, 'Hey, I come here to meet big guys in government, politics, my expertise, and I end up next to Cheryl Ladd.' George said: 'I did it on purpose.' Then he laughed his ass off. He's such a sweet guy.

"He is, you know. Tender. And you know, I was at *his* table at the state dinner. That was on purpose. That was to show people that these rumors he's trying to distance himself from me are all full of shit. It was no accident."

Ailes had worked for Richard Nixon and Ronald Reagan (as well as John Connally in 1980, one of the losing campaigns you never seem to hear about), and I ask him how many Republicans tried to hire him this time.

"Everyone tried to get me but Robertson," he says. "I spent three hours with Haig. He pitched me for three hours. I mean, jeez." Ailes rolls his eyes. "Can you believe it? Dole had me in and I said: 'Hire me as your third guy.' He asked why. And I said: 'Because you're gonna fire the first two. Bush may be out of the race quick and then you can hire me.'

"A lot of guys wanted me. I have a theory, though, and the first rule is that a candidate I support cannot be nuts. Can't take himself too seriously. Whatever else he is, Bush is genuinely sane. He has a balanced view of things. He is genuinely sane and good."

But you sold America on Richard Nixon, I say. He was nuts, wasn't he?

Ailes shifts slightly in his seat. "I was a TV producer. I was twenty-eight, a kid. I didn't know him. But I guess you could say the two Presidents who were nuts were Carter and Nixon."

We start talking about Willie Horton. Ailes points out he never did a Willie Horton ad—he did "The Revolving Door"—and he's going to sue anybody who claims he did.

"If Horton had been white, we would have done more," Ailes says. "We would have done a lot more. But see, it wasn't just a crime issue. It was Dukakis' *insensitivity* to crime. At the [second] debate, Dukakis became a defense counsel for his wife's attacker! I said the question was unfair and I think Shaw wanted Dukakis to win. [Ailes thought the question was a softball designed so Dukakis could hit it out of the park.] Shaw's no Bush fan, let me put it that way. Bernie is angry that he's not Dan Rather or Tom Brokaw."

Ailes began talking about how Shaw's question, however, got to the true coldness of Dukakis. "Gephardt did these focus groups—I don't know how we got the stuff, but we did," Ailes says with a grin, "and it showed the more exposed you were to Dukakis, the less you liked him. So we knew we didn't have to be afraid of too many debates. I went into the negotiations with the knowledge that to know Dukakis was to dislike Dukakis. Now, we fought against a lot of debates anyway, but I wasn't scared of them."

If Ailes wasn't scared of Dukakis, he was scared of one thing: that George—sweet guy that he is—might screw up somehow. Ailes had told *Advertising Age* that the difference between selling a candidate and selling cookies is that "cookies don't get off the shelf and hold news conferences or make gaffes or go on *Meet the Press*."

In other words, his task was to make the candidate as passive and obedient as a package of cookies, a product. And sometimes Ailes would treat Bush like one. *Time* magazine wrote about how Ailes was with Bush as he was about to be interviewed by Tom Brokaw and how Ailes reaches over and "yanks an errant hair from the vice presidential eyebrow. 'That hurt,' winces Bush."

Which is another difference between cookies and a presidential candidate. Cookies don't wince when reporters are around to take it all down.

I know you don't have much respect for reporters, I say to Ailes, but do you actually hate them?

"I have a reputation for being a wild man and press hater and a zealot, but it's not true," he says. "I don't hate the press. I like and understand them. I do think most people on our side are afraid to take the press on, like they are perfect. And did we provide pictures, mistakes and attacks to control the news? You bet. I played the game better than anyone else. *That's* what the press doesn't like about Roger Ailes."

On a panel at Harvard after the election, Ailes said: "That's the one sure way of getting coverage. You try to avoid as many mistakes as you can. You try to give them as many pictures as you can. And if you need coverage, attack and you will get coverage."

Judy Woodruff of *The MacNeil/Lehrer NewsHour* had then said to him: "So you're saying the notion of the candidate saying: 'I want to run for President because I want to do something for this country' is crazy."

"Suicide," Ailes replied.

"The press is part of the negative process they attack," Ailes tells me. "Is Ailes negative? Go read the headlines and you'll see who's *really* negative. A guy plays a wonderful symphony and at the end he falls in the orchestra pit and him falling in the pit will be the story. I knew I could *always* get a headline if I went negative. The press egged me into going negative and then hit me for it."

What about your famous line to Joe McGinniss in *The Selling of the President 1968*: "This is the beginning of a whole new concept. This is it. This is the way they'll be elected forevermore. The next guys up will have to be performers."

"I knew this era was coming," Ailes says to me. "But I was not talking about acting, I was talking about performing. Acting is being something you are not. Performing is being at your best.

"But I'm not saying performance is more important than substance. I'm saying it is easier for a guy to get elected if he is comfortable performing. Dukakis was this rigid guy. Bush was comfortable with the camera. And the camera was friendlier to George because George was friendlier to the camera. It's spooky, almost like the camera had a brain.

"And George's view is that there are a lot smarter people than him, but he'll make the final decision. George made his decisions consciously. Dukakis made his unconsciously. He could never say: 'I'm a screw-up, get me somebody who can help me.'

"In a presidential race the intangibles are more important than the tangibles. And Dukakis missed them all. He didn't understand the symbols: Horton, flags, the goodness of George. He was a man whose feelings were so bottled up, he could not understand the feelings of others."

George Bush did make his decisions consciously. He was a man who knew what he wanted and which guys to hire to tell him how to get it. A man who knew you didn't spend a lot of money for advice unless you were willing to take that advice. A man who knew how to keep his hands clean. A man who knew how to use the hired help, but never to become confused with the hired help.

THE OFFICE OUTSIDE Lee Atwater's private sanctum at Republican National Committee headquarters has a large color picture on one wall of Atwater and Bush jogging. Bush has been captured, amazingly, with both feet off the ground. Bush's fists are clenched in determination, but he looks good, comfortable, as though he knows when the photographer will snap the shutter. Atwater's mouth is a gash of strain—as though he, too, knows when the photographer will snap the shutter. Each has picked his image. And there is one more thing to note. Though Atwater, at thirty-eight, is more than a quarter century younger than Bush, Atwater is jogging a careful half step behind him. It is Atwater's favorite picture and another copy hangs inside his office above his chair.

Atwater motions me forward with two fingers and we enter his office. It is very dark and dignified with dark blue carpeting and blue leather seats. It is almost presidential. As Bush is the first RNC chairman to become President, Atwater is the first professional consultant to become RNC chairman. Atwater sits down at the head of a conference table, tilts his chair back and puts his tasseled loafers against the edge of the table. He is all angles and elbows and edges. He has a piercing gaze. His nose swivels and points at you like a compass needle.

On the walls behind him are pictures of David Letterman, Zsa Zsa Gabor, Donald Trump and Charlton Heston. There are many of Cheryl Ladd and dozens of Bush, one signed: "To my trusted adviser and friend."

There is also a wall of cartoons, some really tough, one depicting Atwater, Willie Horton and the KKK. Atwater shrugs when I mention them. "Doesn't bother me," he says. "I'm a professional lightning rod. I ain't never going to run for office."

I begin by asking him about the negative nature of the campaign.

"There's one thing I don't get," Atwater says. "We were all supposed to be wimps, right? I mean, it was the Wimp Campaign, right? Then, all of a sudden, we're the meanest people in the world. I have a firm code of ethics: I don't give much quarter."

To some it is even more simple than that. Democratic representative Pat Schroeder, for instance, calls Lee Atwater "the most evil man in America."

Today he is tired, however. Maybe he has spent the day mugging Girl Scouts and stealing from church poor boxes. He wipes his hand across his face and says, "Hey, come to Boston with me tomorrow. We'll have time to talk then."

The next day, I wait for him at National Airport as the plane to Boston loads. He and an aide come seconds before departure. Atwater had been working and then went jogging and then jumped in the Lincoln Town Car provided by the RNC, but got caught in traffic. We get the last seats on the plane.

He is wearing a blue hopsack blazer with the lining hanging below the hem of the jacket, gray slacks, tasseled black loafers and a striped shirt. His foot constantly taps against the seat back as he speaks as if keeping time to the blues guitar music he has played since a young man. ("Even as a baby that boy couldn't sit still," his mother, Toddy, once told a reporter. "The doctor said his nervous system wasn't quite right, 'cause his leg shook, his little mouth quivered. He was just a nervous little boy.")

As we talk, his eyes dart constantly over the other passengers in the plane, lingering now and again on an attractive woman across the aisle. Though he doesn't like to be away from his wife and daughters overnight if he can help it, Atwater likes to look at women, hold their hands and pat their shoulders. He even kisses hands, continuing sometimes to the elbow.

As a young man, Harvey Lee Atwater made lists, just like Jay Gatsby. And when he was twenty, Atwater vowed to read two books per week that would contribute to his self-improvement. This actually doubled Gatsby's goal. "Read one improving book or magazine per week . . ." Gatsby had written in his diary.

(George Bush had no need of such vows. He had no need to *be* Gatsby. As people of his class and breeding knew, he could *hire* Gatsbys.)

How long did you spend planning the 1988 race? I ask Atwater.

"At a certain level since 1972 or 1973," he says. "I was twenty and I wanted to be on the presidential level of politics. I developed a thesis, a dogma, a belief, based on work in 1971 and 1972, that if we in the Republican Party could develop a Sunbelt political base, plus the mega-state anchors of California, Texas and Florida, we'd have a 70 percent chance of winning the presidency until the millennium."

You were thinking about things like the electoral college and politics until the millennium at age twenty?

He seems a little disconcerted by the question. "Yeah, well, there's nothing unusual about that, is there?" he says.

No. Perfectly normal. Happens a lot.

We land at Logan Airport, where there is no car to meet us. Atwater's aide gets on a cellular phone. A number of passersby look at Atwater closely as we stand waiting. I ask him if he gets recognized much.

"I get recognized more by blacks than by whites," he says. "I think it's the whole music thing."

Or, just possibly, the whole Willie Horton thing.

A limousine finally pulls up containing Ray Shamie, the head of the Massachusetts Republican Party. Shamie apologizes for the small size of the limo.

"No, it's better," Atwater says. "This way nobody can tell it's a limo and we don't look like such assholes."

We drive to the new Massachusetts Republican headquarters, a renovated warehouse, bare brick and exposed beams, in Watertown. I ask Atwater if he has seen Dukakis since the election.

"I have *never* seen him. Ever," he says, surprised. "He doesn't see people like me."

As we enter the headquarters, Atwater is careful to say hello to the "little" people, who sit at the front table handing out name tags. A young and pretty photographer has been hired to capture Atwater on film at this event, and Atwater kisses her on the forehead.

He goes into a crowded room for a news conference and begins with a small joke: "I'd be glad to answer any questions that I deem appropriate."

He is asked about David Duke, the former Ku Klux Klan Grand Wizard who won election to the Louisiana state legislature in February 1989 as a Republican.

"David Duke is a charlatan and an overt racist and there is no place for him in this party," Atwater says. "But I suggest the Democrats focus on Mr. Farrakhan, who spoke in New Orleans this weekend. We've been loud and clear on David Duke. Ask Jesse Jackson what he thinks about Mr. Farrakhan!"

Atwater is asked about the use of Willie Horton in the campaign.

"It was not about Willie Horton, it was about the furlough issue," he says. "It was about murderers with no chance of parole getting out on weekend vacations without supervision. Willie Horton stabbed a man nineteen times . . . and stuck him in a trash can! I didn't know his race when I first heard of Willie Horton. The furlough plan defied common sense. It was ludicrous. It was wrong. What we did had no racial connotation whatsoever. Our campaign made no TV commercials about Willie Horton. And Dukakis used a Hispanic in a furlough ad in Texas!"

After the news conference, he turns to me. "There's an endless fascination with Willie Horton," he says.

After Atwater gives another couple of speeches, we head back to Washington. Atwater has taken a bag of cheese popcorn onto the plane with him and munches the popcorn as he talks.

"I read three books over and over," he says. "*The Prince*, by Machiavelli. Clausewitz's *On War*. And *The Art of War* by Sun Tzu. The Thomas Cleary translation is very good." He has a copy in his briefcase and pulls it out. "After the presidential campaign, this book has new meaning," he says.

What was the key to your strategy in the campaign? I ask.

"One, stay on the offense. Two, control the political agenda," he says.

Define "political agenda."

"The topic being discussed by the free media," he says. "What is on the free media is the agenda."

In other words, manipulating the press was essential to your victory?

Atwater nods as if it were obvious.

And it wasn't just the big stories, was it? It was the little anecdotes that made Bush look good, a Regular Guy and all the rest.

Atwater smiles. "You do that through an informal process," he says. "That's important."

Atwater knew all about the informal process. He knew the media players. He knew about returning the right phone calls, holding the private breakfasts and the background briefings. He knew whom to leak to and when to leak it.

(According to University of Virginia professor Larry J. Sabato, one reason the press was not tougher in its coverage of the handlers is that the handlers were their best sources. ". . . there is a desperate need for the press to stop treating consultants as the gods of the political wars and to end their sweetheart arrangement," Sabato wrote.)

Atwater and his people knew the value of the little details, like the colorful anecdote. Many newspapers ran potpourri or tidbit columns throughout the campaign that contained political gossip and "color." Such columns were often far better read, one suspects, than the weightier political stories.

And they could make important, though subtle, points. A typical item, from *The New York Times*'s "Campaign Trail" column of October 21, listed the eating habits of the two candidates. Bush was listed as liking "pork rinds, taco salads and tuna sandwiches on Air Force Two during the day, then almost invariably eats dinner at a restaurant . . . where he mingles with patrons in some impromptu campaigning.

"Mr. Dukakis, on the other hand, rarely eats out, dining on room service food . . . On the Dukakis plane, the candidate often has meals that his aides find unpalatable . . . Raisin Bran and milk, which the candidate eats every morning."

The contrast in images is striking. Here is Bush eating tuna sandwiches and pressing the flesh with the common folk in restaurants, while Dukakis is holed up in his hotel room munching his "unpalatable" fiber.

Atwater knew this all helped. It all counted. It was all part of the Message. The Message was whatever the Bush handlers had decided to emphasize for that day: crime, education, patriotism, whatever.

"But for the Message to work, everyone [in the campaign] had to be on board," Atwater says. "Everyone had to have the same Message and not let the media pick you off one by one. Harmony. Like Sun Tzu said: 'Harmony among people is the basis of the way of military operations.' This is what Dukakis never understood. The other side, they just didn't have the discipline."

But for the Message of the Day to work, you had to keep the candidate away from the media, right? Otherwise, the media might find a different message by asking questions.

"Yes," Atwater says, "the companion to the Message of the Day is to limit media access. Mondale in '84 killed himself by giving access to the media."

A few reporters had actually mentioned to Dukakis aides late in the campaign that Dukakis was "stepping on his own message" by having news conferences. Dukakis would try to promote his own Message of the Day, but then he would hold a news conference, which often would produce negative stories he could not control. Dukakis' aides did not have to be told this by the press, however. They had already noticed that the candidate who gave the press the most access got the most negative stories, while Bush, who had cut the press off, got his own Message in print and on the air.

"You give the press access and they don't even respect you for it," Atwater says, shaking his head. "It's give-and-take in our business. We can't limit to the extent we want and we can't give access to the extent the press wants."

Atwater settles his seat back and prepares to take a nap. He invites me to read his copy of Sun Tzu. Sun Tzu lived in China in the fourth century B.C. and was a consultant just like Atwater. His clients were warlords, not presidential candidates, but Atwater thought that made little difference. Conquering the enemy was the same whether it was by the sword or by the ballot box.

As Atwater naps, I flip through the book and notice that more than one of the passages he has underlined deal with Sun Tzu's praise for deception. One is: "A military operation involves deception." Written in the margin at another point in Atwater's hand is: "Unification of wills."

Deception and discipline are big factors in Atwater's planning. Deception to throw the other side and the press off guard. And discipline to keep your own side in line, presenting the same message, the same image, the same act.

In a 1986 profile for *Esquire* magazine, David Remnick captured the essential Atwater. "There is one other rule of political life that Lee Atwater repeats all the time," he wrote. "So far it has kept him afloat: 'Play dumb and keep moving.' "

WE ARE on the Bush press bus blasting down the freeway to Cerritos, about thirty miles to the west of Los Angeles. It is the day after the second presidential debate and the handlers have had their regular morning meeting. Under the direction of James Baker, the Message of the Day and of the Week are determined, based on the input of Teeter, Atwater, Ailes, Fuller and others.

And the Message is: No overconfidence. Keep campaigning hard. But no big departures from the game plan. Fall on the ball until election day.

The Message will be conveyed to Bush, who will have the option of rejecting it, but why would he? It has all worked so far.

As the motorcade roars down the freeway, we notice there are no other vehicles on the road. There are four empty lanes, all cleared for George Bush. And at each entrance ramp, we can see the cars backed up, stopped by state troopers. And by the sides of the cars, angry motorists are standing and steaming and swearing.

And that is why there is nothing on the sides of the campaign cars and buses to indicate this is a George Bush motorcade. No way. The Bush people are not stupid. When you tie up traffic, you make sure nobody knows who you are.

And if Lee Atwater is half the man I think he is, he probably has teams of kids out there at each entrance ramp, going from car to car and saying, "Hey, that's Michael Dukakis in that motorcade! It's Dukakis blocking all this traffic! Can you believe the *nerve* of that guy?"

We pull off the freeway at Cerritos and head down a street where we pass twenty-four yellow school buses all neatly lined up nose to tail. Crowds don't just happen; crowds are created. Crowds are bused in.

At Heritage Park, the people are holding signs that say: "Bush 2, Dukakis 0" and "It's Over." A mini-blimp hangs in a sky with puffy white clouds. On the blimp is a banner reading: "Say Good Night, Mike."

There are high school pompon girls in red blouses and tiny yellow skirts marching up and down with military precision. There is a rock band, none of whose members were alive in the sixties, playing Golden Oldies from that era. Atwater believes in the baby boomer vote and so the rallies have baby boomer music.

Bush emerges from his limousine and goes to a holding room in one of the park buildings. The reporters, about a hundred of us, go to the designated press area in front of the stage.

Sheila Tate, Bush's press secretary, walks up to us to deliver the Message of the Day and we all crowd around her.

"We are going to campaign down to the wire," Tate says. "We think this is going to be a close election." In fact, they do not think this is going to be a close election. But literal truth is not the point. The Message is the point.

"It's not over till it's over," Tate says. "The Vice President wants to keep campaigning hard."

Onstage, the introduction of George Bush has begun, but Tate does not stop speaking. None of us pay any attention to what is happening onstage. It is far more important to get the Message from Tate.

And so we miss it when Representative Bob Dornan says to the crowd: "Didn't the Vice President make it easy for us to say how he *coldcocked* that debate!"

Tate keeps talking. "We are all in a terrific mood," she says. "We're going to continue to inspire crowds and talk about issues."

Onstage, Bush steps up to the microphone and gets an uproarious welcome. "What a fantastic rally!" he says.

Tate does not bother to turn around. She keeps talking. "We want to continue to control the agenda of the campaign, the discussion of the issues," she says. "People have a pretty good sense of who the candidates are."

"I'm glad that the last debate is over," Bush is saying. "I believe I moved my campaign forward by what happened last night."

Tate keeps talking. The reporters continue to huddle around her, pressing up against each other, reaching their tape recorders up close to her mouth to capture her words.

"We're going to hustle," Sheila Tate is saying. "We're going to hustle to the last day."

Onstage, Bush is saying something or other, but the reporters are playing back their tape recorders now, whizzing through them, trying to get a lead paragraph from Tate's briefing.

Off behind the camera platform, where long tables of food have been set up for the press, Lee Atwater ambles into view. The reporters run to greet him. New tapes are popped into the recorders. Fresh pages of the notebooks are readied.

Atwater is eating a pasta salad out of a Styrofoam bowl. "We had a strategy meeting this morning and we decided if we get smug and overconfident, it will be a disaster," he says. "We're not going to attempt to change our strategy. Dukakis has problems. He's gotta draw an inside straight here. We figure we have from 205 to 236 electoral votes."

And they need only 270 to win. We scribble like mad to get all this down. This is good stuff! Hard figures! This is news.

Onstage, George Bush is talking. "Only one man shares the values of the ordinary Americans," he says. "I am that man!" The crowd roars. The reporters move closer to Atwater to hear what he is saying.

Atwater explains how "four or five" states with big electoral vote counts could switch around, but that Dukakis would have to win almost all the big Midwestern states and the Northeast as well as California to win the election.

"If he loses one or two of them, he is out," Atwater says.

Onstage, Bush is finishing up. "I am a Teddy Roosevelt Republican," he says. "I believe we must preserve our natural environment and preserve our economic growth at the same time!"

The reporters begin asking Atwater questions. Only Deborah Orin, a political reporter for the New York *Post*, leaves to go up to the stage after the speech and shout a question at Bush from behind the restraining ropes.

"No, no, there is no overconfidence," Bush responds. "I remember how these polls can change."

Orin comes back to the press area. "I just got a quotation from Bush," she says. "Does anybody want it?"

A few reporters glance at her. Then they turn back to Atwater. One reporter asks him if there has been too much emphasis on handlers in this campaign and whether the public will someday begin to resent their role.

Atwater screws up his face into a hatchet.

"It's a spurious issue," he says. "It won't stick. People don't care about that."

DEATH MARCH

*Q: If Michael Dukakis and George Bush were both on a
sinking ship, who would be saved?
A: America.*

—*Popular joke, November 1988*

Wednesday, November 2, 1988

In 1968, Hubert Humphrey declared his candidacy 120 days before
the Democratic convention. Michael Dukakis declared his 540 days
before the Democratic convention and had actually made his first
campaign trip some 81 days before that.

By now, most people are very weary of it all. Yet Dukakis himself
is beginning a personal transformation. He has finally found some
get-up-and-go just about the time the interest of the American people
has got up and went.

The Dukakis campaign crunches its numbers, studies the electoral
college vote count and comes up with its endgame scenario. John
Sasso announces that Dukakis must win New York and California
plus four out of the five states of Pennsylvania, Ohio, Michigan,
Illinois and Texas to be elected. That's all.

Dukakis feels he has a chance. He knows this because the daily
tracking polls show the gap narrowing between him and Bush. The
tracking polls are breathing life into the candidate and the staff.
Intellectually, many of them know the truth: tracking polls are the
least reliable of all polls. That's because few people have the self-
discipline to look at them properly. A tracking poll will measure, say,
300 voters a day for four days. Each day the poll will add a new 300
and drop the first 300. So taken together, the poll uses 1,200 voters
and is a reasonable national sample.

But you have to look at the four days taken together. What is
virtually irresistible, however, is to look at just the last day, see yourself

within 4 points of George Bush and think: That's it! A trend! We've got him now!

In fact, taking just the last day may be worthless because the sample is too small and too easily affected by transitory events like news stories and small flubs.

This is what the Dukakis campaign aides know intellectually. Emotionally, however, they can feel the spirit. Dukakis is up. The sap is rising.

"There was the spirit it was actually possible," Mark Gearan, deputy press secretary, said. "Nick [Mitropoulos] would call in all the time for the numbers. Dukakis wanted the numbers. All the numbers. Every day. We had our tracking polls and the networks had theirs and Bush had his. Everybody's was different. But still, there was the feeling it was doable. It was real. We felt, somehow, someway, maybe we could still win."

The staff called it the Surge. "I think it's building and it's getting stronger and stronger," Dukakis said, sitting in the back of his car in California. He waved at the crowds through the window. "I think it's that when you're not that well known it takes time to give people a sense of who you are and what your values are and what you stand for and what you believe in."

He admitted that he was just now learning how to really campaign. "Well, look, you've got to find your rhythm, you know?" he said. "I mean, you've got to find what works."

The car passed a group of protesters dressed in prison uniforms symbolizing Willie Horton. Dukakis waved at them, too, and laughed and said: "Hello, guys."

"I think it's beginning to connect," he said. "Look, we have strengths. We have weaknesses like every campaign. If we win on the eighth of November, people will say: 'Well, it was a good campaign.' When we appeared to be doing well, everybody said it was a *terrific* campaign."

And that truly is the wonderful thing about winning. It is the ultimate analgesic. It takes all the pain away. Things that looked like disasters now look like strokes of genius. After the election, I would pose to Lee Atwater the problem of campaign books: everything the loser did looks like a mistake and everything the winner did looks like a triumph. Surely, it really can't be that way.

"The Bush campaign may be the one instance where that stereotype is absolutely true," Atwater said. Then he laughed like hell.

But now, as the last week of the campaign begins, the tracking polls show Bush's lead slipping into single digits. And Michael Dukakis believes it can be done. All he has to do to erase all his mistakes is to win.

Dukakis flies to Philadelphia and goes to Martin Luther King, Jr. High School for an evening rally. He is tired and hoarse, but this is the last major black event he has. Even Jesse Jackson is now allowed on the same stage with him.

In the packed auditorium, Martin Luther King III begins by invoking the ghost of his martyred father. "We must elect Mike Dukakis because it is right!" he says. "I am sure if my father were alive, he'd say the same thing."

Well, it is theoretically possible anyway.

The crowd is on its feet and roaring as Jesse Jackson steps forward. The event is being carried live to thirty-two states by the Black Entertainment Network. Jackson begins by listing all the places he has been campaigning on behalf of Dukakis. This is his "Frequent Flier" speech, proving he has not sat back and done nothing for the Democratic Party even after it has robbed him of his rightful place on the ticket.

"Spoken to more people," Jackson says. "Traveled more miles. In South Dakota on Friday morning. Oakland. Los Angeles. McAllen, Texas. Austin and Dallas and Fort Worth. Jacksonville, Tallahassee. Traveling across this country today from Atlanta, Georgia, to New Haven, Connecticut, down to Philadelphia and on to Baltimore tomorrow. Then to Delaware, Arkansas, Mississippi and Chicago." Everywhere he goes, Jackson registers voters. Voters who can, if they really want to, vote for Michael Dukakis on November 8. But they also may be able to vote for Jesse Jackson on some future Tuesday in November. The thought has crossed his mind.

Jackson mops his face in the sticky heat of the hall. "The race does not go to the swift, the strong or the rich," he says. "But to those who hold out. Judge not by passion, but by priorities. The people supply the passion."

Or at least they must supply it when the candidate does not.

"He will keep hope alive! Michael Dukakis!" Jackson throws out an arm and Dukakis walks to the lectern. The ovation is very large and Dukakis beams. Then he gives his usual twenty-minute canned speech, promising: "Clean air, clean water, clean government in Washington, D.C."

The crowd, expecting poetry, gets prose. Prosaic prose. And the mood ratchets down from enthusiastic to subdued to sullen. People begin drifting out the doors as Dukakis stands on the stage saying: "This race is starting to tighten up! People are focusing in!"

It is the last event of the day and afterward reporters check into the Warwick Hotel. Elizabeth Dole has been campaigning in Philadelphia for Bush this day, and now Bush operatives stand in the Warwick bar spinning the Dukakis press corps. One operative writes down electoral votes on a cocktail napkin. "Texas is ours," he says. "The South, of course. And the West." He goes on and on, listing the states Bush can count on. He stops at 300 electoral votes. And smiles. All Bush needs to win is 270.

Thursday, November 3

Michael Dukakis is fifty-five today. At 8:12 a.m. he appears live on *CBS This Morning* and says: "I am a marathoner. This is the time for a sprint. People are seeing the real Mike Dukakis. The Mike Dukakis who feels deeply about this country."

Dukakis is asked where he is doing well.

"The big states," he says. "As well as the small states."

(Which ranks right up there with George Bush's recent comment: "It's no exaggeration to say the undecideds could go one way or another.")

Dukakis is relentlessly upbeat. "With five days to go we're charging ahead," he says. "One of the things that's been difficult for me to do until recently is give the American people a sense of who I am and what I believe in and the strong passions and feelings for people I have."

In other words, Dukakis has failed to do exactly those things that campaigns are supposed to do. But what was his problem?

"I think I was a little too restrained perhaps," he says.

His next stop is Pennsbury High School in Fairness, Pennsylvania. At 10:35 a.m., Dukakis mounts the stage accompanied by Mark Hamill, best known for his role as Luke Skywalker in the *Star Wars* movies. Hamill goes to the microphone and says: "Dare I say it? The Force is with us?" It gets a small giggle. Bush is barnstorming the nation accompanied by Arnold Schwarzenegger and brings down the house every time he calls him "Conan the Republican." Dukakis is traveling around with a guy whose lines were less interesting than R2D2's.

Dukakis walks to the front of the stage, stops and strips off his suit jacket. The crowd roars.

He is wearing a red tie and a blue shirt and now he rolls up his sleeves. He grabs a wireless mike and stalks the stage like Phil Donahue. "We have five percent of the world's population and we consume fifty percent of the world's cocaine!" he says. "We must set as our goal drug-free schools in the 1990s in every community in America!"

Then a moment comes that will be quoted in article after article. Peter Roberts, ten, from Bristol, Pennsylvania, a fifth-grader at Warren Snyder School, stands up in the audience. "I am supposed to be you in a debate tomorrow. Any suggestions?"

Everyone chuckles.

"Smile frequently," Dukakis says, "and speak slowly." He pauses. "Respond to attacks immediately."

Everyone laughs.

"All kidding aside, be strong, be positive," Dukakis says. "Don't let them get away with anything. Don't let them put any commercials out there."

Sam Donaldson makes an entry in the journal he is keeping for the Gannett Center for Media Studies: "Now this isn't 'boffo,' but from a man who almost never pokes any fun at himself—or anyone else for that matter—and who seldom shows a flash of warmth, it's pleasantly astounding."

But just to prove he has not become too appealing, Dukakis reverts to form. "You can make plastic bags out of cornstarch, did you know that?" he asks the audience.

People look at each other and then look at him and shake their heads.

"And when you're done," he says, "you put them in the compost pile and they are biodegradable!"

There. That ought to tighten up the race some.

He drives back to Philadelphia for a mega-rally in Dillworth Plaza outside City Hall. It is a fine, crisp day and the leaves are bright in their autumn colors. A crowd of 10,000 to 15,000 has gathered. Dukakis stands in front of a giant American flag. He strips off his suit jacket. The crowd roars.

"We're coming on strong all across the country!" Dukakis shouts. The phrases now burst from Dukakis' mouth like star shells. "The Republicans are popping the champagne corks in their penthouses! But I'll tell you something! We're the ones gonna be celebrating! With cheese steaks right here in Philadelphia!"

This is one of Dukakis' "tailored" lines. He changes it for each locale. It can be: "With Old Milwaukee beer right here in Milwaukee!" or "With Kansas City ribs right here in Kansas City!" etc.

"I'm on your side!" Dukakis booms. "I'm on your children's side. I'm on America's side." This is the new "populist" theme that seems to be causing the polls to narrow and has Atwater mildly worried.

"I'll tell you," Dukakis goes on, "I was in Independence, Missouri, and I saw a sign: 'Give 'em hell, Mike.' And I'll tell you, it inspired me. No question about it!"

(As Dukakis knows, virtually all signs at political rallies are made under the direction of the campaign's own advance staff.)

"The tide is rolling! The people are with us! Mike Dukakis and Lloyd Bentsen are going to win this election!"

Balloons are released. The band plays. Dukakis throws his hands into the air in victory.

Bruce Morton of CBS will say: "Mike Dukakis is hot."

Dan Rather calls it a "new, aggressive campaign style."

Sam Donaldson says it is a "new, hard-charging, hard-hitting Dukakis on the trail these days" and calls him "fiery."

Everyone is talking about the new enthusiasm of the candidate. As if Sleeping Beauty had, after twenty-one months, finally awakened from her slumbers. But didn't it used to be the voters' enthusiasm that counted? It is not the crowds that are so fired up (the crowd response in Philadelphia is largely tepid); it is the candidate who is suddenly energized.

Finally, at the eleventh hour, Michael Dukakis has become enthusiastic about . . . Michael Dukakis.

We fly to Bridgeport, Connecticut, where additional star power is added to the campaign in the form of actress Debra Winger. Winger, best known for her performance in *Terms of Endearment*, is enjoying herself, and her raspy voice fills the press bus through the day and into the night. "I'm doing surge control," she says. "Did you hear CBS? They say we're moving ahead in all major states! You should get the lowdown because it's pretty exciting stuff. You've heard of pillow talk? This is surge talk! And if I have to talk surge talk, it's X-rated."

Winger loves to ride in the back of the bus and sing oldies and talk dirty. We have all been on the road for a long time and the air is sexually charged around her. On an earlier campaign trip on the West Coast, Winger was back in the press section of *Sky Pig* when Dukakis poked his head in. As reporters tried to get him to answer questions, Winger said: "If you don't talk to them, they're going to make me the sacrificial virgin." Then she added: "*That* would be stretching the truth a little bit." Dukakis, unsmiling, retreated to first class.

Winger is now kneeling on a bus seat facing backward as we roll through the Connecticut countryside. "There was this really great sign in Philadelphia," she says. "It was a very dignified sign. It said:

'Bush Is a Weenie!'" She laughs a throaty laugh. "I was at this Halloween parade in New York and it's all transvestites and they have a theme and someone said: 'Why do they all look like Marlo Thomas?' And then I realized they were doing *Marilyn Quayle!*"

(In Georgetown in Washington, D.C., on Halloween night, couples dressed up as Michael Dukakis and Willie Horton.)

At 8:30 p.m., with the temperature hovering near freezing, we pull into Ansonia, Connecticut, for a Main Street rally in front of City Hall. The street is brilliantly lit by portable floodlights. The local band is dressed in Revolutionary War garb and Winger has agreed to warm up the crowd. She is dressed in a long coat and a big black hat with a bow and flower on the side, reminiscent of a nineteenth-century suffragette. Winger speaks simply, and her sincerity is effective: "I have an eighteen-month-old son and George Bush is his nightmare. I don't want the co-captains of this administration to pick my next Supreme Court justices. I think of all the people who have been beaten up for the last eight years and it makes me want to get the vote out on Tuesday."

Dukakis takes the stage to the throbbing rhythms of Neil Diamond's "Coming to America." He looks over at Winger and then turns to the crowd and says: "Where did she get that hat anyway?"

Love that Mike.

Friday, November 4

Surge rumors mount. The Presidential Campaign Hotline tracking poll for the day before has Bush's lead down to 6 percentage points among "probable voters." Probable voters are defined as those who voted in 1980 and 1984 and "know where their voting place is."

We begin the day in Forest Hills, Queens, which is Geraldine Ferraro's neighborhood. Dukakis is supposed to have New York wrapped up, but the tracking figures are whipsawing the campaign both ways. Just as good numbers send him flying across the country in the hopes of winning Ohio, they also send him careening back to New York, to shore up those areas where he shows signs of slippage.

The intersection of Austin Avenue and Seventy-first Street has been blocked off for the rally. An arch of multicolored balloons spans the street. About 3,000 people are in the intersection. Squads of plainclothes police mingle with the crowds as dark-uniformed SWAT team members stand on the roof of the Woolworth with scoped rifles. They are protecting not just Dukakis but also luminaries like Daryl Hannah, Cher and Chastity, Caroline Kennedy, Senator Daniel Patrick Moynihan, Governor Mario Cuomo and Mayor Ed Koch.

Dukakis takes the stage. Though it is bright daylight, he is lit by spotlights anyway. He strips off his suit jacket. The crowd roars.

He attacks Bush for stealing his slogan. "Four days before the election," Dukakis says, "after all the slogans and the symbols and the advertising, four days before the election and he tells you he's on your side? Who's he kidding? He's on your side? He's for people who already have it made! *We're* on your side! *We're* on your side!"

We bus back to La Guardia and fly west. In Lexington, Kentucky, at Bluegrass Airport, we are told that Dukakis' official Line of the Day (what the Bush campaign calls the Message of the Day) is: "He's on your side? He's for people who already have it made!"

It has become a point of pride among the reporters to resist being spoon-fed this kind of stuff by the campaigns and the game is to see how low we can put it in our stories. It is difficult to bury it too deeply, however. The Dukakis people have learned—finally—from the Bush people that in order to reinforce the impact of the Line of the Day, you make sure that it is the only new line used all day.

This is an outdoor event and a small stage has been set up on the tarmac. On one side, there is a buffet table with cold cuts for the press. But thunderheads boil up on the horizon and race swiftly toward us. The wind begins to gust and the American flags are soon whipping straight out from their poles. There are about 1,000 people here and they are having difficulty holding on to their campaign signs. The rain begins, lashing the open expanse of the runways. A camera comes crashing down off the press platform. It is 5:15 p.m., the light is fading, the rain is pelting, but Dukakis decides to give his whole speech. Unlike Bush, who considers fifteen minutes a very long speech and five minutes just fine, Dukakis rarely speaks less than twenty minutes. Not even a thunderstorm can stop him.

"I smell victory in the air, don't you?" he says. Actually, all we can smell is wet salami. An aide holds a blue-and-white-striped golf umbrella over Dukakis' head. "The Republicans are popping the champagne corks in their penthouses! But I'll tell you something! We're the ones gonna be celebrating! With Kentucky Fried Chicken right here in Lexington!"

Crash trucks race out onto the runways with their lights flashing as other planes, diverted here by the storm, are forced to land. A Delta jet comes down with a roar and the scream of reversing engines not a hundred yards from where Dukakis stands.

"He's slipping!" Dukakis says. "And we're surging!"

The rain has turned into a torrent by the time Dukakis finishes. We run for the campaign planes and sit inside in our sopping clothes. Soon the cabin smells like it is filled with wet sheep. A flight attendant announces on the intercom: "Ladies and gentlemen of the press, we regret to inform you we were unable to purchase Budweiser for this trip. The nearest liquor store was four miles away. We will have to make do with Heineken and Corona until Chicago."

"Goddammit!" a reporter shouts. "Can't this campaign do *anything* right!"

At 6:30 we land in Chicago for a "torchlight" parade (fluorescent light sticks substitute for torches) and the streets are packed with people. In this city, politics is the leading spectator sport. The parade leads to the Medinah Temple where 200 dignitaries sit on the giant stage. There are so many Chicago pols gathered in one spot, it looks like the waiting area outside a grand jury room.

Also onstage are some of the fallen heroes of the primary campaign: Paul Simon, Bruce Babbitt, Al Gore and Jesse Jackson. Jackson is furious that his name is not on the program and that he is not being allowed to speak tonight. To him this is one more sign of Dukakis' disrespect.

There are 5,000 people in the audience madly waving green, red and orange light sticks. Dukakis takes the stage, and as his introduction begins, Joe Lockhart, a press aide, does what he always does. He crawls up on the front of the stage, crouches down in front of the lectern and holds up a white piece of cardboard for the TV crews. Each TV camera must establish a "white balance" in order to work properly. Lockhart has done this a thousand times without incident. But now, as soon as he crawls to the front of the stage and crouches with his piece of cardboard, Neil Hartigan, the attorney general of Illinois, leaps to his feet. He dashes across the stage, grabs Lockhart and tosses him to the stage floor. He can see the headlines: "Hartigan Foils Assassin!"

Lockhart is on his back, too stupefied to speak. Hartigan looks to the Secret Service agents, wondering why they have not yet taken out their guns and shot Lockhart.

The agents break into laughter. Only in Chicago! "It's O.K.," an agent tells Hartigan. "We know him. He's harmless."

Dukakis strips off his suit jacket. The crowd gives him a standing ovation for eight minutes.

"I remember the days of the Seven Dwarfs," Dukakis says, motioning to Babbitt, Simon, Gore and Jackson. "And let me tell you, these are giants. Giants!"

The crowd beats its hands together.

"You can feel the surge! You can feel the excitement!"

And in the hall, you can. The people in the audience, dripping with sweat, wave their wands and shout Dukakis' name.

He speaks for thirty-six minutes, then walks to the front of the stage, picks up a girl who is slightly too old to be picked up and then leans over and shakes hands with the crowd. This is something Dukakis would not do in the early days. He hated campaigning with children, picking them up, kissing them, using them. But in these final days, he is different. He grabs babies and grabs hands.

The tracking polls for this day will show the same as yesterday: Dukakis 8 points behind overall, but only 6 points behind among likely voters.

Saturday, November 5

Baggage call is at 5 a.m. It is dark and cold, and the Hawk, Chicago's north wind, whistles through the high-rise canyons of the city's Near North Side. Gray waves chop against the ice floes in Lake Michigan. There is little conversation. It is now the last weekend before election day and the press corps is swollen by the "vultures," those assigned to do stories on the loser.

We fly to Rock Island, Illinois, on the Mississippi River. It is 39 degrees and raining. A bus takes us to the Rimco Exhibition Hall, a vast, echoing building with concrete floors. Corn shocks are tied to pillars to try to make things look festive. Volunteers hand out brown bubble-gum cigars that announce the birth of "The Duke in '88."

Senator Tom Harkin of Iowa (which is just across the river) is at the microphone presiding over a piece of theater Dukakis never would have permitted even a few months ago.

"Just as there was no new Richard Nixon in 1968, there is no new George Bush in 1988," Harkin says. "Roger Ailes, who is the real George Bush? Bring him up here."

A man in a rubber Nixon mask mounts the stage, waves both hands in a victory symbol and starts stalking around in front of Harkin.

"Richard Nixon is running again and he's using the name of George Bush!" Harkin shouts. "The real George Bush is Richard Milhous Nixon!"

The crowd is roaring, the press is laughing, even Dukakis is smiling and the TV crews are eating this up. You can bet this will make the news tonight. It is no accident that major campaign stunts happen at the beginning of the day and not at the end. Network TV reporters and their crews must split off from the campaigns in the afternoon in order to produce their stories for that evening's broadcast. So smart campaigns provide their sexiest visuals early in the day. "It is fundamental, it is basic, and the Dukakis campaign still managed often to screw it up," a network producer said.

The campaigns don't especially care what the reporters say along with the pictures. In 1984, Reagan officials told Lesley Stahl they didn't really care what words she chose to speak over the videotape of Reagan. Ever since "it has been very disturbing and I've struggled for four years with the idea that the picture is so powerful," Stahl said. "What is our role here?"

A good question. TV reporters know they are being manipulated when something as obvious as a man in a Nixon mask appears at a campaign event. But what is the alternative? TV is about pictures. And the better the pictures, the happier everybody is. "You can do everything you want to offset it, to balance it and to explain it," the producer said, "but pictures are irresistible."

Dukakis stands up and strips off his suit jacket. The crowd roars.

"President Nixon, thank you for joining us this morning," Dukakis says. "Who is that guy anyway?"

"George! George!" the audience shouts back at him.

"Who's on your side?" Dukakis asks. "Mr. Bush wants to help the people who already have it made!"

Dukakis speaks for twenty-one minutes to the 5,000 people inside the hall. His crowds are consistently large now. But Walter Mondale's crowds were large in his last week, too. And the pros know that large crowds are not necessarily a measure of voter enthusiasm. "Let's face it, you buy crowds," Mark Gearan said. "Crowds are a function of money. They are a function of leaflets saying come down to the plaza at 2 p.m. They are a function of radio announcements. They are a function of hiring buses to take the people there. You don't get 20,000 people out for a rally in Philadelphia by accident. And it's a strange thing. When you're down in the polls, your crowds get bigger."

It's not so strange. Everyone wants to see a creature when it's about to become extinct.

Harkin and Paul Simon flank Dukakis and hold his hands above his head. Illinois is a state Dukakis needs badly.

He will lose it by 238,000 votes.

In Lansing, Michigan, we land in a driving rainstorm. Dukakis is now wearing his black satin "Dukakis for President '88" baseball jacket with the collar turned up. Hundreds of people are packed inside a small baggage terminal, some standing on the luggage carousel, and about a hundred people stand outside in the rain listening over a loudspeaker.

Dukakis strips off his baseball jacket. The crowd roars.

"I smell victory!" he says. He speaks for seventeen minutes, a short speech, and then hurries outside and shakes the hands of the people who have stood in the downpour. "You're terrific," he says to each one. "You're really terrific."

The reporters who witness this are shocked. The old Duke never would have thought to do this. He would have *expected* the people to wait in the rain.

On to Taylor, Michigan, outside Detroit, where Dukakis introduces today's Line of the Day. Bush has just announced that Dan Quayle might head his Crisis Management Group, the team that handles foreign policy crises like hostage takings and small wars.

"Dan Quayle in charge of the most serious problems we have in this country?" Dukakis sneers. "That's a frightening thing. That's enough to make you vote for Mike Dukakis and Lloyd Bentsen *without any other reason!*"

That's his hope anyway.

We head back to the airport, making a brief stop at the Econo Lodge so we can file our stories. Dayton Duncan, Dukakis' press secretary, is sitting on the floor outside the makeshift pressroom. Everybody is exhausted. Texas is the next stop, more than a three-hour flight away. And after that, we will go to Denver, a two-and-a-half-hour flight.

"In the future," Duncan says, "the press will never leave the bus. We will pack everything into a cargo plane. I call it the C-5A approach. You get a permanent seat on the bus at the beginning of the campaign and the bus drives into the belly of the plane. Your food is brought to you at your seat. When we land, the bus goes to events, but you watch the event on a video screen. For a year or so, you never leave the bus."

We laugh, but the truly funny thing is how close to present reality Duncan's future scenario is.

We land at McAllen, Texas, Lloyd Bentsen's hometown. It is after 7 p.m. and pitch dark, but we run into the first warmth of the day: a welcome 78 degrees. We drive to the nearby town of Edinburg, where the rally site is outside the Hidalgo County Courthouse and lit by huge spotlights. The crowd is largely Mexican-American and many of the men are dressed in suits and ties. "*Campañero!*" people shout at Dukakis. "*El Duke! Miguel! Miguel! Viva Dukakis!*" They hold signs that say: "Bush, Your First Decision Was to Pick a Vietnam Dodger" and "No Wimps for President."

It is an emotional moment for Dukakis. Here, the Lower Valley of the Rio Grande, was his first stop after the Democratic convention. This is where his campaign as the Democratic Party's official nominee began in the days when his lead was 17 points and his biggest worry was who he was going to name as Secretary of State.

But tonight, amid the shouts, there is an undertone of sadness, as if this were a farewell address. Some senior Dukakis staff members, smoking big cigars, crawl up on a roof overlooking the rally site and wait for the excitement to build. Dukakis, Kitty and Lloyd Bentsen, Sr., ninety-four, stand on the stage. The senior Bentsen came to this part of Texas after World War I with five dollars in his pocket and now is one of the largest landowners in the valley.

Representative E. "Kika" de la Garza introduces Dukakis. He recounts the heady days of the summer that have now turned to the harsh reality of the fall. Times used to be sweet and now they are bitter. But they all still stand together. "Gentle friend of the sad look and the tender smile," de la Garza says, "we relate to you."

People in the audience nod silently. The Dukakis staff is stunned. They want adrenaline, they want the people pumped up, they want talk of victory. The one thing they do not want is teary nostalgia.

"You are one of us," de la Garza goes on. "No matter the outcome, we shall always be with you. Here are your people."

Onstage, Dukakis is moved. But on the rooftop, his staff is furious. "What is de la Garza trying to do to us!" one says, pulling the cigar from his mouth. "Why is he trying to screw us?"

Dukakis begins speaking in Spanish. ("Dukakis was always more engaging when he spoke in another language like Spanish or Greek," an aide told me after the campaign. Unfortunately for Dukakis, American presidential campaigns are conducted largely in English.)

"*Necesito su ayuda*," he says. I need your help.

"*La tiene*," the crowd responds. You have it.

"*Necesito su voto*," he says. I need your vote.

"*Lo tiene*," the crowd responds. You have it.

"*Los necesito a ustedes*," he says. I need you.

"*¡Nos tiene!*" the crowd responds. You have us!

The band bursts into "La Bamba."

Texas is a must-win state for Dukakis.

He will lose it by 652,000 votes.

On the flight to Denver, the cabin lights are off and many are sleeping. Dukakis comes back to the press section briefly, looks around, doesn't say anything and goes back to the front cabin. He is starting to come back more often now. On an earlier flight, he had come back and a reporter asked him what he was spinning.

"The likability factor," he said with a smile. "Likability."

We get to Denver after midnight, having begun the day at 5 a.m. We have spent a total of eight hours and twenty-eight minutes in the air so that Michael Dukakis could speak for a total of one hour and nineteen minutes. This is modern campaigning.

In his journal, Sam Donaldson writes: "How do I feel about Dukakis as we head into this final weekend? He said early on that he grows on people. Until recently I had not found that to be the case. But . . . I have found myself liking him more. At last he and his aides have gotten their 'act' together. They are now running a coherent effective campaign. It's probably too late."

Sunday, November 6
There are no Sundays this late in a campaign. There is no pretense that this is some kind of day of rest or that Dukakis might actually go to church. We bus out to the Westminster Town Hall, outside Denver. It is an outdoor rally with the white-capped Rockies and black foothills providing an awesome backdrop. The sky is a brilliant blue. But none of us is thinking "beauty" or "the wonder of nature." We take a look and automatically think: Good visual.

"Folks," Dukakis says, "I've always supported the rights of hunters and sportsmen to own their own weapons and use them. A sportsman has the perfect right to use his weapon and use it responsibly and a person has a perfect right to defend himself in his own home."

Dukakis is being forced to say this everywhere. The Bush campaign has been spreading rumors that Dukakis wants to confiscate guns. "I'd like to know a little more about his position when he wants to take guns away from the American people in gun control," George Bush has been saying. So Dukakis must respond.

But every time he talks about how people have a right to defend themselves in their homes, a number of people think: Yeah, just in case Willie Horton comes through the window.

Back on the campaign plane, Dukakis aides begin discussing what they should have done differently. "Dukakis should have resigned as governor months ago," one says. "I think a successful candidate for President has to be unemployed."

You regard Bush's job as Vice President as unemployment? I ask.

"Of course," he says. "And for Dukakis to resign would have been easy. Our legislature is five-to-one Democratic, every constitutional officer is Democratic, the lieutenant governor is Democratic. It would have been *easy* to resign."

So did you ever suggest it to him?

"No," he says with that shocked look all Dukakis aides get when you ask if anybody made a sensible suggestion to their boss. "Nobody seriously suggested it to him. Why? Because nobody ever thought he'd do it."

It was very hard asking Dukakis to do anything he didn't want to do. He once said the "two worst days on the campaign" were the day he fired John Sasso, which was understandable, and, bizarrely, the day in May when he had to accept Secret Service protection. He was snappish and petulant all that day, and outsiders couldn't figure out what the big deal was. Insiders knew: Dukakis didn't like being told what to do, and now there were all these guys in dark suits, talking into their sleeves, telling him exactly that.

Now, on the campaign plane, Sasso makes the big announcement: there will be an Endless Surge. Dukakis will not stop campaigning between now, Sunday, and the Tuesday election. No hotels. No stopping.

So at the end of what would have been an eighteen-hour day in which Dukakis would have flown from Spokane, Washington, to San Francisco, Dukakis will now fly from Spokane to a dawn rally in Cleveland, then a morning rally in St. Louis, and then a noon rally in San Francisco. And he will keep going after that, all without stopping.

"If he wants to sleep, he'll do it on the plane," Sasso says.

Dukakis loves this idea. "We figured the surge was real," Mark Gearan said later. "I mean, stranger things have happened. And so it was Dukakis who wanted this incredible schedule. Sasso laid it out for him, that last fifty-hour 'day.' He lays out all the stops: Colorado, Oregon, Washington, Ohio, Missouri, California.

"And Dukakis just looks at him and says: 'I'll go if Louise goes.' " Louise Miller was his makeup woman.

Is this an example of a rare Michael Dukakis joke? I asked.

Gearan nodded. But, of course, there was a practical side to it. "It got very, very expensive to rent makeup people at each TV appearance, which is why Louise was traveling with us at the end," Gearan said. "For part of the campaign, *I* was the makeup person. I had this list of instructions, like put No. 13 base on his nose and how to deal with his eyebrows."

On the campaign plane, the task for the Dukakis aides is now to persuade the press to do "Dukakis in brave marathon" stories rather than "Dukakis in desperate act" stories. Tom Donilon, a Dukakis aide (who had earlier helped CBS put together the piece on George Bush that led to the Bush-Rather clash), climbs onto the seat in front of me and faces me over the back. "Bush's tracking polls show us ahead a point in Missouri," he says.

What do your own polls show? I ask.

"We didn't poll last night," he says, "but in looking at the other polls, it shows a diminishing Bush lead. A dramatic narrowing. I talked to the NBC pollsters at some length and they say the 'I'm on your side' message is a key determinant. And the Quayle factor is still important. It is worth three or four points right there. And Bentsen is bullish on Texas."

If Bentsen really is, he is the only one. Nobody thinks Bentsen can carry his home state. And some in the campaign now regret having chosen him. The battleground is shaping up in the Midwest, where having Senator John Glenn of Ohio on the ticket might have been extremely helpful.

But Bentsen was chosen because everyone felt Texas was essential. Besides, Dukakis could not resist re-creating the "Boston-Austin Axis" of John Kennedy and Lyndon Johnson. But LBJ managed to carry Texas for the ticket by only 30,000 votes in 1960 and that was when the Texas Republican Party was barely organized. Now that party is powerful—and Bentsen is no Lyndon Johnson.

So Dukakis has Bentsen and no Texas. And one reason is that under Texas election laws Bentsen can run simultaneously for Vice President and reelection to the Senate. Many Texans see this as a good way of getting two Texans in power: vote Bush for President and Bentsen for senator. Which is yet another little glitch the Dukakis campaign never counted on.

Donilon goes on for a few more minutes and then says: "Sasso is spinning a few rows back. You want to catch him? He does this better than I do."

I go catch the Sasso spin. Privately, Sasso has already been analyzing where the campaign went wrong. "The Dukakis campaign did not fully and effectively make the case for change," Sasso will say in a speech after the election. "Everyone in a campaign must be rooted firmly and fundamentally in a unifying and recognizable theme . . . Establishing a theme—a theme that rallies people—is the essence of leadership. You drive your stake into the ground, and you move the country toward it."

This the Dukakis campaign had not done. "Looking back," Sasso will say, "our own lack of a central and sustained theme created the vacuum, a playing field, if you will, that allowed flags and furloughs to dominate."

But now, on the plane, Sasso projects the official Dukakis staff spirit: grim enthusiasm.

"Our polls show California is now within the margin of error," Sasso says. "It is a toss-up. And if it keeps moving in our direction over the next forty-eight hours as it has the last three or four days, we're going to win."

He says it so convincingly that you almost believe he believes it.

We land in Portland, Oregon, where there is a crowd of more than 10,000 people on the rolling landscape of Portland State University.

Dukakis tells them it's just fine if they defend themselves in their homes with guns and that Bush is "slipping and sliding and we're rockin' and rollin', aren't we?"

"On Tuesday," he says, "we're carrying the state of Oregon."

On Tuesday, Dukakis will, indeed, carry Oregon by 57,000 votes. Oregon has 7 electoral votes.

Next stop, Tacoma, Washington, where the same speech is given to another large crowd. The press is getting pretty punchy. It is obvious Dukakis is not going to say anything new or substantive. His actual words no longer count; the act of running is itself the story. The wild plunge across America is the story. Which gives the press very little to do at each stop.

As the reporters line up for food in a holding area, Dukakis and Kitty walk by. Adam Nagourney of the New York *Daily News* starts chanting: "Rally till you puke! Rally till you puke!" The other reporters take it up. "Rally till you puke! Rally till you puke!"

Kitty laughs.

Dukakis shakes his head and puts his face in his hands. "These guys are crazy," he mumbles. "Crazy."

IN WASHINGTON, D.C., Mayor Marion Barry, a Democrat, predicts that Michael Dukakis will lose the election because he failed to generate excitement among blacks. "Obviously," Barry adds, "he'll carry the District."

He will, by 127,000 votes. The District of Columbia has 3 electoral votes.

IN CHICAGO, a story appears quoting Jesse Jackson as saying: "If Dukakis loses on Tuesday, the next political season will begin on Wednesday." Later, Jackson says he was not necessarily speaking of himself.

CAMPAIGNING IN LOS ANGELES, Bush says he's getting tired of Dukakis' "daily whining" about the Republican campaign. "Let me give the governor a little advice," Bush says. "If he can't stand the heat, he ought to get out of the kitchen." And he adds: "I don't like it one bit when the liberal governor of Massachusetts unleashes his minions to call me a racist."

Joan Rivers is trotted out. "Nobody wants to end up with a President that has two mustaches for eyebrows," she says.

"He's too short to be President," Rich Little adds. "And he has no shoulders."

Later, aboard Air Force Two, Bush will admit he's getting tired. "It's the total tension," he says.

Monday, November 7
In this last "Day Without End," the campaign day that lasts from Sunday morning until Tuesday night, Dukakis will visit eleven cities in nine states and fly 8,500 miles.

He catnaps about two hours on his jet before landing in Cleveland. On the ground, he showers, eats some bran flakes and heads out for a dawn rally in a blue-collar suburb, where about 200 workers come out to applaud him.

"Good morning, Ohio," he says. "We took the red-eye to be with the Buckeyes."

Afterward, Dukakis turns to Sasso and says: "How come we weren't doing this earlier? We could have gotten a lot more stops in."

George Bush had been lucky. He had looked into the abyss way back in February. He had seen the real possibility of defeat in New Hampshire and he made the changes he needed to make to prevent it. Dukakis has not faced his abyss until now. More and more, the Dukakis staff is realizing how much luck has helped them up until now. How lucky it was that Gary Hart screwed up. That Biden withdrew. That Gephardt ran out of money. That Simon never caught on. That Gore fizzled in New York. That Dukakis was the last white guy against Jackson. And that Mario Cuomo, Bill Bradley and Sam Nunn never ran in the first place.

Lee Atwater, not exactly an impartial observer, believed Dukakis' early success in the primaries is what doomed him in the general election. In Atwater's view, Dukakis had been passive, just waiting until it was him against Jackson, which assured his victory. And when it came time for an active campaign—the one against George Bush— the Dukakis people simply had no idea what to do. "It was lucky for us," Atwater said.

Dukakis jets out of Cleveland, chasing the rising sun. He is convinced this trip has been worth it. Ohio has 23 electoral votes and is a must-win state for Dukakis.

He will lose it by 477,000 votes.

Dukakis gets to St. Louis shortly after sunup. About 500 people have gathered at Lambert Field. Dukakis bounds off the plane wearing a red St. Louis Cardinal warm-up jacket. The polka band on the tarmac bursts into "Rock Around the Clock."

"This is the Show Me State and I'm here to show you how much I want your help tomorrow and how important Missouri is," Dukakis says.

Dukakis will lose Missouri by 75,000 votes.

He gets back on the plane and heads back to the West Coast. There is almost no conversation on the plane. Sleep deprivation is one of the most insidious forms of torture. This trip from the West Coast to the Midwest and back has been an eleven-hour, 4,100-mile detour. "I don't need sleep; I don't need sleep," Dukakis says. "We're going to win. We're going to win."

Dukakis gets into San Francisco at about 11:30 a.m. and heads for a rally of about 20,000 people in Justin Herman Plaza. Five women in red, white and blue minidresses dance onstage as he arrives.

"Mr. Bush's handlers said they have California all locked up," Dukakis says. "I think California will lock George Bush right out of the White House!"

California, with its 47 electoral votes, is absolutely crucial to a Dukakis victory.

He will lose California by 308,000 votes.

At the Westin Airport Hotel in San Francisco, we wait while Dukakis does satellite interviews. This, he feels, is the future of campaigning. "Dukakis was very savvy about the technology of the campaign, TV and satellites, all the rest," an aide said afterward. "He'd watch himself on TV, study himself. We were doing loads of satellite hookups at the end. We'd buy an hour or two hours and we'd do interviews with local anchors around the country. We'd stand on the tarmac in San Francisco and do Columbus, Ohio, or wherever. The markets were picked by the field director. You'd say: 'What three markets in Ohio do we need to work on?' And he'd pick the news shows. This is the future of politics. It is so much better."

We fly to Los Angeles, where Dukakis returns to the scene of his crime, the Pauley Pavilion at UCLA, the site of the second presidential debate. Now it is crammed with loyal supporters, mostly campaign volunteers. A full line of big names is on hand: Rita Moreno, Jerry Brown, Ted Danson, the Fabulous Thunderbirds, Tom Bradley, Alan Cranston and Rob Lowe.

The hall goes dark. "Coming to America" throbs through the speakers. The lights above the stage pulse. Michael and Kitty walk out arm in arm. Rolls of toilet paper arc through the air as if somebody had just scored a touchdown. Colored streamers crisscross through the cones of light. Even the press is impressed. "It looks just like a movie," one reporter says.

"Don't let them tell you the campaign is over because it's eight o'clock in the East," Dukakis says. "It won't be over."

This is a major fear. NBC, CBS and ABC are planning to announce a winner on election night as soon as a candidate has 270 electoral votes, even if people are still voting on the West Coast.

"Tomorrow, you well may hear some pollsters predict the outcome of this election based on some time zone back East," Dukakis says, and then pleads: "Don't let them tell you it's over. It won't be over until the people of California have their say."

Back on the plane everyone is dopey with fatigue. Some have not slept for two days. A weary-sounding official voice comes over the intercom: "Whoever took the agent's gun, would you please return it?"

The intercom clicks off, then back on.

"And the bullets with it. Thank you."

Election Day, November 8

The lights from the small Iowa towns are pinpricks in the black velvet outside the plane windows. It is 3:30 a.m., but at least 1,000 people are down there waiting for Michael Dukakis.

At the Des Moines airport, the tarmac is lit by floodlights. It is 34 degrees and the sky is brilliantly clear.

About two dozen protesters drive up behind the barbed-wire-topped cyclone fence that surrounds the tarmac. They unfurl a banner that reads: "Willie Horton for Attorney General." They begin to sing: "Hey, hey-hey—goodbye!" This has become the unofficial theme song of the Bush campaign ever since the second debate.

The press plane has landed, but *Sky Pig* still lags behind somewhere. So comedian Robert Klein is asked to warm up the crowd. "Moo!" he says. "My God, look at that dog with the big *things* on it! I'm from the Bronx; I don't know about cows."

The Bush forces kept singing outside the fence.

"I feel like one of those prisoners in the Bush ads," Klein says. "I can't wait to rape and pillage again. I have spoken to Governor Dukakis personally and he has personally assured me he will strip the United States of all its defenses and let all the prisoners out of jail."

People in the crowd look at each other. Is this supposed to be New York sarcasm?

Klein stands on the makeshift stage and shivers in his thin coat. A light snow begins to fall. The audience remains quiet.

Dukakis never understood the comics who traveled with him either. Albert Brooks, the comic actor and filmmaker, tried to break the ice with a joke when he first met Dukakis: "Guy goes to a doctor and the doctor says, 'I need a stool, urine and semen sample,' and the guy says, 'Just take my underwear!' "

Dukakis turned to the aide next to him. "How long is this guy going to be with us?" he asked.

"Does anyone have a credit card so we can refuel the plane?" Robert Klein asks.

The Hotel Savery has brought out one of its portable bars and has set it up on the edge of the tarmac. The reporters walk over, and yes, there is beer, and of course, it is cold.

Sky Pig lands and professionally printed signs are handed out to the crowd. They say: "Welcome Back Mike Where It All Began!"

Dukakis is wearing a zippered suede jacket over his wrinkled white shirt and suit pants and he bounds over to the stage. He doesn't strip off his jacket. The crowd roars anyway.

"It's great to be home," he says with real emotion. He grips the sides of the lectern. "My campaign began here eleven months ago. We have wonderful memories. Learning. Listening. Exchanging ideas. It made the Iowa caucus a special thing for us. We thank you so much for coming early and going out and getting the vote out. You are a very special people in a very special state."

"Twistin' the Night Away" blasts through the speakers, and while it plays, Dukakis goes down into the crowd and shakes hands. The people press against the ropes, reaching out for him.

The atmosphere is so warm and loving and Dukakis is so pleased to be here that it takes an act of will to remember that Dukakis *lost* the Iowa caucuses eleven months ago. He came in third. But, hell, who's counting now?

Today, Michael Dukakis will win Iowa by 125,000 votes. Iowa has 8 electoral votes.

It is raining in Detroit as we arrive at 6:50 a.m. The crowd is small and there is no shelter. The lectern has been draped in plastic. This is the eleventh time Dukakis has come to Michigan. He needs Michigan very badly. Without Michigan and its 20 electoral votes, it is hard to see how he will become President.

"It's a little damp," Dukakis says, the rain dripping from his face, "but our spirits are bright! If we win today in Michigan, we win all across America!"

Michael Dukakis will lose Michigan by 238,000 votes.

"Let's make it happen," he tells the crowd, and then pauses and says a very un-Dukakis-like thing. "I love you," he says. "I love you."

On *Sky Pig*, Dukakis sits in the darkened cabin. The reading light is on above him and the beam sharply outlines his face. He still has his makeup on. He is so weary, though, his face looks like shattered china. Almost everybody around him is asleep.

It was good, he says quietly. The whole thing, the experience, having run for President, was good. No matter what happens, he is glad he did it. "It's been a great experience for Kitty and the kids, you know," he says. "Andrea and Kara really blossomed."

At the very beginning of the campaign, his daughters were reluctant to speak even to small groups. Now, Andrea has been giving speeches to huge crowds.

Dukakis nods. "It was a positive experience," he says. "For my daughters. For John. For my mother. It was positive for Kitty, too. They got to travel all over the country."

He never mentions himself.

A few minutes before the plane lands in Boston, he gets up and goes back and talks to the press. "You look like the walking wounded," he says.

How do you feel? a reporter asks.

"I feel great—all things considered," he says. "It's been an incredible experience and I mean an *incredible* experience."

What have you learned?

"I'll tell you in about a week," he says with a small smile. "Living on this thing is not exactly natural for all of us. You all look a little worse for wear."

Win or lose, what about George Bush? another reporter asks.

Dukakis looked at the questioner levelly. "I feel great," he says.

When the plane lands at Logan Airport, Dukakis, Kitty, Kara, Andrea, Dukakis' son John and his mother, Euterpe, form a receiving line at the bottom of the steps. For the first and last time, the reporters are allowed to exit from the front of the plane, and they come down the steps and shake hands with Dukakis and his family.

After a very brief rally, Dukakis and his family get into the waiting cars and they motorcade from Logan directly to the Theresa Morse Apartments, their polling place, two blocks from their Perry Street home in Brookline.

The whole family except Euterpe (whose polling place is the Putterham Library in Brookline and who will set off wails of protest when she marches ahead of sixty people in line to vote) go in to cast their ballots. Dukakis checks in with the precinct manager and then walks to the center voting machine. "O.K., this is it," he says. He goes in and pulls the curtains shut.

As Dukakis comes out, Sam Donaldson asks whom he voted for. As Donaldson later writes in his journal: "Only if he had replied

'George Bush' would that question and answer have been newsworthy, but somebody had to ask."

Perhaps it was modesty that prevented Donaldson from recording what really happened after he called out: "Who did you vote for?"

"You, Sam, you," Kitty replied.

The family take the limousine home. Dukakis gets out, says nothing to the reporters waiting there and walks inside. Andrea says: "It's good to be home." Euterpe raises two fingers in a "V" sign.

Now, Dukakis doesn't know what to do with the rest of the day. He could, of course, go to sleep. It would be reasonable. But he doesn't feel like it. Instead, he takes a short walk. Then some kids, bused over from nearby elementary schools, come by the house. Dressed now in a red sweater, Dukakis comes out and meets them and jokes about how they are cutting class. He tells them he hopes they consider public service when they grow up.

At Dukakis headquarters, the calls are going out to the field staffs. This thing can still be saved, they are told. "We need to call Michigan," Mark Gearan tells his staff. "Don't you know anyone in Dearborn?"

The field staffs are amazed to find that some Americans, perhaps many Americans, are just today waking up to the fact that a presidential election is taking place.

"Yes," the headquarters receptionist says into the phone, "Mr. Dukakis is a Christian."

Back at the Dukakis home, Jack Corrigan, the campaign's political director, gets an idea. "Let's do more satellites!" he says. "Let's do the West Coast."

Corrigan is told that Dukakis has not slept in days. And it might be a good idea to persuade him to take a nap.

"What? We want him to get some sleep so he can look good for his concession speech?" Corrigan says.

Nobody has an answer to that one. So the arrangements are made, the satellite time is purchased and Dukakis, still wearing his makeup, goes down to WGBH-TV in Boston to do interviews across the United States. He keeps at this until 7:30 p.m. Eastern time, still trying to make it happen in California.

I go to the Four Seasons Hotel, write my column for the next day—writing about events that have not yet occurred is common practice for journalists—and sleep for a few hours.

In the early evening, I catch a shuttle bus to the Dukakis "victory" party at the Boston World Trade Center. There, the drinks are flowing and the rock bands are playing. A small curtained area in one corner has been set up for the press. Dukakis aides wander in and out, looking like bludgeoned steers.

Dukakis is still doing satellite hookups when the word is passed to him: he has lost Michigan. He shrugs. This is a night for shrugs. He goes on with his interviews, completes the fourteenth and goes home. He doesn't wait for any more news. "Up until Michigan," an aide says later, "he thought he had a chance of winning." Dukakis sits down at his kitchen table with Kitty and, writing in longhand, he drafts his concession speech. He calls Lloyd Bentsen and thanks him. At 10:10 p.m. he will call George Bush and congratulate him on becoming the forty-first President of the United States.

A T 9:15 P . M . , CBS projects 266 electoral votes for Bush and at 9:16 p.m. adds Missouri to the total, pushing Bush over the top.

"It's over. George Bush wins," Dan Rather says.

On the West Coast, the polls are still open, people are still voting, or still planning to vote, but CBS has determined that this is unnecessary.

At 9:20 p.m., ABC gives the election to Bush.

At the Boston World Trade Center, it is like a kick in the belly. The air rushes out of the party. Presidential campaigns no longer end with hours of drawn-out tension. They end when the networks say they end. Joe Lockhart, the aide who got tackled onstage in Chicago, refuses to give up. Don't believe those goofy TV exit polls, he says. "Pennsylvania, Illinois, Wisconsin, Ohio, Missouri, Montana, are all cliff-hangers," he says. "It's going well. We've got a good chance."

Reporters ignore him. They have already completed their "Dukakis loses" pieces and are now moving on to their "what went wrong" analysis pieces. They don't want aides sounding hopeful. They want explanations. They want somebody willing to take the blame.

Debra Winger walks into the pressroom. She is livid. "Maybe Dukakis' campaign was poorly run, but Bush's was *rotten*," she says. "George Bush is like bad acting. It's gonna be like four years of being inside the worst B movie you ever saw."

Out in the Trade Center, people wander aimlessly, draining plastic cups of booze. TV body snatchers grab movie stars, Dukakis staff people, Rob Lowe, anybody, to go on TV and fill the time. Dukakis and Bush have agreed that neither will formally concede until 11 p.m. EST, after the polls close in California.

"I should have gone to Nebraska," Winger grumbles, speaking of the state where her former boyfriend, Governor Bob Kerrey, has just been elected to the U.S. Senate. "At least we *won* there."

At 10:17 p.m., comedian Al Franken leaps to the stage and shouts: "Start the music! Start the music!"

Immediately, "Coming to America" begins to blare and the reporters rush out of the pressroom to see Dukakis concede early. And indeed, a smallish, swarthy man with bushy eyebrows walks up to the microphone. "I sent Vice President Bush the following telegram," he says: " 'You *asshole!*' "

There are gasps from the crowd. Then cheers. This is the new, emotional Dukakis they've been hearing about! The speaker, however, turns out to be Jon Lovitz from *Saturday Night Live*.

At 10:30, NBC calls the race for Bush.

At 10:42, CNN calls the race for Bush.

At 10:50, Dukakis and his family arrive at the Trade Center and are whisked to a holding room. His staff gathers around him. You did great, someone says. "When you only win forty-six percent, it's not great," Dukakis replies.

Out in the hall, the final "visual" of the campaign begins. It is a slick, expensive sound-and-light show. The lights go out in the hall. A screen is lowered. Music fills the air and we see pictures of eagles flying and fireworks and other snatches of Americana. At the end, turquoise lasers pierce the darkness of the hall. The lights go up and Dukakis appears onstage. Dukakis hugs his family, walks to the lectern, waves, gives a thumbs up gesture and speaks.

"We had a lot of good days, didn't we?" he says. "There were three thousand people waiting for us in Des Moines, Iowa, this morning! I want to thank the members of the world's oldest and greatest political party. I hope many of you go into politics and public service. It is a noble profession, a noble profession."

The crowd takes up the chant: "Ninety-two! Ninety-two! Ninety-two!" It dies quickly.

In comparison with past Democratic defeats, Dukakis has not done all that badly:

In 1972, McGovern got 28.4 million votes, 38 percent, one state plus the District of Columbia and 17 electoral votes.

In 1980, Carter got 34.9 million votes, 41 percent, six states plus the District and 49 electoral votes.

In 1984, Mondale got 36.9 million votes, 41 percent, one state plus the District and 13 electoral votes.

In 1988, Dukakis gets 41 million votes, 46 percent, ten states plus the District and 112 electoral votes.

But somehow it seems like a terrible, crushing defeat, far worse than in past elections. "It seems so bad because we were expected to really win it," a Dukakis aide says. "We are blamed for losing much more than Mondale was blamed because of the expectations. We had a Republican nominee with the lowest ratings in history. He was called a wimp on the cover of a national magazine. He had Noriega, Meese, everything. And we lost. We lost in a year when people thought it was really possible to win."

When Michael lost one of his three races for the governorship, Kitty described it as "a public death." But nobody knows how this loss will truly affect him. The new pattern for presidential victory seems to be to run once and lose. So perhaps Dukakis still has another chance.

Or perhaps he will be like George McGovern, who ran once against Nixon and was crushed. Sixteen years later, at the Democratic convention in Atlanta, McGovern sat with the other VIPs in a special area of the convention hall as Dukakis made his acceptance speech. And afterward, as person after person sitting around him was summoned to the stage to surround the smiling nominee in the spotlights, McGovern sat alone. Unsummoned, unbidden, he was once again reminded what happened to you when you lost a big one. He had not been invited to a single official festivity the entire week. He was not provided with housing or a car or a driver. "They didn't invite me to anything that would link me to Dukakis," McGovern said later. "I was truly hurt. I wanted to campaign for these guys. I wanted to be a good Democrat." He paused. "Those sons of bitches," he said. "There's not one policy I had back then that they don't have now. But now they don't want to know I exist."

Nobody wanted to be seen with lonesome George. Even though you could make the case that he was one of the last nominees of either party who stood for something instead of standing for nothing, he was a loser. And in politics, you can be forgiven anything but that.

"OUR HEARTS ARE FULL," Dukakis says onstage at the Trade Center. "We love you all. And we love this country."

Silvery Mylar confetti falls from the ceiling onto the heads of Dukakis and the crowd. The final ovation does not last long. Dukakis just leaves the stage. And people head for the exits like suspects leaving the scene of a crime.

IN HOUSTON, George Bush fulfills a pledge at his victory rally in the George R. Brown Convention Center.

"Once in days that were a little darker, I made a promise," Bush says. "And now I'll keep it: *Thank you, New Hampshire!*"

He has a lot to be thankful for: he has received a larger share of the popular vote than any nonincumbent since Dwight Eisenhower.

Bush is surrounded by his family, his friends and campaign aides.

Dan Quayle has been told to spend election night in Washington, D.C.

JESSE JACKSON places a call to Bush to congratulate him. "You ran a tough race," Jackson says. "I hope we can talk soon." Bush invites Jackson to the White House.

Jackson has not yet spoken to Dukakis to offer him any words of comfort. "I couldn't get through," Jackson says later. There, he has gotten his revenge for that vice presidential phone call that never came.

"I DON'T KNOW," Dukakis aide Tom Donilon says to the reporters who huddle around him. "Maybe we should have gotten into the gutter *earlier*."

JOHN SASSO will come up with five reasons for the defeat:
"First, we did not, to my mind, properly or convincingly, make the case for change.

"Second, it is politically dangerous to take for granted that voters will automatically assume the Democratic candidate holds dear the country's basic values: God, patriotism, family, freedom.

"Third, the Republicans routinely field a squad of political professionals, most of them now with years of White House and presidential campaign experience, [while] Democrats somehow field a squad of smart but insurgent players who do not fully understand whole areas of the country and operate far more narrowly.

"Fourth, the media still have not figured out how to deal effectively with negative advertising."

Sasso's fifth reason, however, is the stunner: Jesse Jackson helped do them in.

"If the presidential candidate disagrees with the party's most influential black leader, the candidate must, in my view, break out of his political fright and disagree," Sasso now says. "In some ways voters seem to judge the strength and skill and character of the Democratic candidate on how effectively he gets along with or copes with Jackson. It becomes an unending litmus test."

But what about Dukakis himself? What about the personality and the performance of the man himself? Didn't that play a part?

"It is certainly true that Dukakis is a man who holds his emotions closely," Sasso says. "It is true that supporters inside the campaign and out hoped the candidate would periodically let his feelings fly. But that was not our man, and that was not our campaign. The fact that Michael Dukakis always refused advice to be something he was not, to me, tells a lot about him."

Tonight, it tells us that he's a loser.

EUTERPE IS ASKED if she would like her son to run for President in 1992.

"No!" she says.

KIRK O'DONNELL, the Dukakis issues coordinator, stands against a wall in a hallway outside the pressroom like a fox ringed by hounds. A reporter asks when he knew it was lost.

"When Michigan didn't come in," he says. "But we didn't do badly. We came out of the second debate behind in the high teens and by election day it was down to six points."

If the campaign had gone on for another week, would you have won?

"I'm not saying that," he says.

What did you learn?

He pauses. He thinks.

"Campaigning matters a great deal," he says. "How the actual campaign is conducted; how it is run. Resources used to be a problem for the Democrats, but now we have the resources. But we didn't understand the nature of a presidential campaign. How very intense it is, how you can take nothing for granted.

"I think we just didn't realize how important *campaigning* really is."

Michael Dukakis made his first campaign appearance on February 8, 1987. Today it is 640 days, half a million air miles and $117 million later.

And now, just now, he has finally learned the truth: presidential elections aren't about competence *or* about ideology.

They are about campaigning.

☆ **17** ☆

CURTAIN CALL

"The great test is to win public office without proving oneself unworthy of it."

—*Adlai Stevenson*

THE REPORTER has been on the George Bush campaign for months now and one day she picks up the schedule and learns they are heading for Fort Lauderdale, her hometown. So she calls her mother and tells her she is coming to town and naturally her mother is very, very pleased. Her daughter with the Vice President of the United States! In person!

Bush has some kind of campaign stunt scheduled at Morrison's Cafeteria out on North Federal Highway, where he is photographed eating liver and onions—food that serves to emphasize, of course, what an ordinary Joe he is. The reporter has told her mom to meet her there and they find each other and hug and kiss and chat. After a few minutes, the reporter scoots back over to Bush, just in case she has missed any good liver-and-onions quotes, and Bush is in a chatty mood and so she mentions her mom is in the room.

Bush leaps to his feet. He asks where her mother is, goes over and makes a very big fuss over her. The mother almost swoons from the attention. Bush is being incredibly gracious, lavishing praise, making clear he not only knows her daughter but reads her work carefully, admires it, etc., etc.

Then he motions a White House photographer forward, grabs Mom's hand and has a picture taken. When it is developed, he tells her, he will autograph it and send it to her. (Which, of course, he does.)

The mother is very happy and beaming with pride and the reporter is very pleased that her mom has been treated so nicely. The reporter, highly respected in her profession, is certainly not going to give Bush a break in her stories because of this, but that is not why Bush did it. Bush just does things like this.

Later in the day, the campaign motorcades out to West Palm Beach airport to fly out to the next stop. There is the usual milling around on the tarmac while everybody is getting loaded on the planes and the reporter hears her name being called. She turns around and Bush motions her over.

"See that woman over there?" Bush says, pointing. The reporter looks and sees a small, elderly woman standing on the tarmac.

"Well, that's *my* mother," Bush says. "I said nice things about you to your mother. Now you go over there and say nice things about me to my mother."

The reporter looks at Bush. And he isn't kidding. And so she goes over and tells his mother how nice her son has been.

George Bush wanted people to know what a nice guy he was. Even his own mother.

And of those who knew him, few doubted that Bush intended to be "kinder and gentler" once he became President. The whole campaign had been like promising God that if He'd let you get away with something just this once, you'd never sin again.

To Bush, the campaign had been a role he played and now the play was coming to an end. He had done what was required to win. Yes, he had crushed and humiliated his opponents, and yes, he had used negative ads and low tactics and had exploited race and fear. But, my God, that was something you *did*, not something you *were*. Didn't everybody understand that?

ON THE DAY after election day, Michael Dukakis goes to work. After shining his shoes at his kitchen table, he gets in a limousine and heads for the statehouse. And at 9:30 a.m., he is sitting behind his desk, humming to himself and working on the problem of highway litter along Route 24.

Reporters are ushered in to see him engaged in business as usual. He looks up at them. "I gather we didn't quite make it in California," he says drily.

At 2:02 p.m. in a ballroom at the Sheraton Boston Hotel, Dukakis conducts his final campaign press conference. He stands facing the press beneath a crystal chandelier.

"To the traveling press, especially the last three days, I know it wasn't easy," he says. "I admired you for the way you covered the campaign and covered me."

(Bush has made a gag tape and sent it to his press corps. In it, he talks about how often he had seen the reporters in the snow and cold lugging their equipment from stop to stop. And he had thought to himself: "Tough, too bad, who cares? It's your problem. Get a raise. Get a real job. Get a haircut." He says he also used to see them on the tarmac giving him the "one-fingered salute of friendship and respect." Although Bush had penciled in a few lines of his own, the gag tape was scripted by Peggy Noonan, his speechwriter, and Sheila Tate, his press secretary.)

Dukakis' face is puffy. He has not gotten any real sleep for seventy-two hours. "I think I'll probably take the weekend off," he says. He is not joking. A weekend should be enough.

Did you blow it? a reporter asks.

"Had things gone differently, a different combination of factors, it was winnable," he says. "Obviously I didn't do as good a job as I should."

What about the negative campaigning?

"The use of Willie Horton was cynical and hypocritical," he says. "But that goes with the territory. Some forty million people voted for my record and agenda. I gave it my best shot. But that almost doesn't count in politics. You win or you don't."

If you had more time, a reporter asks, would you have won?

"If I had more time, you'd all be in the hospital," he says, and yields up a small smile. "I wouldn't have done that to you guys. I think too much of you."

Any regrets?

"I'm not a bitter person," he says. "Am I disappointed? Sure. It was a distorted campaign, a campaign that distorted my record. It did not set high standards for the kind of campaign we want for the presidency. And it may well have set a standard we live to regret."

Later the same day, he dismisses his Secret Service agents.

Finally, Michael Dukakis is free.

IN TEXAS, George Bush is asked if he regrets the negative tone of his campaign.

"This is not the day for mea culpas," he says.

"POPULAR WISDOM IS that Dukakis lost because he didn't want it bad enough," Roger Ailes says. "That's horseshit! He wanted it *worse* than George. He just didn't know how to *do* it."

ELEVEN DAYS after the election, Jesse Jackson flies to Des Moines to give a speech to the Iowa Farm Unity Coalition. He tells the farmers that Dukakis lost because he failed to mobilize voters.

Later, Jackson tells me: "Just after the election, many farmers who didn't support me—they wanted to, philosophically, but they didn't support me, actually—the next day they got notices of farm foreclosures.

"And the farmers didn't call Dukakis. They didn't call Bentsen. They didn't call Bush. They called *me*. And I spoke to them. You know, could I get them an appointment with the new Secretary of Agriculture? That's what they asked. Could I call Bush for them? And I did. So I met with Bush on their behalf and I got them an appointment.

"See, they were not looking for a white male; they were looking for a link to the White House. And they called *me*.

"The issue is not who leads us, but who needs us. And that is where I must go. And if I serve their needs, they will let *me* lead *them*."

There are approximately 1,175 days until the 1992 Iowa presidential caucuses.

And the road show has already begun.

INDEX